THE SECOND EMPIRE

Napoleon III

From the picture by Meissonier in the Musée du Luxembourg

By permission of Braun & Co.

THE
SECOND EMPIRE

BONAPARTISM . THE PRINCE
THE PRESIDENT . THE
EMPEROR

BY

PHILIP
GUEDALLA

*Caballero aventurero es una cosa que
en dos palabras se ve apaleado y
Emperador.*
EL INGENIOSO HIDALGO
DON QUIXOTE DE LA MANCHA.

*You have seen better days, dear? So
have I ——*
PRINCE HOHENSTIEL-SCHWANGAU,
SAVIOUR OF SOCIETY.

ILLUSTRATED

G. P. PUTNAM'S SONS
NEW YORK   LONDON
The Knickerbocker Press
1922

CONTENTS

ILLUSTRATIONS

BONAPARTISM

BONAPARTISM

BONAPARTISM stands to Napoleon in the somewhat peculiar relation in which most religions stand to their founder. The picturesque imagination of innumerable ironists has exhausted itself in speculations upon the probable feelings of various divine and semi-divine teachers when confronted with the full glories of their own shrines. But it may be doubted whether the sensations of the central personage at Kamakura or St. Peter's would bear comparison for irony with the thoughts which must rise in that little white-breeched, green-uniformed figure, fresh from a bath of ambrosial *eau-de-Cologne* prepared by an Elysian Constant, as he studies the externals of his career on the painted canvas of Meissonier or spells out his political message from the printed page of M. Paul de Cassagnac. And yet, unlike many teachers, the Emperor apprehended the purport of the gospel which he taught. Napoleon (it is a singular fact) was a Bonapartist. But he did not become one until he had ceased to be an Emperor.

I

THE realities of his career have become almost indecipherably obscured beneath the martyrology and miracles of the Napoleonic myth. Scholastic decorum confined the explanatory exuberance of an Alexandrian commentator to the margin of his manuscript. But the story of that life between the years 1769 and 1821 is a mere palimpsest across which the romantics, the sentimentalists, and the reactionaries have scrawled their distortions of the original text.

Few careers (unless musicians are in question) possess any interest outside the narrow circle of relatives and curio-hunters before the age of twenty is reached. The early years of their subjects are the chosen playground of imaginative biographers, and a full supply of pleasing and significant incident has always been stimulated by the steady demand of those sympathetic students who are perpetually eager to hear their little hero lisping his first prayer, to watch his tiny fingers straining round the pommel of his father's sword. But the child is not, except in fables, the father of the man; and no circumstance of Napoleon's boyhood possesses the faintest European significance beyond the fact, distressing doubtless at the time to his anxious father and more regrettable subsequently to the populations of his fraternal kingdoms of Spain, Holland, Naples, and Westphalia, that he came of a large family. The family lived principally upon expectations from their father's litigation in that somewhat unsatisfactory frame of mind with which Dickens has familiarised his readers, and in a still Bleaker House in Ajaccio Carlo Buonaparte, who was that one figure in life more pathetic than a sick doctor (for he was a litigious lawyer), expected a judgment shortly in an interminable action in which he had cited as respondents the Order of Jesus and the French Crown.

Such judgments are rarely delivered in the lifetime of the parties; and when the plaintiff died, he left little to his widow and his eight children beyond this welter of red tape and their wits.

The boy's education exercised even less than the usual lack of influence upon his development, since he was educated for the army. The world in Napoleon's schooldays was full of that vague atmosphere of Progress which is the invariable indication of a stationary age. The *enfants perdus* of French drawing-rooms were volunteering for service against the English in Rhode Island; and those who stayed at home, whilst Lafayette was crusading in the singular cause of American independence, were learning to quote Rousseau and Montesquieu with that facility which has never failed well-bred persons in the case of authors whom they have not read. But it may be doubted whether any breath of the contemporary movement was permitted to pass the walls of the academy for the sons of gentlemen in which Napoleon received his grounding in French and the rudiments before his education became strictly professional.

Graduating in the paralysing study of mathematics, he obtained the commission of King Louis XVI. and passed out of adolescence as a hatchet-faced subaltern in the Midi. The world was spinning interminably down the long groove of the Eighteenth Century; and life, as the young gunner shaded his eyes to look down the broad avenue of his prospects, must have seemed to hold little beyond a weary alternation of parades on the dusty drill-grounds of the south and polite attentions to the anæmic denizens of provincial *salons,* with a little leave in Corsica and a little leisure for the annotation of Plutarch or re-reading of Goethe for its sole, its ghastly relaxations. But one month and a day before his twentieth birthday a Paris crowd, having some artillery, went against the Bastille, and the Revolution, which had hitherto been conducted as a genteel parliamentary charade among the parterres of Versailles, entered the lives of twenty-five millions of Frenchmen. One of them was a starved-looking young man in a garrison town with an uncertain temper and an Italian accent.

The lessons which Napoleon learned from the Revolution were at once simpler and less unsettling than those which it taught to his more impressionable contemporaries. The forcible reconstruction of the French system by the men of the First Republic, from which the world has learnt so much, taught Napoleon so little; and although he piously muttered the orthodox incantations of the blessed Rousseau and twirled a Jacobin praying-wheel with the rest of his generation, he retained almost to the last the administrative ideals of a sergeant-major.

His contact with the Revolution left him with an extreme distaste for crowds. That tendency is inherent in most orderly minds when confronted by the incalculable and illogical proceedings of large bodies of men, although it is corrected for some by the spectacle of their own oratorical success—it is so difficult to believe evil of one's cheering supporters. But for Napoleon this corrective was absent. In spite of a fashionable armoury of classical allusion and a literary style that is faintly reminiscent of the political platform, he was a poor speaker, and his early triumphs before the Patriotic Club of

Ajaccio (whose Jacobinism, one suspects, was sometimes a trifle Babu, and where a Bonaparte could
always command the respectful applause of his
relatives) were never repeated before more critical
audiences in France itself. It resulted from this
deficiency in his equipment and from the unfortunate
nature of his earliest contacts with the Revolution
that a popular assembly became an object of intense
distaste to Napoleon, and he remained always the
scared subaltern who had faced a country crowd
outside Auxonne in the days when he still wore the
King's uniform. His military instincts had been
scandalised by a mutiny of his own gunners in the
first summer of the Revolution; and as he watched
Danton's republicans sweeping against the Tuileries
in 1792, the policeman in him could find no kinder
name for them than '*la vile canaille*.' Such men
can never be practising democrats; and it was not
surprising that when three years later Barras needed
an artillerist to blow the Parisians off the streets,
he found General Bonaparte.

The second impression left on him by his contact
with the Revolution was a contempt for civilians.
His first experiences of mountain warfare on the
Riviera in the wake of the *Représentants en mission*
must have filled him with a professional distaste for
gesticulating parliamentarians in tricolour sashes. But
he learned it principally in the drawing-rooms of
the Directoire, when the rushing waters of 1793 were
flowing muddily through the shallows of 1798. A
European war had, as usual, washed the army contractors into Society, and they enjoyed a freer field
than usual in view of the recent execution of most
of the people who might have snubbed them. The

spectacle of their purveyors is always peculiarly
exasperating to soldiers, who are apt to recollect the
quality of the stores supplied, and polite society
under the Directoire consisted almost entirely of such
persons with a slight admixture of politicians. These
were still more distasteful to Napoleon, since they
were either rival adventurers, successful public
speakers, or academic persons of a reflective habit
vaguely suggestive of the Common Room. It resulted that Napoleon felt few scruples in substituting
military monarchy for a civilian republic by successive stages of violence and *plébiscite,* although his
wife, a colonial lady whose mild ambitions lay in the
direction of a *salon,* would have been more easily
contented with a *bourgeois* Republic under which
Tallien and a few decorative *aides de camp* might
have grouped themselves solicitously round her couch,
whilst Siéyès in one corner explained the draft of a
new constitution to a circle of respectful stockbrokers.
But Napoleon regarded civilian accomplishments
with the full contempt of one to whom they have been
denied; for him any man who was not in uniform
must be either a sutler or an agitator, and in either
case his proper place was in obscurity. That is how
the French citizens, who had unmade the Monarchy,
dwindled into the deferential supers of a military
pageant. The crowds of the Revolution became the
stage crowds of the Empire, and the high-waisted
civilian of 1800 faded inconspicuously into a cheering
background across which his masters, the soldiers,
clanked and jingled their triumphant way.

But the military intelligence of Napoleon could
apprehend at least one lesson of the Revolution.
Of the three virtues inculcated by the new revelation

the greatest for him was Equality. Liberty was demonstrably bad for discipline, and Fraternity was either a gesture of rhetoric or (worse than that) a piece of feminine sentimentality wholly inconsistent with the axiomatic institution of war. But Equality was a sound lesson of the drill-ground. One could not manœuvre a troop of horse in which each rank enjoyed a peculiar privilege, and the nation which made equal units of its citizens would march more promptly to its master's orders than any old-world welter of castes and classes. To that extent and for reasons comprehensible to any drill sergeant Napoleon was an egalitarian.

But with that exception the contribution made by the Revolution to his stock of ideas was strikingly small. The Jacobin system of local administration possessed irresistible attractions for a disciplinarian and a trifle of loose theory about direct consultation of the will of the people proved a convenient means of eluding the control of its representatives. But apart from these features and a creditable command of the Revolutionary idiom Napoleon had little in common with the men of the First Republic. In regality he was almost completely a man of the Eighteenth Century. His enlightenment was the enlightenment of Joseph II. His secularism was the modish anti-religion of the days when Voltaire had led a dainty crusade against the theological inelegance of the Middle Ages. He would have been thoroughly at home at the Court of Catherine II.

The romantic imagination has persistently endeavoured to see Napoleon as a *condottiere* of the Renaissance born three centuries too late. But no picturesque character of the past could be less indicative of the modern quality of his tight-lipped persistence. He was, as most men are, a man of the type admired in the world in his own boyhood. In its adventure the career of Napoleon has all the flavour of those other adventurers of the Eighteenth Century who climbed to power in countries where they had once been strangers, of Wall the Irishman who became first minister in Spain, of his predecessor the Cardinal Alberoni whose father was an Italian gardener, and (strangest of all) of Ripperda the Dutch diplomatist who turned first Spaniard to become a Duke and then Moslem to become Grand Vizier to the Sultan of Morocco. That, and not the romantic violence of Bartolommeo Colleoni, is the stuff latent in the career of a Corsican gunner who played for a moment with the idea of entering the Turkish service and then made himself Emperor of the French. And in its ideals of monarchy his reign forms an apt pendant to the long chain of genteel tyrannies which had governed Europe in the Eighteenth Century. The true parallel to the first Empire is not to be found in the Caesars. The Emperor's spiritual home was not on the Palatine, but in Potsdam and Schönbrunn. His models lay ready to his hand in the Prussia of Frederick the Great and the Austria of Joseph II. The Empire was an elaboration of the typical monarchy of the Eighteenth Century, and Napoleon was the last (and perhaps the most benevolent) of the benevolent despots.

The principles of his foreign policy were cast in a still more antique mould. It fell to him to direct the course of French diplomacy after the Republic had established itself as the first military power in Europe, and there was strikingly little in the treaties

of 1797 or 1800 which would have scandalised
Frederick the Great or the ministers of Maria Theresa
as a departure from Eighteenth Century statecraft.
In spite of a profession of the fashionable faith in the
doctrines of nationality and natural frontiers, they
exhibited the bland indifference to these principles
which had prevailed in Europe for centuries. Their
simplification of the political geography of Germany
by the abolition of the fragmentary and diminutive
territories of the Church was an unconscious prelude
of German unity, and the establishment of the Italian
republics was an unintentional contribution to the
political education of Italy. But the conscious acts
of Napoleonic policy, of which the most characteristic were the annexation of Belgium and the surrender of Venice to the Austrians, were in perfect
harmony with the diplomatic temper of the century
which had witnessed the First Partition of Poland.

The Imperial reconstruction of Europe was still
more ancient in its flavour. Indeed, the great partition of the Continent between the Emperor of the
French and the Czar of Russia resembled nothing
so much as those allocations of the civilised world
with which the successors of Julius Caesar diversified
the last years of the Roman Republic. The Revolution had sent polite society to its Plutarch; but it
appeared from his foreign policy that the Emperor
had devoted more study to his life of Mark Antony
than to the more fashionable figures of the Gracchi.
The Empire itself was indebted for much of its *décor*
to models that were only a few centuries less antique,
since Napoleon played, like all amateur historians,
at the amiable game of historical parallel and was
unduly impressed by the precedent of Charlemagne.

One looks in vain through this welter of *pastiche* and archaism for any trace of modern ideas. The doctrines of the Revolution found a becoming place in the liturgy of Napoleonic diplomacy. But except where they coincided with French interests, they were rarely permitted to emerge from the area of sonorous repetition. The successive annexations which brought the Empire to its greatest extent in the years preceding the Russian expedition of 1812 displayed the completest disregard of the racial as well as the geographical limits of France. Her eastern frontier, which the most exaggerated demands of Revolutionary geographers had advanced no further than the Rhine, was traced without the faintest justification of contemporary theory from Lübeck to Spezzia; and every canon of nationalist doctrine was violated by the annexation of Amsterdam, the Hansa Towns, and (by a vaguely Carolingian gesture) of Rome itself. The Napoleonic rearrangement of Germany by the creation of the Confederation of the Rhine was a reminiscence, almost equally traditional, of French ambitions under the Cardinals. The fashionable terminology of the day was adapted in the usual manner to the perennial aims of French policy, and by a pleasing irony the fruits of the Revolution were secured to France by political weapons drawn from the rusty armoury of Richelieu.

The farrago of reaction which was the foundation of the Napoleonic state-system produced a remarkable inversion of rôles in the European drama. Napoleon, the heir and legal representative of the Revolution, was confronted by the year 1812 with an almost universal popular insurrection. The Czar of Russia became a symbol of European liberty. King

George III. commanded the undivided allegiance
of his subjects in a war of European independence.
The Bourbons of Spain turned leaders of revolt, and
the Bourbons of France could outbid Napoleon in
democracy by the promise of a constitutional monarchy. The nations of Europe turned against the
Empire its own doctrines of nationality and natural
frontiers, and went to war once more to confine
French government within the scientific limits of
French race and the geography of France. The
reigning Hohenzollern raised the democratic banner
in his proclamation 'To my people,' and when the
reigning Hapsburg set to his lips the trumpet of
nationalism, the walls of the Napoleonic citadel reeled
and fell in.

An odd postscript of modernity was provided by
the brief adventure of the Hundred Days. When
the Emperor swept into Paris from Elba, he was
forced by circumstances into an attitude which was
not his own. If the Bourbons were to be excluded
from France, it could only be done by a more popular
government than theirs. Louis XVIII. had played
the *Charte:* Napoleon doubled and played the *Acte
additionnel,* and France experienced the queer sensation of receiving a Legislature of two Houses, liberty
of the press, and a mild degree of ministerial responsibility from the hands of the most uncompromising
autocrat in Europe. But his actions were not spon-
taneous, and the gesture of constitutional monarchy
which granted the Constitution of 1815 was as
unnatural to Napoleon as the movements of a sick
man. The absolutism of the *Grand Empire* of 1810
had been the true expression of his ideals. The uncertain sketch of a Liberal Empire which he made

in 1815 was little more than an indication of his difficulties. Leaving it half drawn, he drove out of Paris to sweep the Prussians across the Rhine and the English into the sea. He failed; and sentenced, after the custom of that day, to transportation, he sailed into the South Atlantic,

'like some rare treasure galleon,
Hull down, with masts against the Western hues.'

II

At St. Helena Napoleon became a pretender to his
own throne; and in this position of greater freedom
and less responsibility he addressed himself with
enthusiasm to that sport of kings in exile, the drafting
and revision of his manifesto. The alteration of
war and administration in which he had lived during
the Empire left him with little leisure for the elaboration of political doctrine. He had been far too busy
being Napoleonic to find time to be a Bonapartist.
But on his island he had time enough to become a
doctrinaire, and St. Helena was the seed-bed of
Bonapartism. An emperor who is his own Council
of Ministers in peace and his own General Staff in
war is unlikely to leave behind him any considerable
or coherent body of political theory. But the speculations for which the Tuileries had no place were a
welcome exercise at Longwood. Napoleon in exile
became the first of the Bonapartists, and in those
hot afternoons of dictation he laid the foundations
of the Second Empire.

The Emperor had held the centre of the European
stage for fifteen years, and it was improbable that so
experienced a performer would fail to appreciate
the dramatic value of his exile. The lights which
had followed him across Europe were to be swung
on to his rock in the Atlantic, and one can almost

15

catch the tramp of the scene-shifters in the sudden
drop of his tone from the pride of omnipotence to
the resignation of defeat. In the next act the drums
were to be muffled, and in a subdued glare of footlights the lonely Emperor was to be despised and
rejected of men.

Napoleon had discovered that the popularity of
novel creeds is largely derived from the richness of
their martyrology, and with sound judgment he
resolved to become the first martyr of his faith.
Within a year of his arrival at St. Helena he was
talking of a Bonapartist restoration based on his
own martyrdom, and by 1817 that acute publicist
had scandalised his generals with a cynical appreciation of the propagandist value of the Crucifixion:
'If Jesus Christ had not died on the cross, he would
never have been worshipped as God.' The moral
was drawn for the new gospel of Bonapartism: 'If
I die on the cross and my son lives, all will be well
with him.' The Imperial crown was to be exchanged
for a crown of thorns, and Napoleon and his helpers
on the island set to work a trifle clumsily to improvise
a new Calvary. Sir Hudson Lowe found himself
cast for the unsympathetic part of Pilate, and the
evangelists of Longwood prepared their synoptic
gospels for the world.

The new creed had now its martyrology. It remained to provide its doctrine, and the Emperor, in
the words of his step-daughter, 'arranged his life,
his defence, and his glory with the infinite care of a
dramatist lavishing work on his fifth act and elabo-
rating every detail for the sake of the final apotheosis.'
The drama which had been left unfinished at Waterloo was to be provided with a happy ending in which

a younger Bonaparte sat enthroned amid the cheers of a happy people, whilst the founder of the dynasty smiled down through the incense upon the realisation of his dreams. Napoleon's work at St. Helena was much more than a crude and sentimental gesture of martyrdom. It was the first propaganda of Bonapartism.

The new doctrine was designed to compete in the markets of European opinion with the Peace of Vienna, and it became necessary to include in its composition a strong admixture of those liberal principles which had been violated by the old-world diplomacy of Metternich and Castlereagh. A supply of lofty ideals has rarely failed the critics of peace treaties; and if Napoleon II. was to outbid Louis XVIII., he must be prepared to offer democracy to the people of France and nationalism to the populations of Europe. It became the business of Napoleon in exile to demonstrate that these principles had been the political tradition of his House, and the unfortunate circumstance that they had not served only to send him more eagerly to his task.

The problem which confronted those aging and irritable men in their farm-house in the tropics was the adjustment of Napoleon's record to the novel exigencies of Bonapartist doctrine, and it became necessary, if the autocrat of 1810 was to pass for a democrat in 1820, to handle the facts with that peculiar skill which a master of English prose has admired in a master of French painting under the name of 'a marvellous tact of omission.' The Emperor's career was hastily rearranged so as to catch the high lights of fashionable theory, and the long epic of his rise and fall became the mere subject-

2

matter of ingenious exegesis. The material was often
stubborn; and when Napoleon took his place as the
first author of Bonapartist apologetics, he found the
Old Testament of his first reign singularly barren of
helpful texts and had more frequent recourse to the
milder utterances of his New Testament of 1815.
One might catch sometimes an aside to Gourgaud in
which the Emperor confesses his frank disgust for
the democratic expedients to which he had been
driven by the exigencies of national defence after the
return from Elba. But in the main the figure which
it became the business of Bonapartism to present to
the world was the Emperor of the Hundred Days.
The imagination of posterity has been engaged by
a more impressive figure as he sits above the thunder
on the Napoleonic Olympus, holding his eagle, wield-
ing the lightning, surrounded by the minor divinities
of the Imperial mythology.

' Cannon his name,
    Cannon his voice, he came.'

But such visions are unfriendly to prospects of
restoration to the throne of a war-weary people;
and the whole effort of St. Helena was directed towards the evocation of a gentler scene in which the
mild-eyed legislator of 1815 bent a perpetually
attentive ear to the strictly constitutional promptings
of Benjamin Constant. The prospect was *bourgeois*
in the extreme. But now all the world had turned
civilian, and one must move, if one meant to reach
the Tuileries, with the times.

The Bonaparte succession was precluded by the
peace treaties of Vienna. It followed naturally that
the doctrine of Bonapartism must contradict upon
every European problem the principles on which that

settlement was based. The Peace of Vienna was, briefly, the negation of the French Revolution by the assembled monarchies of Europe. Bonapartism was consequently driven to the odd expedient of affirming the principles of 1789 in the name of the man who had used field artillery as a solvent of democracy in 1795, and the Emperor in retirement was graciously pleased to recognise in himself the embodiment of the Revolution. The evidence, apart from his soldierly appreciation of the virtues of Equality, was slender; but the facts were fused in the white heat of Napoleon's new enthusiasm for the First Republic. The returning Bourbons had repainted the lilies on the French flag: Bonapartism, if it was to inherit the future, must hoist the tricolour. The attempt to detect popular tendencies in the *Grand Empire* was heroic. Autommarchi was assured that the Emperor 'consecrated the Revolution and infused it into the laws,' and he made to Dr. O'Meara a still more explicit confession of his secret republicanism: 'I always believed that true sovereignty resides in the people. The Imperial government was a sort of Republic.' If it was, the secret had been admirably kept by Fouché and the police. The real truth slipped, as usual, into Gourgaud's diary: 'It is my opinion,' the Emperor admitted one day in 1816, 'that a constitution would not suit France, which is an essentially monarchical country. . . . there should be no legislative assembly.' Napoleon had inherited the national energy of the Revolution and had employed it to repel the machinery of the Empire. But the engineer who canalises a great stream and harnesses it to his power-house cannot always claim credit for the rush of its waters.

The Emperor's claim upon Liberal gratitude became a shade fantastic when it was founded upon
a sympathetic examination of his record during the
Hundred Days, and posterity was invited to forget
that the First Consul had violated the last parliament
of the Revolution with infantry in a grateful realisation of his embarrassed constitutionalism in 1815.
It must have sometimes occurred to Napoleon that
if he had been a Bonapartist in 1810, he would have
made peace with the world and founded a dynasty.
The evangelists of St. Helena suggested that he had
found the light on his return from Elba and searched
hopefully in the constitution of 1815 for those germs
of Liberalism which had been so distressingly absent
from the Constitution of 1804. But they were con-
stantly discouraged by the Emperor's obstinate candour in confessing at intervals that he had not meant
a word of it. He frequently admitted to the little
circle that if he had won a victory in Belgium, he
would have abolished the Chambers on his return to
Paris; and this inconvenient spirit of the confessional
even impelled him to assure Admiral Cockburn that
he had assumed a Liberal tone in 1815 'simply because my situation at that particular moment made it
necessary for me to yield to popular feeling on that
point.' An equal sensitiveness to public opinion
dictated the draft of a constitution which he produced
in 1820 for the benefit of Napoleon II. But one can
hear the undertone of autocracy through the pious
murmur of its Liberalism, and the exalted claim of
the democratic Bonapartists that Napoleon was the
Messiah of the Revolution must remind many students
of religion that there have been false Messiahs.

An effort of almost equal heroism was made in the

scriptures of St. Helena to demonstrate that the Emperor had been a practising nationalist. The settlement of Vienna, conceived by Austrian statesmen in the Austrian capital, naturally transgressed in every detail the doctrine of nationality; and if the European opposition thrown up by the peace treaties was to be mobilised in support of the Bonaparte succession, the history of the Empire must be ransacked for instances of Napoleon's conformity with the fashionable doctrine. The little group of embittered chauvinists on the island was startled by disquisitions upon the Emperor's affection for the Germans, the Italians, the Greeks, the Poles, and the Spaniards, which had been kept a profound secret from the subject populations of the Empire. Even Iceland, whose claim to independence had rarely been refused by the enemies of England, was admitted to the fast widening circle of his sympathy; and Napoleon emerged from the reflections of his exile with the conviction, which in the minds of Germans, Englishmen, and Spaniards had been fatal to the continued existence of his Empire, that 'there are certain desires with regard to nationality which must sooner or later be gratified' and that the first of those desires is an appetite for national self-government or (to give to it its more impressive, Bostonian name) self-determination. The trace of Napoleon's frontiers had followed at some points the scientific lines of European racial divisions. But his nationalism, which was frankly fortuitous before Waterloo, became dogmatic at St. Helena.

The Empire was now rehabilitated in French eyes by the fashionable democracy of its principles, and its European popularity was ensured by a still more

modish sympathy with 'nations struggling to be free.'
It remained to reassure a nervous French electorate
upon its prospects of continued home life. The
male population of France in 1816 had only recently
become domesticated, and it had no desire to return
to the colours. But when it inquired apprehensively
by what coincidence the government of so enlightened
a dynasty had been a period of uninterrupted European war conducted upon an unprecedented scale, the
Emperor was ready with an answer and demonstrated with a wealth of quotation and argument that the
peace of the world had been continually sacrificed to
the insatiable ambition of the Houses of Hapsburg
and Hanover, whose ministers had forced France into
war after war with an energy only equalled by the hy-
pocrisy with which they denounced Napoleon as the
cause. *L'Empire'* (the words which were to be
spoken by the nephew at Bordeaux were formed by
the uncle at St. Helena thirty years before) *'c'est
la paix.'*

The great Bonapartist of St. Helena had propounded his political doctrine of democracy, nationalism, and peace. It was elaborated in those
interminable talks which alone stood between
Napoleon and madness, until at last in a great storm
of the wind the Emperor, having upon his lips the
name of a military rank or (as some say) of a dead
woman, died also.

III

The destruction of the Empire left an odd gap in France, and it was hardly filled by the return of the Bourbons. The appearance in public life of large numbers of elderly gentlemen, speaking with the accent of the last century and gloomily disapproving of the generation with which they found themselves surrounded, was an inadequate compensation for the disappearance of those bronzed and booted young men of the Empire who had ridden into every capital in Europe. It cannot have been enlivening to be governed by persons who regarded every achievement of the past thirty years as a manifestation of original sin; and for all the memories which it contained of the conscription and the invasion, the roll of the Emperor's drums must have seemed a friendly sound, when it was compared with the dry rustle of the parchments as the King's ministers searched them for royal precedents.

The Restoration of Louis XVIII. was as depressing as any other triumph of age over youth. It seemed to a generation which had served the guns at Wagram and stood in the last trenches on Montmartre that the old men and the priests and the Bretons with their stupid faces had been right after all. The new world which Goethe had seen looming up through

the mist at Valmy wavered and melted away before
the confused gesture of a Peace Conference, and in
France it was as though men came indoors out of the
strong sunlight of the Empire to a long, grey afternoon of deportment and gentility about the house.
The royal troops marched decorously once more behind the white flag and the lilies; King Louis sat
on his throne again; and the Eighteenth Century
seemed to have resumed its interminable course.

It was a queer time, in which half the world was
trying to forget that it had spent the best years of
its life by the waters of Babylon in teaching dancing
and the irregular verbs to the young subjects of
King George III., whilst the other half was almost
ashamed to remember that it had trailed a musket
across the Alps to Marengo or charged shouting
through the smoke of Mercer's guns against the
British squares at Waterloo.   So long as French
politics were directed by that generation, there was
little disposition to find fault with the unimpressive
exterior of Louis XVIII. and the blameless tedium
of his ministers.   The lives of most Frenchmen had
been sufficiently eventful before 1815 for them to
acquiesce with relief in the sedative provided by the
restoration; and France, which has more generally
regarded parlimentary institutions as a source of
scandal than as a form of government, sat comfort-
ably back in the public galleries of the Chamber to
enjoy the deep notes of MM. Guizot and Royer-
Collard.   Faint echoes of the Emperor drifted up
out of the South Atlantic.   Gaunt old men (one aged
rapidly on the road from Moscow to the Beresina),
who had once been the masters of Europe when they
trailed the *sabretache* of the *Cuirassiers* or wore the

schapska of the Lancers of the Guard, tilted hats over their eyes and drew up rickety chairs in provincial cafés to mutter about 'the Man' and 'the Son of the Man.' There was a feeble sputter of insurrection. But Napoleon went to his grave *dans une petite vallée d'une île déserte, sous un saule pleureur;* and whilst the old King lived, France was profoundly and excusably indifferent to the fascinations of political experiment.

This temper prevailed among the men who had returned home from the two exiles of the emigration and the conscription until they grew old and faded out of politics. But after the angularity of Charles had succeeded in 1824 to the gentler curves of Louis XVIII., a new, more incalculable generation began to come of age, and the children of the First Empire gathered in the wings, prepared to shoulder their way on to the stage of French affairs. The uneasy temper of the age was described a few years later, when Alfred de Musset set down the *Confession d'un Enfant du Siècle:* 'During the wars of the Empire, whilst husbands and brothers were away in Germany, anxious mothers brought to birth a hectic, sickly, nervous generation. Conceived between two battles, schooled with the sound of rolling drums in their ears, boys in their thousands eyed one another gloomily, as they tried over their frail muscles. At intervals their fathers appeared from the bloodshed, held them to the gold braid on their breasts, set them down, and to horse again.'

These young men, round whose cradles the slim draped Victories of the Empire had sounded upon trumpets the names of Austerlitz, Iéna, Eylau, Friedland, Wagram, were the new factor in French

politics.   Peace is never in greater danger than when
a generation grows up which has not in its own person
known war; and as the children of 1810 grew up
into the young men of 1825, their imagination played
fitfully round the glory of their fathers.   In literary
taste they were Romantics.   In politics (since it
seemed tragic that old men should govern when all
the world was young) they were Liberal.   But imperceptibly their politics became touched with romance as they began to regard the Empire in kindly
retrospect.   Napoleon had been a name at which
the men of 1816, according to their politics, stood to
attention or looked nervously behind them.   Gradually the sharp outlines of that little figure melted
into the distance, and the Imperial scene began to
glow for the men of 1825 through a gentle haze of
romance.

The revulsion at this stage was merely sentimental.
Bonapartism, outside the dwindling ranks of old
irreconcilables, was not yet adopted by any considerable body of Frenchmen as a political faith.   The
Emperor was dead, and Napoleon II. could hardly
be said to be alive.   Few eyes turned eastward
towards Vienna, where the dim figure of a pale
young man, whom the imagination of a poet and
the genius of a great actress have conspired to present
to posterity as a stoutish woman in a white uniform
with a queer, haunting voice, might be seen moving
vaguely behind the ordered solemnity of the Austrian
Court.   Even Béranger, so responsive always to the
requirements of his public, felt no deeper emotion
at this spectacle of predestined futility than the mild
irony which inspired *Les Deux Cousins, ou Lettre
d'un petit Roi à un petit Duc:*

' Les rois m'adoraient au berceau,
Les rois m'adoraient au berceau;
Et cepedant je suis à Vienne!'

This lyric of gentle sympathy was hardly a marching
song to which a prince might come to his own again.

But the Emperor himself was a more inspiring
subject for young poets under a dull dynasty, and
the declamatory possibilities of his career seemed
inexhaustible. Victor Hugo invoked

' gloire au maître suprême!
Dieu même a sur son front posé le diadème.'

His imagination was excited by *'Toujours Lui!*
Lui partout.' Even Béranger, who had found a
more powerful vehicle in the *chanson,* was inspired
to an ode of fashionable sensibility by the Emperor's
death:

' Sa gloire est là comme le phare immense
D'un nouveau monde et d'un monde trop vieux.'

But his real contribution to the renascence of the
Imperial legend was made in those simpler verses
which both recorded and stimulated the traditional
Bonapartism of the countryside. It was the peasant
who had felt most acutely the return of the gentry
under the Restoration, and when the shadows of his
new masters fell across the cottage window, the ex-
soldier of the Imperial armies was half inclined to
regret the past. Napoleon became a name for all
the fine freedom and brave endeavour of the past;
and that odd alliance between the Emperor and the
Liberal cause to which all his work at St. Helena
had been directed was realised by the chansonnier
of the *Roi d' Yvetot.* At that gentle music the cold

figure of Caesar came alive and stepped down from
his niche, and the conqueror of the world became the
people's friend.

> ' On parlera de sa gloire
>   Sous la chaume bien longtemps,
>   L'humble toit, dans cinquante ans,
> Ne connaîtra plus d'autre histoire.
>
> .   .   .   .   .
>
>   Le peuple encor le révère
>   Oui, le révère.
> Parlez-nous de lui, grand'mère,
>   Parlez-nous de lui.
>
> Mes enfants, dans ce village,
> Suivi de rois, il passa.
>
> .   .   .
>
> Il avait petit chapeau
> Avec redingote grise.
> Près de lui je me troublai:
> Il me dit: Bonjour ma chère.
>   Bonjour ma chère.
> —Il vous a parlé, grand'mère!
>   Il vous a parlé!'

That is how Napoleon passed from history into folk-
lore.

A similar movement steadily became noticeable
in the printsellers' shop-windows. During the
Empire his representations had been strictly confined to a somewhat dreary canon of official pictures.
Napoleon was to be seen in large canvases crowning
his Empress with a frozen gesture or distributing
eagles to his legions with a statuesque immobility
which owed almost more to David than David himself owed to the antique. Court painters posed him
bare-headed in the centre of obsequious princes and

A Review at the Tuileries under the First Empire

From the picture by Bellange in the Musée de Versailles

Grands Cordons, extending an inexpressive hand of friendship or clemency to the Emperor Francis, the Czar of Russia, the burghers of Madrid, or the Queen of Prussia; whilst their more martial colleagues sent him caracoling across battle-fields which they had never visited with a complete lack of horsemanship which is only attainable by a lay figure in a studio. The Emperor was depicted upon every conceivable occasion of civil dignity and military triumph without any deviation from his Imperial imperturbability, whether the foreground was obstructed by a conquered people or the French dead. Indeed, almost the sole concession to human weakness which it was permissible to record in this solemn series was his unforgettable wound in the right foot at Ratisbon, borne bravely in a circle of solicitous shakoes and with the unwounded foot in the stirrup of that incomparably, that incredibly Arab steed.

Adversity in the field checked the majestic flow of official art, and Napoleonic portraiture entered upon a new phase in defeat. The symbolic possibilities of the lonely Emperor on his distant rock were exhausted with pitiless persistence. But the effective appeal of the Imperial legend in art was not made by the sea, the sunset, the reflective eye. It was couched in the less tortured perspective and the simpler scenes of the military draughtsmen of the Restoration. They began in the mere depiction of uniforms and a simple enjoyment of crowded foregrounds in which the big, bearded Pioneers swung along eight abreast and the massed drums brought on the Guard, with the long line of level bayonets rising and falling to the swing of the bearskins and the mounted field-officers riding like tall ships along

the stream.   Avoiding the stately banalities of
official art, Raffet and Bellangé brought the crowded
battle-fields of the Empire within range of the normal
imagination or appealed to sentimental reminiscence
with the invisible sweep of great cavalcades past the
dead Emperor at midnight, or the resurrection of
lost legions to the roll of a dead man's drum.

> 'C'est la grande Revue
> Qu'aux Champs Élysées,
> A l'heure de minuit
> Tient le César déchu.'

But while they were accomplishing this in their
more crowded canvases, their smaller works began
to do for Napoleon's memory something of the service
which had been performed for it in verse by Béranger.
His praetorians, whom an indignant countryside
under the Restoration had been apt to set violently
about as 'brigands,' were displayed by Charlet in
an endearing light of mild comedy.   Their hardships,
their gallantries, their potations, and their heroism
reinstated them in the national affection; and slowly
the grognard with his growling repartee, his bearskin and his long moustache climbed to a popularity
which in a more recent war has been earned by a
still older soldier with a still more ragged moustache.
The Emperor himself was popularised by a more human attitude, as the laurels and the purple were sent
back to the costumier's and he assumed a more natural
dress:

> 'Il avait petit chapeau
> Avec redingote grise.'

The smirk of official portraiture passed from his
lips, and he was seen, hunched and anxious, by the

camp-fires of 1814. The little figure stepped out
of the formal surroundings and heavy gilt frames of
command portraits into reality; and the change
carried his image into every little room in France.
He galloped along cheering lines or watched the
gun-fire with folded arms. Tall Grenadiers were
called out of the ranks to have their ears pinched
and to exchange memories of the campaign of Italy.
Sleepy sentries awoke to find the Emperor on guard.
Napoleon himself confessed to human frailty in
innumerable snatches of sleep before Austerlitz.
Cottagers entertained him unawares, and artillery-
men stood aside to watch the master-gunner lay a
gun at Montereau. Gradually the spell was broken,
and the dead Emperor came to life on every wall as
the saviour, the guardian, and the hope of his country.

A deeper note of pictorial Bonapartism was struck
in the eccentric blend of piety and patriotism which
inspired a popular engraving of *'Saint Napoléon,
Martyr'* and displayed the canonised Emperor in
the Roman pallium and short, curling beard of one
of Diocletian's Christians, holding the palm in one
hand and mildly deprecating with the other the be-
stowal of a wreath by a foreshortened angel. But
sometimes mere hagiology proved insufficient, and
Napoleon passed into the more rarefied atmosphere
of theology itself. A grateful Church had repeated-
ly acknowledged his services to religion; and Bellangé lent a Napoleonic flavour to religion itself,
when his peasant pointed to a familiar outline and
exclaimed to the village priest: *'Tenez, voyez-vous,
Monsieur le Curé, pour moi le v'là le père éternel.'*
Bonapartism could fly no higher.

The drift of the Liberals towards Bonapartism

was determined by the new presentation of the Imperial legend in art and letters, and it was without infidelity to their master that his old officers found themselves brigaded with the young rioters of 1830. That sudden, summer insurrection jerked Charles X. off his throne; and by the effort of the young men who ached to follow the new ways the slow, grinding machinery of the Eighteenth Century was stopped for ever.

The Orleans monarchy endeavoured for eighteen years to satisfy the needs of France. A desperate attempt was made to flatter the national vanity by restoring some of the national playthings. The tricolour flag fluttered once more to the masthead. A forward foreign policy recalled the brave days before the Peace of Vienna. And Napoleon's statue dominated Paris again from the top of the *Colonne de la Grande Armée*. But in its effort to be Napoleonic without a Bonaparte the reign of Louis Philippe resembled nothing so much as a production of *Hamlet* by a company which not only omitted the Prince but rarely got beyond Rosencrantz and Guildenstern.

The enunciation of the Imperial legend rose, under official encouragement, to a crescendo. Poets and historians became incapable of other topics, and the Napoleonic illustrators flooded the bookshops with pictorial Bonapartism. The shadowy reign of Napoleon II. closed, as that dim light flickered out at Schönbrunn in 1832. But in Paris men were still quoting the full-mouthed eloquence of Victor Hugo's *Ode à la Colonne,* and at half the theatres French audiences were staring open-mouthed whilst round-shouldered actors in grey overcoats took snuff, pinched ears, or raked the footlights with that single field-glass. Thiers passed from the history of the Revolution to the Consulate and Empire. The *Mémorial de Sainte-Hélène* appeared with Charlet's drawings, and Raffet illustrated a mediocre *Histoire de Napoléon.* Whilst the King's ministers were struggling with the Egyptian question, epic poets were collaborating to produce *Napoléon en Égypte* in eight cantos with decorations by Vernet and Bellangé; and Heine found Napoleonic engravings on every wall in France.

This queer fever, which produced almost the whole mass of Imperial bric-à-brac now extant, raged in verse, prose, politics, and statuary; and Louis Philippe set solemnly about to cure it by a desperate homœopathy. The Orleanist King made himself the first Bonapartist in France. The Arc de Triomphe was completed and consecrated to the myth of the Emperor. The Château of Versailles became a museum of Imperial battle-pictures and was dedicated in great letters '*à toutes les gloires de la France.*' And by a supreme gesture of Bonapartism the frigate *Belle-Poule,* commanded by the Prince de Joinville, sailed in 1840 to St. Helena to carry out the second clause of the Emperor's will: '*Je désire que mes cendres resposent sur les bords de la Seine, au milieu de ce peuple français que j'ai tant aimé.* They brought him into Paris on a November day of frost and bright sunshine; and as Napoleon passed to the Invalides there was a great cry of '*Vive l'Empereur!*'

THE PRINCE

THE PRINCE

I

On an April morning in 1808 there was French gun-
fire along the Pyrenees.   A son had been born in
Paris to the Queen of Holland, and the Emperor was
in Bayonne.   The heads of the French columns were
thrusting down through the passes into Spain in the
first movement of the Peninsular War, and on the
day that the child was born King Ferdinand VII.
drove into Bayonne by the great south road from
Irun.   That night he dined with Napoleon and
received in his lodgings after dinner a message,
brought by General Savary, that the Emperor felt,
on consideration, that the House of Bourbon should
cease to reign.

The boy was born in the dark hours of a Wednesday morning (it was the 20th of the month).   But
it was not until the fourth day that the news came
from Paris to Bayonne.   Napoleon found time to
write a few lines and pass them to a secretary:

> 'Ma Fille, j'apprends que vous êtes heureusement
> accouchée d'un garçon. J'en ai éprouvé la plus vive joie.
> Il ne me reste plus qu'à être tranquillisé et à savoir que
> vous vous portez bien. Je suis étonné que dans une
> lettre du 20, que m'écrit l'archichancelier, il ne m'en
> dise rien.   NAPOLÉON.'

And all along the frontier the salutes boomed up the
valleys of the Pyrenees.

II

HE was the third child of an unhappy marriage.
But the news of his birth gave pleasure almost everywhere except to his ailing and indifferent father.
Louis Bonaparte, King of Holland, might have been
a happier man if he had found himself in a less remarkable family. He presents a vague and shifting
outline against the clear-cut background of the
Bonapartes. There is an odd flavour of modernity
about his nerves, his diffidence, his introspection,
his perpetual cures which hardly accords with those
bright figures of romance; and as he circulates nervously among the thrusting brothers and exuberant
sisters of the Imperial family, he has the air almost
of an incautious Hellenist introduced suddenly into
the company of some of the more primitive members
of the House of Atreus. His career was one long
struggle waged by his nerves against his promotion.
He had worked at his schoolbooks in the little lodgings in the Midi where Lieutenant Bonaparte polished his buttons and read history. But the tense
atmosphere of that hired room at Valence can hardly
have been congenial to a youth who, as he informed
the grateful author some years later, wept copious-
ly over the mild sentiment of *Paul et Virginie*. The
elder brother, who had paid his school bills out of a
subaltern's pay, taught him the rudiments of soldier-
ing in the campaign of Italy. He was a quiet boy,
combining in an unusual degree physical courage

38

with taciturnity; and as the family got strenuously
on in the world, the young Louis seemed to sink
steadily deeper into himself. It was an age in which
dyspepsia was frequently mistaken for intellect; and
when the First Consul brought peace to France and
set up his little suburban Court at Rueil, his younger
brother was mostly to be found regarding the bois-
terous relaxations of Malmaison with Byronic gloom.

Louis was of the melancholy stuff that unmarried
uncles are made of. Indeed, the Emperor and his
mother-in-law subsequently disagreed as to whether
it was the study of Rousseau or his digestion that
made him impossible. Undisturbed by family life
such a man, who was described in the English idiom
of 1800 as a person of sensibility, might have passed
his time agreeably enough between the elegant patronage of Canova and a polite correspondence with
Goethe. But with a wife to share his infelicity, he was
bound inevitably to become the unhappy husband of
an unhappy woman. Unfortunately his brother's
wife had a daughter.

When Josephine de Beauharnais married General
Bonaparte, that lively widow from Martinique
brought to him the two children of her first husband.
The younger of them was a fair schoolgirl with large
blue eyes, named Hortense-Eugénie. In the closing
years of the Eighteenth Century, when the Revolution
seemed to have spent its force in the feeble movements of the Directoire, she was trained in the accomplishments requisite for polite society at Madame
Campan's celebrated academy for young ladies,
where that indomitable Minerva kept alive under
the tricolour and Phrygian cap the traditions of
French gentility. There Hortense received instruc-

tion in perspective, deportment, correct sentiments and the use of the globes; and she displayed that aptitude for playing on the harp and painting in water-colour which was universally recognised to be the most elegant enhancement of a pair of drooping shoulders and two downcast eyes.

This accomplished young lady became an ornament of the Consular circle at Malmaison in the days when her mother was beginning to feel the weight of a republican crown. That amiable widow had consented to become the wife of Napoleon without anticipating either his bewildering promotions or the somewhat volcanic nature of his affections, and towards the year 1800 she found herself balanced a trifle precariously at the head of French society. The Bonapartes had always resented their brother's choice of a West Indian wife, and her conduct during his absence in Egypt provided ample material for the disapproval of his family. After his return he considered the possibility of a divorce upon grounds which were at once more human and less royal than those upon which he acted ten years later. But he could not put out of his life the woman whom he later called without irony 'the best woman in France,' in whom he saw *'la grazia in persona,'* whose name died on his lips in the dark at St. Helena.

Josephine resumed her place at the head of the Consular household with an increasing fear of her husband and the future. But in such a situation any step was welcome which would bind her fortunes more closely to those of the Bonapartes. Now if her daughter were to marry a Bonaparte, the two families must rise or fall together; Hortense might even raise up children who could become the heirs

The Empress Josephine (1798)

After the drawing by Isabey

of Napoleon himself. With some such design she
marked down the reflective Louis to be her son-in-
law. The prospect was uninviting to both parties.
Hortense would have preferred the more decorative
Duroc, and Louis would have preferred another lady
in spite of the discouraging circumstances that she
had suffered in the past from the small-pox and
continued to suffer from the obstinate longevity of
a husband. But the First Consul and his wife were
insistent. It was an age of submissive daughters;
and Hortense, who might with a little firmness have
become the wife of the youngest Marshal of the
Empire, acquiesced in her mother's choice. Louis
was more restive. But, after at least two refusals
and a determined avoidance of the young lady's
company in the absence of witnesses, he succumbed
to the fatal atmosphere of a ball-room and consented
to the designs of his implacable relatives. Napoleon
retained a lively recollection of the conversation for
nearly twenty years and recorded it at St. Helena
in language more appropriate to the sudden storm of
a fortified position: *'une attaque aussi vive qu'in-
attendue lui arracha son consentement.'* The result
was a winter wedding in the Rue de la Victoire, and
in the first week of 1802 Hortense led her blushing
bridegroom to the altar.

The young people were set up in a château in the
Ile de France, and in the autumn their first child
was born. But whilst the little Napoléon-Louis-
Charles struggled through his first ailments, his
father and mother were drifting from indifference
into hostility in the gardens of Saint-Leu. The Consular circle had become the Imperial family and, in
view of the continued childlessness of the Empress,

Hortense's child was a small boy of extreme political importance. But his parents (it may have been due to some fault in Madame Campan's excellent curriculum) lived in a dismal atmosphere of domestic debate. A second boy was born in 1804. But Louis' health deteriorated as his curses became more frequent, and apart from her two little boys the prospect for Hortense became increasingly dreary.

At this point the Emperor, who was a trifle inclined to regard his relations as a successful player of draughts regards his pieces when they have reached the far end of the board, conceived the unfortunate design of converting the Dutch Republic into a monarchy and promoting Louis to be its king. A conscientious monarch may well prove a depressing husband, and family life in the Dutch palaces varied between tedium and disagreement. When Napoleon sent a French nominee to The Hague, he did so in the reasonable anticipation that French interests would not be disregarded by the new monarch. But Louis, whose sentiments were now dyed a deep Orange, was perpetually insisting on the ancient liberties of Holland and exasperated his brother with a fervent patriotism for the country of his adoption. His wife was treated to a still more irritating affectation of Dutch austerity. Her French light-mindedness became distasteful to the successor of De Witt and William the Silent, and the solemn conduct by Louis of his royal duties and diversions called down a reproof from the Emperor in 1807 which lights up the domestic scene in which Hortense was living:

> 'Vous gouvernez trop cette nation en capucin. La bonté d'un roi doit toujours être majestueuse et ne doit pas être celle d'un moine. . . .

*Vos querelles avec la Reine percent aussi dans le public.
Ayez dans votre intérieur ce caractère paternel et efféminé
que vous montrez dans le gouvernement, et ayez dans les
affaires ce rigorisme que vous montrez dans votre ménage.
Vous traitez une jeune femme comme, on mènerait un
régiment. . . .*

*Vous avez la meilleure femme et la plus vertueuse, et
vous la rendez malheureuse. Laissez-la danser tant qu'elle
veut, c'est de son âge. J'ai une femme qui a quarante
ans: du champ de bataille je lui écris d'aller au bal;
et vous voulez qu'une femme de vingt ans, qui voit passer
sa vie, qui en a toutes les illusions, vive dans un cloître,
soit comme une nourrice, toujours à laver son enfant? . . .
Malheureusement vous avez une femme trop vertueuse; si
vous aviez une coquette, elle vous mènerait par le bout du
nez.'*

Like so many men, Napoleon would have made a
perfect husband to another man's wife. But through
the interstices between his excellent advice one may
catch a vivid glimpse of that dismal Dutch interior.

The Emperor, whose view of married life had become so debonair, was campaigning at the far side
of Europe. He had fought the battle of Eylau in
the winter, and he was now tasting the discomfort
of operations conducted against the Russian armies
at the end of eight hundred miles of communications.
But his letter had hardly reached Holland from East
Prussia when the long shadow of bereavement fell
across Hortense, and her eldest boy died in her arms
at The Hague. For a time grief made her husband
seem almost tolerable. The surviving child was sent
to his grandmother, and the King and Queen of
Holland passed the summer of 1807 in a dejected
little honeymoon in the Pyrenees. The news took
more characteristic effect upon Napoleon. After a
stream of kindly letters of consolation to Hortense

and her mother, he began to look into the causes of
their loss. The child, it appeared, had died of croup,
and on a June morning the Emperor dictated a note
from headquarters to his Minister of Foreign Affairs:

> *'Monsieur Champagny, depuis vingt ans il s'est manifesté
> une maladie appelée* croup, *qui enlève beaucoup d'enfants
> dans le nord de l'Europe. Depuis quelques années elle
> se propage en France. Nous désirons que vous proposiez
> un prix de 12,000 francs, qui sera donné au médecin auteur
> du meilleur mémoire sur cette maladie et sur la manière
> de la traiter.*   NAPOLÉON.'

The rest of the day's work included a minute to the
Minister of Marine on naval supplies and the defence
of Toulon, a note to Daru on an increase of the
tobacco ration of the forces in the field, and a decree
awarding public lands for meritorious service in the
Polish army. Napoleon also found time for a line
to Jerome Bonaparte on his operations in Silesia
(with hints on the management of a discarded General
of Division), some notes on the conscripts of 1808
for the guidance of the commander of his general
reserve, and a strong hint to Fouché as to the prompt
removal from Paris to some small provincial town
of two ex-colonels of the royal army and a sham
baroness who had been spreading disloyal rumours.
Administrative life was sufficiently variegated at
Imperial headquarters without excursions into path-
ology. But the Finckenstein decree on croup, which
elicited two completely erroneous prize essays from
practitioners in Bremen and Geneva, was a neat ex-
ample of Napoleonic versatility in the manner of the
classical *Décret de Moscou* which was to date from
the Kremlin in 1812 a thorough reorganisation of the
Théâtre Français. Ten days after that busy morning

among his papers the Emperor fought the battle of
Friedland and ended the Continental war which had
opened at Ulm and Austerlitz.

But the death of the Prince Royal of Holland at
the age of four possessed an importance beyond the
unsound conclusions of the medical *concours* of 1807.
'*Ce pauvre Napoléon,*' as his uncle called him, had
been the heir to the French Empire; and with his
death the Emperor turned once more to that project
of divorce and re-marriage which haunted Josephine
among her flowers at Malmaison. The surviving
child of Hortense could not take both the Dutch and
the French succession, and something must be done
for the perpetuation of the dynasty. The unpleasing
subject was opened to the Empress early in 1808,
and that aging, pretty woman with her forced smile
stared miserably down the prospect of desposition and
official widowhood. The Emperor postponed a decision, and there was still a hope that Hortense would
provide an heir. 'It is your Majesty's business,'
as the urbane M. de Talleyrand had observed, 'to give
us princes; we may depend on you.'

So it was good news, when the boy was born in
April, to his mother, who longed for the company
of children since she had lost that of her husband,
and to the Emperor, as he sat in Bayonne watching
the Spanish Bourbons stumble heavily into his net.
But it was best of all to the weary, bright-eyed woman
who waited at Bordeaux, because she was still an
Empress and the child in Paris might serve to keep
her so and then one day be Emperor of the French.

III

IMPERIAL infancy under the First Empire was apt
to be uneventful, but impressive. Even the comparatively human business of getting born was conducted, for a little Prince of Holland, with a wealth
of ritual. Late in the afternoon of April 20, 1808,
three Princes of the Empire, one Cardinal, the Dutch
ambassador, a French minister, a Grand-Duchess
who was sister to the Emperor and Murat's wife,
and the alarming old lady whom Napoleon called
Madame Mère came to the door in the Rue Cérutti,
and an official *acte de naissance* was executed for
publication in the next day's *Moniteur*. Respectful
crowds cheered their King under a palace window
at Amsterdam, and Hortense was overwhelmed by
visits of ceremony in Paris. She had inherited her
mother's tropical taste for flowers; but although she
was never without the scent of Parma violets, which
she introduced into France, the scent of M. de Talleyrand's powder came near to overcoming her.

There was some official correspondence from
Bayonne on the subject of the boy's name. The
Emperor, like all the world, had forgotten the child's
father; but with an effort of piety he recalled the
shadowy figure of his own and wished the new prince
to be called Charles-Napoléon. This desire was expressed in a short note to The Hague, dictated on the
morning after the *Dos Mayo,* when the Spaniards

46

rose in resentment of the detention of their royal family in Bayonne and the streets of Madrid were cleared by French cavalry. The volleys of Murat's firing-parties were still echoing in the ears of the Madrileños and the news of the *émeute* was boiling slowly up through Old Castile, when the Emperor, after sending some orders into Spain and answering letters from Fouché and the Viceroy of Italy, considered the problem of his small nephew's name. But the first proposal was modified by a sudden recollection of the existence of King Louis; and a few weeks later the world was informed through the *Moniteur* that the boy was to be called Charles-Louis-Napoléon. He bore, a trifle ominously, the names of two failures and an emperor.

The little prince started life with both parents and a small brother of three. He had a king for his father and an Empress for his grandmother. But before his third birthday Josephine was dethroned in Paris and Louis had ceased to reign in Holland. The nightmare of divorce had seemed to fade in the early months of 1808. The Emperor had yielded to her unanswerable argument of tears in March. When he moved to Bayonne to direct the Spanish operation from the frontier, the Empress followed him as far as Bordeaux, where the news of the child's birth reached her. A few days later she was presiding over the combined Courts of France and Spain in *villeggiatura* which must have been a trifle congested, since Napoleon and his Empress, Charles and his Queen, Ferdinand and Godoy were comprehended with an appropriate suite within the straining limits of a provincial château. The Emperor was in the wildest spirits, and Josephine retained his favour, which was indicated, as was usual with him, by the most distressing practical jokes. The couple travelled together as far as Paris, and Napoleon posted alone across Europe to the Congress of Erfurt. There, in a rarefied atmosphere of diplomacy and without the distraction of a pretty woman's tears, he could regard the divorce of Josephine in the cold light of foreign policy, and Talleyrand was instructed to open negotiations with Russia for a Grand-Duchess. In the autumn he was back in Paris on the road to Spain, and as the *berline* left the Tuileries for the south, they kept the Empress from taking the road with her husband.

From Spain, where the *Grand Armée* swept Palafox into Saragossa and brought King Joseph back across the Guadarrama into Madrid, the Emperor furnished Josephine with a curt but conjugal series of notes on his health, whilst the embers of the Spanish insurrection were vigorously scattered and the English were driven into the sea at Corunna. Early in 1809 Napoleon crossed France once more on his way to break Austria at Wagram. He took the Empress with him as far as Strasburg, and during the ensuing campaign he entrusted her with various official duties. The tone of his letters gave no hint of the impending divorce. Hortense and the baby, who was now a year old, had gone with her other boy to the waters at Baden-Baden. The Emperor was busy fighting the Archduke Charles outside Vienna; but a week after the battle of Aspern-Essling, in that busy military interlude in which the French army prepared to re-emerge from the island of Lobau and move upon Wagram, he found two minutes for the composition of an indignant family letter. Hortense was sharply reminded that valuable French princes must not be hazarded on German territory. Peremptory orders came to her from Schönbrunn to interrupt her thermal exercises, and she was given precisely one hour in which to send the boys back over the Rhine to Strasburg. The Empress was delighted at this evidence of the value which Napoleon still placed on Hortense's children, and her confidence may well have been increased by the geniality of his tone in the correspondence which came from Vienna after the victory of 1809. It had been for many years his pleasing habit to threaten her with the prospect, so alarming to wives in war-time, of a sudden midnight return of the wronged husband from the distant wars. The picture seemed to attract his somewhat primitive sense of humour, and it had become a standing family joke in his letters to Josephine, which abound in wild imaginary scenes of nocturnal farce. So late as the month of September in the year of the divorce the Emperor found the heart to send to his wife a comic admonition from Schönbrunn:

> *'Ne te fie pas, et je te conseille de te bien garder la nuit; car une des prochaines tu entendras grand bruit.'*

But after his return to France the end came quickly. The first hint was given by a closed door in the palace. The poor lady endeavoured to retrieve the first evening by a new dress and a wreath of blue flowers; but her husband gloomily observed that they had taken an hour and a half to put on. The autumn of 1809 slowly deepened for Josephine in rain and wretchedness. Napoleon pleaded for a divorce, and the Empress went about the Tuileries holding her head low so that they should not see how red her eyes were.

Her grief was bitter and genuine; but she was not
unaware of its value as an argument, and once at
least with a full appreciation of the dialectical advantages of unconsciousness she interrupted a swoon to
warn a solicitous courtier that she was incommoded
by his sword-belt. The swoon was satisfactorily
resumed, but the Emperor remained unmoved. The
Court calendar with a ghastly ineptitude brought on
the fifth anniversary of the Imperial coronation, and
the unhappy Empress went weakly through an evening of official felicitation at the Hôtel de Ville. After
that she broke down, and a few days later the
Bonapartes sat solemnly round a table in the Tuileries
to hear Josephine, in white and without jewellery,
renounce her husband. That evening she stumbled
to his room, and on the next day she drove out of
Paris through the rain to Malmaison.

The little Prince had lost an Empress for his grandmother before his second birthday. But as the year
1810 opened, his father was still a king. That dismal,
if conscientious, monarch had consistently failed to
give satisfaction in the Napoleonic hierarchy. His
morbid sensitiveness to the interests of his subjects
became increasingly distasteful to the Emperor, and
the Continental blockade of England provided frequent topics for dissension between Paris and Amsterdam. In this controversy Louis proved himself
no better than a Dutchman, and Napoleon was
indisposed to bargain with the Dutch as to the precise
measure of their co-operation in the economic war.
Shortly after the divorce he put in a French army of
occupation and took control of the Dutch coast and
custom-houses. It was the end of Holland, which
was not even accorded the comparative dignity of

partition. The King, whose monarchy had ceased to be even nominal, abdicated in favour of his younger son, and abandoning his family at the same time as his throne, retired alone to the Austrian Alps. But the little Prince never reigned in Holland, which was promptly annexed to the French Empire. He was reserved for a more devious ascent to a greater throne.

Late in the year, when Napoleon had inflicted upon the Hapsburgs the supreme humiliation of matrimony and the Empress Marie Louise simpered at the head of French society, the child was baptized at Fontainebleau in an impressive galaxy of Dukes and Counts of the Empire. The new Empress stood godmother. But in spite of this encouraging beam from the rising sun, Hortense, as the daughter of an ex-Empress and the deserted wife of an ex-King, occupied under the later Empire a position which was somewhat effaced. Having consoled herself for the absence of King Louis with the presence of the Comte de Flahaut, she bore him a child who, as the Duc de Morny, was to take part in the family adventure of the Second Empire. But the greater part of her time was passed with her two little boys in consoling the official widowhood of Josephine at Malmaison. There were occasional interludes of a more alarming character when they breakfasted at the Tuileries with the Emperor; he invariably bore down on his small nephews and lifted them by the head on to a table, a practice discouraged under medical advice by their mother. But their recollections were mainly of Malmaison, where a smiling lady with sad eyes let them run riot among the flowers and gave them the most exciting presents, whilst their mother was taking the waters

amongst all the fine gentlemen at Aix. The little
Louis, dressed in the costume which delights the
admirers of Miss Kate Greenaway, was sufficiently
delicate to become the favourite; and his health was
carefully preserved by the precaution of a governess
who, when he watered the flowers, filled the watering-
can with warm water. In the years of the Empire's
decline a small boy, who was to see little more of
France until he returned to rule it, was walking in
the woods round Malmaison or drilling the big
Grenadiers of the Guard who stood sentry at his
grandmother's door, and rewarding them shyly with
a furtive biscuit.

Before the child was six, the Emperor had fought
a rearguard action across Europe which brought him
from Moscow to Leipzig and from the Rhine to
Champaubert. The Empire went down in the spring
campaign of 1814, and for the two children there was
a confused recollection of an excited mother and a
night drive out of Paris to the sound of the guns.
When the news came to Josephine that the Emperor
had ceased to reign in France, the tired woman that
he had put away sat weeping in the night and crept
back to Malmaison to die.

IV

SMALL boys of six are rarely intrigued by the changing fortunes of their uncles. Indeed, the little Louis probably welcomed the disasters of 1814, which were for him the excuse for exciting journeys and delightful visits to strange houses. The interval between the collapse of the Empire and the return of the Emperor in the following spring was a crowded interlude of foreign visitors. There was a tall fair gentleman with curly hair and such high collars to his uniforms, who particularly engaged the Prince's affections. He was believed to be a mysterious dignitary known as the Czar of Russia, and became one day, by a sudden and furtive gift from an embarrassed little boy, the possessor of Louis' only ring. Then there was an unhappy-looking German gentleman, who was the King of Prussia and brought with him to Malmaison two small boys, to one of whom fifty years later Louis was to send his sword on the hill of La Marfée above Sedan. Other gentlemen came to conspire in the drawing-room about his uncle, and a rather alarming lady, whose excess of petticoats was noticed about the same time by another youthful observer, asked one a great many questions and answered to the name of de Staël.

Then came a fascinating evening in March, 1815, when the boys were back in Paris with their mother at the house in the Rue Cérutti. An Englishman had told Hortense the news that Napoleon had broken out of Elba and landed in the south, and his raid spelt danger to such members of his family as were in the capital of King Louis XVIII. That night there was a party downstairs. In the children's room there was a little hasty packing, and a governess delighted them by taking them across a dark garden into the streets. It was inadvisable to be a Bonaparte in Paris whilst the eagles were advancing from Grenoble to Lyons, and for twelve days Hortense shared with her boys a lumber-room in the house of an old nurse. But the Emperor swept into Paris; and when he came back to Elba to find his first Empress dead in the church at Rueil and his second enjoying beyond the French frontier the society of a one-eyed Austrian count, Hortense stood at his side and her boys became a small part of the Napoleonic legend.

The sudden course of the Hundred Days seemed to sweep the little Louis into the direct line of the Imperial succession. Hortense, who was in mourning for her mother, had gone to the Tuileries in black on that March afternoon when the *personnel* of the Empire resumed possession of the palace. Whilst the Emperor was driving up the white road from Fontainebleau, the ladies and gentlemen of his Court passed a happy evening of hysterical recognitions, diversified by the pleasing discovery that one could pull the *fleurs de lys* off the carpet in the throne-room and reveal the Imperial bees. Towards nine o'clock there was a roar from the courtyard, as a closed carriage clattered in with a cavalry escort and Napoleon, his eyes closed and a fixed smile on his lips, was carried into his palace on the shoulders of men.

That night he saw Hortense; he said a word to
her about her brother Eugène and seemed vexed at
her residence in Paris under the Bourbons. But the
absence of the Empress brought her into prominence,
and during the hurried reign which preceded the
campaign of Waterloo Napoleon drove out more
than once to be her guest at Malmaison. Sometimes
she took the boys to him at the Tuileries or the Élysée,
and once he presented them to the troops outside the
palace windows in the Place du Carrousel. His own
son was a hostage in Allied hands; and if the Emperor
ever found leisure in the desperate improvisation of
the Hundred Days to think of the succession, he must
have looked curiously at his small nephews. But
their greatest excitement was the day of the Champ
de Mai, when they were taken in a box with their
mother and the ex-Queen of Spain to see their uncle
take oath to the new Constitution and give eagles to
his new armies. There was a salute of six hundred
guns, as the Lancers of the Guard jingled across the
Pont d'Iéna and the Emperor, with four Marshals
riding beside his coach, drove on to the ground and
took his place for the ceremony. The small boys,
whose places were immediately above the throne, enjoyed from behind the unusual and fascinating
spectacle of their uncles Lucien, Joseph, and Jerome
in white velvet, wearing short capes *à l'espagnole*
embroidered with golden bees, and carrying remarkable feathered hats which hesitated in style between
the Renaissance and the *toreador*. It was a warm
afternoon of June sunshine; and the programme,
which was generously punctuated with salutes of one
hundred guns and included an open air service, eight
other events, and a *Te Deum*, was admirably calcu-

lated to minister to the enjoyment of two schoolboys with good seats.

Ten days later, as the last army of the Empire was moving slowly up to the Sambre and anxious caterers in Brussels were preparing for the Duchess of Richmond's ball, the children were sent for to say goodbye to their uncle before he took the road for the northern frontier. Popular history, always so responsive to the exigencies of drama, has set a pleasing scene in Napoleon's room. To the Emperor and Soult, deep in the maps and papers of the approaching campaign, enter a weeping nephew of seven; he clings to his uncle and begs him not to go, not to go because the wicked Allies want to kill him. The hero falls silent, kisses the child, and, as they lead him away, turns quietly to Soult: 'There, Marshal, kiss the boy: he will have a good heart and a high mind—he may be the hope of my race.' The Emperor is left thinking, and the curtain descends slowly upon the applause of a Bonapartist posterity. But the trlue facts are a trifle less Sophoclean. There was a family party at the Élysée on the evening before Napoleon drove out of Paris to the army. All the small nephews were allowed to come in to dessert, and the Emperor, unaware for once of the dramatic possibilities of an occasion, abstained from histrionics and was in thoroughly good spirits. His brief exhausting masquerade as a citizen king was at an end, and he was once more in command of the armies of France.

When the news came to Hortense that Napoleon had lost 'that last weird battle' in the north, she sent her boys to cover at a dressmaker's in the Boulevard Montmartre and stood up bravely to receive the

Emperor in defeat. Three days after Waterloo he drove into Paris at eight o'clock in the morning, and for three days more he struggled with the unfamiliar forces of parliamentarism and Fouché. Then one evening at dinner he turned abruptly to Josephine's daughter: *'Je veux me retirer à la Malmaison. C'est à vous. Voulez-vous m'y donner l'hospitalité?'* That night she posted out of Paris to Rueil, and on a summer afternoon the Emperor drove for shelter to his dead wife's house. For three days Hortense made for him a home among the June flowers. Her boys were fetched from their hiding-place to see him once more. His mind was busy with plans for America, for a scientific career, for a second campaign of France. But for long intervals at Malmaison he seemed to see nothing but the lost, slim figure of Josephine bending above her roses. There was a great coming and going of military messengers bearing the wishes of the Provisional Government, the news of the Prussian advance, and the last offer to France of the sword of her greatest soldier 'not as Emperor, but as a General whose name and reputation may still affect the nation's fortunes.' At last in the lengthening shadows of a June afternoon, dressed strangely as a civilian, he passed through a little gate and drove away. They did not speak until the carriage reached Rambouillet.

V

THE First Empire was at an end. But Prince Louis had more than thirty years to wait for the Second Empire to begin. The Bonapartes after Waterloo were hardly likely to begin it. Elaborate measures of international police excluded them from France, separated them from any common centre, and dictated the smallest details of their provincial existences. The King of Rome was learning to wear a white uniform in Vienna with anaemic distinction. *Madame Mère* resided at Rome in a mild aureole of Papal courtesy. Joseph was on the banks of the Delaware. Louis and Lucien lived lives of Tuscan ease at Florence and Frascati; whilst Jerome and the sisters were in the neighbourhood of Trieste. All of them were pitiably quiescent and eager for the comfort of oblivion. There was little truth in the complaint of an impatient nephew: 'All the Bonapartes are dead.'

In this dismal Diaspora Hortense and her two boys travelled a long and embittering road. Peremptorily ordered out of Paris by a Prussian general, they followed the traditional route of royal exiles and headed for Switzerland. But by her brave refusal to desert the Emperor in his downfall she had acquired an inconvenient reputation as a Bonapartist firebrand, and Geneva was rendered unpleasant by the excessive degree to which the local Swiss had developed the

national instinct for rallying to the winning side.
There was even held at her hotel a banquet of Swiss
officers to celebrate the defeat of Napoleon by almost
every other army in Europe; and Hortense, under
Allied supervision, left with relief for Aix-les-Bains.

At this stage she lost her eldest boy by the mysterious operation of French justice. Her husband had
commenced proceedings in the royal courts to recover
the custody of his two children. The litigation can
only have been inspired by spite, since it is difficult
to believe that the dismal Louis, who was one of
Nature's solitaries, was genuinely anxious for the
uninterrupted society of two small boys. An embarrassed tribunal, following the principles of
jurisprudence laid down under somewhat similar
circumstances by King Solomon, bisected the disputed
family and awarded the eldest son to his aggrieved
father. But before the judgment could be executed,
Napoleon had returned from Elba and Hortense
enjoyed a brief respite. The decree of the King's
courts revived in the autumn of 1815, and the elder
boy was removed to his father in Italy, leaving his
mother to take the road with the little Louis.

Hortense in exile developed to an alarming degree
that tendency towards mild virtuosity which had
made her the youthful prodigy of Malmaison. When
ill-health followed her judicial bereavement of a son,
they found her sketching feebly on the hills above
Aix. Her accomplishments, which included poetry,
drawing, painting, singing, and musical composition,
were something more than queenly; sometimes she
carried them to a pitch beyond the ladylike which
positively verged upon the professional. The air of
Partant pour la Syrie, which became the official

anthem of the Second Empire, was her work; and her Creole origin was never more clearly indicated than by a *Marche Impériale* for six pianos and a military band. This indomitable amateur became, naturally enough, the tutor of her remaining boy, and her instruction was eked out with a succession of French gentlemen of mild erudition.

The exiles had money; but it became the business of the Holy Alliance to see that they had little peace. An Allied Conference met in Paris and considered the grave menace presented to the peace of Europe by the continued residence on the shores of the Lac du Bourget of Hortense and a child who was now almost eight years old. It was decided, as the winter was coming on, to transfer them under circumstances of the greatest possible discomfort to Constance in Baden. This Bonapartist invasion, which was accommodated with some difficulty at an exceedingly bad hotel, struck the government of the Grand-Duchy with consternation; and the poor lady was promptly requested to leave. With a gesture of heroism that was almost Napoleonic Hortense defied Europe and took a house; and Constance became for two years the place of her exile. It was a dreary period, in which the little Prince was instructed in the rudiments and developed a startling and hazardous form of charity for which authority exists in the life of St. Martin; it appears to have been his practice to respond to mendicant appeals with the immediate gift of his clothing in a manner which both embarrassed himself and alarmed his mother. But after little more than a year of residence in Baden, the wheels of Allied policy began to revolve once more, and the lady and her little boy were moved on into Bavaria.

By the accident of royal courtesy at Munich Louis
became a German schoolboy, and the first stage of
his training for the throne of France was conducted
at the St. Anna Gymnasium of Augsburg. He took
a French tutor with him, and during the first four
years of his residence his mother had a house in the
town. But in the main his education was in the hands
of German teachers who observed in him those signs
of ability which academic persons have never failed to
detect in royal pupils. It resulted from his instruction at Augsburg that he acquired a German accent
and a vague flavour of Teutonic romance; the atmosphere of German education in the year 1820 was
unfriendly to undue precision of thought, and the haze
which it engendered can hardly have been dispelled
for Louis by the desultory predilections of Hortense.
His holidays were spent in travel, which took him to
every resort in Switzerland in pursuit of his mother's
health, to the South German palaces where he had
friends and cousins, or on more alarming visits of
duty to his father in Italy. In the years between
1820 and 1830, when the whole western sky of Europe
was alight with the afterglow of Byron and the young
lions of French Romanticism were beginning to roar
in Paris, the young Louis Bonaparte was a mild-eyed
German schoolboy, learning to seek philosophy in a
sunset and romance in a ruined castle.

By this time Hortense had succeeded in securing a
permanent home. The Canton of Thurgau redeemed
the Swiss reputation for political hospitality by a
definite invitation to the ex-Queen and her son, and
with some hesitation she bought a château at Arenenberg on the Swiss shore of the Lake of Constance.
The Allied governments weighed this dangerous step

with their accustomed gravity, and Stratford Can-
ning, who was serving his diplomatic apprenticeship
at Berne, corresponded solemnly with Lord Castlereagh as to the possibility of effectively overlooking
a lady who lived on the banks of a lake. But she
proceeded with the preparation of her home. The
reception rooms were all decorated in the tented style
which had been so modish under the Consulate, and
the house was filled with the swans' necks and the
gleaming gryphons of her Empire furniture. While
his mother sketched the lake with all the persistence
of a determined amateur, Louis passed out of boyhood in an atmosphere of rural gentility, driving his
cabriolet up and down the road to Constance, riding,
shooting, swimming, doing acts of feudal beneficence,
and performing generally all those duties which are
believed to qualify an English landowner for a seat
on the local Bench. He emerged from his training
as a sportsman of tolerable proficiency who scandalised an English peer in 1829 by riding at full gallop
through the streets of Rome.

But swimming the lake and winning prizes at the
local *Schutzenfest* were not his only interests. A
Bonaparte, even if he were a younger son, must learn
the family trade of war. The French army was closed
to him. But in 1829, when Diebitsch was moving on
Silistria, the Byronic appeal of a campaign against
the Turk proved irresistible, and he begged his father
for leave to serve with the Russians. Had it been
granted, the prospects of the Second Empire might
well have ended abruptly in a scuffle in the Dobrudja.
But Louis at fifty was unsympathetic to a young
man's romantic predilection for crusading under a
foreign flag. His permission was withheld in a letter

which denounced as barbarism all war except a war
of national defence, and the Prince was left to satisfy
his military inclinations nearer home. With a drop
in the scale of romance he joined the Swiss artillery.
There was a volunteer unit which went into camp at
Thun, and route-marching had no terrors for a young
man who had walked over the Splügen with his tutor.
Under commanding officers who had learnt their
experience in the wars of the Empire he acquired that
familiarity with the details of military equipment
which is indispensable to monarchs, and when the July
Revolution swept Paris in 1830, he was learning the
elements of gunnery on the Polygon at Thun. The
news brought him to the frontier, and from Geneva
he strained his eyes into France.

In the autumn he went into Italy with his mother
on a visit to her elder son at Florence. His brother,
from whom he had been separated by the French
courts, was now happily married to a cousin, and
in default of politics he had devoted himself to industrial enterprises. After a few days Prince Louis
went on with Hortense to Rome and proceeded to
render himself impossible in the eyes of the Papal
police by attending a suspicious meeting of the male
members of his family and emphasising the revolutionary nature of his sympathies by a shameless
exhibition of the tricolour. He was conducted to the
frontier under escort and rejoined his brother at
Florence. Early in the new year Hortense warned
the young man against futile adventures. But her
advice came too late. When the Romagna rose
against the Temporal Power in February, she posted
after them to Florence. But her sons were nowhere
to be seen, and their destination was clearly in-

dicated by a note from Louis which she found at her
hotel:

> 'Your affection will understand us. We have accepted
> engagements, and we cannot depart from them. The name
> we bear obliges us to help a suffering people that calls
> upon us. Arrange that my sister-in-law may think that it
> was I who carried off her husband; he is pained by the
> idea that he has hidden one action of his life from her.'

History has been exercised as to the precise nature
of the 'engagements' assumed by the young men.
The titillating spectacle of a future Emperor in a
secret society has inspired the hope that Louis had
actually joined the *Carbonari*. But there is a distressing lack of evidence, and it may well be that
they had merely enlisted in the rebel forces which
were campaigning in the Papal States. Upon either
view there can be no question that by the year 1831
the German schoolboy of 1820 had become an Italian
romantic.

The two Princes were in the field with the insurgents. But their mother, who was a Beauharnais
and had kept house for Napoleon in the Hundred
Days, was disinclined to inactive lamentation and
was perfectly capable of fetching them out of the
firing-line. On the following morning she had an
interview with her husband; and the meeting after
twenty years between that independent, cultivated
lady and her morose relict must have resembled the
rencounter, if one may employ an expression of
Mr. Thomas Hardy's to describe a situation of Mr.
Bernard Shaw's, of Mrs. Clandon and Mr. Cramp-
ton at the seaside hotel where Gloria met her dentist.
The husband was flurried and faintly ridiculous. He

proposed to the wife whose frivolity had shocked him twenty years before that she should fetch the truants from the army; for himself he reserved the manly task of interviewing the Austrian ambassador. Hortense hesitated to compromise her political reputation by a journey to the rebel forces in the Papal States and remained in Florence, where her husband subjected her to a daily series of futile suggestions. Meanwhile the Princes were in command of the insurgents before Cività Castellana. The town was carried by an attack projected by Prince Louis in accordance with the principles prevailing in the Swiss army, and the two young leaders of revolt threatened Rome itself. The Pope opened negotiations with the Princes. But at this stage they were removed from the command on the pretext that their leadership might prejudice the insurrection in the eyes of Europe. An Austrian army, true to Metternich's policy that the world must be made safe for reaction, was in the field against the insurgents, and it was ominous that its commander had omitted their two names from his announcement of an amnesty. Early in March Hortense, alarmed by this threat of outlawry, started from Florence in pursuit of her sons. She went first to the army, but found that they had left it. At Perugia she was told of their achievements in the field; they were further to the east, and there was fever in the country. She quickened her pace towards Ancona, and on the road she met a messenger with the news that the elder Prince had taken the sickness. At Pesaro they told her that he was dead, and she was carried fainting into Louis' house.

He had ceased to be a younger son; but he was ill and an outlaw. At Ancona the Austrians came

5

up with them, and Headquarters were actually installed in Hortense's house. But although the whole town believed that Prince Louis had left by the sailing packet for Corfu, he could not be moved from his room; and through eight days of fever Hortense, who had no intention of losing her last son by an Austrian firing-party, nursed him in silence with a door between her patient and the room of a polite but deluded Austrian commander. She had a British passport for a journey across France to England, and at dawn on Easter Sunday she drove out of of Ancona with Louis in the full glory of Miladi's footman (it was the golden age of Jeames) on the box. In his Odyssey across Italy he enjoyed the advantages which would have fallen to the hero if Calypso, instead of being one of the obstacles, had formed one of his party. Hortense lavished her charm on Austrian officers and Italian police, and she gave evidence of a real gift for theatricals which should have found a place among her more advertised accomplishments. The road from Ancona to Genoa lay between the Scylla of inquiring officials and the Charybdis of undue recognition by incautious friends. But Louis travelled successfully from the Adriatic to the Mediterranean, sometimes in livery, sometimes in the character of a young English gentleman with a remarkable accent and a charming but (Hortense's English was confined to her passport) inarticulate mother. From Genoa they entered France by sea; and on a spring evening in 1831 the Prince looked out at Paris from his hotel windows in the Rue de la Paix.

The journey from the Riviera had been broken at Fontainebleau, where Hortense showed her son the font where the Emperor had stood his godfather,

and all along the road he saw French towns, French
men, French women, French soldiers. The Government was promptly informed of their arrival, and a
suspicious Prime Minister presented himself at the
hotel. On the next day Hortense was taken to the
Palais Royal with an air of operatic secrecy. She
was shown into a small bedroom, and almost to slow
music King Louis Philippe arrived with his sister
and his Queen in an impenetrable atmosphere of conspiracy. The royal family of France was hardly
adapted to furtive entrances, and when Hortense had
reassured them that she had no intention of remaining
in Paris, the interview became more genial. But on
her return to the hotel she found her son suffering
from a virulent return of his illness, and utterly
unable to leave for London. The Government, which
regarded without enthusiasm the presence in Paris
of a Bonaparte Prince, displayed a touching anxiety
as to his health; and when great crowds honoured the
day of the Emperor's death by piling flowers round
the base of the *Colonne de la Grande Armée,* its
concern at his continued inability to leave became
positively maternal. Anxious inquirers from the
Tuileries pressed into his bedroom, and their solici-
tude was followed up by a curt order to leave Paris.
It was injudicious for the Orleans monarchy to
tolerate a Bonaparte in the Rue de la Paix with a
crowd of Bonapartists in the Place Vendôme; and at
some risk to himself Louis took the road again for
London. His journey across France had taught him
in wayside talks and printsellers' windows that the
memory of the Empire was not dead. He had heard
the roar of a great crowd surging up the street to do
honour to the Emperor, and in that spring journey

which followed on his Italian escapade Louis
Napoleon became a Bonapartist.

The subjects of King William IV. were undisturbed by the arrival of Hortense and her son at a
hotel in St. James's Street. The world was far too
interested in the prospects of the Reform Bill, and the
even flow of Mr. Greville's diary was not broken by
their appearance in polite society. The news that a
nephew of Napoleon was ill with jaundice so near to
the new glories of Regent Street was of less interest
than the cholera scare; and while Mr. Greville was inquiring in what pattern of crown Queen Adelaide
desired to suffer coronation, Hortense took a house in
Holles Street and began to look up her English
friends. The Whigs have always displayed a *pen-
chant* for the enemies of their country, and she had
formed a few English connections during the interval
of peace before Trafalgar. Whilst Talleyrand looked
on with suspicion from the French embassy, the great
ladies whose husbands were following Lord John into
the lobby on Reform sent cards to Holles Street; and
Hortense was presented everywhere by the Duchess
of Bedford, whilst her son perseveringly inspected
the sights of London. The city had been transformed
by the reconstructions of the Regency into a dream of
elegance in stucco, nor were the miracles of science
disregarded in a visit to the Thames Tunnel. At one
moment the Prince wrote to Louis Philippe begging
for permission to serve his country; but a cautious
Prime Minister insisted that he should discard the
dangerous name of Napoleon, and the young man
preferred to remain in exile. The travellers proposed
to return to Switzerland by way of Belgium, and this
choice of route alarmed Prince Leopold of Saxe-

Coburg, whose bereavement had just been consoled by the gift of the new Kingdom. It became necessary for Louis to declare that he had no sinister designs on Brussels. The Belgian route was abandoned, and he retired with his mother to Tunbridge Wells to wait for passports.

Early in August they landed at Calais, and Louis re-entered the atmosphere of the Empire. Hortense had decided that an excitable young man had better be kept away from the somewhat explosive atmosphere of Paris; but she employed the journey across France to improve his Bonapartist education. When the Army of England was in the Pas de Calais a quarter of a century before, she had been a frequent visitor at the cantonments. She could tell him in those summer days of 1831 which were the old French lines and the moorings of that fleet which never sailed. He saw the Emperor's camp from the top of the column behind Boulogne, and the little house at Pont-de-Briques where the orders were dictated which swung the *Grande Armée* from the English Channel to Austerlitz. Then they went driving along the dusty roads of France by Chantilly to the northern edge of Paris, and at every turn of the road Hortense banked the fires of memory with tales of the Empire. At Rueil they found that a rich man had bought Malmaison and admitted only ticket-holders: Josephine's daughter had no ticket except her memories. But the church was open, and they stood together by her mother's grave. Circling round Paris, they passed Versailles and took the great road to the south by Melun. France seem full of voices murmuring the Imperial story. There were old prints on every wall and old tales on every tongue which set Louis wondering vaguely whether the past Empire had perhaps a future; and when at last they repassed the Swiss frontier, the young man who had left Arenenberg as a romantic lover of Italian liberty returned to his exile as the youngest and bitterest recruit of the Bonapartists.

VI

His brother's death gave Prince Louis a step in the Napoleonic hierarchy, and he found himself at twenty-three the heir of Queen Hortense. But he was not yet the heir of the Empire, and family discipline was too well maintained for any change in the succession. For the faithful there was still an Emperor; the King of Rome had succeeded to his father, and somewhere beyond the mists Napoleon II. was reigning in Vienna in spite of Metternich and the long illness under which he was fading into a figure of pale romance. Louis had offered to join him in captivity; but no word came from Schönbrunn, and perhaps the letter was never delivered.

The Prince returned to his lake in Switzerland with a new faith in his dynasty. He could not fail to see that of the younger men he stood next to the dying Duc de Reichstadt, and he turned from the life of a sporting Swiss landowner to the more serious interests of an heir presumptive. His rooms were furnished with maps and accoutrements, and when a Polish deputation arrived to offer him the leadership of a hopeless insurrection, he seemed to have entered the full stream of European politics. The national movement in Warsaw had a curiously French flavour. The tricolour cockade was reverently carried in procession on a cushion like a sacred relic, and there were queer tales of a French army half seen marching in the mist at night. The ghost of the *Grande Armée* walked Lithuania in 1831; and it seemed natural to appeal for the assistance of '*un jeune Bonaparte apparaissant sur nos plages* (the coast of Poland has much in common with the seaboard of Illyria; but Polish patriotism has never been confined within the narrow limits of literal exactitude) *le drapeau tricolore à la main.*' But the invitation was refused. Prince Louis was vowed to another quest; and he was no longer prepared to crusade promiscuously in the cause of liberty.

All through the autumn and winter of 1831 he worked in his room at Arenenberg, and in the spring a pamphlet appeared which contained his first manifesto as a Bonapartist. There was not yet an organised body of Bonapartists to which he could appeal; but France under Louis Philippe was full of a vague, thwarted belief in the sovereignty of the people. It was an age of lost illusions. The Revolution of 1830 had opened with a flourish of republican trumpets and ended with a deadening roll of *bourgeois* drums, and Paris began to stir uneasily. As in all periods of discontent, there was a rank and bitter growth of political caricature, in which the genius of Daumier cut savagely at the unheroic figure of the King. The country had begun to despise its new masters, and men would believe any meanness of the Government. They came together easily into crowds, and as they learnt that it is not difficult to force up a few paving-stones and turn an omnibus on its side, the barricades began to become a political habit. There was an intermittent rattle of musketry in the streets of Paris, as the National Guard defended royal law and *bourgeois* order; and the

Orleans monarchy drifted steadily further from its popular origins.

In this air of discontent Prince Louis propounded in his *Rêveries Politiques* a republican type of Bonapartism which was intended to unite behind Napoleon II. all the parties of opposition. His doctrine was broad-based upon quotations from Montesquieu, and he introduced himself as a republican in theory. But his affection for the Republic was purely platonic, and under the pressure of practical politics and the exigencies of national defence he avowed himself an Imperialist. *'Si le Rhin était une mer, si la vertu était toujours le seul mobile, si le mérite parvenait seul au pouvoir, alors je voudrais une République pure et simple. Mais . . .'* There is a faint irony in the circumstance that it was the Second Empire which lost the Rhine frontier in 1870 and the Third Republic which reconquered it in 1918. But in the *Rêveries* of 1832 France was directed away from the middle-aged expedients of the Orleans monarchy and the visionary idealism of a Republic towards the superior merits of *'un gouvernement qui procurât tous les avantages de la République sans entraîner les mêmes inconvénients,'* and the author obligingly appended the draft of an Imperial constitution in which the hereditary principle was tempered by *plébiscite.*

The gospel of St. Helena was closely followed in the *Rêveries* of Arenenberg. Democracy was assured by a parliamentary constitution and the right of the people to approve by direct vote the succession to the throne. Peace without conquests was to be the programme of French foreign policy; and the doctrine of nationality, so fashionable since the Peace of

Vienna and so interesting to a young man who had
seen service in Italy, was respected by a declaration
that France was the natural ally of all free nations and
by an insistence that their sovereign should grant to
them the institutions which they demand. Provision
was even made for the career of an energetic cousin
of an ailing Emperor: on a demise of the Crown *'si le
fils ou le plus proche parent du dernier Empereur ne
convient pas à la nation* (and one's uncles would
afford a strikingly uninviting prospect), *les deux
chambres proposeront un nouvel Empereur, et toute
proposition passera à la rectification du peuple.'*
Louis was indisposed to pass his life as a Prince
of the Empire; and although he was not prepared to
supersede Napoleon II., he had few doubts as to who
would be Napoleon III.

In a few weeks his time came, and on a July day
in 1832 the Duc de Reichstadt faded out of life.
His father was dead; his uncles were insignificant
and old. But he left a young cousin by a Swiss lake
who was the heir of the Empire. When Louis
Napoleon became the Bonaparte pretender, he was a
horse-faced young man of twenty-four. He wore
a pointed beard with a romantic air and might, to
all appearances, have fluttered round George Sand
or set cheering on a *strapontin* at the first night of
Hernani. His portrait was painted about this time
by Cottrau, a cheerful young painter whose loud
laugh, straw hat, and Byron collar must have sent
a breath from the Quartier Latin over the Lake of
Constance; and one sees in the picture one of those
bearded young men in a high cravat who formed the
public of Victor Hugo and the raw material of the
Vie de Bohême.

But with his accession to the full dignity of a French pretender Prince Louis assumed a more solemn aspect. It became his business to assure public opinion by the publication of political studies that he had found a statesmanlike employment for his leisure, and with the assistance of his barber he proceeded to the first of those modifications of his appearance which were to make him the delight of caricaturists. A moustache was retained as an indication to the world that he was a soldier, although his uncle had contrived to make this obvious with the shaved face of a priest. But the beard vanished, leaving no trace except a slight imperial; and in his uniform he looked much like any slim young officer of the French army which marched against Antwerp with Marshal Gérard in 1832.

With his new responsibilities he proceeded to the composition of a second book, interrupting his work in the autumn with a second visit to London. On the way through Belgium he drove out with his maps to Waterloo; and as he explored the ground, it is to be feared that he did not escape the more obvious reflections which haunt that undulating but platitudinous neighbourhood. In London he became unwell, suffering, as a tribute to English local colour, from 'le spleen,' and he reported to his mother that M. Hugo's new novel *Notre-Dame de Paris* was unsuitable literature for an invalid. Then, as the winter came on, he returned to Switzerland and abandoned himself to the allied pursuits of composition and proof-reading.

The *Considérations Politiques et Militaires sur la Suisse,* which appeared in 1833, formed an impressive addition to his published works. The title alone had

an air of dull distinction which was worthy of any
reigning family in Europe; one would hardly have
been surprised to find it among the *juvenilia* of Prince
Albert.   But the book was something more than an
inventory of the political virtues of the Swiss Republic. Opening with an ominous apology for the number
of his references to France, the Prince proceeded to a
restatement of Bonapartist doctrine. The necessities
of his subject compelled him to display a tedious
knowledge of cantonal constitutions and the organisation of the Swiss army; but in the digressions from
which, like *Tristram Shandy,* the book derives its
main interest he returned to more familiar ground.
Napoleon reappears as *'Empereur plébéien.'* His
policy is to be judged by his intentions rather than
by his achievements; and in the true spirit of the
gospel according to Las Cases Prince Louis sketched
the programme of the Liberal Empire which was to
have followed a victory at Waterloo:

> '*S'il eût été vainqueur, on aurait vu le duché de Varsovie
> se changer en nationalité de Pologne, la Westphalie se
> changer en nationalité allemande, la vice-royauté d'Italie
> se changer en nationalité italienne.   En France, un
> régime libéral eût remplacé le régime dictatorial; partout
> stabilité, liberté, indépendance, au lieu de nationalités
> incomplètes et d'institutions transitoires.*'

The bright picture which the First Empire had left
unfinished might be completed, as the Prince hinted
broadly, by a Second Empire which should be *'un
pouvoir national, c'est-à-dire un pouvoir dont tous les
éléments se retrempent dans le peuple, seul source de
tout ce qui est grand et généreux.'* Such were the prospects for France and Europe at which Prince Louis

Queen Hortense

After a picture in the Arenenberg Collection

glanced in the intervals of his more relevant reflections on the political importance of Zurich and the
military responsibilities of Appenzell.

His quiet life by the lake was resumed with appropriate interludes of gentlemanly recreation. In
the four years which intervened between his accession
to the pretendership and his first attempt to seize
power in France there was little change in the even
tenor of his days. In the summer he went into camp
with the artillery, and in the winter he skated on the
lake until tea-time, whilst his mother wore all her furs
and ventured on the ice in a little sledge. At nights
he read and wrote and corrected proofs, with an occasional game of billiards, and by day he planned
roads and bridges in the grounds or watched the
fuliginous progress of the steam-boat (it was the year
1835) across the lake. Hortense became the centre
of a little French colony, and there was a gentle flow
of amusing visitors to the château. Madame Récamier
came, all in black, to exchange Directoire gossip about
the *Incroyables*. Chateaubriand called after a correspondence of exhausting chivalry with his hostess;
and a large negroid gentleman named Dumas, half
genius and half journalist, was asked to dinner. That
night there was a little music in the drawing-room,
and Hortense sang one of her old songs:

> ' *Oui, vous plairez et vous vaincrez sans cesse;*
> *Mars et l'amour suivront partout vos pas:*
> *De vos succès gardez la douce ivresse,*
> *Soyez heureux, mais ne m'oubliez pas.*'

It was the song which she had sung to the Emperor
on the night before he drove away to the campaign

of Wagram, and Josephine had sat watching his face, because there was something of her own story in the words. At the end of the song, Napoleon told his wife that she was the kindest thing on earth and kissed her and turned unhappily away. The Empress had sat weeping in the *salon;* and twenty-five years later, when the Emperor and his Empress were both dead four thousand miles apart, Hortense sang the old song in exile for Dumas.

The Prince was a grave young man to whom the world was beginning to pay the compliment of slight attention. Switzerland honoured him with the freedom of Thurgau and a captaincy in the Bernese artillery. Rumour joined his name with the Queen of Portugal as an intending consort and afforded him an opportunity for the publicity of a *démenti.* Energetic friends urged upon him the possibilities of the Tagus as the starting point of a progress by way of the Manzanares to the Seine itself. But he was indisposed to make the detour. His correspondence was increasing, and in 1835 he brought out a *Manuel d'Artillerie,* which demonstrated that the family interest in gunnery originated at Toulon in 1793 had been maintained. The book was long, laborious, and technical, and by its solid qualities it incurred the suspicion that the Prince owed something to collaboration. But it was a serious achievement, and he distributed it broadcast to the military profession in France and the rest of Europe. It was something to have convinced the world that there was still a Bonaparte.

But he found this distinction unsatisfying. Like his brother, he was in love with a handsome cousin; and he might have married her at some little Swiss

church and subsided into happiness. But it was
the family *métier* to sit upon thrones; and since
thrones are not conquered by publicity alone, he went
forward.

VII

BONAPARTISM in the year 1836 was a barren enthusiasm for the memory of a dead man. It was an historical sentiment rather than a political cause. Frenchmen were prepared to stand cheering as the statue of Napoleon swung once more into place on the Vendôme column or to watch the workmen carving the names of victories on the Arc de Triomphe. They bought the innumerable Napoleonic picture-books and crowded to any theatre where an actor could be found to play the part of the Emperor. But they made no conscious connection between this pleasant exercise of the imagination and the real politics of the day. The reign of Louis Philippe was a dismal triumph of middle age, an age of reason as depressing as the administration of Walpole; and old men might stir their memories and young men their imaginations with the picture of a more vivid period when the Grenadiers of the Guard went swinging through the Carrousel and France was unacquainted with the less heroic figures of M. Thiers and M. Guizot. But they saw their visions without any practical desire to reinstate a Bonaparte in the Tuileries. The Empire was over. The Emperor (it was the most dramatic turn of his story and gave it a modish flavour of romantic sentiment) had died on an island four thousand miles away, and one knew nothing of his family: perhaps

they were dead also. Politicians were either Orleanist
or Republican or Legitimist; but they were never
Bonapartist. The great movement which multiplied
little bronzes of the Emperor and filled the printsellers' shops with scenes of his career was not
Bonapartist: it was Napoleonic. Prolific of poetry
and perorations, it was without a practical programme
or dynastic loyalty. The eyes of France were turned
to St. Helena; but they did not look towards
Arenenberg.

But slowly in Switzerland a Bonapartist group
was beginning to form round Prince Louis. His
mother's friends respected his ambitions, and gradually the circle round her fire became a conspiracy
which was to grow in time into the Second Empire.
Queen Hortense possessed that remarkable attribute
of royalty, a reader. Her reader had a husband; and
when Mlle. Cochelet married Colonel Parquin of the
Guard, the Prince enlisted his first recruit. But it was
not enough to sit in a corner and talk over old times
whilst Hortense played softly on her piano to enter-
tain the ladies; and when an excitable young man
named Fialin arrived from England with an introduction, the Prince's conversation became more practical.
His new friend, who called himself for no very obvious
reason the Vicomte de Persigny, had begun life in the
Hussars; but discouraged by the tedium of barracks
in peace-time, he transferred his activities to the
more bellicose atmosphere of Parisian journalism.
Bonapartism came upon him under circumstances
which Imperialist writers have not hesitated to com-
pare to those in which St. Paul came by a greater
faith. On a business journey into Germany, as he
was driving along a road for the sufficient reason that

7

he hoped to meet a lady whom he had seen once before,
his coachman stood up on the box, and, at the sight of
a young man, waved his hat with a strange shout of
'Vive Napoléon!' The young man, it seemed, was
familiar in those parts as a nephew of the Emperor
and the son of Queen Hortense. The names set
Persigny dreaming of the Empire; and when he
reached the end of his journey, he impolitely forgot
the lady for whom he had taken it in a queer revelation which came to him in the garden of a German
palace. He seemed to see through the summer night
a great march of the armies of France roaring their
loyalty to a new Napoleon; and he returned to Paris
with a revivalist faith in the dynasty. His exuberant
style had been contained with difficulty within the
narrow limits of the *Temps,* and he proceeded with
enthusiasm and relief to the publication of a magazine
of his own, of which there was one number. Pitched
in the shrillest key of Bonapartism, it advocated the
return of France and the whole western world to the
true faith; the motto of this remarkable periodical
was a quotation from Napoleon—*'J'ai dessouillé la
Révolution, ennobli les peuples et raffermi les rois'*—
and its sole contributor roamed from politics to
economics with a haunting refrain of *'l'Empereur,
tout l'Empereur.'* The calm of Paris was undisturbed
by his eloquence. But Persigny, who regarded himself as an apostle, was endeavouring to attract the
attention of his Messiah. He called on King Joseph
in England with the full programme of a Bonaparte
restoration. But his host, who had reigned in Madrid
during the Peninsular War, was already sufficiently
instructed as to the discomfort incidental to the occupation of thrones by uninvited persons; and Joseph

passed him on to Prince Louis in Switzerland with a polite letter.

Persigny came to Arenenberg with an ideal and left it with a plan. The young man whom he had met in the way to his *rendezvous* had grown up. The two became allies, and there was some close talk among the maps in the Prince's room. It was agreed that the time had come for an attempt on the French throne, and there can be little doubt that much of the Prince's impulse and more of his plan were derived from Persigny. He was launched on his career as a pretender by the susceptible young man whom he had passed on a road in Germany; and that singular journalist, who lived to write a book on the Pyramids, did much to promote a sphinx to be Emperor of the French.

The conspirators in Hortense's drawing-room felt that among civilians there might be a pardonable lack of enthusiasm for any change of dynasty. King Louis Philippe undeniably satisfied the somewhat limited aspirations of the *bourgeoisie,* and revolutions were always bad for trade. But there remained (had not Prince Louis published a work on artillery and Persigny served in the Hussars?) the army. The temper of the French army under the Orleans monarchy was peculiar. Its professional grievances were rarely appreciated by a government which was so essentially civilian, and it still contained men who had served under Napoleon. French policy was ostentatiously pacific, and it offered to the army no substitute for the glories of a European war, beyond frequent changes of uniform and the extreme discomfort of campaigns in Algeria. It was even a trifle effaced as the guardian of domestic order by the faintly ridiculous figures of the National Guard.   In such a service it might well be that a return to the Empire would be welcomed, and it was resolved to raise the army against the King.

The plan which was adopted was vaguely modelled on the return of the Emperor from Elba.   The bloodless revolution of 1815 was to be repeated by the pretender in 1836.   He was to appear suddenly in a frontier town, show himself to the troops with a Napoleonic gesture, and as the scene rang with the familiar *Vive l'Empereur!* to march at their head on Paris.   The fortresses of the eastern frontier were accessible from Switzerland, and the irrespressible Persigny flitted from garrison to garrison testing the state of opinion.   Eventually it was decided that the attempt should be made at Strasburg, where the civil population was largely republican and at least one unit of the garrison had Napoleonic traditions: the 4th Artillery had been Napoleon's regiment when he wore the King's uniform before the Revolution, and it had joined him at Grenoble on the seventh of the Hundred Days.

As the summer went on, Prince Louis established himself in German territory at a convenient distance from Strasburg; and since it was frequently necessary for the officers of the French garrison to recuperate at Baden-Baden from the exertions of the barrack-square, the Prince found it easy to make useful acquaintances, to bow in the right direction, to drop a gracious hint in a Casino or stir the ambition of a subaltern with a grievance.   In this way he enlisted in his enterprise a dozen young men, of whom Lieutenant Laity of the Engineers was the most ardent.   But one can hardly precipitate a military *pronunciamiento* without a senior officer, and the Prince made the fortunate discovery of a disappointed colonel. The 4th Artillery, with its faint flavour of the Imperial legend, was commanded by a colonel of the Empire. Colonel Vaudrey had taken his guns into action at Waterloo with a division of D'Erlon's corps which was sent against La Haye Sainte, and his kindly recollection of the Empire was stimulated by the Government's recent refusal of a post and a perquisite. But colonels, even colonels with griev-ances, are not readily accessible to pretenders, and it was found necessary to adopt a peculiar means of approach. Vaudrey (the story becomes faintly Gallic) was, though married, a lively, a susceptible colonel, and Prince Louis numbered among his sup-porters an operatic contralto of undoubted charm whom he cast for the part of Delilah. This young lady, who was the widow of an Englishman of exotic tastes, had adopted the Napoleonic cult with the irrational fervour of her type. She was devoted to the Prince, but, as she said, *'politiquement,'* because, *'à dire vrai, il me fait l'effet d'une femme';* and from the loftiest motives she undertook the more congenial task of fascinating the colonel. He heard her sing on summer nights in Strasburg drawing-rooms; and when he saw her with the Prince in the Casino at Baden-Baden, he asked for an introduction. Louis improved the occasion by explaining his political principles. But the colonel had no head for politics, and returned to Strasburg with a simple-minded devotion to duty and his contralto. The Prince fol-lowed up the acquaintance with a mysterious letter in which a lady named Louise Wernert appeared to avow her affection for the colonel with unmaidenly explicitness: it was a cypher by which he desired to convey his reliance on Vaudrey. But the decisive blow in the conversion of the colonel was struck by his contralto. With the directness of an enthusiast she informed him that his advances would be refused until he joined the conspiracy, and Vaudrey (what else could a susceptible colonel do?) succumbed.

As the autumn came on, the happy pair went on leave in a kind of Bonapartist idyll, and the Prince went on with his preparations. The Military Governor was approached without success. But one evening Prince Louis rode across the bridge of Kehl into Strasburg and addressed a roomful of officers on the sanctity of his cause and the bitterness of exile. It was a small room, and his audience did not number more than twenty-five; but the Prince was impressed by their enthusiasm, and he returned to Switzerland with a strong conviction of success. He left his home again in the dawn of an October morning, and as he went Hortense put on his hand a plain gold ring engraved with the names *Napoléon Bonaparte* and *Joséphine Tascher*. It was the Emperor's wedding-ring, and with this rather tragic talisman he took the road for Strasburg.

The unwearying Persigny had gathered all the characters of the piece. Colonel Vaudrey and his Éléonore were recalled from their peripatetic dream of Bonapartist bliss, and the young gentlemen of the Strasburg mess-rooms were warned that the moment was approaching. On the evening of October 28, 1836, the Prince, who had entered France at Neuf-Brisach, drove into Strasburg by the south road from Colmar. He passed the night in the town at some lodgings which Persigny, true to the spirit of *opéra bouffe,* had taken in a false name. The next day was spent in paying furtive calls, and after nightfall he met the conspirators in a ground-floor room. The order of events was arranged, and he read out his manifestoes. They consisted of proclamations addressed to the citizens of Strasburg, the army, and the French people, and signed in the Imperial style *'Napoléon.'* Opening with the familiar invocation *'On vous trahit!'* they reproached the government of Louis Philippe with *'des institutions sans force, des lois sans liberté, une paix sans prospérité et sans calme, enfin, un présent sans avenir,'* and demanded a National Assembly to be followed by the more alluring prospect of a young man who presented himself *'le testament de l'empereur Napoléon d'une main, l'épée d'Austerlitz de l'autre.'* In a bolder figure he exclaimed: *'Du rocher de Sainte-Hélène un rayon de soleil mourant a passé dans mon âme'*; and the proclamation closed with one of those chronological appeals that are so dear to French politicians, to the men of 1789, of March 20, 1815, and of 1830. That night he did not sleep and wrote two letters to his mother. One was to be sent in case of success, and the other announced a failure.

In the morning five men slipped out of the house in the darkness at six o'clock and walked through the falling snow to the barracks of the 4th Artillery. The Prince was transformed into a colonel in the French army; and Colonel Parquin, by one of those sudden promotions which form a pleasing feature of all military revolutions, had become a general. One of the group carried a tricolour surmounted by the eagle of the Empire, and they hurried past a mounted guard into the barrack-square. Vaudrey, who had

paraded his command at an early hour, received his
new sovereign respectfully. There was a roar of
'Vive l'Empereur!' and the Prince responded with a
speech congested with historical allusions and diversified by some dramatic business with the eagle. He
was applauded, and the standard was solemnly
entrusted to Vaudrey. The band struck up, and the
regiment marched out of barracks with its new
Emperor at its head. Persigny went off on the congenial errand of arresting the *Préfet,* and the main
body proceeded with the Prince and the colours to the
barracks of the 46th of the Line. On the road they paid
an early call on the Military Governor, who declined
in the lightest of underwear to recognise the Prince as
Napoleon II. Parquin was detailed to deal with him
and pursued him about the house through a multi-
plicity of doors in the best tradition of Palais Royal
farce. But in his hasty transit the Governor found a
moment to complete his dressing, and with the moral
support of a general's uniform he emerged victorious
from a struggle in which the royalist cause was
sustained by his wife, his mother-in-law, and some
stray officers.

Meanwhile there was a confused scene at the barracks of the 46th of the Line. The infantry seemed
unwilling to take its tone from the artillery. The
sergeant of the guard was strikingly unresponsive
when the Prince announced himself as the son of the
Emperor, and a subaltern declined to parade the
battalion. A dangerous suspicion began to spread:
perhaps the short young man was an impostor. Someone shouted that he was the nephew (if no stronger
expression was used) of Colonel Vaudrey, and the
whole conspiracy foundered on the incredulity of a

Prince Louis Napoleon (1836)

From an engraving by Hall and a drawing by Stewart

few privates in a barrack-square. The colonel of the 46th roused his officers and drove the conspirators back against a wall. There was a scuffle in which Vaudrey lost his epaulettes. But the Prince declined to permit his men to use their swords on the infantry: the return of the Emperor from his exile was to be as bloodless as the march on Paris in 1815. He was arrested by a young officer who lived to repent his energy, and by eight o'clock in the morning the attempt on Strasburg had failed. The piece had been carefully staged; but a few badly rehearsed supers had caused it to break down in the second act.

Later in the day the Prince was lodged in the town gaol, and the Military Governor proudly reported to Paris that order reigned in Strasburg. But the message went by semaphore, and there was fog on the line. No news reached Paris until the evening of the following day, when King Louis Philippe and his ministers received a disquieting fragment:

'*Ce matin vers six heures Louis-Napoléon, fils de la Duchesse de Saint-Leu, qui avait dans sa confidence le colonel d'artillerie Vaudrey, a parcouru les rues de Strasbourg avec une partie de. . . .*'

That night there was little sleep at the Tuileries; the royal ladies flitted anxiously in and out of the council which sat through the night, and the Duc d'Orléans was on the point of starting for Strasburg on the next day, when the full news arrived and the King turned to the more congenial business of conferring a peerage upon the Military Governor. The pretender was in prison with his conspirators, and it remained for the Government to decide upon their future. On receipt of the news Hortense had got into

France in a false name and was staying outside Paris, appealing to the King for her son's life. After an imprisonment of twelve days the Prince was driven to Paris in a post-chaise. He protested against this separation from his friends and was informed that the adroit King Louis Philippe had avoided the unpleasant publicity of a state trial by granting him a free pardon. The pretender was to have no opportunity of impressing public opinion by his demeanour in the dock, and his attempt on the throne was systematically ridiculed by a stream of reports and caricatures of a half-witted young man who had dressed himself up in his uncle's uniform and was repenting his grotesque adventure in floods of tears.

But the quality of the King's mercy was diluted by the further decision to deport the Prince to America. Hortense was not permitted to visit him in detention, and he wrote begging her not to follow him into further exile. On a November morning he drove out of Paris by the road to the western ports which the Emperor had taken twenty-one years before him, and instead of Rochefort and the *Bellerophon* he went to Lorient and (by a variation in mythology) the *Andromède*. As he went on board the French cruiser, the *Sous-préfet* handed him a *viaticum* of 15,000 francs: the King was generous, but as he had secured 200,000 francs from the Prince's pockets at Strasburg, he could afford to be. On November 21, 1836, the *Andromède* sailed from Lorient into the Bay of Biscay; and, in a scene which has rarely provoked historians to reflect or Academicians to paint, Louis Napoleon left France in a warship.

VIII

NAPOLEON had been exiled on a rock in the Atlantic:
his nephew (it was typical of the more crowded atmosphere of the later age) was exiled to New York.
It was a sweeter, simpler New York, unguarded as
yet by Ellis Island or the menacing gesture of colossal
statuary and with a skyline not yet serrated by the
spectacular application of steel construction to
architecture, a "small but promising capital," as Mr.
Henry James described it, "which clustered about the
Battery and overlooked the Bay, and of which the
uppermost boundary was indicated by the grassy way-
sides of Canal Street." In the clear light of Emerson-
ian America and across this mild urban scene Prince
Louis Napoleon walked in the early months of 1837,
when Washington Square was 'enclosed by a wooden
paling, which increased its rural and accessible appearance; and round the corner was the more august precinct of Fifth Avenue, taking its origin at this point
with a spacious and confident air which already
marked it for high destinies.'

On the voyage out the Prince had been profoundly
wretched. He had failed, and it appeared from his
intention to become a farmer in the New World that
he regarded his failure as final. He wrote bravely
to his mother about his prospects in agriculture, and
he endeavoured to buy some land from his uncle
Joseph. But that cautious potentate, who had retired

to gentility in England, declined to answer his nephew's letters; and the disapproval of his family was still more deeply marked by the action of King Jerome. He had a handsome daughter, and before the expedition to Strasburg Louis had courted her in Switzerland. It was understood that they were to marry, and the dark Mathilde would have made a noble Empress of the French. But her father was scandalised by the young man's rashness or by its failure, and he expressed his sound parental instincts by breaking off the engagement. The news reached Louis before his ship sailed; and he took the blow, if one may judge from his letters, in the best taste of contemporary romance:

'Lorsque je revenais il y a quelques mois de reconduire Mathilde, en rentrant dans le parc, j'ai trouvé un arbre rompu par l'orage, et je me suis dit à moi-même: Notre mariage sera rompu par le sort.'

In his isolation on board the *Andromède* the Prince was almost a tragic figure, and one can hardly wonder that (it was the year 1837) he stated his tragedy in terms of Lamartine. The cruiser had sailed, in the best tradition of maritime romance, with sealed orders. The cautious government of Louis Philippe intended to isolate the pretender in the obscurity of a long sea voyage until his memory had faded, and the captain was directed to take his ship to the United States by way of South America. They passed the Canaries in mid-December, as Prince Louis sat writing on deck; and early in the New Year the *Andromède* ran into rough weather off the coast of Brazil, whilst the Prince sought inadequate consolation in a set of Chateaubriand from the ship's library.

There was a long wait at Rio, which so far stirred his inherited virtuosity that he sketched the bay. But at last, in the month of March, 1837, his imprisonment on a French cruiser came to an end, and Prince Louis walked ashore at Norfolk, Virginia.

After a little dinner to the ship's officers he went on board the steamboat for Baltimore, and eluded the persistent inquiries of a gentleman who followed him twice round the deck in the interests of the infant publicity of the United States. The journey to New York was resumed by way of Philadelphia, and on an April evening in the year of Queen Victoria's (and President Van Buren's) accession the Prince was installed at the Washington Hotel, Broadway, in a growing metropolis which trailed rapidly away to the north in incipient streets with high numbers.

His arrival in New York, which produced a pleasant stir, brought him once more into touch with the news from France; and it was of a character to distract him from the prospects of agriculture in America and to revive his ambitions as a pretender to the French throne. He read in the papers that seven of the conspirators of Strasburg had been prosecuted in January and acquitted by an Alsatian jury. The irrepressible Persigny had eluded the police and was conducting propaganda from London. But the French authorities had secured Laity, Parquin, Vaudrey, and his contralto, whose white satin hat and black side curls were an ornament of the dock. The trial, which lasted twelve days, abounded in irrelevant eloquence in the best tradition of French criminal jurisprudence, and a pleasing element of delay was introduced by the necessity of translating the entire proceedings into German for the benefit of several Alsatian jurymen who knew no other language. The prosecution called ninety-one witnesses: but as every prisoner and their six counsel delivered an almost uninterrupted succession of political speeches, the trial, which was largely attended by the public, turned into a political meeting with a strong Bonapartist bias. When Maître Thierret by a masterpiece of advocacy disclosed the conclusive fact that the prisoner Laity had a mother, the prosecution was shaken. But when Maître Parquin went one masterly step further and added that his own client in the dock had a mother also and (better still) a mother of eighty-two, there was not a dry eye in court. The jury retired and returned in twenty minutes with a verdict of 'Not guilty': there was a scene of wild excitement in which the prisoners embraced their counsel preparatory to an evening of conviviality and public serenade at their hotel.

The news was profoundly interesting to a young man in New York. The expedition to Strasburg had demonstrated that the French army was not indifferent to a Bonapartist appeal. But from the acquittal of his friends he learnt the far more gratifying fact that there was a civilian public for his views. This discovery, which he owed to the collapse of the Strasburg prosecution, modified his intention to stay permanently in America and threw him once more into the attitude of a French pretender. The tone of his letters to Europe became less resigned, and it was with the cursory glance of a distinguished visitor rather than the more anxious scrutiny of an immigrant that he surveyed the American scene.

On his first evening in New York he was invited to step along Broadway to the Old City Hotel, where a party of assorted senators, generals, and clergymen entertained him. This circle, from which he received a good deal of hospitality, found him well-mannered but somewhat silent, with an odd tendency to discuss his destiny and his future reign on the throne of France. An American poet even described him with that licence which is permitted to the most respectable poets, as 'a rather dull man of the order of Washington,' and he was believed (it was so delightfully French of him) to exhibit a preference for ladies' society. But he made occasional excursions beyond the somewhat oppressive gentility of his new friends; the American *monde* was apt, as Disraeli said, to resemble 'the best society in Manchester'; and he was sometimes to be found playing billiards in the public room or taking a glass of claret with the initiated of the Order of Owls in the cupola of Holt's Hotel. But these gaieties, punctuated with a more sober course of visits to a great-aunt of Mr. Roosevelt and a camp meeting of Wesleyan Methodists, hardly sufficed to occupy the Prince; and as a serious student of the great republic he resolved to survey its principal sights by visiting the falls of Niagara and Mr. Washington Irving. Once, as he drove through Brooklyn, he took the salute from the military. No self-respecting foreigner can spend a month in New York without solving the problem of the United States, and Prince Louis recorded his impressions with due solemnity:

> '*Un mineur qui se déclare indépendant à seize ans, quelle que soit sa force physique, n'est qu'un enfant. Les États-Unis se sont crus nation dès qu'ils ont eu une administration. . . . ils n'étaient et ne sont encore qu'une colonie indépendante.*'

It was, in spite of an intelligent prevision of the slavery contest, a fatal illusion for a man who was one day to encounter American policy. The Prince never recovered from the hallucination that he understood the United States, and it was not until thirty years later, when he had sent Maximilian to Mexico, that he learnt his error.

But his investigations were suddenly interrupted by the mail. One evening in June, as he was driving with a clergyman in New York, he opened a letter from his mother. It was a brave letter announcing an operation, but on the outside a doctor had scrawled 'Venez! venez!' Louis was a good son: his American plans were abandoned at once, and he booked a passage in the sailing packet for Liverpool. Before it sailed he conveyed, with the courtesy of a crowned head, his apologies to Mr. Martin Van Buren for his omission to visit him at the White House, to which the President had omitted to invite him. The voyage of the *George Washington* was uneventful in spite of the presence on board of two English actors and one of the few men whom Prince Louis could beat at chess, and he landed at Liverpool in July with a desperate hope that the French embassy in London would give him a passport for the journey across France to Arenenberg. It was refused; and at the end of the month, when the crowds in the London streets were respectfully cheering the young Queen, he left the Thames in a Dutch boat with a borrowed American passport. Hortense was slowly dying on a couch in her garden, as her son drearily worked his way up the Rhine from Rotterdam to the Swiss frontier. When he came to Arenenberg, she was asleep and they would not let him see her. But on the next morning (it was an August day on the lake outside) he came to her bedside. Seeing her son again, she lingered into the autumn. It was her belief that they would meet once more and for ever; when he was in America she had written to him: *'Bien sûr on se retrouve: crois à cette douce idée: elle est trop nécessaire pour ne pas être vraie.'* And in that belief, with her face towards her son, Hortense died on an October morning in the year 1837. She had lived too long without happiness to regret life; but she had given much pleasure in the world, and she had made an Emperor of the French.

7

IX

HORTENSE was dead, and between the dripping trees of Arenenberg the long avenue of exile without her to share it opened before Prince Louis. But he could not face the empty house, and within a few months he moved round the Lake of Constance to another château of Gottlieben. A quiet winter which he passed with a few of the acquitted prisoners of Strasburg raised the suspicions of the French government, and it was resolved in Paris to remove this danger from the eastern frontier. Early in 1838 the French minister at Berne made a semi-official suggestion that the Prince should be expelled from Switzerland. But the proposal, which by a pleasing irony came from a son of Marshal Lannes, was received without enthusiasm and referred by the Federal government to the Canton of Thurgau. The Canton declined and emphasised its refusal by electing the Prince to the local council and the presidency of its shooting club, whilst the exile was intensely gratified by the publicity which he owed to the French *démarche* and struck heroic attitudes before Swiss audiences.

Bonapartism was taken more seriously at the Tuileries than elsewhere in France, and at this stage the French government was still further alarmed by the publication in Paris of an account written by one of the conspirators of the attempt on Strasburg. A wise policy had dictated the endeavour, which had been almost completely successful, to ignore the pretender and to ridicule the entire affair. But it was now feared that a serious narrative might show it in a graver light, and the pamphlet received the incomparable advertisement of suppression. Publicity and martyrdom are the two essentials of successful agitation, and by the new policy of the French government both these stimulants were generously administered to the Bonapartist cause. The author of the book, Lieutenant Laity, was arrested and brought before the Peers on a charge of treason. The prosecution condescended to plead the claims of the Orleans monarchy and afforded to Laity an admirable opportunity to expound the superior political virtues of Prince Louis. But the Peers of France were not a Strasburg jury, and with an egregious lack of proportion they sentenced to five years' imprisonment and a fine of 10,000 francs the historian of an unsuccessful conspiracy whose actual participants had been uniformly acquitted. The gravity of the sentence won sympathy for the unfortunate pamphleteer, and no jury of Bonapartists could have done better work for his cause. Before the trial the Prince had written to Laity that there was no Bonapartist party, only a Bonapartist state of mind. But after it no Frenchman could doubt that a movement which had startled the Government into vindictiveness and the Peers into brutality was a serious competitor with the reigning dynasty.

This impression was deepened by the wholly disproportionate anxiety with which the Government pursued the trivial question of the Prince's place of residence. The French minister at Berne returned to this topic in a Note of portentous solemnity; and the Swiss, who resented this interference with their traditional (and not unprofitable) right of giving sanctuary to foreigners, entered with gusto upon the happy round of circumlocution for which a federal constitution affords such unrivalled opportunities. It was debated in the Diet; the debate was adjourned; the Note was referred to the Canton immediately concerned; the legal talent of Switzerland was mobilised to advise on nice points as to the Prince's national status; the Prince wrote letters full of grave eloquence; the French minister read Notes full of vague menace; and the world at large was made to appreciate to a degree beyond the wildest dreams of Bonapartist propagandists that there was in existence a living heir of the First Empire. The summer passed away in these fascinating exercises. Meanwhile the French government lost patience and paid the Prince the supreme compliment of a mobilisation in his private honour. An army corps was concentrated at Lyons to operate against the Swiss frontier; and Louis, whose resemblance to William Tell had never been marked, became a national hero. Cantons rained republican honours on him, patriotic *guerrilleros* were recruited in Lucerne, and the excitement rose to a crescendo. Then, having sufficiently apprised the world of his existence, the Prince gave a regal display of his magnanimity and withdrew to England with a graceful gesture. The aimless fatuity of his persecution had assured his position on the European stage, and in October the silent young man who had crept back into Switzerland as an obscure failure took the road again between cheering crowds as a figure of international importance.

He arrived in London in the late autumn of 1838.

It was four months after the coronation of Queen Victoria, and society before the pervasion of railways and the Prince Consort was faintly reminiscent of the Regency. The age of Count D'Orsay and Lady Blessington was an echo of the great days of Mr. Brummell, an odd survival of the allied elegances of dress and duelling into the gathering gloom of the Nineteenth Century. There was a compact little world of wits and beauties, where Mr. Greville kept his wicked diary and ladies shook their curls at gentlemen in stars and ribands. The long shadow of Prince Albert had not yet fallen across the bright Victorian scene, and under the urbane consulate of Lord Melbourne the young Queen rode out daily with her Court. It was the modish period of the Books of Beauty; and when Prince Louis Napoleon came upon the town, his career was an exercise in Disraelian *bon ton*.

He made a quiet entrance at his old hotel in St. James's Street. But after a migration to a second hotel in Waterloo Place, he was soon more magnificently established in a peer's house which he took in Carlton Terrace, and the imagination of Mr. Disraeli, always so inflammable by royalty, was kindled by the Prince's reception in London society. His horses became familiar in the Park, and the world learned to look for the quiet young man who drove to the opera with his equerries and had the Imperial eagle painted on his carriage doors. His suite included the ubiquitous Persigny and the more impressive figures of Colonels Vaudrey and Parquin; and he was sometimes attended by General Montholon, the authentic Montholon of St. Helena, author of the latest and least reliable of the Napoleonic gospels, or by the more

questionable presence of Colonel Bouffet de Montauban, who had varied his retirement with service in the
Colombian army and the management of a soap works
at Richmond.

Part of his first winter was spent in instructive
travel. After exhausting the attractions of the Bank
of England and the Lord Mayor's Show, the Prince
visited the spa of Leamington and the more forbidding
centres of the industrial North. He succumbed at
Manchester to the delights of an Industrial Exhibition
in the Mechanics' Institute, and the managers of
provincial theatres proudly displayed him to cheering
audiences in decorated boxes. When he returned to
London the great house was opened, and half a
century later Endymion remembered his entertain-
ments. 'The appointments were finished and the
cuisine refined. There was a dinner twice a week . . .
to which Endymion, whom the prince always treated
with kindness, had a general invitation. When he
occasionally dined there he met always several foreign
guests, and all men apparently of mark—at any rate
all distinguished by their intelligence. It was an
interesting and useful house for a young man, and
especially a young politician to frequent.' Since
society was mildly interested to meet the celebrated
pretender who had given Louis Philippe such a scare,
he was well received and was much seen at Lady
Blessington's. The French government followed his
progress with an anxious eye and requested Lord
Melbourne to exclude the Prince from London. But
the Prime Minister, who was rarely at a loss to find
excuses for inaction, blandly explained the unfortunate state of the law; and Prince Louis continued to
go the round of the clubs.

The world found him a romantic figure, and
D'Orsay (it was the height of elegance) made a
portrait of him. He escaped by a few months the acid
etching of Mr. Creevey. But when Mr. Greville met
him at a party, he saw 'a short thickish vulgar-looking
man without the slightest resemblance to his Imperial
uncle or any intelligence in his countenance'; but the
old gentleman had never felt at home at Lady
Blessington's, and the injudicious combination on
that evening of Lord Durham with Captain Marryat,
Alfred de Vigny, and Bulwer Lytton may well have
disturbed his observation. But the more sympathetic
Mr. Disraeli found in him 'that calm which is rather
unusual with foreigners, and which is always pleasing
to an English aristocrat.' The Prince even satisfied
the more exacting tests of tailoring; and the member
for Maidstone, who matched at this time the yellow
of his waistcoats with the bottle-green of his trousers,
declared that 'his dress was in the best taste, but to
a practised eye had something of a foreign cut.'
There could be no higher tribute in the whole length
of Savile Row.

But the Prince was not satisfied with his drawing-
room successes. It was pleasant to walk over to
Lord Eglinton's for a rubber after dinner. It was
delightful to breakfast with Lytton up the river, even
if one rowed Persigny and Mr. Disraeli on to a mud-
bank afterwards and endured the shrill invective of
Mrs. Disraeli as the grounded boat rolled in the wash
of the passing steamers. But Louis Philippe was
still King of the French, and a pretender must do
something more for his name than explain his destiny
to dinner-tables. Mysterious gentlemen flitted up
and down the steps of Carlton Terrace (and later of

Carlton Gardens) with the preoccupied air by which
the French spies in the street learned to distinguish
secret agents. Money went to Paris for the formation
of Bonapartist clubs and the foundation of that depressing type of newspaper which derives its sole
revenue from the proprietor. Behind the respectable
façade of his social position the Prince was busy with
his dynastic ambitions, and in the summer of 1839 he
produced a fresh statement of Bonapartist doctrine.
Des Idées Napoléoniennes was issued in London
by Mr. Disraeli's publishers. But its real public
was in France, and a cheap edition was printed in
Paris at half a franc, bound in the green of the
Empire and bearing on its cover the Emperor's
eagle.

The book, which was a more ambitious affair than
its predecessors, followed the familiar lines. The
more obtrusive facts of Napoleonic policy, which had
been largely due to the Emperor's lamentable ignorance of Bonapartism, were relegated to a secondary
place, and Napoleon was revealed by his nephew as
a social reformer distracted from his benefactions by
a fortuitous connection with the *Grand Armée*. The
revelation was in the direct tradition of St. Helena,
and it was made with a creditable command of eloquence. The author professed to be free from all
party ties and, like most adversaries of party, praised
his own. The sound revolutionary pedigree of
Napoleon was carefully established: he was the
'*Messie des idées nouvelles,*' the executor (not the
executioner) of the Revolution, whose monarchy was
the fullest expression of the First Republic. His
absolutism was an accident of the European war,
forced on a blushing Emperor by an impetuous pub-

lic opinion. But he was a democrat at heart, and in
the intervals between his victories he had reconstructed
France on a basis of equality. The codes, the colleges,
the conscription were all founded on the broad base
of democracy, *'un colosse pyramidal à bas et à tête
haute.'* It would all have become obvious after a
victory at Waterloo: *'Sous le rapport politique,
l'Empereur n'a pu organiser la France que pro-
visoirement; mais toutes ses institutions renfermaient
un germe de perfectionnement qu'à la paix il eût
développé.'* The bright prospect closed at Waterloo, but it might reopen under a Second Empire.

In Europe, it seemed, Napoleon had been still
more anxious to make a better world. His Italian
Kingdom had been the rough sketch of a free Italy:
*'Le nom si beau d'Italie, mort depuis tant de siècles,
est rendu à des provinces jusquas-là détachées; il
renferme en lui seul tout un avenir d'indépendance.'*
German unity and Polish independence were vaguely
foreshadowed in the Emperor's manipulations of the
European state-system, and his whole creation moved
towards the confederation of Europe, with a code
of European laws administered by a European court
of justice, in a single league of free nations, *'la sainte
alliance des peuples,'* in which war would survive only
as a crime and mankind would at last set up its
eternal rest. It was a remarkable design which had
more influence upon the imagination of Prince Louis
than upon any of his contemporaries; and he left his
readers with a vague gesture towards world peace and
a more detailed recitation of the virtues of a popular
monarchy. The Napoleonic idea, as the Prince expounded it, was *'une idée sociale, industrielle, com-*

merciale, humanitaire,' promising to France *'à travers la gloire des armes une gloire civile plus grande et plus durable.'*

This adroit and intelligent piece of propaganda had an immediate success. But while it was running through its editions in Paris, Prince Louis was less usefully employed in Ayrshire. Lord Eglinton held a tournament at his house in Scotland which lived for a generation in the memories of British humourists. It was to be a costume affair, and mediæval costume was supremely ridiculous to a generation which wore rectangular hats and strapped its trousers under its boots. Even Mr. Disraeli, so tolerant of sartorial eccentricities, was still laughing forty years later at 'the Knights of the Griffin, and the Dragon, and the Black Lion and the Golden Lion, and the Dolphin and the Stag's Head, and they were all always scrupulously addressed by their chivalric names, instead of by the Tommys and the Jemmys that circulated in the affectionate circle of White's, or the Gusseys and the Regys of Belgravian tea-parties.' It was all vastly entertaining, and the Prince went up to Scotland to play a leading part in the pageant. He proposed to appear in the lists in a dazzling combination of bright steel and crimson satin, with a somewhat ill-advised creation of green velvet for evening wear. His horsemanship, which was excellent, would have made him a more formidable pretender to the throne of England, where such accomplishments are highly valued; and with Persigny as his faithful squire, he figured prominently in the jousting. The first day of the Tournament was held in pouring rain, and the knights adjourned to the ball-room, where Prince Louis tilted on foot. He

was at home in the air of chivalry, since he was himself the author of a ballad in which

> 'Brightly each targe and burgonet
> Was glancing in the sun,'

and a number of knights displayed a laudable recollection of the works of Sir Walter Scott. His
remaining poetical works in English might have
appeared without attracting attention in any Book
of Beauty or Landscape Annual to which Mrs.
Hemans contributed. They included a thoughtful
elegy by Napoleon on

> 'My dearest thought—my darling Son—
> My beautiful Napoleon,'

in which the Emperor's reflections were pitched in a
tone of melancholy platitude and literary reminiscence more usually associated with prize composi-
tions. The French armies pass across the stage

> 'Fearless as lions when they haste
> Athwart the long Numidian waste,'

and their master soliloquises to an extent which is
fatally facilitated by the simplicity of the metre:

> 'Farewell! ambition—lofty schemes—
> Heroic deeds—and daring dreams!
> Farewell! the field of death and doom—
> The pealing gun—and waving plume!'

There is also a Byronic set of *Stanzas to Ireland* of
which the sentiment must have been more pleasing
to Mr. Moore than the poetry.

In the autumn, when the polite world was reopen-

ing its doors in London, the Prince resumed his life
in Carlton Terrace. Mr. Greville met him again at
Lady Blessington's and he found himself engaged in
an unpleasant dispute with a Mr. Kinglake for the
wandering affections of a blonde lady whom he had
met at Gore House. The Prince was successful, as
princes generally are; and Miss Howard became his
unconsecrated consort for a long term of years. But
Mr. Kinglake bore malice and lived to demonstrate
by his subsequent depiction of the Emperor of the
French the unwisdom of exasperating a historian.
Early in 1840 the Prince resumed his politics, and
Persigny published in the *Lettres de Londres* an inspiring picture of the pretender as the hope of his
country, in which his views were fairly represented
and his appearance considerably improved. He appears as the living image of the Emperor, *'le même
nez aux belles proportions et les mêmes yeux gris'*;
and an elaborate game of historical parallel is played
between Prince Louis and Octavius, Caesar's nephew.

Meanwhile he was going quietly about the West
End with his vague eye and his black stock. Politicians professed themselves impressed by his reserve,
and the great world was interested to make the discovery of a foreigner who could be a sportsman. The
unwearying Doyle made a drawing of him on horseback, which was to be seen among the 'Equestian
Sketches' in McLean's window in the Haymarket.
At one moment the public esteem of him was almost
heightened by his appearance as a duellist. An
unpleasant person named Léon developed a sudden
repugnance for the Bonaparte family (although he
subsequently so far overcame it as to live in official
charity under the Second Empire), and the Prince

found himself challenged and standing on Wimbledon
Common with the exquisite D'Orsay for his second.
But it was three weeks after the marriage of Queen
Victoria to her Consort, and the light had died out
of English life; the police intervened, and the intending duellists were bound over at Bow Street. It was
time for the Prince to return to a larger, a less confined
activity. He had made himself known to the world
as the heir of the Empire, and he could write proudly:
*'Tous les Bonaparte étaient morts. Eh bien, j'ai
rattaché le fil.'*

X

FRENCH opinion in 1840 was not unprepared for a return of Bonapartism in a militant form. A generation whose fathers had marched across Europe as conquerors felt vaguely humiliated by the continuance of peace, and there was little in the sober spectacle provided by the existing dynasty to appeal to the French imagination. An elderly king, a devoted royal family, and a succession of Liberal ministers formed an inadequate substitute for the rolling drums and the Man of Destiny; and it became steadily more difficult for a Government that was so eminently Victorian to control a people which was preponderantly Romantic. France under Louis Philippe was haunted by the little figure of the Emperor; one could catch on every wind the echo of old names, and men turned to the crude memories of the Empire for an escape into romance.

It was four years since Prince Louis' first experiment in pretendership at Strasburg, and the Orleanist government had unintentionally employed the interval in advertising his cause with a thoroughness which might more usefully have been reserved for the advertisement of its own virtues. The shrewd policy which had cynically denied him the publicity of a state trial in 1836 was forgotten in a new temper of irritable vindictiveness, and the Bonapartist cause derived

more benefit from the ponderous victimisation of
Lieutenant Laity and the aimless persecution of the
exiled Prince than it had ever drawn from the apocalyptic fervour of Persigny. France and Europe
were made aware by the ministers of Louis Philippe
that Napoleon had left a nephew, and the world
inferred from their obvious anxiety that he was a
formidable person.

His own propaganda was vigorously sustained, but
for effectiveness it bore no comparison with the fatuity
of the French government. His emergence from the
obscurity of Switzerland into the brighter light of
London society, which he owed entirely to M. Molé
and his minister at Berne, was an object of mild interest in France; and when he stated his political faith
in the intermittent perorations of the *Idées Napoléoniennes* he was regarded with increasing attention by
a widening circle. His claims were pressed on the
attention of Paris by the baroque eloquence of two
newspapers, whose expenses exceeded their revenue
in spite of the attractive circumstances that one of
them was edited by a claimant to the throne of
Hungary; and there was a steady flow of pamphlets.
True believers were offered opportunities of congenial
society in Bonapartist clubs, two of which were formed
in Paris. One was a genteel receptacle for retired
officers, whilst the other was commended to public
favour by the more enlivening company of the contralto of Strasburg.

But the verbiage of the *Capitole* and the enter-
tainments of the *Club des Cotillons* were of less service
to the Prince than the slow drift of French opinion
towards the Napoleonic legend. The national taste
for drum and trumpet history was vaguely thwarted

by a king who carried an umbrella; and his drab combination of a judicious foreign policy with the family virtues, which might have captivated an Anglo-Saxon electorate, fell bitterly short of the more picturesque requirements of the French. His appearance was irredeemably uninspiring, and his public utterances provoked M. Thiers to the conjecture that his monarch's morning prayer was 'Give us, O Lord, our daily platitude.' His ingenious and unheroic adjustments of European affairs were resented as a national humiliation; and when it transpired that his Egyptian policy was breaking down, the country was thrown into a wholly disproportionate paroxysm of indignation. The French imagination had played round the Eastern Mediterranean for almost a century, and these vague ambitions had been incorporated in the Napoleonic tradition by the operations of General Bonaparte and his *Régiment des Dromadaires* in 1798. The Napoleonic atmosphere was heightened by the career of the Pasha of Egypt. Born by a pleasing coincidence in the year of the Emperor's birth, Mehemet Ali began life in the tobacco trade but soon found a more congenial occupation in the Bashi-Bazouks. The simple-minded blend of homicide and intrigue by which he rose to power inspired French observers to a flattering comparison with Napoleon, and it became an article of patriotic faith that in the intermittent warfare between Egypt and Turkey the Pasha deserved every encouragement. His armies were moving slowly up into Asia Minor, and at Nisib on the upper Euphrates they met and broke a Turkish force whose operations were conducted in strict conformity with the views of the accompanying judicial and religious authorities and in defiance of the more

exacting requirements of a Captain Helmuth von
Moltke. This young officer, who was not yet under
the necessity of confronting the world with a wig of
transparent artificiality, was attached to Turkish
headquarters and succeeded by hard riding in escaping
from the rout into European history. The Egyptian
victory startled the world, and it was resolved in
London to check Mehemet's too Napoleonic career.
This initiative was fiercely resented in France, and
M. Thiers struck heroic attitudes before enthusiastic
audiences. But his protest was overborne, and the
humiliation left French opinion in a state of acute
self-consciousness.

The government of Louis Philippe regarded its
high-spirited young charges with the anxious eye
of an elderly nurse and decided to distract their
thoughts from the inadequacy of the present by another of their favourite stories about Napoleon. The
fractious public already had an armful of Napoleonic
toys and picture-books. The Arc de Triomphe looked
down the Champ Élysées, an army of historical
painters had converted Versailles into a gallery of
Napoleonic pictures, and there was a statue of the
Emperor on the Vendôme column. But it was now
decided that Paris should have the Emperor himself.
Early in 1840 M. Guizot, who had achieved a European reputation as an English historian without ever
visiting England, was appointed ambassador in London in the mistaken belief that relations with Lord
Palmerston would be facilitated by a thorough grasp
of the constitutional struggles of the last century but
one; and within a few months of his appointment
he applied for the surrender of Napoleon's body to the
French nation. This somewhat emotional application

8

was granted by the sardonic Foreign Secretary, and in
July a French cruiser commanded by a royal prince
sailed for St. Helena. The challenge to a Bonaparte
pretender was obvious. The political funeral has
always been a favourite vehicle of French propaganda,
and it seemed almost indecent that the Orleanist
monarchy should be permitted to monopolise so
Bonapartist an occasion as the second funeral of
Napoleon. If the Emperor's body was to return to
Paris, the Emperor's nephew should be there to receive it; and Prince Louis resolved to make a second
attempt on the throne of France before the frigate
Belle-Poule could anchor at Havre.

His project at first took the romantic form of a
piratical attack to be made on the French cruiser at
sea on its long voyage from St. Helena to the English
Channel. But the attractive design of hoisting a
Bonapartist Jolly Roger in the South Atlantic was
abandoned, and it was decided to attempt a military
revolution in Fance on the lines which had so nearly
succeeded at Strasburg. Lille was selected as a suit-
able garrison town, lying close to the Belgian frontier
and commanded by an officer who had risen from
the ranks under the First Empire. The Prince's
agents began to appear at the officers' club, and one
of the conspirators of Strasburg was seen walking on
the fortifications. The genial Parquin arrived on the
scene, and a retired staff officer, who had been converted to Bonapartism by the Prince's prompt
condolence upon his retirement, secured an invitation
to dine with the commander of the garrison. As the
guests on this occasion included the royal *Préfet,* the
circumstances were hardly favourable to an attempt
to enlist his host in a Bonapartist conspiracy. But in

the course of a call which he paid after this entertainment, he conveyed to the General a somewhat crude offer from the Prince of 400,000 francs if the attempt succeeded. The simple soldier steered a cautious course by declining to join the conspiracy but omitting to arrest the Prince's agent. But his refusal to co-operate determined the conspirators to transfer their activities from Lille, and in its final phase the conspiracy centred on Boulogne.

The selection of a seaport presented obvious advantages to an expedition which was bound to start from England. The garrison was small, and great hopes were built on the sympathy of a subaltern named Aladenize, part of whose regiment was sta-toined at Boulogne. The plan was simple: the Prince was to appear in the town with a strong party in the uniform of the infantry battalion which was stationed at Calais, and it was hoped that the Napoleonic appeal, heightened by this iliusion of initial success, would secure the 42nd of the Line and the port of Boulogne. During the summer mysterious bales of second-hand French uniforms arrived at Carlton Gardens, and button-makers in St. Martin's Lane were bewildered by orders for military buttons of outlandish foreign patterns. Muskets were ordered from Birmingham, and Dr. Conneau, who had attached himself to the Prince after attending his mother, divided his time between sewing buttons on the uniforms and printing Imperial proclamations on a hand-press in a locked room. The Prince's style had crystallised slightly since the manifestoes of Strasburg, and his staccato appeals to the army and the people of Boulogne and France had the authentic Napoleonic ring:

'Soldats!

La France est faite pour commander et elle obéit. Vous êtes l'élite du peuple et on vous traite comme un vil troupeau. Vous avez recherché ce qu'étaient devenues les aigles d'Arcole, d'Austerlitz, d'Iéna. Ces aigles, les voilà! Je vous les rapporte.'

The customary references to *la grande ombre de l'empereur Napoléon'* and *'le martyr de Sainte-Hélène'* were salted with lively denunciations of the competing dynasty, whose reign was dismissed as *'dix ans de mensonge, d'usurpation et d'ignominie,'* whilst its pretended respect for the memory of the Emperor was stigmatised as *'hypocrites et impures hommages.'* Promotion was promised to all classes and Europe was reassured as to the Prince's peaceful intentions. There was also a curt decree in the name of the French people declaring, in the true Imperial style: *'la dynastie des Bourbons d'Orléans a cessé de régner.'* M. Thiers, who had not been consulted, was graciously appointed President of a Provisional Government, and the Prince, who abstained from proclaiming himself Emperor before a decision of the people had been obtained, promised to summon a National Assembly on his arrival in Paris.

This happy transformation was to be effected by Prince Louis and fifty-five other persons, mostly armed with muskets. The party was oddly recruited for the adventure, and the Prince was supported in his endeavour to impersonate the 40th of the Line by a company consisting largely of men-servants. It was the need for numbers rather than an affectation of royalty that led him to take his *chef,* his butler, his tailor, and his fencing-master to Boulogne, and the rank and file of the expedition was recruited almost exclusively from below stairs at Carlton Gardens. General Montholon, who had ridden through the campaign of Waterloo with Napoleon and sat with him through the long afternoons at St. Helena, lent a flavour of the First Empire to the enterprise, and five other veterans took the field again. Of Prince Louis' inner circle, Conneau and Persigny went on active service, and five of the heroes of Strasburg resumed their familiar rôles. But the remainder of the company, which included some footmen, an Italian banker, and two Poles, was of strangely miscellaneous origin.

Early in July a foreign gentleman hired a paddle steamer for a month, and the Prince mobilised his forces. Dining at Lady Blessington's for the last time in the first week of August Prince Louis, who was wearing 'a large spread eagle in diamonds clutching a thunderbolt of rubies,' caused a mild sensation by inviting the company to dine with him that day twelvemonth at the Tuileries, whilst an indifferent stevedore was watching men at the Docks load the *Edinburgh Castle* with a remarkable cargo consisting principally of fancy dress and refreshments. In addition to the uniforms and two dozen cases of wine and spirits, two carriages and nine horses were slung on board; and the Bonapartist Armada was complete. The steamer left London Bridge on an August morning, as M. Guizot was proceeding to France by a more regular route; and before it left, Colonel Parquin, with an infelicitous taste in mascots, bought a vulture at a bird-fancier's in the City. The Prince went on board at Gravesend, and as the *Edinburgh Castle* dropped down the river to the Nore, the remainder of the party was picked up unobtrusively at various points between Blackwall and Ramsgate. The night was spent at sea, and the majority of the company were profoundly mystified as to the object of an excursion which rapidly became uncomfortable. There was a vague idea on board that it was to be a pleasure trip to Belgium, until on the next morning the Prince paraded his force on deck and startled them with the information that they were the companions of his destiny, bound for the port of Boulogne in the interest of the Bonaparte succession. Uniforms were served out, and there was an additional issue of one hundred francs to each member of the party. Calumny has added a more convivial scene; but nervous men are rarely intemperate two days out from land, and the malicious propaganda of the Orleanists has suppressed the presence on board among the stimulants of considerable quantities of ginger-beer and soda-water. There was little enthusiasm outside the Prince's immediate circle as men stood talking together behind the paddle-boxes of the *Edinburgh Castle* and the steamer moved slowly towards the quiet coast of France.

They anchored off Wimereux in the dark hours of the night, and the ship's boat put off to land this singular invasion. It was about three in the morning of August 6, 1840, when Prince Louis Napoleon stood once more on French territory. Somewhere in the darkness there was an argument going on with two *douaniers* whose professional instincts had been outraged by the nocturnal arrival of fifty persons from a suspicious steamer. It was explained to them that it was a party of the 40th Infantry proceeding down-Channel to Cherbourg and delayed by trouble to the paddle of their transport. They were invited to guide the party to Boulogne; but a dramatic colonel scared them with a revelation of the Prince's identity, and at the sight of their genuine alarm Louis mildly permitted them to go back to the village. As the sun was rising, the little column marched over the shoulder of the hill to Boulogne. The Prince had come to his own again with a standard-bearer and fifty men. Towards five o'clock they entered the town and tramped through the silent streets in the early light of a summer morning. A sergeant turned out the guard at the sight of this galaxy of officers, but he declined to leave his post and join the party. An officer, who was stirring early, was presented to the Prince; but failing to appreciate the honour, he slipped down a quiet street and warned the incorruptible Captain Col-Puygelier of the 42nd Infantry of the remarkable invasion. Meanwhile the detachment had arrived at the infantry barracks. The guard turned out respectfully, and they took possession of the barrack-square. Whilst Prince Louis was promoting non-commissioned officers in Napoleonic attitudes, a crowd of early loiterers began to gather at the barrack-gates; an officer invited them to shout *'Vive l'Empereur!'* and under the stimulus of a distribution of silver the seditious cry was raised. Lieutenant Aladenize, who was an officer of the battalion, paraded the 42nd, and the Prince addressed them at some length. He then proceeded to the agreeable business of promoting and decorating such non-commissioned officers as had not yet been presented to him. But at this stage the officers of the battalion began to arrive in barracks, and the truculent Captain Col-Puygelier forced his way past the sentries into the square. He rallied his men and commenced a violent

altercation with the Bonapartists. Someone began
to shout *'Vive le Roi!'* and there was a confused scene
in which Persigny was narrowly prevented from killing the royalist captain and a pistol went off in the
Prince's hand. The attempt to win over the infantry
had failed, and his party marched out of barracks as
the drums of the 42nd began to alarm the town.

The Bonapartists moved off in the direction of the
upper town, where there was a small arsenal. It was
about six o'clock, and a few people were beginning to
move about the streets. They were offered money
and manifestoes by this eccentric detachment of infantry, and enjoyed the unusual spectacle of the
Sous-préfet summoning the invaders to disperse and
being struck full in the chest with the brass eagle of
a regimental standard. After this achievement the
company reached the upper town and endeavoured to
force the Porte de Calais. But the gate resisted their
axes; and the expedition, having failed at two objectives, became a retreat. Some of the older men
broke away towards the harbour, but the Prince led
the survivors out into the open country at the back
of the town. With a sudden reminiscence of the
exigencies of drama he had resolved to make a last
stand under the *Colonne de la Grande Armée* and to
fall fighting on a windy ridge at the foot of his uncle's
monument. The gesture, which was in the taste of
M. Victor Hugo, was an effective one; but it was not
appreciated by his friends. Some mounted police and
the National Guards of Boulogne were coming up
the hill, and the Bonapartists scattered in all directions. A small party forced the Prince to leave his
flag fluttering at the top of the column and join them
in a dash for the seashore. A breathless run brought

them down to Wimereux; but their pursuers were
close behind, and the majority surrendered on the
beach. The ringleaders were less cautious, and the
Prince plunged into the sea with Conneau, Persigny,
and a few others in a desperate attempt to reach a
small boat. The exhausted men tried wildly to
climb into it under a heavy fire from the shore. Two
men were lost, the boat sank, and the Prince was hit.
Two boats put off towards them, and by a supreme
humiliation the survivors were rescued rather than
arrested.

It was about eight o'clock when Prince Louis was
driven up, shivering in a borrowed coat, to the Château
in the upper town and went straight to bed. He had
spent five hours as a free man in France. The *Sous-
préfet,* whose contusions were amply avenged, reported proudly to Paris that 'Louis Bonaparte is
under arrest' and proceeded to an inventory of the
eccentric cargo of the *Edinburgh Castle,* which had
been brought into harbour. It included vehicles for
the Prince's triumphant progress and a sumptuous
provision of clothes for his appearance at an evening
celebration. Colonel Parquin's vulture, which had
remained disconsolately on board during the expedition, was consigned to the town slaughter-house; but
being a bird of spirit, it escaped and ended its days
in a more honourable captivity with a coal-merchant
at Arras, after providing the humourists of a continent with a succession of jokes of which they never
wearied on the subject of the new Emperor and his
eagle. The authorities at Boulogne prolonged the
excitement by restricting the use of post-horses, and
Lord Hertford and Mr. Croker were delayed for
as long as two hours on their way from Calais to

Paris by this impudent intrusion of French politics. But the town subsided gradually into its provincial repose, and the attempt on Buologne was at an end.

On the next day King Louis Philippe enjoyed the story in his family circle at Eu with a humorous appreciation which did not prevent him from taking prompt decisions as to the disposal of the prisoner; and on an August morning about fifty hours after his first landing on the coast of France the Prince drove out of Boulogne by the Paris road. He went in a closed carriage, wearing under a greatcoat the dismal relics of his military adventure and the police on the seat facing him had orders from Paris to shoot their prisoner if an escape was attempted. Sentries were posted along the road, and as the *berline* rumbled through the *Boulonnais* he could see out of the windows the First Empire silhouettes of his Lancer escort and the great Dragoon helmets of the *Gardes Municipaux*. On the road he spent a night at the unpleasant Château of Ham, and on August 12 he came into Paris. The Emperor had arrived in his capital; but they brought him in at midnight, and he drove through the empty streets, over the dark river to the Conciergerie. Whilst the preparations for a state trial went slowly forward and a valet in Carlton Gardens was packing for Paris some bed-linen marked with N and a crown, the old King made a solemn progress to Boulogne and the fountain of honour played gently upon his 'dear comrades of the National Guard, the 42nd Infantry and the *Douanes.*' Louis Philippe struck triumphant attitudes in the north; the valet in London kept for himself the Prince's 'old pink hunting coat, the leather breeches, the white breeches, the top-boots, the big green coat with trousers to match, the shooting-boots, the big brown coat, and the hats'; and for six weeks the pretender sat in a cell in Paris translating Schiller. A letter of condolence came from the elegant D'Orsay, and one day Madame Récamier called to see him. The prison was full of sentries (the Prince informed his counsel that he proposed, when he came to the throne, to make certain modifications in the uniform), and some offence was caused by the Government's choice of a cell for him. It had recently been in the occupation of the man Fieschi who had endeavoured without success to assassinate the King (and to anticipate the Gatling gun) with an elaborate complication of gun-barrels. Political prisoners are notoriously particular as to their prison comforts and dignities, and it was felt that the association was vaguely insulting to the Prince. It was even resented by his father; and the strange old gentleman, who was still living in Italy and maintained intermittent communications with his son through the medium of a rather peevish correspondence, sent to the French newspapers an emotional statement of his own patriotism and infirmities and a somewhat futile defence of Prince Louis as the victim of false friends and even, conceivably, of Orleanist *agents provocateurs*. The Prince was disinclined to elude his responsibility in this manner and replied with some eloquence:

> '*Fier de la mission que je me suis imposée, je me montrerai toujours digne du nom que je porte et digne de votre affection.*'

As the weeks went on, counsel were instructed for the defence, and the Prince retained for himself and his friends a galaxy of political advocates. They were

recruited from every group of the Opposition, and
the court was provided with the engaging spectacle
of the Legitimist Maître Berryer and the republican
Maître Jules Favre expressing their respective attach-
ments to Charles X. and the Convention by defending
the Bonapartist prisoners.

The trial opened in the last week of September
before the Peers of France. It was an odd tribunal
for the indictment of a Bonaparte, since the roll-call
of the full court was a Napoleonic litany. Davoût,
Marmont, Lannes, D'Erlon, Suchet, Grouchy,
Lauriston, Sébastiani were strange names for
Orleanist judges; and with a certain delicacy they
abstained from sitting. But by a crude irony Molitor,
Daru, Déjean, Claparède, Excelmans, and Pajol sat
under the presidency of Chancellor Pasquier, an ex-
Prefect of Imperial Police, to try the Emperor's
nephew for treason. The prisoners were all neatly
dressed with white gloves, and the Prince wore on his
coat the great *plaque* of the Legion of Honour. He
sat in the dock behind Berryer and next to old General
Montholon, and after hearing the indictment read,
he rose to make a full statement of his political ideals.
The opening was effective:

> 'Pour la première fois de ma vie il m'est enfin permis
> d'élever la voix en France et de parler librement à des
> Français. Malgré les gardes qui m'entourent, malgré les
> accusations que je viens d'entendre, plein des souvenirs de
> ma première enfance, en me trouvant dans ces murs du
> Sénat, au milieu de vous que je connais, messieurs, je ne
> peux pas croire que j'aie ici besoin de me justifier, ni
> que vous puissiez être mes juges.'

The young man was ceasing to be ridiculous. He
expounded his principles and claimed that the Bona-

parte succession represented a decision of the French
people. Of the attempt on Boulogne he spoke with
real courage: '*Je n'ai point eu de complices. Seul
j'ai tout résolu, personne n'a connu de l'avance ni mes
projets, ni mes ressources, ni mes espérances. Si je
suis coupable envers quelqu'un, c'est envers mes amis
seuls.*' The attitude was effectively struck. Then,
with a drop to the staccato eloquence of M. Victor
Hugo, the Prince settled into his peroration:

> '*Un dernier mot, messieurs. Je représente devant vous
> un principe, une cause, une défaite: le principe, c'est la
> souveraineté du peuple; la cause, celle de l'Empire; la
> défaite, Waterloo. Le principe, vous l'avez reconnu;
> la cause, vous l'avez servie; la défaite, vous voulez la
> venger.*'

The Prince's speech almost reversed the effect of
his failure at Boulogne. The grotesque masquerade,
the eagle, the capture in the water had seemed to
make of the pretender a figure of *opéra bouffe*. But
by his statement from the dock he raised himself
once more into serious politics, and none of the efforts
of the prosecution could recreate the congenial atmosphere of farce. The trial dragged on for four days;
Berryer was cruelly ironical to the solemn rows of
Counts, Barons, and Marshals of the Empire who sat
to condemn Bonapartism; and Persigny was char-
acteristically suppressed half-way through a voluble
exposition of the Bonapartist idea and published his
undelivered peroration in a newspaper. But the conviction of the prisoners was never in doubt, and the
court was only concerned to consider its sentence.
Prince Louis Napoleon was sent to imprisonment for
life in a French fortress, and the conspirators received

sentences varying from two to twenty years. All except four were confined at Doullens, where Parquin died in prison. But the Prince, Conneau, and Montholon were reserved for the dismal Château of Ham, and the bright adventure of Boulogne seemed to end in the trailing mists of the Somme.

XI

PRISON life, to judge from the criminal classes, is an odd school of character, and it is rarely included in the normal curriculum of princes. Ex-convicts have a strange habit of silence, and Louis Napoleon owed much of his manner and something of his character to the six silent years which he spent in the citadel of Ham. When a young man goes into a cell at thirty-two and remains in prison until he is thirty-eight, the experience will inevitably deflect or deepen the normal lines of his development. Louis in 1840 was a silent man, and prison only deepened his silence. His mother's visitors in Switzerland had always thought him quiet. Madame Récamier found him *'poli, distingué, taciturne,'* and Chateaubriand saw *'un jeune homme studieux, instruit, plein d'honneur et naturellement grave.'* The little world of New York in 1837 had remarked his silence, and the defect of taciturnity, which Continental observers regretted, was highly appreciated in London society as a genteel reserve. Six years in a feudal fortress varied with a little writing, an afternoon walk on the ramparts, and an evening game of whist with two friends and the governor of the prison drove him still further within himself, and the queer, silent potentate who was to mystify Europe from behind the dull eyes of the sphinx of the Tuileries owed much of his impenetrable manner to his six years as a political prisoner at Ham.

The prison was a massive fragment of the Middle Ages, less interesting to its occupants than to amateurs of military architecture, since the view commanded by its admirable bartizans consisted almost completely of mist. The situation was uncomfortably damp, and the Prince's two rooms were inadequately furnished in the style of the lodging-house rather than the cell. There were a few planks fixed along the sitting-room wall to serve as book-shelves, and the innumerable draughts contended with a large screen of which the prisoner mitigated the ugliness by cutting out and pasting on some of the less sympathetic of the *Charivari's* caricatures of the reigning dynasty. His life within these narrow limits was of a distressing regularity. In the morning he worked in his room; after lunch there was a little dismal exercise on the ramparts in view of a few trees and a depressing reach of the St. Quentin canal with a detective in attendance who never let the Prince's red *képi* out of sight, or a pitiable attempt at horticulture in a little garden planted with mignonette, and at one time (until the expense became too great) he rode gloomily round the courtyard while the guards were doubled on the castle walls and the governor of the prison officiated as ring-master; then he worked until dinner and passed the evening with Conneau, Montholon, and a pack of cards. In that quiet, grey school, as the sentries tramped up and down in the mist and the barges slid by on the St. Quentin canal, Louis Napoleon learned the gift of silence.

His mental life was inevitably more active, and in the six years which he passed by the light of his reading-lamp the Prince received an education unusual to royalty. He filled his book-shelves and wrote steadily behind the white curtains of his room. The ministers of Louis Philippe, with financial caution more worthy of a landlady than a government, had allowed the extravagant sum of 600 francs for the preparation of his apartments; but since the loan of books is comparatively inexpensive in cases where the borrower is in prison, they permitted him to draw freely on the national libraries, and he read with the persistence of an invalid. Indeed, it became his boast in later years that he had 'graduated at the University of Ham,' and the degree of that non-existent faculty was more laboriously earned than the more impressive academic distinctions with which royal persons are frequently decorated. His reading was rapidly transferred into a full correspondence and a queer series of miscellaneous writings. He reached his prison on October 7, 1840 (it was the day on which a French cruiser four thousand miles away was anchoring respectfully off St. Helena to bring his uncle's body to France), and before the year was out he had plunged into *'trente-six mille choses à la fois.'* The return of the dead Emperor to his capital inspired the Prince to an eloquent exercise on the contrast between the uncle at the Invalides and the nephew in prison, and in a desperate hunt for employment he converted a corridor into a miniature shooting-range. Like so many solitaries, he turned to invention, and early in 1841 he was on the track of a minor improvement in French musketry which he proposed to submit to the War Office. With a touch of his mother's virtuosity he copied a picture of his prison for Lady Blessington, and then as an escape from the present he plunged into English history. French politicians have always been careful students of

British revolutions, although they appear to have learnt little from them beyond the names of the characters. The contemporaries of Napoleon talked fluently about Cromwell and Monck, and now Guizot had brought into fashion a parallel between the Glorious Revolution of 1688 and the July Revolution of 1830. The Prince was disinclined to admit the accuracy of his comparison of Louis Philippe to the heaven-sent William III. and plunged into the authorities for a refutation. Hume, Smollett, and the French historians were sent to Ham, and in the spring he published the *Fragments Historiques, 1688 et 1830.* The pamphlet was a skilful succession of variations on a theme of Guizot, demonstrating that the true analogy to William of Orange was rather to be found in a young man who should invade a country at the head of a small force proclaiming as his intentions: *'Je renverserai un gouvernement, en gardant intact le prestige d'autorité; j'établirai la liberté sans désordre, et le pouvoir sans violence. Pour justifier mon initiative et mon intervention personelle dans une lutte si grave, je ferai valoir pour les uns mon droit héréditaire, pour les autres mes principes, pour tous les intérêts communs. . . .'* The approximation of Boulogne to Torbay was complete, and the pitiless pursuit of his parallel even led the Prince to indicate vaguely an analogy between the Seven Bishops and the acquitted conspirators of Strasburg which was highly complimentary to Colonel Vaudry and his operatic brunette. The tables were ingeniously turned on Louis Philippe, and it was demonstrated with a wealth of quotations from Guizot that the real prototype of the King of the French was to be found in the 'political atheism' of Charles II., in the Restoration cynicism which substituted material advancement for national honour and glory and destroyed faith by cunning. The comparison was startling to French readers familiar with the private life of their elderly King, but there was an effective ring in the peroration:

> *'Elle est triste, l'histoire d'un règne qui ne se signale pas que des procès politiques et des traités honteux, et qui ne laisse après lui au peuple qu'un germe de révolution, et aux rois qu'un exemple déshonorant.'*

The moral was sharply pointed, even if it had been necessary slightly to adorn the tale. The argument was occasionally lit up by a flash of Napoleonic eloquence (*'l'armée est une épée qui a la gloire pour poignée'*), and there were passages which show a queer prevision of the *coup d'état*:

> *'Un gouvernement peut souvent violer impunément la liberté. . .'*
> *'En général, les révolutions conduites et exécutées par un chef tournent entièrement au profit des masses; car, pour réussir, le chef est obligé d'abonder entièrement dans le sens national, et, pour se maintenir, il doit rester fidèle aux intérêts qui l'ont fait triompher.'*

The epilogue was still more characteristic of the coming reign:

> *'Marchez à la tête de idées de votre siècle, ces idées vous suivent et vous soutiennent. Marchez à leur suite, elles vous entraînent. Marchez contre elles, elles vous renversent.'*

So the Prince sat writing in his little room through the spring of 1841, with a line of Guizot written large on the wall: *'Pour les peuples comme pour les in-*

dividus, la souffrance n'est pas toujours perdue.' The
damp of the place was gaining cruelly on his health;
but he was permitted to see a few visitors, and one
of them remembered for years the look which he
caught on the Prince's face as he turned to go and
the lonely man stood staring after him. In the summer he set out in pursuit of a sound historical parallel
and began to collect material for a book on Charlemagne, in which that misunderstood German primitive
would doubtless have received a strongly Napoleonic
flavour. He even elicited a bibliography of the subject from Sismondi. But as the year wore on, history
was neglected in favour of the more active delights of
chemistry. An empty room was converted into a
laboratory, and a local chemist was permitted to assist
his experiments. Faithful Bonapartist correspondents
were alarmed with strange problems about the density
of gases, and the Prince's electrical work even received
the mild commendation of a learned society. Then he
returned to more familiar ground and began to revise
his *Manuel d'Artillerie* for republication. But his
attention was caught by a new subject, and in the
summer of 1842 he startled his supporters by publishing a substantial work under the forbidding title
of *Analyse de la Question des Sucres.* Beet sugar
is an odd topic for a pretender, and Prince Louis
treated it with a wealth of established and agricultural
technicality. It created some interest in the sugar
trade, went into a second edition, and stands in the
Protectionist severity of its doctrine as an ironical
contradiction of the Free Trade policy pursued by its
author when his ministers negotiated with Mr. Cobden
the treaty of 1860.

But the Prince's attention was not fixed exclusively

on carbonic acid gas and sugar islands. He studied through the newspapers the slow drift of French opinion, and in a letter of rare self-revelation he showed that hope had not died in him:

> 'En 1833 *l'Empereur et son fils étaient morts; il n'y avait plus d'héritiers de la cause impériale. La France n'en connaissait plus aucun. Quelques Bonaparte paraissaient, il est vrai, ça et .là sur l'arrière-scène du monde comme des corps sans vie, momies pétrifiées de fantômes impondérables; mais pour le peuple la lignée était rompue; tous les Bonaparte étaient morts. Eh bien, j'ai rattaché le fil; je me suis ressuscité de moi-même et avec mes propres forces, et je suis aujourd'hui à vingt heures de Paris une épée de Damoclès pour le gouvernement. Enfin, j'ai fait mon canot avec de véritables écorces d'arbres, j'ai construit mes voiles, j'ai élevé ma rame et je ne demande plus aux dieux qu'un vent qui me conduit.'*

There was always *'au foud du cœur le seul soutien, le seul guide certain dans des positions exceptionnelles, la foi dans ma mission.'* It was a queer doctrine:

> '*Je crois qu'il y a certains hommes qui naissent pour servir de moyen à la marche du genre humain, comme ces animaux qui naissent, soit pour détruire d'autres animaux plus nuisibles qu'eux, soit pour servir de germes, quand ils sont morts, à d'autres êtres plus perfectionnés. Je me considère comme un de ces animaux, et j'attends avec résignation mais avec confiance le moment, ou de vivre de ma vie providentiell, ou de mourir de ma mort fatale, persuadé que, des deux manières, je serai utile à la France d'abord, de l'humanité ensuite.'*

In this temper he became an active contributor of anonymous articles to the provincial press. They covered almost the entire field of political and economic organisation with a system of lucid and dogmatic

views from many of which their author had the
courage to dissent when he had reached a position to
enforce them.   When he approached the military
problem, the irony deepened, and he became the advocate in 1843 of the system of recruiting with which
Prussia broke his Empire in 1870.   Meanwhile he
corresponded promiscuously with Bonapartists and
democrats and entertained his leisure with the preparation of an elaborate history of artillery.   His principal assistant was an early friend whom he had known
at Malmaison; she had already conducted painful
researches for him into the sugar problem, and she
was now sent round the booksellers and libraries in
pursuit of information about early bombards and
Renaissance ballistics and the effect of gun-fire in
Algeria.

The prince sat by his reading-lamp at Ham, surrounded with notes on gunnery and sketches of
limbers.   Sometimes he seemed almost to lose hope
and wrote: *'La prison est une mort anticipée.   On
ne m'écrit plus, on m'oublie. . . .'*   And sometimes
he trailed off into introspection and religious reflections.   But he kept a brave face before his callers;
Chateaubriand and Louis Blanc and his friends from
London (and even on one delightful occasion the
frivolous but accomplished Mlle. Déjazet) saw a
pale man with a slight foreign accent who received
them in a dismal little room and talked eagerly
through the few rationed hours of their visit.   His
interest in the outer world was undiminished by his
excursions into the early history of gunpowder, and
in the spring of 1844 he entered the field of popular
economics with a pamphlet on the problem of poverty.
The *Extinction du Paupérisme* was not a subtle or a

profound work; with engaging simplicity it advocated the abolition of unemployment by means of the transfer of surplus labour to agricultural colonies formed for the development of the waste lands of France. The workers were to be brigaded in a semi-military organisation, and the project blandly ignored the pardonable distaste of the poor for regimentation and the limited qualifications for agriculture possessed by an unemployed texile operative. But it was well received in those advanced circles which were to succumb four years later to the similar fascinations of the *Ateliers Nationaux,* and the Prince received polite letters from such oddly assorted democrats as Béranger and George Sand, while large numbers of French working men were favourably impressed by this evidence of the pretender's gracious interest in their condition. A few months later King Joseph died after his long exile, and Prince Louis published a polite memoir of his uncle. The ex-King of Spain and Naples was not an impressive figure, but the occasion seemed to merit a muffled roll of Bonapartist drums. His biographer even asserted that Joseph had been so imperfectly acquainted with the brother, the Emperor, as to identify his views with the *Idées Napoléoniennes.*

But gradually, as the fifth year of his imprisonment wore on, the writing-table in the mist at Ham became intolerable to the Prince. Visitors were a faint echo of the world, and the young lady from the local laundry, whom her friends (and students of historical scandal) knew more picturesquely as 'Alexandrine la Belle Sabotière,' was a very pale reflection of the gaiety of princes. But the echo and the reflection seemed to trouble the lonely man. He began to trifle with one of those vast designs which fascinate men in small rooms, and discussed with a Central American diplomat the possibility of an inter-oceanic canal. Nicaragua, with a laudable instinct for names which look well on a prospectus, made a flattering offer to the Prince; and he seemed to contemplate leaving Europe to assume the governorship of the canal zone of the *Canale Napoleone de Nicaragua.* That coy republic jilted a Belgian syndicate in favour of Prince Louis; deferential gentlemen came to Ham from the Nicaraguan Legation to convey the wishes of their government; the Prince made sketch-maps and composed an eloquent pamphlet in which he demolished the claims of Panama and Chagres in comparison with the maritime glories of Realejo and San Juan; and the whole strange episode left him with a vague attraction towards Central America which was to make the tragedy of Mexico. Slowly the fascination of the outer world began to gain on him, and it steadily became less possible to make a life out of pamphleteering at long range and archaeology at second hand. An English friend was asked to make a move for his release; but it produced no result. Then, towards the end of 1845, his father asked that he might see his son once more and for the last time. The strange old man, who was still living in Italy, had reached that advanced age which is rarely attainable except by chronic invalids. Since the day in 1810 when he abandoned his family and the throne of Holland King Louis had played little part in his son's life except as an irritable correspondent and the exacting host of dutiful visits. The Prince's efforts at filial virtue had been consistently discouraged, and when he was an active pretender to the throne of

France, he received from his father an almost illegible letter in which patient research has deciphered an angry request that he should write more distinctly. But although Louis regarded his father without enthusiasm, the old man's request to see his son was turned to excellent account. The Prince approached the Government in the attitude of a grieving son. Filial virtue makes an irresistible appeal to French opinion, and when the young man undertook to return to prison from his father's death-bed, it was difficult to see how Louis Philippe could refuse. An agitation was started in Prince Louis' favour among the deputies of the Opposition, and the rotund eloquence of M. Odilon Barrot was enlisted in his support. But the Government insisted that its prisoner should take the tone of a suppliant; and having struck his attitude, he refused to humiliate himself. The negotiation failed, and the Prince remained at Ham.

It was the year 1846, and Louis Napoleon was still a prisoner. His mood was becoming a little desperate, and he wrote: '*Je ne sortirai plus de Ham que pour aller aux Tuileries ou au cimetière.*' The Government had made an escape morally possible for him by its refusal of leave of absence to visit a dying father and its recent release of the other prisoners of Boulogne. With his friends at liberty (except Parquin, who had died at Doullens) the Prince might honourably dream of prison-breaking, and in the dark evenings of the first months of 1846 he found a more immediate topic than the artillery of the past or the canals of the future. A little money was raised for the purpose by the *opéra bouffe* expedient of a treaty with another claimant to a throne, and the escape of an imprisoned Emperor of the French was financed by an exiled

Duke of Brunswick. His plan was told to Conneau in May; the doctor's sentence had expired, but he stayed in the Prince's service at his own request and he opposed the desperate project of an escape. The Prince insisted, and that month he borrowed a British passport from one of his visitors. His servant bought a suit of workman's clothes in the town, and in the last week of May the plan was ready. The Prince's building was under repair, and he proposed to walk out of his room among the workmen and, in the character of one of them, to pass the gate into the open country. At six on a Monday morning (it was May 25, 1846) the Bonaparte pretender put on a blue blouse and stood up as a builder's labourer. He was a pale man, but his face was rouged. Soon after seven he shaved off his moustache, and a few minutes later he stepped out into the passage carrying a plank which had been one of his book-shelves. He took a knife with him, since he had formed a cold resolve never to be recaptured. In the passage a workman spoke to him, and at the door he passed two gaolers. With a pipe in his mouth and a plank on his shoulder the Prince walked across the courtyard under the eyes of the guard on duty at the gate. Half-way across his pipe dropped and broke, and with an effort of control he stooped to collect the fragments. At the gate the sergeant of the guard was reading a letter. The Prince's servant and a little dog had gone down the road in front of him, and with a plank held between his face and the sentry he walked slowly out of the citadel of Ham. On the road beyond he met two workmen, and just outside the town he threw away his plank and sat down to wait. There was a cross in a graveyard by the roadside, and the Prince knelt suddenly and gave thanks for his escape. His man came up the road with a cab, and they drove to the outskirts of St. Quentin. There the valet went into the town to hire a chaise, and Louis Napoleon walked across to the Valenciennes road. The chaise followed, and about two in the afternoon they drove into Valenciennes after exasperating their driver with a continual *'Postillon, cent sous de pourboire.'* For two hours they sat wretchedly in the railway station. An official looked at the British passport and someone in the station asked the valet after his master the Prince. Then, about four o'clock, a train steamed out of Valenciennes and passed the Belgian frontier. Whilst Conneau at the prison was delaying the alarm with an elaborate comedy of medicine and a dummy in the Prince's bed, Louis Napoleon was a free man in Belgium on the road to England with the memory of his years in prison and an old reflective habit which he took with him from Ham to the Tuileries.

XII

THE Prince resumed his life in London on a May
morning in 1846, and for two years he re-entered
English society. He put up at a hotel in Jermyn
Street, and on his first walk up Bond Street he met
Lord Malmesbury. That evening he dined with
Lady Blessington at Gore House, and the elegant
D'Orsay was offended by the spectacle of a half-
shaved Prince who was regrowing his moustache and
imperial after a brief appearance as a smooth-faced
artisan. He was even to be seen at a breakfast of Mr.
Monckton Milnes' with D'Orsay, Disraeli, and Sulei-
man Pasha, who had been at Nisib and refought the
battle with spoons and tumblers on the table-cloth;
Mr. Cobden, who was of the party and feeling a trifle
anxious about Sir Robert and the Corn Bill, found
the Prince 'evidently a weak fellow, but mild and
amiable.' The world was kind to him on his arrival
in town, and he hastily assured the governments of
Great Britain and France that his intentions were
purely peaceful. He made every effort to obtain a
passport for the visit to his father at Florence. But
France and Austria were hostile, and the Grand-
Duke of Tuscany became frankly panic-stricken at
the prospect of his arrival. His application was refused, and in July the old man died, as he had chosen
to live, alone. Before the news came, Prince Louis
spent an evening at the play to hear Rachel; it was

his first contact with classical French tragedy, and he made it in a London theatre.

In the summer he went off to Bath for his health. The formative soliloquies of Ham had done much for Prince Louis' intelligence; but the dripping walls of the citadel and the white mist of the St. Quentin canal had made a rheumatic of him, and when his *Études sur le Passé et l'Avenir de l'Artillerie* were published in the early autumn of 1846, he was seeking health on the hills above Clifton. Lady Blessington was at the waters, and Mr. Landor left cards on the Prince. Louis Napoleon returned the call, and there was an exchange of courtesies. His French friends were urged to come to England by the packet from Ostend and to pay especial attention to the marine beauties of Ramsgate; Prince Louis offered to meet them in London and escort them to Bath by the old broad-gauge Great Western Railway. But when the visit took place and the Prince's faithful correspondent on matters of artillery and agriculture arrived in England, she and her husband were met by another Bonaparte. Jerome's ill-natured son Napoleon had joined his cousin Louis at Bath, and there were great walks of the little French party along the English hills.

Late in the year the Prince was back in London, wearing his buttoned frock-coat and his strapped trousers in the world where Lord Eglinton played whist and Lady Jersey displayed her well-bred impertinence. Although he was living somewhere in St. John's Wood, he was a member of two good clubs and saw something of Bulwer Lytton at Craven Cottage and more of Lady Blessington at Gore House. He even designed artistic stalls for Lady Londonderry and Lady Combermere to facilitate their charitable sales at the great military bazaar held at the Guards' barracks in Regent's Park in aid of the starving Irish. But the sands were running a little low; he seemed to be without prospects as a pretender, and the long solitude of Ham had sharpened his appetite for life. The association with the blonde and beautiful Miss Howard was resumed, and the Prince installed her in a house in Berkeley Street. But the advantages of this relation were not one-sided; the lady had gathered a considerable fortune in the course of a varied career which earned her the successive esteem of a gentleman rider, a major in the Guards, the fastidious D'Orsay, and several members of the aristocracy; and when she became the Prince's un-licensed consort, she was able to give considerable financial support to his fortunes. Such assistance was not unnecessary at this stage of his career, since he had elected to seek entertainment on the turf. Early in 1847 he established himself expensively in King Street Houses, the embryo of King Street, St. James's, and his expenses there and at Crockford's steadily exceeded his income. Financial embarrass-ment, which may serve to private gentlemen for a social distinction, is vaguely discreditable in a prince; and Louis' public reputation had suffered a little from the fashionable atmosphere of mortgages and promis-sory notes in which he passed the year 1847. His expenditure included the maintenance of a considera-ble pension list; Napoleonic veterans, Swiss villagers from Arenenberg, Bonapartist sympathisers of every sort felt little diffidence in relying upon Prince Louis' charity; a practice had to be bought for the faithful Conneau when he emerged from imprisonment to

medicine; and although the Prince kept a good balance
at Baring's, there must have been moments in 1847
when he backed horses with something less than a
sportsman's indifference to the result of the race.
There was even an attempt to raise money on the
great Nicaragua Canal scheme from a financial
gentleman who lived in Hyde Park Street.

It almost seemed, in the last year of his long exile,
as though the light of that star with which he had
for so long entertained genteel dinner-tables was
beginning to burn a little low. He was almost forty,
and he had risen no higher in the world than Lady
Blessington's drawing-room. The French king was
very old; but he would leave an innumerable family.
Louis kept up an intermittent flicker of Bonapartism
in a perfunctory correspondence with a French historian about his own record, and a gesture of despairing exile when they brought his father and brother
home to their graves in France. But France with
its politics began to seem so far away; and England,
where one could at least live like a gentleman, was
near at hand. One might even marry a charming
Englishwoman with sloping shoulders. There was
a pretty Miss Seymour; but she preferred a gentleman
from the west of England, and the Prince had the
infelicity of attending her wedding. Then there was
the rich Miss Burdett, whom the world had almost
married to the old Duke of Wellington and the course
of time was to solemnise into the Baroness Burdett-
Coutts. But the nearest of Prince Louis' matrimonial
ventures was his successful offer to Miss Emily
Rowles. The young lady received some charming
presents from the Prince; but she was shocked by the
little house in Berkeley Street, and the affair was

broken off. Her parents had a delightful house at Chislehurst. It was called Camden Place; and when strange news came from Paris early in 1848, Louis Napoleon set out to reach it by way of the Tuileries and Sedan.

THE PRESIDENT

THE PRESIDENT

I

THERE was an agreeable spontaneity about the
Revolution of 1848 which it shares with the best
earthquakes. On the morning of Febuary 22 Louis
Philippe was King of the French: before sunset on
February 24 France was a Republic. The King's
ministers were tolerably unpopular. But then M.
Guizot rather cultivated his unpopularity; and besides
it was one of the advantages of constitutional government that one's ministers could be unpopular without
imperilling the dynasty. There was a faintly nauseous
atmosphere of financial scandal. But revelations have
always titillated rather than scandalised French
opinion, and it was hardly possible to govern a nation
with a lively imagination and a peasant tradition of
rapacity without giving cause for some deviation from
financial probity. The edifice of the middle-class
monarchy was not impressive; but it had an air of
bow-windowed security which seemed to promise an
indefinite future. An incautious minister had just
commented on the stillness of affairs: it was the same
calm which deluded Mr. Pitt into promising the
House of Commons fifteen years of peace six months
before his country went to twenty-three years of war,
which led Mr. Hammond of the Foreign Office to ob-

serve to his Secretary of State that there was not a cloud in the sky as the black wrack of 1870 was driving up towards France. But the world seemed very still in France by the grey light of February 1848. There was peace in Europe; but its blessings are rarely appreciated until after an outbreak of war. French opinion was a little restless. The domestic felicity of an elderly King was becoming almost exasperating to a generation whose appetite for sensation had been pleasantly stimulated by the more adventurous morality of M. Eugène Sue and his less remembered colleagues of the *feuilleton*. A more disturbing taste for political heresies had been provoked by the almost simultaneous return of MM. Michelet, Louis Blanc, and Lamartine to the more spacious age of the Revolution of 1789; and it was improbable that imaginations which were playing round the great gestures of the Convention or the last drive of the Girondins would derive any lasting satisfaction from the parliamentary ingenuity of M. Guizot. The reigning dynasty was beginning to seem a trifle dull; its attractions were ceasing to appeal to an increasingly indifferent public, and it was possible for Lamartine to summarise the shrug of a nation's shoulders in his bitter phrase *'la France s'ennuie.'* But revolutions are rarely the result of boredom, and France in February 1848 seemed very far from revolution. A number of preposterous persons had distilled from the tedious science of political economy a queer nostrum called socialism, with which they mystified their patient proletarian audiences. But their doctrine seemed at once too good and far too logical to be true, and their strange incitements cast hardly a shadow on the political scene. The centre of the stage was held by a more blameless company. A number of rather solemn gentlemen who formed the constitutional Opposition raised the respectable banner of Reform; their impeccable programme included an extension of the franchise and the exclusion of public servants from politics, and they exploited with a rather childish glee the British institution of the political dinner. The *Banquets Réformistes* were a novelty in French political agitation; provincial caterers were delighted with enormous orders, and long tables were spread in public gardens at which prominent politicians gave sonorous displays of their public virtues. There was a post-prandial alliance of Orleanist radicals and the more respectable republicans, and the deep notes of M. Odilon Barrot mingled with the shriller accents of MM. Garnier-Pagès and Ledru-Rollin in condemnation of the existing government. It was regarded officially as a harmless exercise until the reformers proposed to conclude the series with a monster demonstration in Paris. After a little fumbling the function was proclaimed by the Government. It was to have been held on February 22. On that morning Louis Philippe was still King of the French: two days later France was a Republic.

The day of the great meeting (it was a Tuesday) opened in rain over Paris. Soon after nine a crowd began to form outside the Madeleine, and there was a little aimless singing under the grey sky. For lack of any better employment they made a move across the Place de la Concorde and marched over the river to the Chamber of Deputies. The building was empty, and a few minutes later the Dragoons trotted out of the barracks on the Quai d'Orsay and cleared the

approaches. The old King was watching through
field-glasses from a window of the Tuileries. He
turned from the window to his papers; and as he
scattered some sand to dry a signature, he said to
Horace Vernet, *'Quand je voudrai, cela se dispersera
comme ceci.'* It seemed so on that first morning of
the Revolution. A few windows were broken, and
there was a little hooting; the crowd sat round the
fountains in the Place de la Concorde to watch small
boys throw stones at the mounted police, and the
Deputies began to walk across to the Chamber. In
the afternoon the streets were gleaming with rain,
and there was infantry massed outside the Palais
Bourbon. The Dragoons sat their horses in their
long grey cloaks, and somewhere outside a cavalry
band was playing trumpet marches in the rain.
Inside the Chamber an interminable debate dragged
on about the Bank of Bordeaux, and on the great
square the police were charging the crowd. There
was a barricade at a corner of the Rue de Rivoli,
and a few shots were fired. That night there was a
great blaze in the Champs Élysées, where someone
had made a bonfire of all the park chairs, and in the
late hours of Tuesday, February 22, the troops
marched back to the barracks. Paris seemed quiet,
and there was little to show that by Thursday the
Orleans monarchy would be a memory.

The night was very still. But on the next morning
the town had an air of revolution. The rioters were
entrenching themselves in the streets, and the paving-
stones of Paris resumed their dismal duty on the
barricades. Long columns of cavalry and infantry
were marching in from the outlying barracks, and
the drums were beating to call out the National

Guard. The mobilisation of the middle class in defence of its monarchy seemed an obvious resource; but by a queer irony it proved fatal. The *bourgeoisie* of Paris had made the monarchy in 1830, and by a singular inadvertence they unmade it in 1848. Touched a little by the general indifference to the King's difficulties, they inclined to the cause of Reform. But as they mustered at the *Mairies* on that February morning, it was suggested to them by some queer inspiration of vanity or kindliness that they might play a larger part, and it became the ambition of the National Guard to keep the peace of Paris as mediators between the troops and the crowd. When the harassed military moved against the insurrection, they found that the auxiliary force had interposed itself in the attitude (if with something less than the grace) of the Sabine women; and the National Guard, which should have been the last police force of the monarchy, melted into a vaguely cheering mass of middle-class politicians. This odd transformation paralysed the troops and startled the King. With the unheroic gesture of a cautious man in a hunted sleigh, he lightened the cargo and dismissed Guizot. The old man in his buttoned coat announced his resignation to the Chamber, and mounted police rode round Paris in the failing light of a winter afternoon with the news that Guizot was out. That day M. Victor Hugo was late at the House of Peers and went down into the town to watch the crowds. The King, without yielding upon the question of Reform, had summoned M. Molé to form a cabinet, and the change of ministry was entirely satisfying to the middle-class *deus ex machina* of the National Guard. The honest *bourgeois* returned home with the proud consciousness that they had made history, and in the better quarters of the town there were lights in the windows and cheers for the King. But revolutions are apt to continue after their promoters have been satisfied with the rate of progress, and it was always easier to fill the streets of Paris than to empty them. The shopkeepers might cheer for M. Molé; but there was a rougher type under arms behind the barricades, for whom there was little to distinguish M. Molé from M. Guizot. A roaring mob paraded the roadways with a vague taste for disorder, and the contented *bourgeois* took an evening walk to watch them from the pavement. The crowd went singing through the streets by torchlight and yielded cheerfully to a pardonable impulse to break M. Guizot's windows. But a battalion of infantry barred the way. It was about half-past nine in the evening. The crowd was friendly and cheered the troops. Then, as a rioter in front of the dark mass of the procession flourished his torch in the colonel's face and shouted abuse at him, a sergeant of infantry (he was a Corsican) resented the man's insults and shot him dead. The shot broke the strained nerves of the infantry: and at the sound, without an order, they poured an irregular volley into the crowd. The street cleared in a moment; but there were about fifty men and women on the ground. Somewhere in the town a young man named Flaubert thought that he heard firing. Down in the street the crowd had crept back to the ghastly corner, and as they saw the bodies, there was a great cry. There had been little in the parliamentary niceties of Reform to inflame a passion; but by that chance shot at a street corner a demonstration was converted into a revolution. A great open van drove by, taking some emigrants to the Gare Saint-Lazare. It was stopped and emptied; and when it drew up in the circle of torchlight, angry men piled the poor bodies onto it. Slowly the van moved off through the dark streets in a glare of torches; and as it went, the mood of Paris flamed into revenge and insurrection. The queer French aptitude for political funerals was exercised to the utmost, and the last hope of the monarchy went down before that slow, heavy van in the torchlight. When the news came to the Tuileries late at night that M. Molé was scared and would not take office, there was no sleep at the Château.

In the dark hours of Thursday, February 24, the old King made his last throw. Marshal Bugeaud, who was a master of street-fighting, was appointed to the command of the troops, and a general fetched M. Thiers to the Tuileries at two in the morning. He was to form a cabinet before sunrise, and the little man spent a busy night picking his way over the barricades to visit sleepy statesmen. The bells were chiming in the church towers as the dawn broke, and men were forcing the shutters of gun-makers' shops to arm themselves. In the early light the new ministers mustered at the Tuileries. Their master was uneasy, and in the streets outside the rioters were manning the barricades. The troops had been thrust out of Paris in long columns; but it was hoped that there would be no fighting if they could spread the news that MM. Thiers and Odilon Barrot were in office and the King would grant Reform. M. Barrot even rode through the streets to announce his own appointment; but somehow the rare spectacle of a middle-aged politician on horseback failed to rouse enthusiasm. At the Tuileries there was a dismal

coming and going of statesmen with good advice and
soldiers with bad news. The troops were falling back
on the palace and had lost their guns; a great crowd
on the march through the streets had halted in the
Place Vendôme to present arms to the *Colonne de la
Grande Armée* and to send up a roar of '*Vive
l'Empereur!*' M. Thiers was muttering '*la marée
monte, monte*' and urging his master to leave Paris
until the civil war was over. The King had ordered
his carriages for Vincennes, when he decided to review
his forces in the Place du Carrousel. Slowly the old
man rode out of the palace in the uniform of the
National Guard, with M. Thiers walking at his horse's
head. As he passed along the ranks, the cheers
turned to shouts for Reform; and as the King caught
the new tone of his faithful *bourgeois,* his nerve gave
way; he was seventy-four and it was a wild morning.
The National Guard had been the praetorians, the
janissaries to the Orleans monarchy; and as they
broke their ranks to shout with the mob, it seemed
that the reign was over. The old man turned his
horse sharply and entered the Tuileries for the last
time. There was a hurried debate, as a mob surged
towards the palace, and the sharp sound of firing
could be heard in the room. Then Louis Philippe
abdicated in favour of his grandson and drove away
into exile up the long hill past the Arc de Triomphe.

In its final phase the Revolution of 1848 was staged
in the Chamber. By the act of abdication a boy of
nine was King of the French, and his mother became
Regent. It was a dramatic gesture to present the
young widow and her child to the chivalry of the
Parliament; and as the people made free with the
deserted palace, a little party walked across to the

Chamber of Deputies. A confused session was in progress, and the Duchess of Orleans made an appealing entrance with her two boys. But before the Chamber could take a decision, there was a roar at the doors, and the mob surged across the floor of the House. M. de Lamartine proposed the appointment of a Provisional Government, and the Regency was at an end. Crowds swept into the Chamber, and the five gentlemen of the Provisional Government went off to the Hôtel de Ville to govern France. Someone in the Tuileries was playing the *Marseillaise* on the Queen's piano, and M. de Balzac was exploring the palace. Outside in the street an excited gentleman named Baudelaire was waving a gun and shouting, and all Paris was roaring with the intoxication of a successful riot. The *bourgeois* with a singular inadvertence had made possible a revolution which they did not require, and by a sudden turn France was swept into the Second Republic.

II

WHILST Paris was striking republican attitudes,
France and the world looked on with mild surprise.
The old King lay for a night at Dreux and posted
on into Normandy towards the coast. Behind him
in Paris a committee of public speakers and literary
men was improvising a republic and conducting the
business of government before cheering audiences.
There was an outburst of sentimental allegory in the
printsellers' shops, and engravers luxuriated in the
upturned eyes of virtuous soldiers and workmen or
a symbolic profusion of broken chains, wings, lightning, and lions harnessed to chariots; sometimes there
was even a queer intrusion of Christian imagery
amongst the Phrygian caps and masonic symbols of
orthodox republican art. The streets slowly emptied,
and men who had shouldered a musket on the *Trois
Glorieuses* of February began, as the echoes died
away, to make small jokes about '*Louis file-vite*' or to
sing little songs about the end of the reign:

'*Philippe s'désespère;*
Mironton, mironton, mirontaine.
Il part pour l'Angleterre,
Ne sait quand reviendra.'

At the Hôtel de Ville ten harassed gentlemen and
an inarticulate workman were sketching a new world
with large, free strokes. It was inaugurated under
the best literary auspices, and Lamartine was to be

156

seen in the recesses of a window offering to Victor Hugo the portfolio of Public Instruction. Universal suffrage was re-established, and the needs of labour were met (and the exigencies of economics defied) by the guarantee of work for all and the establishment of the *Ateliers Nationaux*. Projects of betterment pullulated, and some one proposed the establishment of a Ministry of Progress: it was a happy anticipation of the administrative method for the solution of any problem by the formation of a Ministry of it, which was subsequently adopted in almost every country under pressure of war.

The news from Paris sent a quiver through Europe. Italy began to stir uneasily in the grasp of Austria; South German Liberals held strange language to their masters; democracy alarmed the Cardinals by returning to its birthplace in Rome; there were barricades in the streets of Berlin, and the King of Prussia went riding down the *Linden* hawking his new principles to the passers-by; the Viennese swept into the dance, there was a little shooting at the Hofburg, and Metternich was hounded out of office; even the Spaniards took the contagion, and there was a faint movement in the calm air of Madrid. Queen Victoria and her correspondents spent themselves in a feverish outpouring of exclamations and underlinings on the subject of 'these *awful, sad, heart-breaking* times' and such 'an *awful, overwhelming, unexpected* and *inexplicable catastrophe.*' But the news found a more favourable reception in King Street, St. James's, where Prince Louis' carriage waited at his door and the twopenny post began to bring a steady stream of letters from France. One night, before the old King had been forty-eight hours on the road out of Paris, the Prince sat talking to his Italian banker after twelve. Early the next morning Louis Napoleon left London by the train for Dover, and about midday on February 27, 1848, the pretender was once more on French territory. He landed with his face in a muffler and (since he had no luggage) made a rapid passage through the *Douane*. Like most travellers, he lunched as the train stood in the station. At Amiens there was a long wait, and the station rang with the shouts of a queer party of released convicts. The train went on, and the Prince was exasperated by a conversational traveller. Somehow the long journey drew to an end, and on the next morning Prince Louis drove into Paris. They were restoring the roads and taking the paving-stones off the barricades, and someone asked him to lend a hand. 'My good woman,' he answered, 'that is just what I have come to Paris for.'

The arrival of a Bonaparte four days after the disappearance of Louis Philippe was a matter of some interest. King Jerome had been in Paris before the Revolution; but neither he nor his son were persons of any popular importance. Louis Napoleon was a more sensational figure, and after midnight he sent Persigny to the Provisional Government with a letter announcing his arrival *'sans autre ambition que celle de servir mon pays.'* The Government, which had no desire to see a pretender added to its troubles, requested him to leave the country in twenty-four hours; and the Prince, having made known his existence, withdrew 'for the moment.' He went from Boulogne by the *Lord Warden* steam packet and landed at Folkstone about the time that Louis Philippe, shaved, disguised, and without his wig, was

making a wretched arrival at Newhaven with his
thin-faced Queen under the unimpressive designation
of Mr. and Mrs. Smith, uncle and aunt of the British
consul at Havre.

As the Orleans family gathered in exile at Claremont to receive the solicitous inquiries of Prince
Albert, Louis Napoleon returned to King Street.
But his attention was distracted from the turf to
the larger speculation of the Second Republic. M. de
Lamartine and his divergent collaborators were
struggling with a proletariat which was too excited
to work and a *bourgeoisie* which was too indifferent to
moderate it. The public service was recruited from
the ranks of the agitators, and it grew in consequence
more voluble than orderly. A young man named
Émile Ollivier represented the Republic in the south.
Life in Paris became a succession of demonstrations,
and in the disorders the cry of *'Vive l'Empereur!'*
began to be heard in the streets; Persigny had remained in France and, although the caricatures of
the day exhibited a marked distaste for pretenders
with eagles, a small Bonapartist committee was
formed which included Montholon and one or two
more of the army of Boulogne, the Corsican Piétri,
some stockbrokers, and the faithful contralto of Strasburg. The Provisional Government struggled
through the spring, whilst the wind of the Revolution
was sweeping Europe; and the Prince in London was
sworn in at Marlborough Street Police Station as a
special constable to stand between British society and
the menace of the Chartists. He carried a truncheon
for Queen Victoria on a beat in Piccadilly between
Park Lane and Dover Street and was heard to say
that 'the peace of London must be preserved.' It

was a queer gesture for a foreign prince who was beginning to attain some reputation among the republicans of his own country. But a gentleman who kept his horses and lived in King Street was expected to attest; and besides it was the Bonaparte tradition to keep order in revolutions.

Two weeks later France went to the polls for the election of a National Assembly. The Prince, who had taken competent advice, was not a candidate; but two of his cousins were elected in Corsica, and Vaudrey and Persigny were defeated in the provinces after prodigious professions of their republican convictions. The mood of the country was becoming steadily more favourable to any name which embodied the idea of order, and the increasing cries of '*Vive Napoléon!*' in the Paris streets expressed a growing distaste for government by processions. The Provisional Government had been an experiment in dictatorship; but its history had disclosed a singular failure to dictate. A crowd, which began as a demonstration in favour of the Polish insurrection, had rushed the Chamber in May; there were a hundred thousand workmen in Paris ploughing the sand in the *Ateliers Nationaux;* and M. de Lamartine made speeches to the gathering storm. It was small wonder that the propaganda of Bonapartism began to raise its head, and the world grew familiar with engravings of '*Les Troix Neveux du Grand Homme*' and of Prince Louis himself (with the invariable superscription '*né à Paris*' to correct the malicious misstatement that he was a Swiss). By a strange irony, just as his name began to gather force as a symbol of order, the crude economics of his pamphlet on unemployment won for him a considerable popularity

in the stormy world of socialism; and the young man
in King Street simultaneously became the rising hope
of the harassed *bourgeois* and the theatening proletariat. It was an odd position for one of Lord John
Russell's special constables.

In the last week of May he made a serious move
into French politics. When the Chamber was debating the exile of the dethroned dynasties, he wrote
an indignant letter to the President demanding his
rights as a French citizen; and his friends had already
taken drastic steps to enforce them by a vigorous
candidature opened in his name at the by-elections
which were to take place early in June. Whilst M.
Piétri was moving that the Chamber should revoke
the banishment of the Bonapartes and the Government was agreeing in the most generous terms, a
handful of workers, canvassers and billposters by
turns, were covering the town with hand-bills, small
posters, and brass medals detailing the virtues, the
credentials, the sufferings, the principles of Louis
Napoleon Bonaparte, author of the *Extinction du
Paupérisme*. Persigny, Laity and a financial gentleman named Ferrère walked the streets all day, listening to arguments at street corners, distributing
portraits of the Prince, and leaving small bills in cafés
and at tobacconists. The Bonapartist committee
worked desperately; street musicians were even hired
to give a Napoleonic turn to their performances and
prophetic sleepwalkers murmured the Prince's name.
A great crowd waited outside the Hôtel de Ville to
hear the results. The Prince was in, and the hats
went up with a great cheer. Louis Napoleon had
arrived, in June 1848, at his first public position in
France; he was a Deputy for Paris.

By that queer pluralism which is possible in French elections, he was returned by the Departments of the Seine, Corsica, the Yonne, and the Charente-Inférieure. An excited meeting of workmen sent a petition to the Assembly demanding that he should be made First Consul; one district offered him a colonelcy in the National Guard; and in the provinces he was regarded without affectation as a future Emperor. In Paris there was a steady increase of excitement. The elections had been held on a Sunday, and the results were known during the following week. On the Saturday, when the Prince might take his seat, a great crowd waited on the Place de la Concorde and the Chamber was guarded by three regiments of infantry. That night the Government circulated to all *Préfets* and *Sous-préfets* a police description of the Prince with orders for his immediate arrest. Louis Napoleon stayed quietly in King Street, walking across after dinner to a paper shop by the Burlington Arcade for the last news from Paris. But every evening there were Bonapartist meetings on the *boulevards,* and the *camelots* hawked him in profile, full-face, or in pamphlet form as M. de Persigny took the air after his dinner at the Café de Paris and listened to the talk of the streets. There was a spate of little papers with cuts of the Emperor and his nephew, echoing with prophecies from St. Helena and voices from the dungeons of Ham, reporting the soliloquies of Napoleon on his column in the Place Vendôme or in the great sarcophagus at the Invalides. On June 12 there was almost a Bonapartist *journée.* Crowds paraded the streets all day shouting *'Vive Napoléon!'* and the Place de la Concorde was full of men selling little tricolour flags seditiously in-

scribed *'Vive le prince Louis!'* The old soldiers and
the workmen seemed to have joined the enemies of the
Republic. The republicans took fright and called out
the National Guard. There was an obscure scuffle
in the great square outside, and with the sound of
drums rolling through the Chamber Lamartine moved
that Prince Louis should remain in exile. At the
same time Persigny and Laity were arrested, and
the state was saved by its rather self-conscious consuls.
On the next day, with a delightful lack of consistency,
the Assembly ratified the Prince's election on sound
democratic principles. The rioting continued, and
there were great crowds in the centre of Paris. Shouts
of *'Vive —poléon!'* drifted into the Chamber as M.
Jules Favre was justifying the election, and men wore
little eagles in their hats. The police were hustled,
and someone began a barricade at the fashionable
corner of the Rue Castiglione and the Rue du Mont-
Thabor. But the Prince was a cleverer tactician than
the rioters, and on the next day he asked the President
for leave of absence. His letter to the Assembly expressed a dignified regret for the disturbances of
which he had been indirectly the cause. But it contained the ominous phrase which scandalised republican opinion:

> *'Si le peuple m'impose des devoirs, je saurai les remplir;
> mais je désavoue tous ceux qui me prêteraient des in-
> tentions ambitieuses que je n'ai pas. Mon nom est un
> symbole d'ordre, de nationalité et de gloire. . . .'*

The protest of the Chamber was immediate and
violent; and when the news reached London, Louis
showed his skill with an immediate resignation of
his seat. With a rare mastery of himself he chose

to wait, like a cautious fencer, for a better moment.
It was preferable, in the suspicious mood of French
opinion, to remain for a short time the Prince over
the water, hoped for and half seen; and the new
idol of the Paris streets stayed in St. James's, whilst
his virtues were celebrated in pamphlets and medals,
by old soldiers and young workmen, in Paris and
across the provinces. The papers (he had no regular
press) might affect to regard him as a stupid young
man from Switzerland who wore his uncle's uniforms
and was habitually accompanied by an eagle. But
the elections of June had made him a figure in French
politics. Men had heard the name of Napoleon
spoken loudly; and when the moment came, they
would not easily forget it.

The spring disorders deepened, as the year drew
on, into the flaming horror of civil war. The facile
expedient of the *Ateliers Nationaux* had concentrated
in Paris an army of 117,000 workmen at a daily cost
to the state of 170,000 francs, and an attempt to
demobilise this force sent the workers to the barricades in a desperate attempt to substitute the
République sociale for the parliamentary Republic
of 1848. The men were starving, and they fought
without hope, without leaders, without cheers, shooting sullenly in a dreadful silence behind great
barricades of stone. For four days Paris was alight
with the dull glow; guns were brought up against
the barricades; a great storm broke over the smoking town; women were shot without pity, and on a
ghastly Sunday a general in parley with the barricades
was shamefully murdered; the Archbishop of Paris,
with a supreme gesture of reconciliation, went out at
sunset to make peace and was shot and died. It

was a time of horror, and for four summer days Paris was tortured by the struggle. Then the rebellion broke, and the Republic survived. But in the servile war it had changed its character: during the struggle France had found a dictator, since the Assembly within sound of the guns had turned from the Provisional Government with a terrified gesture and handed every power of the executive to the Minister of War. General Cavaignac was one of those rare soldiers who manage to remain soldierly in politics. The martial virtues of taciturnity and decision rarely survive the change of occupation, and military men in civil affairs are too often garrulous and irresolute. But Cavaignac had learnt silence to the north of the Sahara, and he retained in the Chamber the gaunt air, the strong will, the staccato utterance of an Algerian general. Coming of a republican family, he regarded the Second Republic with an affection that varied between religion and pedantry; and when he was called to save the state in the June days of 1848, he saved it without swerving, without ambition, a little fiercely. His iron repression of the rebellion, the stern employment of military methods and martial law followed by the classical gesture of divesting himself of all power when the work was done, made a picture that was full of republican reminiscences of Camillus on his farm, of Washington at Mount Vernon. The Assembly replied by retaining him in office, and France was dominated by the gaunt figure of the republican soldier who had crushed the social revolution.

As the echoes died away, the wise men of the Chamber began to draft a constitution for the Republic, and France returned to work. Paris had still

a strange air; there were Dragoons in the Champ
Élysées, and the sudden sound of trains at the Gare
du Nord brought nervous citizens to their doors. The
country was governed with military precision, and
Cavaignac distributed punishment and multiplied
his enemies with the strict impartiality of an honest
man. But republican austerity is sometimes a little
trying; and the country, although it had called for a
man after the confused experiment of government by
committee, began to wonder whether there was not
perhaps another man. Men had heard the name
of Napoleon earlier in the year. It had been shouted
then across the Paris streets by a rather disorderly
element. But after the insurrection of June and a
dismal summer spent in the heavy grasp of General
Cavaignac the old name began rapidly to make new
friends. To the orderly classes it seemed to promise
(as it had once performed) the reorganisation of
France after revolution; the workers saw in it a hope
of escape from the General and his martial law; and
in the broad fields, where the Emperor had never been
forgotten, the sound of it made countrymen think
that he was still alive. There was to be a fresh series
of by-elections for the Chamber in the autumn, and
the propaganda of Bonapartism was vigorously resumed. The Prince announced his re-entry into
politics in a skilful letter, and his friends in France
returned energetically to the organisation of opinion.
Letters were sent from London to men of influence,
and his posters began to appear on the walls. Montholon pleaded his cause in print, and every class was
invited to rally, according to its tastes, to his
democracy, his love of order, or his incipient socialism.
He even had a mysterious interview with Louis Blanc

at a hotel in Leicester Square; and by a skilful turn of his political facets towards every class of elector he was returned once more to the National Assembly. On September 17 Louis Napoleon was elected Deputy for Paris, Corsica, the Yonne, the Charente-Inférieure and the Moselle; and when the results were announced at the Hôtel de Ville, a prophetic bugle-band played the old official anthem *Veillons au salut de l'Empire*: it was a just comment.

The Assembly was disinclined to exclude a Deputy who had been twice elected, and eight days after the poll M. Louis Bonaparte took his seat. There was a great turning of heads towards one of the benches of the Left, and the President took up his opera-glasses to stare: he saw a small man dressed in black with a heavy moustache. A little later the new member rose to speak. Since he disliked the tribune (he had condemned it for its dramatic possibilities in an article written at Ham), he was about to speak, in the English fashion, from his place. But the Chamber valued its stage effects, and he was hurried up the steps with cries of '*A la tribune! à la tribune!*' In a still House he read a short speech declaring his devotion to the Republic; and as he slipped out into the lobby, someone introduced him to a dapper military gentleman in a brown wig named Changarnier whom he was to know better.

In the weeks which followed the Prince frankly became a candidate for the Presidency, since the new Constitution included a President on the American model. He was rarely in his place at the Chamber; and when he went, he took a revolver in his pocket; but he was busy finding a way into the world of politics. He took a suite at the Hôtel du Rhin, with

a view of the Emperor on his Column, and there was
always a crowd round the door in the Place Vendôme
to see him.   Old soldiers waited for a glimpse of the
Emperor's nephew, and the world made little jokes
at the gaunt old men who cocked their hats and wore
tight, buttoned coats.   Daumier modelled the type,
threadbare and lean and swaggering with a great
stick, and called it *Ratapoil.*   Cham poked exquisite
fun at it in the *Charivari.*   But the crowds in the
Place Vendôme grew larger; and inside a short man
with dull eyes was receiving his callers.   He stooped
a little, and he had the thin legs of an ostler; London
had done much for his clothes, but once at least with
a strange lapse (or an ill-timed reminiscence of Mr.
Disraeli) he startled a visitor with a green plush
waistcoat and trousers that were distinctly yellow.   In
the morning he rode in the Bois, and in the evenings
he received at his hotel or was seen in drawing-rooms.
Sometimes he gave dinner to a journalist, and once
he met Proudhon, the Pope of contemporary socialism.   M. Odilon Barrot took him out in November to
dine in the country, and before dinner they went over
to Malmaison.   There was a little difficulty at the
gate; but the porter yielded to the Emperor's nephew,
and they saw the old rooms, the old furniture, even
a little chair that he remembered.

Through the autumn the Chamber was debating
the new Constitution, and it paid to the Prince the
compliment of an extreme anxiety as to the powers
of the President.   Once he was forced to speak by
an amendment to exclude from office all royal and
Imperial families.   The house was excited, and Louis
Napoleon was unprepared.   He spoke badly, with
pauses and in sentences which did not end.   But his

halting denial of sinister designs sufficed to defeat the
proposal and to convince an Assembly which always
measured ability by eloquence that the Republic had
little to fear from this inarticulate young man with a
foreign accent. He had learnt to be silent in his
rooms at Ham and in the cold drawing-rooms of London,
and parliaments are rarely captivated by silent
men. It became the fashion to treat him as a faintly
comic figure; his career as an *opéra bouffe* pretender,
his docile attendance on his adviser, M. Vieillard, his
inability to speak, set the lobbies tittering; and his
eagle, his uncle's hat, his English constable's truncheon
became a blessing to caricaturists. But the rising
tide of Bonapartism was unaffected. The *salons*
might raise a polite laugh with the story of his accent
or lift an eyebrow at the '*fils d'Hortense*.' But down
in Paris crowded meetings were cheering loud-voiced
men as they perorated confusedly on his sufferings in
prison, his burning patriotism, his melting pity for
the people. The provinces were frankly Imperialist,
and the rococo eloquence of countless local papers
answered the scorn of the clever gentlemen up in
Paris who multiplied little jokes about

> '*un faux Napoléon*
> *Qu'on met en circulation.*'

There was a vigorous campaign of Bonapartist sheets
financed by his friends, by the sale of his establishment
in King Street, by unknown soldiers of the
Grande Armée. Gradually as the crowds in the
streets sang:

> '*Nous l'aurons,*
> *Nous l'aurons,*
> ——*poléon!*'

the politicians began to feel the infection. M. Berryer
sank his loyalty to the Bourbons in support of a
Bonaparte interregnum; M. Guizot did the same;
Marshal Bugeaud saw a possibility of order in the
Presidency of the Prince; M. Thiers saw a possibility
of office. Late in October he even recovered something of a position in the Chamber by a dignified
defence of his own candidature:

> *'Eh bien! oui, je l'accepte, cette candidature, parce que
> trois élections successives et le décret unanime de l'Assem-
> blée nationale contre la proscription de ma famille
> m'autorisent à croire que la France regarde mon nom
> comme pouvant servir à la consolidation de la société. . . .
> Ce qu'il lui faut, c'est un gouvernement ferme, intelligent
> et sage, qui pense plus à guérir les maux de la société qu'à
> les venger.'*

The young man was beginning to take a sound tone,
and his elderly preceptors redoubled their good advice.
M. Thiers even suggested, after consultation with
M. Molé, that he should shave his moustache for the
election: it was felt (since they were both clean-
shaven) that Presidents should not wear moustaches.
As the day came nearer the Prince published his
manifesto. It spoke of the defence of society and
removal of taxes. Foreign policy was to be peaceful
but firm (*'Une grande nation doit se taire ou ne
jamais parler en vain'*) ; it might even be possible to
reduce the burden of military service. The conclusion
had a restrained eloquence:

> *'D'ailleurs, quand on a l'honneur d'être à la tête du
> peuple français, il y a un moyen infaillible de faire le
> bien, c'est de le vouloir.'*

The Prince stood upon one side. Against him on the other (there were other candidates, but they barely signified) was General Cavaignac. He had won a great victory in June; but men could not forget that he had won it over Frenchmen. The agony of the barricades was recorded in the tortured perspective and hectic colouring of popular prints, and France had no wish to see a perpetual reminder of it in the President's chair. His honest figure had become almost forbidding, and his republican virtue received, as it had merited, the reward of Aristides. On December 10, 1848, Louis Napoleon was elected by a majority of four millions in a poll of seven millions, and the strange figure whom the world addressed indifferently as *Prince, Altesse, Monsieur, Monseigneur,* and *Citoyen* was President of the French Republic.

III

FRANCE had a new master; but the statesmen were too clever to know it. Little M. Thiers tittered discreetly about *'notre jeune homme,'* and Lord John Russell sagely informed his sovereign that 'Bonaparte may probably play the part of Richard Cromwell' and clear the stage for a more sober Restoration of the dear good Orleans people at Claremont. Queen Victoria invited her uncle Leopold to rejoice with her at the election of Louis Napoleon although 'that one *should have to wish for him* is really wonderful'; but she showed a better judgment than many grave people in Europe in the reflection that 'it will, however, perhaps be more difficult to get rid of him again than one at *first* may imagine.' Stupid provincials felt vaguely that they had elected an Emperor; but in Paris, where they knew everything, he was only a President. M. Louis Bonaparte (it was an effect of his English reticence and his expressionless stare) seemed to the wise man of the Chamber so mild, so stupid, such a good listener, a patient, backward pupil. Ten days after his election they sat round solemnly on a winter afternoon to watch him take the oath. The austere Cavaignac sat with his hand in the breast of his coat, as someone announced the figures. The General said a few words of resignation, and there were some tears among his audience. Then the President was proclaimed, and 'the citizen Charles

Louis Napoleon Bonaparte, born at Paris' was invited to take the oath to the Republic. He followed it with a short speech, and General Cavaignac folded his arms. The President spoke of his duty to the nation and his detestation of usurpers; his French accent gave entire satisfaction. He was dressed exactly as he had been for his trial eight years before, in black and wearing the Legion. As he left the tribune, he turned with a gesture which he might almost have learnt in London (although M. Thiers claimed credit for suggesting it) and held out his hand to Cavaignac. Then he left the Chamber; the officers of the Assembly proposed to escort him to his official residence, M. Victor Hugo shouted something, and the ceremony was over. It was about half-past four of a December evening. There was a bitter wind blowing and a queer flicker of winter lightning, as the Dragoons trotted across the bridge and the Prince came home to the Élysée with the Lancers behind him: it was thirty-three years since the Emperor had driven out of that gate and taken the road for Malmaison and St. Helena.

The Presidential Court in 1848 had a delightful air of impromptu. Persigny and Mocquard wrote the letters; and a young captain of *Spahis* named Fleury, whom he had met at the Hôtel du Rhin before his election, formed the nucleus of the Prince's personal staff. It already contained a Ney and a Meneval, and the reminiscences of the First Empire was to grow stronger as his own gestures became more Napoleonic. There was a little dinner at the Élysée on the first Saturday of his term. The workmen were still in the building, and behind the flowers on the great staircase one could feel the indefinable

atmosphere of a recent removal. There was a Murat
and a Ney at the table, and M. Victor Hugo with
poetic licence was half an hour late for dinner. The
President was inclined to be apologetic about his new
establishment, and the china was deplorable; but the
band from the Opera played during the evening, and
his guests had the felicity of listening to the *Marche
républicaine* and a *pot-pourri* of the favourite airs of
Queen Hortense. One or two people came in after
dinner, and the President, after telling M. Victor
Hugo how he saw the last of the Emperor in the
large room downstairs, had a few words with the
British ambassador. On the next day (it was the
first Sunday of the Presidency) the Prince rode out
to his first review. The troops marched past on the
Place de la Concorde opposite the Tuileries, and someone in the crowd flew a kite in the shape of a great
eagle over Louis Napoleon's head: General Changarnier with a sudden reminiscence of the constitution
had the string cut. The Prince wore a general's uniform in spite of his purely civic position in the state
and the advice of M. Thiers (which was not uncon-
nected with his own sartorial possibilities) that the
President should always dress as a civilian.

The Presidency opened in a mild round of official
visits; and the Bourse, some hospitals, and a few
works had an opportunity of receiving with polite
applause the short gentleman with a heavy moustache
who was the anodyne substitute for monarchy provided by the Constitution of 1848. Early in the New
Year he heard Rachel at the Français; and there were
a few evening parties at the Élysée, where the names
of the Second Republic—Cavaignac, Thiers, Changarnier, Marrast, Montalembert—were mixed with

The Prince President (1848)

From a daguerreotype formerly in the possession of the Duc de Morny

faint echoes of the First Empire—Bassano, Came-
rata, Otranto—and the scene was set by the slowly
advancing men of the Second Empire. Twice he
called on Béranger at Passy; but the old man was
out. Concerts and balls afforded an opportunity of
exhibiting the President to the great world, and in a
more systematic succession of engagements he was
displayed to the army. The Dragoons were visited
in their quarters on the Quai d'Orsay; the reviews
went on; and there was even an interesting negotiation in which the President contracted with the pro-
prietors of a panorama for the troops of the Paris
garrison to see the battle of Eylau at wholesale prices.
At an infantry camp in the Luxembourg Garden he
was found in a still more Napoleonic attitude, tasting
the rations and demonstrating to the army that it was
no longer the servant of a disembodied committee of
politicians.

French politics in the early months of 1849 were
in an agreeable state of confusion. Constitutionally
the President had entrusted the government to an
impressive array of those elder statesmen of whom
M. Odilon Barrot was the most solemn representative and M. Thiers the private inspiration. But his
affections were with the more adventurous group of
his personal adherents; and, on the proposal of the
President, Persigny, Conneau, Laity, Vaudrey, and
Bouffet de Montauban were decorated by a Government which gravely disapproved of them. His
ministers constituted what would have been considered
under Louis Philippe a progressive administration.
But their principles were at once too conservative for
the Republic and insufficiently monarchical for the
President. He complained to Ney that they wished

to make him 'the Prince Albert of the Republic,' and he refused the part in a peremptory letter to the Minister of the Interior demanding the files of 1840 relating to his own sedition at Boulogne and insisting on the submission of all telegrams to the Élysée. There was an indignant flutter among the statesmen, and the President apologised politely; but it was obvious that he was disinclined to confine himself to purely ceremonial duties. Towards the end of January there was a vague threat of disorder in Paris, and the Prince supported his ministers in a vigorous display of force. The centre of the town was occupied by troops, and the forts were taken over by the regular forces. In the afternoon the Prince showed himself in the streets, and there were some shouts of *'Vive Napoléon!'* in the ranks. Queen Victoria, to whom (as his official *'Très chère et grande Amie'*) he had written a polite letter on entering office, paid him the compliment of informing her uncle at Brussels that 'everybody says Louis Napoleon had behaved extremely well in the last crisis—full of courage and energy, and they say that he is decidedly straightforward, which is not to be despised.' The Prince-President was beginning to take his place in the European hierarchy.

IV

On an April afternoon in 1849 twelve hundred men marched through a cheering crowd down the Corso into Rome. They swung along in the spring sunshine wearing green cloaks, and at the head of them went a bearded man on a white horse; he rode slowly in a white *poncho* with a great mane of golden hair that hung to his shoulders, and a tall negro rode behind him on a black horse with a lasso at his saddle-bow, wearing a blue cloak. His officers marched in red shirts, and in the ranks men wore those tall Calabrian hats which are inseparable from the picturesque calling of operatic brigandage and delighted the assembled artists of Rome, who had almost exhausted the *pifferari* and *contadine* of the Campagna. The little column marched away to bivouac in an empty convent, and all Rome knew that Garibaldi and his Legion had come in from the north to defend the Republic.

He was a queer, spectacular figure, whose patriotism was of that peculiar intensity which a man derives from being born on the extreme limit of his country and passing most of his life outside it. As a boy he had lived at Nice, which owed an interchangeable allegiance to France and Piedmont, spoke a Provençal *patois,* and regarded both the Italian and the French languages as genteel affectations; and as a young man he saw as much of the world and as little of any single part of it as a captain in the merchant service may, working mostly in the Mediterranean and Levantine trades. Once he commenced to tutor in an Italian family at Constantinople. But he went back to the sea, and in a sailors' inn at a Black Sea port he found a young man from Genoa who told him that there were men in the world hoping to build up a strong and single Italy from the welter of kingdoms and duchies over which the Pope and the Bourbons and the white coats of the Austrians kept guard. Then at Marseilles, in the house where Émile Ollivier was a boy, he met Mazzini and vanished into the twilight of false names and secret societies in which that spare, gaunt figure flitted vaguely beckoning to young men to follow, follow round the world and into prison and to the galleys the faint light which might one day dawn on Italy. The masters of Italy had reduced patriotism to a conspiracy, and Garibaldi took service in the Piedmontese navy with the simple object of permeating the fleet with the ideal of insurrection. The movement failed, and a courtmartial in Genoa sentenced to death as a bandit of the first class 'Garibaldi, Giuseppe Maria, son of Domenico, aged 26, captain in the merchant service and sailor of the third class in the Royal service.' He did not wait for the sentence to be carried out, but bolted to Marseilles, went two voyages under the French flag, and sailed for South America. For twelve years he was half seen across the great distances, buccaneering on the Rio Grande, commanding gunboats against the Emperor of Brazil, riding across the great plains of Uruguay to dine at an *estancia* on beef and *maté* with the *capataz,* and charge with the sword or the whirling

bolas as the army thundered out the battle hymn of
the Republic and the negro lancers crashed home. It
was a queer life of long marches and sudden fights,
and the little towns of Italy must have seemed very
far away as the great moon came up over Corrientes
and the *gauchos* off-saddled in the long grass. He
found a wife by a Brazilian river, falling in love (as
few men do) through a telescope and opening his
first conversation with a proposal in Italian, which
was fortunately overlooked, since the young lady
spoke only Portuguese. But he lived mostly among
Italians; and when Rosas marched against Montevideo, he raised an Italian legion for the defence of
the Republic. They marched behind a black flag
emblazoned, for remembrance of Italy's mourning
and her hope, with a burning mountain; and since a
shipper had failed to find a market for some scarlet
woollens imported for wear in the Argentine
slaughter-houses, they wore red shirts. They fought
well with the bayonet; and sometimes Garibaldi served
in command of the young Republic's younger navy.
But as the guns boomed across the River Plate, men
from Venice and Genoa began to remember Italy.
Their leader had kept touch with Mazzini; and when
a new Pope seemed about to lead his people out of
captivity, they offered their swords to the Holy See.
An embarrassed Nuncio replied politely with his
prayers. Five months later the *Speranza* sailed from
Montevideo with Garibaldi and sixty-two Italians;
they had learnt to fight, and their desire was to fight
for Italy. They brought with them into European
warfare a queer flavour of South America, with their
great saddles and their lassos, sitting their horses in
long *ponchos* and rounding up cattle under the heights

of Palestrina as though the Anio had been the Rio Grande.

Italy in 1848 was a seething cauldron. There was a Pope at Rome to whom men looked for liberty; Piedmont, Tuscany, even Naples found their rulers growing apprehensive and almost constitutional; the Milanese rose and swept the Austrians behind the four great fortresses of the Venetian border, whilst in Venice Manin and his men made a republic once more among the lagoons. Piedmont drifted nervously into war with Austria; but Radetzky was too strong for the Italians, and they were driven westwards out of Lombardy. There was a flicker of insurrection among the mountains in the north, where Garibaldi and his Legion hung on the Austrian flank. On the road to Como he met Mazzini marching with a great banner, and for a few weeks he fought an ingenious rearguard action among the lakes. Then he passed the Swiss frontier and Italy seemed to lie helpless again before her masters. There was a vague stirring with nervous protests towards Liberalism. But there is a stage in political history at which Liberals are more distasteful to a people than the frank reactionaries. Measured progress is a poor substitute for revolution, and its Liberal exponents owe their frequent unpopularity to their judicious and exasperating blend of moderation and enlightenment. The Pope took a minister who had learnt the art of government in Paris; but the reforms which would have satisfied opinion under Louis Philippe were an ineffectual gesture under Pius IX.; and Rossi, who might have organised the States of the Church in a year, was murdered after a month in a Roman crowd. There was a yell of triumph, and a young lady from Boston, who was honoured with the acquaintance of Mr. Emerson and Mr. Carlyle, sat down to convey her satisfaction in terms which must have startled her mother in New England. The Pope was disinclined to preside over a chaotic democracy; and after a few days of disorder, he dressed as a parish priest and drove (railways had been prohibited by his predecessor) down the Appian Way into the Kingdom of Naples, whilst behind him the people of his capital settled down in the last weeks of 1848 to the confused experiment of the Roman Republic.

The Italian nature and the unexampled splendour of the Roman background invested the affairs of this struggling commonwealth with an irresistible atmosphere of charade. The great mass of the Colosseum and the broken columns of the Forum were a constant temptation to impressionable politicians, and they would have been less than human (and far less than Latin) if they had omitted to strike classical attitudes against the Roman sky. The *fasces,* the wolf of the Capitol, the civic crown were conscientiously produced as properties on the crowded stage; and when the austere Mazzini was called to save the little state, he found himself draped with the impressive title of a Triumvir. A Mr. Arthur Clough of Rugby, Balliol, and (until recently) Oriel was worrying the dictator for a permit to see the Vatican; but the principal preoccupations of the new government related to its foreign policy. From the first the Republic lived under the shadow of foreign intervention. Even when Pius was playing gently with reform, Metternich had lamented at Vienna that he should live to see a Jacobin Pope and discussed intervention with the French, and Louis Philippe in his last weeks of power mobilised a few thousand men in the Mediterranean ports to sail for the Tiber. But when the Pope suffered the final indignity of flight and appealed to the world in the cold eloquence of Papal Latin, there was a touching rivalry between the competing defenders of the faith. Naples was his host at Gaeta; and the Neapolitan army was massed on the Roman frontier, ready to retreat with alacrity from any enemy and observed across the border by Garibaldi and his Legion, who were drifting southwards through Italy in search of insurrection. Austria was putting troops into Romagna from the north, marching with an unaccustomed air of victory since Piedmont had flung convulsively into war in the spring days of 1849 and crashed into disaster at Novara. Even Spain was fumbling with her army in her own fashion, as though time stood still and Philip was still king and Olivares and his heavy infantry were taking the road again for Italy. But France was too quick for them, and three brigades and a few guns were moved on Toulon and Marseilles to form (it was an ominous name) the Mediterranean Expeditionary Force and bring the Pope to his own again. It was a singular Crusade. The motive, apart from a desire in the new Government to please the Catholic masses of the French countryside, was a simple jealousy of Austria, a fear that France might be forgotten in the world if Radetzky's armies, which had struck down Piedmont at Novara, became the masters of Central Italy, a sudden return of the old desire to *porter haut le drapeau de la France*. So it was that Louis Napoleon, and not Franz-Joseph or King *Bomba* or Queen Isabella became defender of the faith, and a French fleet anchored off Civitavecchia on an April afternoon in 1849, and the Legion came marching into Rome with Garibaldi riding at its head to defend the Republic.

An embarrassed French general (he bore, with a faint flavour of old battles, the name of Oudinot) was instructed to occupy Romagna and to settle the dispute, to protect the Romans from the Austrians, from the Spaniards, from the Neapolitans, from themselves: there was no reference in his instructions to the course to be followed in the event of any reluctance on the part of the new Republic to have its destinies decided at French headquarters. His troops were landed, and there was a friendly air in the port. But at Rome the murmurs swelled into a roar. The Garibaldians marched in with Masina's lancers; and two days later the Bersaglieri from the north, nine hundred strong, sent their cocks' plumes waving through the streets. So Rome would defend itself, and on an April morning the French marched up the white road from the sea. They marched for two days, and in the dawn they moved against the Vatican hill. There was a great wall round the city, and the *Chasseurs à pied* went with sloped arms against the gates. Two guns spoke from the wall, and the French artillery unlimbered. Their infantry went at the old fortress with the bayonet; but the Italians shot from behind their ramparts, and the attack failed. Mr. Clough walked up the Pincio and saw the smoke; then he went home to write a letter, and the sound of gunfire drifted across Rome.

There was a flutter in Paris when the news came. The Chamber began to ask questions about the use of republican guns for the suppression of young republics. But there was a Bonaparte at the head of the state, and his inherited tradition after a defeat was to issue a mendacious *communiqué* and send more troops. In the month of May, whilst General Vaillant of the Engineers was considering whether to make his breach in the walls of Pope Urban or to trace his parallels against the line of more interesting antiques which the Emperor Aurelius had built beyond the Tiber, France was assured that the flag would not be dishonoured; and the siege-guns were slung on board at Toulon. Meanwhile there was an odd attempt to end the war: an energetic person named de Lesseps, who had graduated in a course of civil disorder at the French consulate in Barcelona, was sent from Paris with instructions to please all parties, from the Roman Republic to the exiled Pope, and to co-ordinate with more than consular ingenuity the general in command before Rome, the French ambassadors in Italy, and in European conference which was in intermittent session round the Pope's door at Gaeta. He hurried cheerfully from Paris to Toulon and from Toulon to Rome. He made an armistice and drove busily up and down between Mazzini and the French camp, while Mr. Clough hovered round the Sistine Chapel and Garibaldi moved out into the Campagna and drove the Neapolitans off the Alban Hills. The Legion rode out with its lassos and its queer American habits of indiscipline; but King *Bomba's* army displayed its customary ingenuity in sudden and silent withdrawals, and the armies were rarely in contact. At Rome Mazzini was negotiating at the Quirinal with the fascinating M. de Lesseps, and a treaty was even drafted between the two republics. But the busy consul from Barcelona found it easier twenty years later to reconcile Suez to Port

Said than to align Mazzini with French headquarters in 1849. His treaty was denounced by General Oudinot; Garibaldi's raiders swept into the city after their easy victories in the south; and the war went on.

Rome was besieged *en règle* through the month of June. The French rushed an advanced post in the still dawn of a Sunday morning; the Italians went running through the empty streets and Garibaldi was brought out of bed by the sound of the guns; there was an early parade of the garrison on the great square before St. Peter's with every bell in Rome reeling and clanging in its belfry, and in the early light the young men went charging up the hill against the French. The red shirts went shouting at the double, and Garibaldi sat his horse in his great white cloak; there was a sound of bugles coming up the hill from Rome, and the Bersaglieri drove at the French line. But it held firm, and the young men on the hillside learned to die for Italy. The sun came up over the city, and the Italians spent themselves up the slope against the Villa Corsini in wild, attacking waves. At last, in the full blaze of afternoon, forty men from the great meres beyond Ravenna rode madly on horses against the French entrenchments and galloped unbelievably up the hill, up the steps, into the battered house. Half Rome surged cheering after them. But the place could not be held, and the French swept back into the position. It was almost night, and the guns were still booming on the Janiculan; Garibaldi's white cloak was vaguely seen in the darkness, and half the night they served the guns by moonlight. Then, for three patient weeks, the siege went on. The French trenches crept slowly towards the city, and their shells went singing over the

Trastevere. Mr. Clough heard the muskets 'at it, at-at-at it' and the dull slam of the mortars, as he walked about and polished his hexameters about

> 'a great white puff from behind Michel Angelo's dome, and
> After a space the report of a real big gun—not the Frenchman's !'

or perfected a smoother elegiac

> 'in a Roman chamber,
> When from Janiculan heights thundered the cannon of France.'

The long June days passed slowly, and in the last week of the month the French developed their attack. There was a long roll of firing for eight days, and the besiegers broke into the town. For a week and two days the Italians fought across the slope of the Janiculan, over a fragment of the old Imperial wall, through houses and up gardens, until the houses melted into ruins and the ruins faded into the dust of Rome. Then, in the dark hours of the night after a flare of illuminations (it was St. Peter's day) had died away from the black roofs, a great storm of rain swept down on the city, and the French moved silently to the last attack. Garibaldi stood sabring the besiegers in the darkness; and as the dawn broke, the Bersaglieri died grimly in a reeling house. Slowly the firing died away; Rome had fallen.

Garibaldi rode desperately across the city under the midday sun; his sword was bent, and his great negro was dead. He offered to march out into the Campagna carrying the Republic with him, as he had seen the Republic of Rio Grande years before go out into the great plains of South America in the bullock-waggons of a retreating army. But the Assembly surrendered to the French. Two days later, before Oudinot's *képis* could march down the Corso, there was a vast crowd in the great square between St. Peter's and the sweep of Bernini's columns; Garibaldi rode slowly through the roaring throng and sat his horse by the obelisk in the centre of the square; then, in a great voice, he called for volunteers, offered them *'fame, sete, marcie forzate, battaglia e morte,'* and turned his horse through the massed faces and the tears of Rome. That night four thousand men formed under the Lateran and marched slowly out of the city. They marched through the night, and they saw the sun in Tivoli. For four strange weeks they toiled across the hills by Orvieto and Arezzo and Macerata, while the blind armies of France and Spain and Austria fumbled on their tracks and the paths climbed the Apennine and trailed down eastwards into the Marches. Garibaldi went in his white cloak, and Anita rode with him; and the waggons and a great herd of bulls had an air of the Rio Grande as they came down to San Marino under the Italian sun. In an August night he rode out again, and the Austrians were close behind. Then he came down to the sea and put out in the moonlight. The Austrian fleet took some of his ships at sea; but he ran for the shore, and where the waves break along the sandhills by Cesenatico he waded through the surf with a dying woman in his arms. There was a little farm by a great mere, and its windows looked across to the long forest of sad pines by Ravenna. On a bed there in his arms Anita died, and Garibaldi was left alone in Italy. The hunt was after him, but he hid and wandered and marched once more across the mountains, until on an autumn morning he put out to Elba with a loud cry of '*Viva l'Italia!*'

In Rome the French marched in, and Mr. Clough, who had been at Rugby under Arnold, commented unfavourably on the *vivandières*. Mazzini and Garibaldi had helped the young men of Italy to dream a great dream. But the Pope had come to his own again, and the French bugles sounded the *diane* down the long Italian streets until a day in August of 1870, when the red trousers marched away to the sea and the great guns were booming above Metz. The siege of Rome was the prelude of the Second Empire, and in its queer melody one may catch the dull roll of the last movement.

V

The comedy of French politics proceeded briskly through 1849. The President continued to take the air in cheering crowds and to scandalise his ministers by appearing in Council with the unauthorised magnificence of striped military trousers, whilst the judicious politicians of Paris began to regard their new acquisition a trifle dubiously, to wonder vaguely whether they had really made the wisest choice, to feel, as they contemplated that mild-mannered, mysterious figure, a faint unconfessed apprehension. But the elderly gentlemen who were the rising young statesmen of the Second Republic and had occupied the same promising position under Louis Philippe (and, in some cases, Charles X.) were very sure of themselves. At first they regarded their President with amiable contempt; the young fellow had been so very ridiculous in his youth, and M. Barrot talked of *'notre jeune homme'* with the benevolence of an indulgent pedagogue, whilst the blameless M. Thiers appeared in the unusual character of a man of the world with his debonair declaration: *'Nous lui donnerons des femmes et nous le conduirons.'* General Changarnier was even heard to refer to the chief magistrate of the Republic as 'a dejected cockatoo.'

The President went quietly about his business, presenting colours, visiting schools, inspecting troops. One day he went to mass at the Invalides; it was the Emperor's anniversary, and as he knelt under the great dome, he saw in the crowd a line of tall

189

old men wearing the great boots and braided coats and swinging capes which they had carried through Europe under the Empire. But in the streets outside he lived in the grey light of the Republic. France was electing a new Assembly, and the post was filled with the conflicting eloquence of circulars. The wise men in Paris were nervous of a victory for the revolutionary socialism which Cavaignac had blown off the streets in 1848, and the active Persigny was sent into the country to consult the greatest soldier of the day. Marshal Bugeaud was in command at Lyons, and the Prince's young man went by the new railway to its terminus and finished his journey by boat. The Marshal was prepared to concentrate eighty thousand men round Lyons and, if the socialist won too many seats for his taste, to march northwards and join hands with Changarnier in the Paris command. All one night he sat with Persigny as the results came in, and in the morning they could see that the country had voted against socialism and there was not yet a need for the army to save (as the expression went) society. In Paris the elder statesmen were still more militant. There were a few arrests, and when a respectful crowd shouted *'Vive Napoléon!'* Changarnier thought his President a fool for postponing a *coup d'état*: it was an opinion which the General was to revise. There had been a vigorous campaign by the Bonapartists; a committee of old soldiers demanded a Chamber of true believers; an enterprising banker urged in a circular that the Presidency should be prolonged into a Consulate of ten years; and the loyal group which had fought the Prince's elections in 1848 took the field again. The results were a singular rebuff for the Bonapartists. Five million voters had sent the Presi-

dent to the Élysée. But they were not equal to the
mental effort of sending his supporters to the
Chamber and he was only represented in the Assembly by a small group; the rest of the Chamber was
preponderantly conservative, but it was completely
out of sympathy with the Prince. A majority could
more easily have been obtained in the Assembly of
1849 for a Bourbon restoration than for any concession to Bonapartism; and M. Bonaparte presided imperturbably over France with an executive which
he did not control and a legislature in which his
views were barely represented.

But the Prince was not, was never in a hurry.
He had waited for forty years to return to France.
Now he was in France, he was President of the
Republic; and if his friends were beaten at the polls,
if policy was controlled for the moment by an hierarchy of solemn old gentlemen, he could afford to
wait. It was enough for him in 1849 that the country
had accepted the Prince; one day, if all went well, it
would accept Bonapartism as well. But the socialists
were in no such easy mood. They, like the Bonapartists, had been submerged in the conservative flood
at the elections. But they were disinclined to accept
the decision and invoked once more the democratic
argument of the barricades. In the second week of
June, while the guns were booming on the Janiculan
and Paris was fighting dismally against the cholera,
they used shrill language in the Chamber, printed
wild abuse of the Government, and invited Paris to
demonstrate by a great procession against the war on
Rome. It was a manifestation of the familiar type
which had made history twelve months before. Under
the Provisional Government men in thousands would

have marched shouting through the streets and M.
de Lamartine would have addressed them (eloquently
or inaudibly, according to their position in the crowd)
on the great square before the Hôtel de Ville.   The
Presidency was less sympathetic.   As the procession
passed down the *boulevards* (it was a little before one
o'clock in the afternoon of June 13, 1849), the
Dragoons came riding up Rue de la Paix from the
Place Vendôme.   The great crowd was crossing the
end of the street; and the troops took it sideways, cut
the procession in two, and cleared the streets.   The
manœuvre was an unheroic but welcome substitute
for the more familiar forms of street-fighting.   Across
Paris at the Conservatoire there was a faint attempt at
insurrection.   A few deputies, with the loud voice of
M. Ledru-Rollin at their head, startled the curator
and seized the empty building.   But four companies
of infantry and a few shots scattered the defenders;
and when the President with a staff of generals and
a squadron of Lancers rode out in the afternoon, the
crowd stood cheering in the Place de la Concorde.
It was about six o'clock when he stood in the Élysée
again, and he turned with a significant laugh to the
trim Changarnier, saying: 'Yes, General, it has been
a good day, a very good day.   But you rode me very
fast past the Tuileries.'

France had once more a government which could
keep order in the streets of Paris, but it was not yet
the government of the Prince.   He seemed content
in that first year of the Presidency to make ceremonial
gestures before provincial audiences.   Whilst the
Chamber was asserting its devotion to authority and
his ministers were curtailing the freedom of the press,
the Prince was deferring amiably to his advisers (he

never was heard to say '*Je veux,*' but always '*Ne vous semble-t-il pas?*') or touring the provinces with a repertory of blameless speeches. At Chartres he opened a railway and spoke of Henri IV.; at Amiens he presented colours and spoke of the blessings of peace; at Ham he proposed a toast and spoke of the wickedness of pretenders. With practice and in spite of an excellent education he was acquiring that air of happy commonplace which among public speakers distinguishes reigning princes. The summer went on, and the President went mildly up a royal avenue of foundation stones. Railways, which had so recently been the speculative rage in England, were spreading irregularly across France, and each new section of the system was opened by a dull-eyed President with a large moustache. At Angers a bishop blessed him as the protector of the Pope; all down the Loire to Nantes he steamed between cheering crowds and clanging belfries; and at Tours he struck an attitude of injured innocence and denied the malicious imputation that he was an ambitious man. His hearers were gravely adjured to observe his modesty and to dismiss all suspicion as to his intentions. But this effective display of political virtue was marred, in official circles, by an unfortunate question as to his private behaviour. The blonde Miss Howard had followed him to France. In Paris, by a concession to romance more familiar under the monarchical than the republican form of government, she occupied an equivocal position as his unofficial wife, and he was even accompanied on tour by this unusual consort. At Tours she was accommodated, by some official indiscretion, in the house of an irritable public servant, then on leave; in a temper of prudery or patriotism he resented the intrusion of the blonde lady from Berkeley Street; a complaint was made to Paris, and the President was called to account by his elderly preceptors. He replied in a romantic vein, lamenting his loneliness in France without friends, without family, without (it was the sad fate of princes) a wife, and taking a tone of proud apology (*'Je m'avoue coupable de chercher dans des liens illégitimate une affection dont mon cœur a besoin'*). It was queer to see the chief magistrate of a Republic, who was holding great audiences in Champagne and Normandy, pleading to his ministers like a nervous nephew before a tribunal of inexorable uncles; but it was a clear sign that the old gentlemen still held him captive.

Slowly, in his patient way, the Prince turned to the government of France and began gently, blandly, without hurry, to lay hold on the executive. He seemed inclined at first to secure a control of foreign policy through the embassies; his explosive cousin Napoleon was sent to Madrid and rocketed through that solemn gloom in a blaze of indiscretions, whilst Persigny went off into Germany and startled Berlin and Vienna with a vivacious course of lectures on the mission of the Bonapartes. French diplomacy was controlled officially by the judicious M. de Tocqueville and a discreet *personnel*. But the President seemed to give it a more lively turn when he urged an ambassador bound for Rome to look up his old Italian friends in the *Carbonari*. Gradually he took a hand himself; and as the Pope fumbled suspiciously with the resettlement of Rome, Louis Napoleon accelerated the deliberations of the Cardinals with a calculated indiscretion. An officer was sent from Paris with a letter stating the President's views; they were lucid and Liberal, with a firm injunction to the Pope to secularise the public services and confer upon the Romagna the modern blessings of the *Code Napoléon*. The letter drifted about Rome, got into print, and came echoing back to France. The Pope nervously withdrew to the more restful neighbourhood of Vesuvius. The Cardinals fluttered apprehensively about Rome. But the agitation was greatest in the solemn shades of M. Barrot's ministry, where the elder statesmen were startled into vivacity by the spectacle of their gentle President in an unaccustomed attitude of command. The rash young man had formed a policy; he had sent a curt order to the Pope through a Colonel Edgar Ney; and, worst of all, he had spoken in the name of France, which the Constitution had put so scrupulously into commission. If France was to be found anywhere, it was believed in political circles to reside in M. Thiers' drawing-room when a number of old gentlemen were present sufficient to form a quorum. There was a genteel explosion in Paris when the President's *démarche* became known, and the level tones of his advisers rose an octave. They defended him without enthusiasm in the Chamber; and as the autumn went on, he persisted steadily in his independence. A fresh instalment of the veterans of Strasburg and Boulogne received decorations, and the paladins of Bonapartism were enrolled in a Friendly Society. An urbane figure was brought to the Prince's table by a friend, and Louis saw for the first time his mother's other living son. M. de Morny, who was to personify so much of the Second Empire with his elegant patronage of the stage-door and his faint flavour of the Bourse, was an adroit person, something in the taste of one

of Balzac's heroes: he would have known the
Nucingens and married well. He had started (since
he was Flahaut's son) in the cavalry. But he drifted
from Algeria into business and then (since politics
were business also) into the Chamber under Louis
Philippe. He had his mother's charm, pleased all
the world, and smoked cigars, with a great reputation
for political sense. The Élysée was slowly developing a party of its own; and as the President stiffened
his grip upon policy, his ministers withdrew to their
studies and waited for the bowstring. Suddenly, on
an October afternoon, he sent a message in the American fashion to the Assembly. It announced with
perfect assurance that there had been a change of
government; the President felt that control of the
executive should be undivided and had appointed
ministers 'who had as much regard for his responsibility as for their own.' Their policy was simple:

> 'Le nom de Napoléon est à lui seul tout un programme.
> Il veut dire: à l'intérieur, ordre, autorité, religion,
> bien-être du peuple; à l'extérieur, dignité nationale.
> C'est une politique, inaugurée par mon élection, que je
> veux faire triompher avec l'appui de l'Assemblée et celui
> du peuple.'

The President was master of the executive; and his
elderly advisers observed his gesture of authority
with something of the bewilderment with which hens,
in Persigny's pleasing image, observe the first navigation of a duck whom they have unintentionally helped
into the world.

The ministry with which Louis Napoleon faced the
world at the end of October 1849 was unimpressive;
but it was his own. There was no Prime Minister,
since the Prince intended to preside at his own

Council; and amongst the names there were some—
Rouher, Parieu, Fould—which have the metallic ring
of the Second Empire. One was a banker; two were
lawyers from the provinces whom Morny had recruited
for the Élysée. Rouher, who was under forty, was a
persistent young man from Auvergne, who had come
to Paris from his country town with high professional
abilities and that appetite, with which they are so often
accompanied, for public employment. His affections
were transferred with a rapidity which kept pace with
the movement of affairs from the King to Lamartine,
and from Lamartine to Cavaignac, and from Cavaignac, when his time came, to the President. In an
age of fanatics he was a political agnostic and, if he believed anything, believed only that men required to be
governed since they could not govern themselves. He
possessed as a speaker and a thinker the fatal facility
of a good advocate, and there was something of the
successful lawyer in his almost total illiteracy. Un-
touched by the great movements which had set young
men brawling over the perspective of M. Delacroix
of the verses of M. Victor Hugo, he was to be found
in his early days roaring choruses or dancing in un-
critical quarters where Classics and Romantics met
on equal terms, and as a minister declining to claim
for the state the copyright of Saint-Simon's *Mémoires*
because the state could have no use for 'the Memoirs
of that fool of a socialist.' In the Chamber and in
administration he was as efficient as any other mechanical device, and he began in 1849 an association
with the Prince which was hardly to end until the
German cavalry rode round his great house at Cerçay.

The President had formed his ministry, and it remained to govern France with it. He had absorbed

the executive, and the world, which had known him
as 'M. Bonaparte,' was learning to call him 'Louis
Napoleon' and sometimes 'the Prince.' At first he
seemed to be supported by the Assembly. His
ministers stood firm in the rising tide of socialism,
and their firmness was appreciated by politicians who
were increasingly alarmed by the waning popularity
of government and its symptoms in the emergence of
M. Victor Hugo as the organ-voice of democracy and
the election of M. Eugène Sue for Paris on a platform
artfully combined of socialism and serial stories.
Public meetings were restricted; journalism was
supervised; the franchise was reduced. It almost
seemed in the first months of 1850 that the President,
having mastered the executive, would live in peace
with the Chamber. The elder statesmen resumed their
consultations and talked interminably with a wealth
of historical parallel and good advice: perhaps the
prodigal President would repent of his independence,
recall them to office, or at least act on their advice.
But gradually, in the steadily growing uproar of
Bonapartism, their voices grew fainter and died away,
and the noble figures who had once posed as a Roman
Senate became the twittering chorus of a Greek
tragedy, recording in a minor key the course of events,
upon which their ululations produced not the slightest
effect. M. Thiers was torn between the duties of
a parliamentary Opposition and the increasing royal-
ties of the *Consulate and Empire*. But when the tone
of the Bonapartists rose and distinguished journalists
began to write openly of the Empire, the politicians
took fright. It seemed slowly to dawn on the
Orleanists that the Presidency was unlikely to end in
a Bourbon restoration, and the republicans began to

be uncertain whether, when it ended, the Republic would still survive. This queer mixture of motives aligned the Assembly against the President, and French politics in 1850 became a duel between the executive and the legislature.

Whilst the Chamber gave an exhibition of its peevishness in a puerile attempt to limit the President's expenditure, Louis Napoleon continued to cultivate his popularity in the provinces. Wherever a new line of railway was to be found, the Prince was at the station in a cheering crowd. In the summer he went into the north with the bataillon *sacré* of Bonapartism, Conneau, Vaudrey, Ney, and Fleury. At every town the bells rang, the fire brigade was inspected, and there was a speech about the President's love of his country. Then he turned southwards, and the shouting rolled away down France. At Sens he fought his way through a battle of flowers; at Dijon there was a great ball, and two days before the Prince drove in, there was not a pair of gloves to be bought in the town and a single tailor had taken more than 5000 francs in dress coats: it was an inelegant function for a friend of Lady Blessington. The provincials stood in the sunshine roaring *'Vive Napoléon!"* and sometimes *'Vive l'Empereur!'* and the President scarcely heard the name of the Republic until he was on the Steamboat between Mâcon and Lyons, when the official *cortège* on the paddle-boxes was scandalised by the sudden protrusion from the river of a hygienic socialist wearing the simple uniform of Eden and shouting *'Vive la République sociale!'* At Lyons, which French administrators have always regarded with a nervous eye, the cheers were louder than ever. But at Besançon, as the Prince moved up towards the

eastern frontier, there was a mutter of hostility. Then,
by way of Belfort and Colmar, he came to Strasburg:
it was fourteen years since he had driven in by the
Colmar road to a lodging taken in a false name. The
cheers, the flowers, and the speeches went on in the
summer weather of 1850. Alsace and Lorraine ran
shouting by his carriage; at Metz the King of Prussia
sent his respects, and on the bare hill of Gravelotte
(the war and the Prussian guns were twenty years
away) they had made a little triumphal arch. Then
the cheers rolled westwards beyond Paris, and he
went into Normandy. The quiet man seemed suddenly to catch their meaning, to see that France
wanted something further of him. His tone rose, and
at Caen he spoke of his new duty to the state:

> 'Si des jours oraguex devaient reparaître et que le
> peuple voulût imposer un nouveau fardeau au chef du
> gouvernement, ce chef, à son tour, serait bien coupable
> de déserter cette haute mission.'

He had appealed from the Chamber to the country,
and the crowds had answered him. Parisian politicians might gesticulate angrily at his name. But
before larger audiences he was remembered by church-
men as the defender of the Pope and by the mass of
Frenchmen as the nephew of the Emperor. It remained
only to captivate the army. The Napoleonic incanta-
tion had a strange power over the troops, and the
President had taken every opportunity to make himself known in the service. But the Chamber, in its
duel with the Prince, clung to the hope that it would
retain the affections of the armed forces of the
Republic. Armies are rarely enamoured of parliaments; but the dominant figure of the French army

in 1850 was a Parliament man. General Changarnier, who held the Paris command and was at the head of the National Guard, was a trim military gentleman with a supreme sense of his own importance. In an age when a Mexican profusion of generals abounded in French politics, he carried himself with the air of France's only soldier. There were moments when he was half inclined to yield to the Prince's vague offers of a golden future and a Marshal's bâton; but they came to him mostly when he was on horseback with the thundering cheers of an army in his ears. In his great headquarters in the Tuileries he decided, under his brown wig, to maintain an impassive exterior (they called him the Sphinx) and to become the chosen soldier of the Assembly. The *salons,* which were still Bourbon territory, abused their master and tittered more divertingly than ever about the *'perroquet malade'* under whose Presidency they lived. At the autumn reviews of 1850 the President tested the feelings of the army. The guns and the Line passed the saluting base in silence; but the cavalry went by with a great roar of *'Vive Napoléon! Vive l'Empereur!'* There was an issue of treble pay and extra rations, and anxious politicians began to complain that the Republic's reviews at Saint-Maur and Satory had been turned (there was a considerable consumption of cold ham and stimulants) into *al fresco* Bonapartist picnics. A dithyrambic gentleman of the press was inspired to an ode in one hundred and twenty verses, terminating with an apocalyptic invocation to Napoleon as *'Empereur Messie'* and *'Christ-Soldat.'* But Changarnier openly expressed his disapproval of the demonstrations and stood boldly between the President and the control of the army.

Bonapartist enthusiasm rose to a shriller pitch.
Someone published a historical study of the blessings
of military dictatorship; questions began to be asked
about the great *Société du Dix-Décembre,* and a
minister (he was Baroche, a name of the Second
Empire) explained the harmlessness of Friendly
Societies; but there was a growing throng round the
Élysée of gaunt, hungry figures wearing long buttoned coats in the image of *Ratapoil,* avid for employment and ready to flourish their great *muscadin* sticks
and shout for '—*poléon*' on the streets of Paris. The
executive made a move against Changarnier in the
transfer of his best subordinate to a provincial command. The General retorted with elaborate discourtesy in Council and a prohibition in army orders
of demonstrations on parade. The politicians stared
suspiciously at every act of the Élysée; and the
demand for a plot, to which Titus Oates had reacted
so sympathetically in his own generation, stimulated
an obliging official to produce a fantastic story that
the Bonapartists had drawn lots for the murder of
Changarnier. The conception was too garish even
for the leaping imagination of Persigny, and the feud
proceeded through the winter of 1850 without ever
deepening into melodrama. Early in the new year
the dapper *Changarlot,* whose imagination was
haunted by Cromwell and Monck and the other
soldierly figures familiar to French historical analogy,
assured a cheering Chamber of his devotion *'durant le
combat.'* Morny and Persigny caught the menace of
his tone and slipped out to warn the President.
But Louis Napoleon was not easily alarmed by the
General's heroics. It was only a few weeks since he
had said in his quiet way to Rouher: *'Vous êtes bien*

*jeune, monsieur Rouher. Si l'on venait m'apprendre
à l'instant même que le général Changarnier marche
sur l'Élysée avec les troupes qu'il commande aux
Tuileries, j'irais au-devant de lui avec les chasseurs
à pied qui me gardent, et ses soldats se réuniraient
immédiatement aux miens. Monsieur Rouher, ma
destinée n'est encore accomplie; je serai empereur!*
In the same level tone he informed his ministers in
the first week of 1851 that Changarnier must go.
This intimation was repeated with courtesy to the
elder statesmen who shortly bore down upon the
Élysée to discharge a heavy cargo of good advice.
There was a nervous shower of resignations, and
the President was left to search for a ministry with
courage to dismiss the General. Persigny ran round
Paris; and one cold morning when M. de Morny
was out with his phaeton, his energetic friend met a
general in the street who felt equal to the effort.
The government was hastily reconstituted; but its
nerve was uncertain. They sat half the night in
Council, and before dawn the Prince was offering to
replace them with a ministry of militant Bonapartists. But the threat sufficed, and with the consent
of his ministers the President removed Changarnier
from his command: the heavens, in spite of all
predictions, did not fall, and the judicious M. Thiers
remarked that the Empire had come.

The executive had struck the last weapon from
the hand of the legislature; and as the duel moved
to its end, the focus of French politics shifted to a
fresh problem. The Constitution of 1848 prohibited
the re-election of the President for a second term.
The Prince was disinclined to return to private life
in 1852, and sane parliamentarians were unwilling

to drive him to extremes by maintaining the prohibition. The amendment of the Constitution was debated through the spring and summer of 1851 to a running accompaniment of threats upon either side. The Chamber denounced the slow dawn of the Empire in every tone from the falsetto invective of M. Victor Hugo to the more studied chest-notes of General Changarnier's *'Mandataires de la France, délibérez en paix.'* The President replied, wherever there was a railway to be opened or a statue to be unveiled, with the grave resignation of a reluctant man accepting fresh responsibilities. And the streets of his capital rang with an appropriately Parisian chorus, of which the refrain was:

> *'Révision!*
> *Révision!*
> *Des lampions!*
> *Poléon——*
> *Nous l'aurons!'*

The Assembly was forced to make an embarrassed choice between the distasteful alternatives of installing Louis Napoleon in the Presidency for a second term or driving him to prolong his power by an act of violence, and about midsummer it chose wrong. The Constitution stood unamended, and the Chamber decided that in 1852 the Prince must leave the Élysée: since he was a Bonaparte, he could leave it for the Tuileries.

The struggle had become inevitable, since the purists of the Assembly insisted that there could be no legal prolongation of the Prince's term; and on an August day in 1852 Morny, Persigny, and Rouher met the President and his Prefect of Police at St. Cloud: their business was to arrange a *coup d'état*. Opinion had been prepared for the shock in the long weeks of the Prince's tours. He was the greatest figure in the country, and his emergence was favoured by a vague fear of social revolution. The Church was friendly, the crowds would cheer, and the army obeyed orders. It remained only to make the plan and to select (since politics had become a military problem) the soldiers. France had lived for twenty years in the shadow of military reputations made in the Algerian wars of Louis Philippe. Cavaignac, Changarnier, and Lamorcière filled something of the position held in the later reign of Queen Victoria by Lord Roberts, Lord Wolseley, and Sir Evelyn Wood. The French public had lost the habit of European warfare, but its patriotic appetite found an agreeable substitute in the more picturesque operations in Algeria. The public imagination was obsessed by the hot African glare, the slow march of the French armies across the sand, and the pounding drums of the *Turcos* as they went in shouting with the bayonet. It had its Rorke's Drift at Sidi-Brahim, and the Algerian *razzia* became the favourite background of French heroism. The Caucasian races have always preferred their heroes slightly bronzed, and the *vieux Africains* stood high in the favour of that great mass of civilians whose vicarious militarism is the mainspring of wars. But the senior generals were, without exception, Parliament men; and the Prince turned for his collaborators to a younger group. Reputations had been won on the frontier since the older generals went into politics, and in 1851 Fleury was sent to explore the African garrisons for a likely team; his excursion was financed with some difficulty on borrowed money. On the way up to Sétif he stayed at Constantine with a brigadier named Saint-Arnaud. He was a queer, raffish figure who had commenced life in the army, abandoned it for a mysterious interlude behind the footlights or a counter, and returned to the service to make a name under Bugeaud. The man was past fifty; but his ambitions remained. He was still hungry and, like all ambitious men outside the circle, he hated politicians. The disorder of democracy disgusted him; and (he had seen the streets in 1848) he could write *'Je ne me laisserai jamais dominer par la rue.'* Fleury reported to Paris that he had found a man for the work; but his discovery was short of laurels, and the President took the singular step of fabricating a reputation for him with an unnecessary war. The Republic gravely took the field against the Kabyles; Saint-Arnaud was in command and his operations were followed breathlessly by the Parisian press. He marched into the interior, startled the tribes, and restored the peace which he had interrupted. There was an impressive fanfare of bulletins, and France had a new hero. Late in the summer they brought him to Paris. The President had found in the *jeune Afrique* his counterpoise to the older reputations. Saint-Arnaud was given a division, and he brought with him a Colonel Espinasse who was well qualified to purge a parliament by his three failures at the Staff College. There were likely men among the Paris brigadiers, Forey had a command (the Empire was to send him into Mexico), and with him a colonel of Zouaves named Canrobert. Slowly in the African sunshine the soldiers of the Second Empire seemed to be taking their places for the piece: Pélissier, a Crimean reputation, commanded at Oran; Vinoy (one seems to hear in the name the slow booming of the Prussian guns over Paris) was still in Africa, and the *Turcos* marched behind a dark young colonel, whilst all the world sang:

> *'Ce chic exquis*
> *Par les Turcos acquis,*
> *Ils le doivent à qui?*
> *À Bourbaki!'*

It was a man who was to see the running fights across the snow of 1871 and the slow, trailing march of a beaten army over the Jura into Switzerland. And somewhere in the shadow there was (the names are growing ominous) a Colonel François Bazaine.

The cast for the *coup d'état* was almost complete. General Magnan, who had refused a Bonapartist bribe at Lille in 1840, was brought to the Paris command: he asked no questions. Saint-Arnaud began to study his part hastily, and the plan grew in cold precision under the quiet hands of the President. In the autumn the piece was ready. Opinion was duly alarmed by a lurid publication on the *Spectre rouge,* and it was thought that society was willing to be saved. The date of the production was fixed for a day in September; but Saint-Arnaud declined to proceed until the Chamber was sitting. There was a shuffle of ministers. An energetic official named de Maupas was promoted *Prefect* of Police, and Saint-Arnaud went to the Ministry of War. The Assembly met in a nervous mood. Paris was full of odd stories, and the President was to be

seen in the autumn mist riding in the Champ de
Mars to have a word with General Canrobert and
watch his men on parade.   Whilst the Chamber was
drifting into a wrangle as to its own authority to
command the army, the Prince told half the truth
of his design in a public speech:

> 'Si jamais le jour du danger arrivait, je ne ferais pas
> comme les gouvernements qui m'ont précédé, et je ne vous
> dirais pas: "Marchez, je vous suis." Mais je vous dirais:
> "Je marche, suivez-moi!" '

The days grew shorter and colder.   The Paris streets
began to sing:

> 'Nous l'aurons!
> Nous l'aurons!
> —Louis Napoléon!'

The President was challenged daily by his Parliament, and in his slow way he prepared to answer
the challenge.   His reply was conveyed curtly in
a December night by three divisions and some heavy
cavalry.   That evening M. de Morny was seen at
the theatre.   After the play he looked in at the
Jockey Club, and two hours later they had changed
the history of France.

VI

On the night of December 1, 1851, there was a winter
mist over Paris. At the Élysée there were lights in
the windows, and a sound of dance-music drifted
into the night. It was one of the Prince's Monday
evenings, and the President moved slowly among
his guests, smiling vaguely under his heavy moustache. He said a few words to a young *Préfet* named
Haussmann; and as the dance went on, he stood
by the fire and talked to a colonel of the National
Guard. The elegant M. de Morny came on from a
first night at the *Opéra Comique,* and after ten he
walked through the rooms with the President on
the way down to his study: in the last room there
was a portrait of their mother. Saint-Arnaud and
the Prefect of Police had slipped out of the party,
and some one fetched Persigny. In the study six
men talked quietly whilst the band in the ball-room
was playing a *cotillon.* Maupas and Saint-Arnaud
went through the time-table of the night. The
Prince took up a file of papers and gave out the
draft of a lecree and some proclamations: on the
outside of the packet he had written the word
Rubicon. Then he handed 10,000 francs to Saint-
Arnaud for issue to the troops. Morny said something apt, and the President took each of his men
by the hand. Before eleven the carriages drove away
in the darkness, and the lights went out at the Élysée.

Across Paris in the winter night the printers were
setting up the proclamations with armed men standing at every door. Saint-Arnaud sent his orders to
General Magnan for the troops to move before dawn,
and then (he was a desperate man of fifty-three, but
he had once been on the stage) he yielded to the
conventions of French drama and wrote eloquently
to his mother. At the Prefecture of Police M. de
Maupas sat writing by his lamp in the night; it was
two o'clock when his men were fetched out of their
beds by an order to report to the Prefect, and between then and half-past four they filed through his
room to get their orders. One by one he instructed
them to arrest the party-leaders of the Chamber in
their beds before dawn, and at five in the morning
his men began to move across Paris: it was the
Prince's answer to the Assembly. At the Chamber
itself Colonel Espinasse slipped in through a gate;
some officials were arrested, and the 42nd of the Line
marched in. An early train from the south steamed
into the Gare de Lyon, and M. Émile Ollivier went
quietly home across Paris. It was still dark when the
police began to knock at the doors of the statesmen.
Changarnier came out with two pistols in his hands;
Cavaignac banged a table and relapsed into gloomy
indifference; M. Thiers sat on his bed in a night-shirt
and delivered a considerable speech. But by seven
o'clock they were all at Mazas, and the collective
wisdom of the Chamber had been transferred by a
simple operation to the courtyard of a prison. Outside in Paris the troops were marching through the
empty streets in the grey light; six brigades moved
silently into position, and in barracks forty thousand
men were under arms in support. Before dawn bill-

posters under police escort had covered the town with proclamations by the Prince, and at the Ministry of the Interior M. de Morny was explaining to a startled minister that he was his successor. The Prince had struck his blow; and as the sun came up over Paris, the *Deux-Décembre* passed into history.

It was broad daylight when the town began to read the news on the hoardings. They found a curt decree by the President dissolving the Assembly and proclaiming martial law. It was accompanied by a more reasoned appeal to 'the one sovereign that I recognise in France—the people.' The factious opposition of the Chamber was denounced; the Prince's high mission—'to end the age of revolution' —was proclaimed; and the country was asked to vote upon a new Constitution with a head elected for ten years. It was a Consulate on the Napoleonic model. In the streets they stared at the proclamations and hurried on to work. Scared Deputies began to get the news, and someone brought it to M. Victor Hugo as he was working in bed. On the Place de la Concorde a captain of *Chasseurs à pied* was reading a proclamation to a circle of his men. It was addressed to the army, reminding the troops of their humiliation by the crowds in 1830 and 1848; it spoke of their common interest with the Prince (*'Votre histoire est la mienne. Il y a entre nous, dans le passé, communauté de gloire et de malheur . . .'*) and it made a grave appeal:

> *'Aujourd'hui, en ce moment solennel, je veux que l'armée fasse entendre sa voix.'*

The men cheered: Paris was indifferent, but the army was with the President. At the Élysée there was a

great coming and going of mounted men, and about
ten o'clock the Prince rode out of the great gate to
a shout of *'Vive l'Empereur!'* from the *Cuirassiers*
in the courtyard. He trotted out into Paris with his
staff behind him, riding clear of the escort without
turning to speak. Saint-Arnaud, Magnan, Fleury,
Excelmans, and Ney rode with him and the old
King of Westphalia: it was a queer procession of
the two Empires. On the Place de la Concorde there
was a roar of *'Vive l'Empereur!'* and then they fell
to shouting *'Aux Tuileries! Aux Tuileries!'* The
great gates swung open and the Prince went in at a
gallop. But the old King said a word in his ear;
and before they reached the palace he turned his
horse. Then they rode through the streets for an
hour and more. The troops cheered steadily, but
sometimes there was a shout of *'Vive la République!'*
from the pavement. Paris had not quite lost its
taste for politics.

There was a feeble gesture by the politicians.
Their leaders were in prison; but there was still,
there was always, M. Odilon Barrot. At his house
and others breathless statesmen held little meetings
in the morning. There was even an abortive sitting
of the Chamber itself, where a few Deputies slipped
in through an unguarded door. But a peroration
is an unhandy weapon against the bayonet, and these
gatherings pursued a uniform and unheroic course
of striking Roman attitudes until the arrival of the
military and then dispersing under protest. Even
M. Victor Hugo caught the infection of futility.
When someone asked him at a meeting, *'Hugo, que
voulez-vous faire?'* he replied in his best staccato
vein *'Tout.'* But since time was not available for

this comprehensive programme, he confined himself
to a more limited proposal that one hundred and
fifty Deputies of the Left should march *procession-
nellement'* through the streets decorated with tricolour sashes and ejaculating at regular intervals
'Vive la République! Vive la Constitution!' It was
a strange expedient; and his colleagues, who were
less habituated to the theatre, refused their parts.
They preferred to spend a confused morning in
drawing-room meetings, in the street, arguing with
soldiers, with passers-by, with one another, until they
were headed off by a chance suggestion and tramped
hopefully down the road to a *Marie* near the
Chamber. A polite crowd began to shout *'Vive
l'Assemblée!'* and about eleven in the morning, when
the President was riding on his rounds, more than
two hundred Deputies met in a large first-floor room
for the last sitting of the Chamber. After an agreeable interval for the exchange of anecdotes they
settled down under the direction of M. Berryer to
an orgy of rapid legislation comparable to the best
efforts of governments in war-time. They decreed
that the President was deposed; they decreed that
executive authority was vested in the Assembly;
they decreed that the National guard should be called
out; they decreed that their colleagues should be
released from prison; they decreed the transfer of
the military command to General Oudinot, and even
that someone at the door should refrain from ob-
structing the entrance. But their proceedings were
closured by the arrival of the military, and General
Forey's infantry cleared the room. The Deputies
filed out under arrest, and the *Chasseurs à pied*
marched them in the grey December afternoon be-

tween fixed bayonets to the barracks on the Quai
d'Orsay. The President had made his reply to the
Chamber.

There was a little shouting in the streets, but Paris
did not move. Constitutions in 1851 seemed made
to be violated, and the outrage left no impression
on the public mind. Loud-voiced men sang the
Marseillaise with an air of defiance, and M. Victor
Hugo startled an omnibus on the *boulevards* by
protruding suddenly from its window to convey to
a passing regiment of *Cuirassiers* his opinion of their
degradation. But the scattered sounds seemed to
echo in a dismal silence. The church bells were not
clashing in alarm, and there were no drums beating
to call out the National Guard, because a cautious
executive had stove them in. The town was still; and
as the evening closed in after the short December day,
there was a fine rain falling and the streets were
filled with the clank and jingle of heavy cavalry on
the move.

The President had devised a singular celebration
of the anniversary of Austerlitz, and his capital
seemed strangely indifferent. Paris on that Tuesday
night was almost quiet. The great vans rumbled
out of the barracks on to the Quai d'Orsay taking
the Deputies to prison, and up on the *boulevards*
some men hooted a regiment on the march. M.
Victor Hugo hurried down back streets pullulating
with laconic eloquence, and there were a few sketchy
attempts at barricades. But the great town lay
silent under the night mist, and M. de Maupas' discreet agents, in their anxiety for public repose took
the belfries under police protection and cut the
bell-ropes. M. Victor Hugo spent the night on a sofa

and slipped out in the dawn to pursue the agreeable pastime of tearing down the President's posters. In the morning there was a sputter of insurrection. The troops were out at sunrise, and before ten they were shooting at three carts and an omnibus which lay across the street: a Deputy named Baudin struck a brave attitude and was shot dead. But the barricades were cleared, and M. Victor Hugo was left shouting abuse out of a cab at a general on the Place de la Bastille. A few Deputies flitted about Paris legislating in little rooms, abounding in republican eloquence, muttering to workmen, gesticulating obscurely in the shadow of a city which declined to revolt. The troops marched back to the barracks, and the streets were left to the crowds; General Magnan was indisposed to fumble with the barricades, and his plan was to withdraw his men, to let the insurrection gather and take form, and then to return in force and break it. All that night Paris was filled with strange stories of revolt: Rheims had risen, Lyons and Marseilles were up, the army was marching on Paris, and, strangest of all, the Comte de Chambord, who reigned in theory as Henri V., was at Saint-German in the uniform of a trooper of Dragoons. They were all false. Nothing moved in Paris on the night of December 3 except the torches, where they were building barricades in the darkness, and two prison vans which turned into the Gare du Nord between midnight and dawn behind a Lancer escort to set down Cavaignac and Changarnier. The *coup d'état* consigned them, by a pleasing irony, to Ham.

When the sun came up on December 4 (it was a Thursday morning), there were no troops in the streets of Paris. The barricades were up, and the police were busy tearing down the placards of the insurrection. The morning was uneasy, and it was after one o'clock when the barrack gates swung back and the army of Paris came marching out into the town. The infantry went in silence without bands or bugle-marches, and the field-guns clanked down the streets past the shuttered shops; sometimes a crowd on the pavement shouted '*Vive la République! Vive la Constitution! À bas les prétoriens!*' The columns formed up, and before dark the army had broken the barricades. At one point it had done worse and fired, with an evil sense of power which was never forgiven to the soldiers of the Second Empire, into the crowd. By the evening of December 4 the *coup d'état* was over; and the Constitution, which the Chamber might have amended by a majority of three-quarters, had been forcibly revised with a loss of something more than one hundred and less than five hundred civilians. The Prince was still President of the Republic, and in a few days M. Victor Hugo stepped out of a train in Brussels dressed with some care as a workman whose luggage consisted almost entirely of the first draft of *Les Misérables*.

France was still a Republic, and the electors were invited in the third week of December 1851 to approve the new Constitution outlined by Louis Napoleon in his proclamation, with its decennial Presidency and its Senate and *Conseil d'État* and its strong flavour of the Consulate. Since Paris was under control and the provinces had been systematically captivated by the President in his official peregrinations, it was thought that society would signify its willingness to be, as they said in 1851, saved. The Prince had promised to interrupt the long course of revolutions in France, and the vague menace of an outbreak in 1852 seemed to reconcile the country to his claims. He was assisted further by a strange flicker of revolution on the eve of the *plébiscite*. As the news of the *coup d'état* ran through France, there was a stir among the advanced parties, and with that rare ineptitude which is the surest indication that men are following their natural instincts they flung suddenly into insurrection. Up and down the country wild-eyed men cursed the allied institutions of property and the police; the red flags came out, and there was some hoarse singing of the *Marseillaise*. A little killing in the south flung across France the long shadow of the *Spectre rouge,* and the Prince-President alone seemed to stand for social security. The army, which was the natural guardian of order and property, was in his hands, and religion (had he not sent troops to Rome?) seemed safe under his authority: even M. de Morny was lecturing his *Préfets* on the observance of the sabbath. It was not surprising that on December 20, 1851, the French electorate affirmed by *plébiscite* the conversion of the Second Republic into the Second Consulate; and when they did so by seven million votes, the Second Empire was not far distant.

VII

IN its last phase, through which it passed in the year
1852, the Presidency became without affectation the
prelude of the Empire. The news of the *coup d'état*
reverberated impressively in the high places of
Europe. Baron Stockmar composed a memorandum
which proved conclusively that it could not succeed,
and Queen Victoria took almost the gleeful tone of a
schoolgirl with a novelette when she wrote to her
dismal uncle at Brussels about 'the *wonderful* proceedings at Paris, which really seem like a *story* in a
book or a play!' Firm government was such a comfort in those days of Radicals and Red Republicans,
even though one owed it to one of Lady Blessington's
peculiar friends. But that dreadful Lord Palmerston
quite spoiled it all with his irresponsible confidences
to the French ambassador when he called with the
news. The *coup d'état* might be a blessing; but it
was intolerable that the French Government should
be told so by Lord Palmerston, and his sovereign
(with the assistance of several memoranda by her
Consort) insisted that Lord John Russell should demand explanations. Palmerston, who had gone a
little far, explained nothing. Someone had told him
at dinner that the Orleans family was packing its
trunks at Claremont for a raid on France, and Mr.
Borthwick of the *Morning Post* had been offered
exclusive narratives of a civil war which the Prince

de Joinville and the Duc d'Aumale were about to initiate at Lille; Joinville got as far as Ostend, and Aumale posted overland from Italy. But the President got his *coup* in first, and the Orleanist *rendezvous* was never kept: the Queen confessed to a 'fear that poor Joinville *had* some *mad* idea of going to France,' and his Brazilian princess was left lamenting to her ambassador—'*et pauvre moi qui devois être à Paris le 20!*' Orleans princes and French statesmen were equally distasteful to Lord Palmerston, and their double defeat by the *Deux-Décembre* evoked from him that candour which is fatal to Secretaries of State. The Queen pressed her advantage; Lord John was taught from Windsor to be firm, and before the year was out she was writing to Brussels almost in falsetto that '*Lord Palmerston is no longer Foreign Secretary,*' whilst that bland old gentleman explained to his friends that state papers were sometimes 'written in anger by a lady as well as by a Sovereign and that the difference between a lady and a man could not be forgotten even in the case of the occupant of a throne,' and clever Mr. Disraeli summed it all up in his enigmatic way on the stairs at the Russian embassy (one really met him everywhere) with the queer epitaph: 'There *was* a Palmerston!'

But in Paris the Prince-President was imperturbably installed. He had become a European fact; and Prince Albert, who was a student of facts, was patiently reading the *Idées Napoléoniennes* to find out, if he could, what it all signified. The meaning became increasingly obvious as the new government developed: it was the Empire in that queer preliminary phase through which the first Napoleon had put upon his coins the two contradictions *Napoléon Empereur* and *République Française.* The Republic still existed, but it had found a master. Since he was to rule according to a constitution, he was a constitutional monarch; but he had the rare advantage that he was to draft his own constitution. The churches prayed for his name—*Domine, salvum fac Ludovicum Napoleonem*—as though he was already a king; M. Barre of the Mint was modelling his profile for the new coinage in place of the heavy features of the Republic; and the eagles, which in the years of victory had grown to be the crest of his family in the eyes of Europe, reappeared by his decree on the standards of the French army.

Repression, since he had saved society, was the first business of his ministers. The prisons of the Republic were full of its supporters. The elder statesmen were in their cells at Ham; Mazas, Mont-Valérien, and Vincennes were filled with Deputies of the late Chamber; and arrested democrats overflowed from the gaols of Paris and the provinces into half the barracks in the country. The politicians were carefully classified by M. de Morny's officials; statesmen were deported with permission to return to France, agitators (of whom Victor Hugo was one) were exiled from the territory of the Republic, and innocuous persons were shown politely to the prison gates. But a larger problem was presented by the common prisoners. Four thousand men in Paris and five times that number in the provinces were still in custody; their offences varied from active sedition to unpopularity with the police, and a hasty investigation was conducted by *ad hoc* committees without the technical distraction of evidence, procedure, or appeal.

The decisions of the *Commissions mixtes,* on which a general sat with a lawyer and an official, cleared the prisons. There were no death sentences; but three hundred men were transported to Cayenne, the *guillotine à sec* of the Directoire. Less than two thousand were exiled, and ten thousand more were shipped to Algeria. The rest were sent to prison or set at large, and by the spring of 1852 society was as good as saved.

It had for long been the tradition of French revolutions that the brisk, decisive days of insurrection should be followed by a grey period of constitutional debate in which a National Assembly travelled slowly up the long road back to first principles, formulated interminably the Rights of Man, and drafted with statesmanlike deliberation a constitution which should be (unlike its three or four predecessors) indisputably final. The Prince-President was disinclined for these solemn exercises. Three competent lawyers were requested to produce a draft. But since they failed to reach finality in a fortnight, the circle was narrowed, and the industrious Rouher retired for twenty-four hours with the Constitution of 1800 and a quantity of paper: he emerged with a constitution in eight sections and fifty-eight articles which became by a simple process the law of France. With a queer ingenuity it combined an omnipotent electorate with a paralytic legislature. The voters would choose their master by *plébiscite;* but, as he said to the Austrian minister, *'Je veux bien être baptisé avec l'eau du suffrage universel, mais je n'entends pas vivre les pieds dans l'eau.'* The President, who was elected for ten years, absorbed every power of the executive and even exercised a remarkable control over the Chamber. It met at his discretion to debate legislation introduced on his behalf; its amendments were to be submitted for the approval of his *Conseil d'État,* and it had no power to consider Bills of its own. Its debates were to be unreported except for an official minute; and since their only subject-matter was to be official legislation, it was unlikely that the reading public would feel the loss. There was a Senate with vague powers of interpreting the Constitution (its meaning seemed clear enough) ; but the Chamber had become a debilitated debating-society, and it was hardly surprising that ministers of state were not required, were even forbidden by statute, to waste time in that futile precinct.

Until an election could provide France with this noble organ of legislation, the Prince-President governed the country without further assistance. Legislating by *décret-loi,* he rapidly cleared the ground for the new system by elaborate measures of police; trade unions were dissolved, publicity was controlled by an ingenious press law under which newspaper offences were tried without the embarrassment of reporters or a jury, and the President's ministers displayed a complete appreciation of their own policy by directing the removal from all buildings of the unfashionable words *Liberté, Égalité, Fraternité*: it was time. Their social programme wore an expression of despotic benevolence. Governments which annihilate the political rights of their subjects are normally solicitous as to their creature comforts, and the decrees of the Presidency displayed a laudable anxiety as to the material prosperity of France. Railways, electric telegraphs, Friendly Societies, land banks, pawnshops, and all the apparatus of economic efficiency in the year 1852 were poured from the President's cornucopia upon the country whose institutions he had silenced. But he was disinclined to permit at this early stage a free expression of opinion as to the blessings which he had forced upon his countrymen. The election of the muted Deputies of the new Chamber caused grave misgivings, and the discreet Morny coached his *Préfets* in the use which should be made of their 'legitimate influence.' Those anxious men had already been promoted by the new system to a position of black-coated local omnipotence comparable to Darius' satraps or Cromwell's Major-Generals; their duties included the control of public opinion by every form of censorship and delation, and they were now invited to tamper discreetly with the exercise of the suffrage, to mobilise their subordinates in defence of the existing order, and to give official support to candidates of a becoming docility in the name of *'ce gouvernement loyal et paternel.'* Preference was to be given to successful business men whose practical knowledge was believed to be more valuable to the state than the less reliable activities of 'what are generally called politicians': the new Chamber was to be (the ideal has survived) a parliament of experts supporting (the conception is familiar) a business government. This simple-minded manipulation of the electorate became a standing feature of the Empire; but within a few days of his contribution to political science Morny left office. His retirement was accelerated by a regrettable aptitude for applying official information to Stock Exchange transactions; but a more dignified pretext was found in his objection to the predatory policy which confiscated by decree the property of the late

dynasty. There was an unpleasant flutter in Paris;
a few ministers resigned, and someone made a joke
about *'le premier vol de l'aigle.'* But whilst the
susceptible consciences of M. de Morny and (it
seemed at Windsor *'too* dreadful and monstrous')
Queen Victoria received a simultaneous shock, the
Prince-President's government was carried on by the
less tender intelligence of Persigny. Absorbing with
a heroic gesture the Ministries of Commerce, Agriculture, and the Interior, he bluntly urged his *Préfets*
to assist their Departments to return *'deux-cent-
soixante et un députés, animés du même esprit,
dévoués aux mêmes intérêts et disposés egalement à
compléter la victoire populaire du 20 décembre.'*

The elections took place in a queer silence. It was
not easy for malignants to find printers to multiply
their detestable opinions or workers to distribute them,
and Persigny's wishes were respected by the constitu-
encies almost to the letter. The new Chamber contained eight Deputies of the Opposition; the rest were
sealed with the approval of the *Préfets*. In the spring
they travelled up to Paris. The President received
them at the Tuileries and took a high tone:

> *'Depuis trop longtemps la société ressemblait à une
> pyramide qu'on aurait retournée et voulu faire reposer
> sur son sommet; je l'ai replacée sur sa base.'*

But in 1852 the Prince had passed beyond metaphors,
and he warned his legislature that if his authority
was questioned, if society was once more in its perennial need of being saved, why then he would make a
change:

> *'Il pourrait être raisonnable de demander au peuple,
> au nom du repos de la France, un nouveau titre qui*

fixât irrévocablement sur ma tête le pouvoir dont il m'a revêtu.'

There was a nervous silence, and the assembled nonentities went dismally about their legislative duties in the shadow of the Empire.

That shadow grew longer as the summer drew on. The Prince-President began to take the airs of a reigning monarch, drove to great functions at the Tuileries, stood in the Champ de Mars as the Emperor had stood, giving eagles to the army. Paris, in the intervals of seeing the *Dame aux Camélias* at the Vaudeville, was learning to line the streets and cheer, to make its bow in a new court dress to the Prince-President, to step imperceptibly out of the Republic into the Empire. In the provinces Imperialist petitions were being signed, and local authorities passed loyal resolutions. In the summer the President opened his last railway line at Strasburg; with an eye to the Queen at Windsor he decorated the judicious Stockmar, and a Colonel von Roon of the Prussian service watched him drive standing and bare-headed through the streets. Then for the last time he took the road again with his suite and his speeches to test the temper of his subjects. He said at the Élysée that his tour was a question asked of France. He knew the answer and would perhaps have been content to let it come unassisted. He believed in stars and destiny; but Persigny was not above assisting his faith with works. Preferring art to nature, he prepared a demonstration with the instruction to his *Préfets: ' "L'Empire! Vive l'Empereur!" et ne nous trompons pas.'* The cheering crowds, the flags, the arches overhead were ordered for *Son Altesse* (M. Bonaparte was rising in

15

the scale), whom one circular abbreviated by a felicitous anticipation of the Empire into *'S. A. I.'*; and when he faced his first audience at Bourges, a general (after a word with the discreet Maupas) took the troops by with a roar of *'Vive l'Empereur!'* The cry went on into the south, and at Lyons the Prince-President made it his text, spoke thoughtfully of his uncle, hesitated to decide *'sous quel nom je puis rendre les plus grand services.'* Down the river to the sea the shouting grew louder; all Avignon was roaring on the walls; Arles, Marseilles, Montpellier joined the dance and set their flags waving in a flutter of Bonapartism. He was *Caesar Imperator, protector Franciae,* lapsed into the vernacular as *sauveur de la propriété* and *'le bienvenu dans ce pays où Charlemagne et Saint Louis ont régné.'* Then, as the cheering died away, he stood up in October to make his last speech at Bordeaux. For a month he had lived in roaring crowds, and slowly, in his quiet way, he explained the lesson. France, as it seemed, was grateful for its salvation, tired of revolution, eager beyond all else for confidence and security. *'Voilà pourquoi la France semble vouloir revenir à l'Empire. Il est une crainte à laquelle je dois répondre. Par esprit de défiance, certaines personnes se disent: L'Empire, c'est la guerre. Moi, je dis: L'Empire c'est la paix.'*

Within seven weeks the President of the Republic was Emperor of the French. His Senate petitioned for the Empire. There was a faint protest from the exiles; but on November 21, 1852, a *plébiscite* approved the change by a majority of seven millions and a half on a poll of eight millions: *'Le paysan,'* in Jules Favre's phrase, *'voulut couronner sa légende.'* On a December night (it was the first of the month, and the Prince kept as an anniversary the eve of Austerlitz and the *coup d'état*) the sentries stood in the mist outside St. Cloud. Some mounted men rode up with torches, and a long line of carriages set down the men who were to tell Louis Napoleon that he was Emperor. The Presidency was over. If it had run its term under the Constitution, it would have left him in 1862 with victories to his name and success for his reputation; Maximilian would never have gone to Mexico or Bazaine to Metz, and the world would have missed the gas-lit tragedy of the Second Empire.

THE EMPEROR

THE EMPEROR

I

When the curtain went up on the Second Empire and M. Bonaparte became in 1852 the *bon Frère* of Queen Victoria, the stage seemed hardly set for the tableau. France had an Emperor, and he came riding down into Paris through the Arc de Triomphe on a winter morning. Saint-Arnaud and Persigny rode with him, and they trotted down the long hill to inspect the troops on the Carrousel where the Emperor had once taken the salute on his white barb, and the old King had walked his horse with M. Thiers at its head on a wild morning in 1848. Then he dismounted and passed into the Tuileries; on the Place de la Concorde Persigny was proclaiming his Emperor to the National Guard. That evening Napoleon III. walked through the rooms of his new palace; they were full of bowing uniforms, and the official world turned gently on its axis to take the first beams of the risen sun.

France had an Emperor; but as yet the rest of the Empire seemed hardly to exist. One might improvise a Court from the dinner-table at the Élysée. Saint-Arnaud and Magnan were promoted Marshals, and the fountain of honour played in a steady drizzle of decorations over the public services. It was entertaining enough to make a bishop into one's Grand-Almoner and to call Vaillant, who had trained the guns on Rome, Grand-Marshal of the Palace. The active Fleury might seem more picturesque as *Premier Écuyer,* and the Imperial hunt derived and added dignity from the appointment of Marshal Magnan to be *Grand Veneur.* The titles had all been worn under the First Empire, and they returned with the eagles and the bees and the crowned N. Even D'Orsay appeared in a sinecure having some relation to the fine arts. But the scene, as the players were redressed for the new tableau and the lights were centred on the throne, seemed half unreal, a great charade staged by a single player and hanging on his life, an Empire without a dynasty.

Whilst the Emperor drove bowing through his streets, twisted a long moustache, and thought of marriage, Europe was looking on. Anxious gentlemen in Vienna argued that the second Emperor could not be Napoleon III., turned up the Treaty, and pulled long faces over his recognition, whilst the Czar declined to be the *bon Frère* of a Bonaparte. But the Empire had returned, and the Emperor sat wondering before the *Almanach de Gotha* where he should find an Empress. One could hardly, if one was the eldest son of the Church, found a dynasty with the blonde Miss Howard: she must be titled, repaid her loans, and (if the revenue would run to it) pensioned. There had been an offer under the Presidency to a young lady in Germany; she was called the Princess Vasa, and Napoleon had dethroned her grandfather for Bernadotte. But her hand was promised, and in Paris they went back to the pedigrees. The Duke of Cambridge had a daughter; there was a Braganza girl; and a discreet ambassador in London was perpetually asking Lord Malmesbury for the address of Princess Adelaide of Hohenlohe-Langenburg. The young person was a Protestant; but she was niece to the Queen of England, and a sudden conversion might carry an alliance with it. The subject trailed away into courtesies, and by a queer chance the Emperor half considered a Hohenzollern-Sigmaringen. He never married her, and she lived to see Count Bismarck almost make her brother King of Spain, and in the attempt bring down the Empire in the dull thunder of its last war.

II

PARIS was an Imperial city once again, and the French army was the army of the Empire. It re-entered the long tradition which had ended at Waterloo, and the trumpets which rang out in the dawn of the Second Empire were a faint, retarded echo of the trumpets of Austerlitz. The new government was in its beginnings a military government, and the army remained throughout the course of the Empire the most brilliant symbol of the iridescent transformation which France had undergone. In its jaunty reminiscence of the First Empire, its elegant protest against the dowdy age of Louis Philippe, in the swagger of its easy victories and the sudden downfall of its last defeat it expressed the whole temper and career of the Second Empire.

The soldiers of the First Empire had been equipped with a heavy magnificence; tall bearskins, great helmets of Dragoons, and the long lines of shakoes had been the background of Napoleon.

> 'Voici les Mamelucks!—Tiens, là je reconnais
> Les plastrons cramoisis des lanciers polonais!
> Voici les éclaireurs culottés d'amarante!
> Enfin, voici, guêtrés de couleur différente
> Les grenadiers de ligne aux longs plumets tremblants
> Qui montaient à l'assaut avec des mollets blancs,
> Et les conscrits chasseurs aux pompons verts en poires
> Qui couraient à la mort avec des jambes noires!'

That pageant had ended in 1815, and the Restoration hastily redressed the French army in uniforms which avoided so far as possible all risk of dangerous reminiscences. The cavalry assumed an appearance that was positively British, and even in the infantry the rigid propriety of the Napoleonic tradition was gradually modified by the exigencies of service in North Africa. The inelegance of the reign of Louis Philippe had found immediate expression in military uniform, and the army was disguised in a rather lumbering gaudiness. At a time when the surroundings of society were swathed dustily in red rep, the classical red trousers became universal in the French service and the slatternly *képi* crept into use from Algeria. Strange units of Zouaves and *Spahis* and *Turcos* were beginning to appear along the African border; but Paris knew little of the burnous and the fez, and the prosaic flavour of the age was neatly conveyed by the *bourgeois* shakoes of the National Guard.

With the second advent of the Empire the lights were turned up on the military scene, and the French soldier reappeared in a scintillation of new decorations. A twisted moustache and a fierce imperial united with an ideal of wasp-waisted elegance to give him a fresh character, and he took the stage with *panache.* The eagle reappeared on the standards of France, and the bearskins mounted guard once more at the Tuileries. The Line swung past in red and blue, and the green epaulettes of the *Chasseurs à pied* went by at the quick step behind a clanging bugle band. Rossini was asked to compose a new trumpet march for the dandy gentlemen of the *Guides;* they lounged in green and gold with blue Hussars, and the dull gleam of the *Cuirassiers* sent the mind back to the pounding charges of the First Empire. Light cavalry dangled an eagle *sabretache* or trailed a braided dolman; there was a galaxy of helmets, busbies, shakoes, *colbacks, schapskas*. But it culminated in the blue and silver magnificence of the *Cent-gardes,* and the military ideals of the Second Empire found complete expression in the tall, rigid figures which lined the stairs of the Tuileries on grand occasions. Their great helmets with the Imperial cypher towered over a sea of rustling guests, and with the elegance of the age of Offenbach they wore a uniform of the age of Murat.

III

On a May morning in Granada the dull mutter of
an earthquake brought the people into the streets.
It was the year 1826, and Ferdinand VII., who displayed a perfect appreciation of his time and place
by closing a University and endowing a school of
bull-fighting, was king in Spain. Andalusia lay in
the spring sunshine, and at Granada in a house in the
Calle de Moret opposite Santa Maria Magdalena the
Countess of Teba was suffering. Because the house
was not safe, they took her out to a tent in the garden,
where a child was born. They named it Eugénie
after an uncle, and the father succeeded a few years
later to the title of Montijo.

The Count had followed the tradition of his country
and was a man of family. He fought with some distinction on the French side in the wars of the First
Empire, and with the elegant pluralism of the Spanish
nobility he bore the surnames of Guzman, Portocar-
rero, and Palafox. His Countess, who was painted
by Goya, had been addressed by the honourable
but simpler name of Kirkpatrick. As his politics
were a trifle advanced, he found it necessary to leave
Spain. A kindly government detained his property,
and when he removed his lady and his little girls to
Paris, their lodgings seemed small after the arid
magnificence of a Spanish house. But they had
friends in France; there was a M. Mérimée who came

to talk about Spain and had from the Countess the
story of a *Gitana* who fascinated a Dragoon, left him
for an *espada* of Seville and died by the knife outside
a bull-ring; and more than once he brought with him
his friend M. Beyle, who knew so much history.
Sometimes, when they were not learning their lessons
from the sisters of the Sacré-Cœur, M. Beyle called
and told them stories about the wars of Napoleon
which he illustrated with the brightest, most military
little pictures; and once M. Mérimée took Eugénie
down the Rue de la Paix to have a cake when King
Louis Philippe was living in the great palace at the
end of the street.

Whilst they were all in Paris, there was a change in
Spanish politics and the Count went back to Granada.
But he died before his girls had grown up into young
ladies; and his Countess brought them back across
the Pyrenees to complete their education in the sterner
air of New Castile. The English conversation of
Miss Flowers was substituted for the more casual
ministrations of M. Beyle and the sisters of the Sacré-
Cœur, and she even added to the repertory such
literary amenities as 'Lalla Rookh and the Irish
Melodies of Tomas Moor.' But there was a steady
correspondence with Paris in which M. Mérimée sent
dresses from Palmyre and Chinese lanterns and seeds
for the garden by the embassy bag (which only
reached the limits of its capacity when he endeavoured
to insert a barouche), receiving in return *mantillas*
for his friends and Spanish bread and *fosforos* which
put all French matches to shame and really lit. After
the Paris lodgings their life in Spain was a period
of greater magnificence. Espartero was still pounding the Carlists in the north; but one could dance and

go to Court and sing all the airs from *Norma*. Paca, the eldest girl, married the Duke of Alba; and M. Mérimée's commissions at the dressmakers increased. The Countess was a fine lady, with her culture and her French friends and her daughter the duchess; and when Eugénie began to go into the world, her mother had a great place at Court and was *Camarera mayor* to Queen Isabella. The girl was tall and had white shoulders, but her beauty (since she had beauty) was the red gold of her hair. Once, when they were at Pau, she heard a dark lady sing operatic airs in a French drawing-room. Deep songs were always so romantic; but the contralto had her own romance, since all the company knew that she had once plotted with a Prince—'*mon prince*' as she always called him —and had been carried off to prison. Now she was singing for them, while her Prince was a captive in a distant tower. The Gordon, who had once fascinated Colonel Vaudrey, spoke to the tall girl and her Spanish mother, told them that the Prince was lying helpless at Ham and that she was going to him. The girl, whom M. Beyle had told about the Emperor, pitied his nephew; it was sad to fall so low; it would be exquisitely romantic to visit him; it could, it must be arranged for her. The *diva* was gracious, and the Countess (was she not a woman above prejudice?) consented to the trip. But Spanish politics swerved once more towards revolution; the Montijos posted back across the mountains to Madrid, and Eugénie never saw her Prince behind his bars.

The young Countess of Teba was twenty-one when Europe reeled through the first months of 1848, and in the next year at a turn of the wheel in Madrid (Narvaez went out of power, and there was a change

in the Ladies of the Bedchamber) her mother removed once more to Paris. Her Prince, if she still
thought of him, was President of the Republic, and
one evening a friend presented them at the Élysée.
She made her reverence and startled her host with
an allusion, unusual in the polite world, to the faithful Gordon. Followed a little dinner on a summer
evening at St. Cloud. It was laid for four at a small
lodge in the park; but when the President offered
his arm for a stroll in the evening, Eugénie held back
and bowed him to her mother. The invitation was
not repeated; but the Spanish girl was seen about
Paris under the Republic; and when society resumed
after its salvation, she was asked to Fontainebleau and
Compiègne for the hunting. The girl looked well on
horseback, and the Prince began to ride by her side,
to watch her in the evenings, to talk to her sometimes
about his future. The ladies of his circle used their
tongues, and in the dawn of the Empire a spiteful
word sent her almost sobbing to the Emperor at a
supper-table in the Tuileries. That night Eugénie
and her mother packed their trunks for Italy; but
in the morning a letter from the palace asked for
an Empress, and before the month was out, they
married at Notre Dame. The doubts of Princess
Adelaide, who had been fluttering at Langenburg
in a delightful uncertainty, were sharply solved. The
Emperor had eluded a bride of the indeterminate
nationality affected by German royalty, and in Lord
Palmerston's view he had chosen well since 'he had
no chance of a political alliance of any value, or of
sufficient importance to counterbalance the annoy-
ance of an ugly or epileptic wife whom he had never
seen till she was presented to him as a bride.' France

was informed early in 1853 that the Emperor had
made his choice *'en conservant son caractère propre
et en prenant franchement vis-à-vis de l'Europe la
position de parvenu, titre glorieux lorsqu'on parvient
par le libre suffrage d'un grand peuple.'* Miss
Howard withdrew into the nobility of the Empire as
a countess, and the costumiers settled down to the
agreeable preparations for an Imperial wedding. M.
Mérimée drafted a wonderful marriage contract with
an interminable recital of his young friend's dignities
and quarterings, and Félix wrestled with the problems
of *coiffure* presented by a veil, a wreath of orange
blossoms and an Imperial crown. On a clear day
of winter sunshine they drove across Paris to Notre
Dame. The Empress looked pale in the great vault
hung with velvet and banked with flowers. There
was a blaze of gold and candle-light, a band crashed
out the march from the *Prophète,* and it all seemed
to Lady Augusta Bruce 'like a Poet's Vision.' That
night they drove to a little house at St. Cloud, and
in the morning two people rode out in a phaeton on
the road to Trianon. The lady beside the driver had
a queer taste for memories of Marie Antoinette, and
her husband drove happily along in the frosty sunshine. He had found a leading lady for his strange
play, and the cast for the Second Empire was
complete.

16

IV

IT is the tragedy of Napoleon III. that he did not
die until twenty years after his life had lost its
purpose. He had lived, since he came of age, by
the light of a single star which shone above the
Tuileries and would make him, as he believed,
Emperor of the French. The steady gleam of it,
first seen above the hills in Switzerland, then dancing
bright above Strasburg, faintly visible in the night
sky over New York, then lighting a room in London,
and shining through a barred window at Ham, had
drawn him across the world to France. He followed
it; and at forty-five, a pallid man with dull eyes, he
was Emperor of the French and the husband of a
beautiful woman. But the star flickered and failed,
since on attaining his purpose he had lost it: it was
the tragedy of an *arriviste* who arrived.

In his odd, silent way, behind the dull mask and
the great moustache, the man had known he would
be king. Since it was pre-ordained, his actions were
unhurried, and he said always, '*Il ne faut rien
brusquer.*' He had seen a man follow his destiny out
of exile, out of prison, to a predestined throne; and
he was left with a queer faith in predestination. He
had followed a star; and a King, a Republic, and
seven millions of men had gone down before the
inevitable event. But he knew nothing more of the
future. It was written, and a wise man would watch

the slow movement of events without thrusting rashly across the stream. His attitude was always that of a man who, in his own phrase, *'attend un événement.'* 'I never form distant plans,' he once told a king's secretary, 'I am governed by the exigencies of the moment.' It was an odd confession; yet it was the wisdom of a man who had seen one thing happen inevitably and was left with a belief that all things were inevitable. The world thought him designing. Palmerston warned Gladstone that he was 'an able, active, wary, counsel-keeping but ever-planning sovereign.' An ambassador in Paris was even informed by his jaunty minister that 'the Emperor's mind seems as full of schemes as a warren is full of rabbits.' But he made few plans; he was indifferent in the choice of men to act for him, because he believed that without plans or men that which was written would come to pass; and when it came, he faced it quietly, saying as he had said to a Carlist prince, *'Quand le vin est tiré, il faut le boire.'* So it was that for twenty years he seemed to drift, since it was useless to strive against the stream; a sphinx, since he answered no questions; an enigma to the world, since his own intentions were an enigma to himself.

He had been a man of one idea; and when it was accomplished, he was left without one. It was as though a man should climb a ridge of high hills and then have no direction for the great walk along the summits. Yet there was one principle which seemed to gleam vaguely through his opportunism. He still believed, as he had written in 1839, that the world should be made up of free nations, and he was haunted through his policy by a half-formed idea (had he not trained Italian guns against the *Papalini* in 1831?)

that Italy must be freed by a Bonaparte. 'Tell them,' he had said to a woman in 1848, 'that my name is Bonaparte, and that I feel the responsibilities which that name implies. Italy is dear to me, as dear almost as France, but my duties to France *passent avant tout.* I must watch for an opportunity. For the present I am controlled by the Assembly, which will not give me money and men for a war of sentiment, in which France has no direct immediate interest. But tell them that my feelings are now what they were in 1830, and repeat to them that my name is Bonaparte.'

But Italy was not in play in 1853, and the Empire drifted into its first war without even the guidance of a sentimental instinct. The polite world of Paris was busy table-turning (and the Austrian ambassador was gravely confiding this outbreak to his diary) when the long cloud of the Eastern Question showed above the horizon and climbed slowly up the European sky. The Nineteenth Century, which was in so few respects an age of faith, believed passionately in the power of Russia. This singular faith, which was handed on unimpaired to deceive a later generation, found various expressions. At St. Petersburg it produced an exaggerated truculence; in Paris, where oriental affairs had been a French hobby ever since the Most Christian King had sought the alliance of the Grand Turk, it set men watching the Near East with a jealous eye; and in London, since Leadenhall Street was in London and India was governed from Leadenhall Street, it sent a shudder through patriotic statesmen at every lurch forward in that sprawling advance which was described in serious circles as the expansion of Russia. The new master of French policy was indisposed to take the Russian side, since

The Empress Eugenie

From a miniature by Ross at Windsor Castle

he valued English friendship and could strike a Napoleonic attitude by defying the Cossacks. He might even appear in his favourite character of a son of the Church by supporting the Catholics of Palestine against the Orthodox priests; and a slow debate developed in which judicious Moslems at Constantinople held the scale between the French and Russian conceptions of Christian duty at the Holy Places. But the issues were sharply broadened. Early in 1853 the Czar was at an evening party, and he spoke mysteriously to the British ambassador about Turkey in the metaphor (there is something deeply impressive about the birth of a *cliché*) of a sick man—'*nous avons sur les bras un homme malade, ce serait un grand malheur s'il devait nous échapper avant que les dispositions nécessaires fussent prises.*' It was his amiable intention to absorb the Balkans, whilst England was to be satisfied with Egypt. But the ministers of Queen Victoria were unequal to this dramatic conception of *haute politique* as an intrigue of highly placed persons carried on in whispers at a *soirée*. It might have flattered the richer imagination of Mr. Disraeli to partition Turkey in an exchange of metaphors with a Romanoff. But he was out of office; and the colder intelligence of Lord John Russell was unimpressed by the prospect. A little stiffly the Englishmen refused the invitation to conspire, and the Czar was left alone in the sick-room. As the year drew on, he became assiduous in his attendance at the Turkish bedside. Two army corps were mobilised in South Russia, and a truculent ambassador appeared in Constantinople with instructions to find a *casus belli*. At the French Embassy a nervous *chargé d'affaires* named Benedetti (one can see moving in

the clear dawn of the Second Empire the little figure
which was to cast so long a shadow as the evening sun
went down over Ems) sent long reports to Paris,
whilst bland Russians demanded from the Sultan a
protectorate over his Christian subjects. The Turks
refused, and Europe was alarmed. In the summer a
Russian army passed the Turkish frontier, and with
a vague gesture of protection a Franco-British fleet
anchored in Besika Bay. The *ikons* were brought out
in St. Petersburg; harassed gentlemen posted across
Europe with clever drafts; and there was a slow drift
towards war, while Princess Lieven was left lamenting among her screens in Paris, '*Mais c'est embêtant
ca; c'est détestable, et tout pour* a few Grik Prists!'
But in the heat of the larger questions the world had
forgotten the little issue about Palestine. It was
settled or adjourned, and France was aligned with
England in defence of Turkey against the sudden
aggression of the Czar. The Sultan seemed so helpless, and men began to feel almost chivalrous about
the Bashi-Bazouks. Late in the year a Russian fleet
used its guns in the Black Sea, and the Allies passed
the Dardanelles. Lord Palmerston scandalised Mr.
Bright with a jaunty speech at the Reform Club;
Napoleon curtly ordered the Russian troops out of
Turkish territory; and in March 1854, the diplomatists
were hurried into the wings and the curtain went
slowly up on the Crimean War.

Whilst the Queen was enjoying the spectacle of
her departing Guards from a balcony at Buckingham
Palace, the Army of the East formed unhurriedly in
the southern ports of France. It was unmistakably
the army of the *coup d'état,* since Canrobert had a
division and Saint-Arnaud was in command. But

there was a faint omen of the future in the name of a
Colonel on the Staff: he was a dark man called
Trochu, and he waited for sixteen years until in the
last scene of all he commanded a starving city against
the Prussians and had, had always (and never acted
upon) a *plan.* In the summer weather of 1854 the
white sails of the transports went eastwards beyond
Italy and the headlands of Greece and faded into the
Levant. At Paris the Emperor was conversing
gravely with the Duke of Cambridge and impressing
that ripe intelligence that he 'never would say what
he did not mean.' At the turn of the year the armies
began to silt slowly into the Black Sea by way of
Gallipoli and Varna, and the Queen desired her Prime
Minister to convey to the Archbishop of Canterbury
her view that a special form of prayer for the cholera
was '*not* a sign of gratitude or confidence in the
Almighty' and was distinctly undesirable. The Prince
Consort was considering an invitation to visit the
Emperor of the French in his camp behind Boulogne;
Baron Stockmar was favourable to the idea; and on
a fine morning in the first week of September Mr.
Dickens listened to the French salutes, as the royal
yacht steamed up the harbour, 'the Prince, in a blazing
uniform, left alone on the deck for everybody to see—
a stupendous silence, and then such an infernal blazing and banging as never was heard.' The two men
met at the foot of the gangway, and Prince Albert
was hurried off into a round of inspections and reviews
which were all narrated to the Queen in letters written
in the intervals of changing uniforms. The Imperial
entourage alarmed the Prince a little by its '*ton de
garnison,* with a good deal of smoking,' and even the
Emperor took part in these excesses after dinner,

when 'I withdrew with him to his sitting-room for
half an hour before rejoining his guests, in order that
he might smoke his cigarette, in which occupation, to
his amazement, I could not keep him company.' But
in spite of this indulgence (and a bed that was too
short for his guest) Napoleon made a favourable impression. He was examined *viva voce* upon every
branch of royal accomplishment from reformatories
to finance, and his answers in the French and English
languages satisfied his examiner and left him *'im
ganzen recht zufrieden mit ihm.'* The Prince was
charmed to detect a German accent in his speech and,
almost, in his thought. The Emperor won his heart
with reminiscences of the Gymnasium at Augsburg
and a recitation from Schiller; he even confessed with
emotion that the sight of Queen Victoria opening Parliament in 1837 had been one of the great impressions of his life. At the same time the judicious
host, controlling his raptures sufficiently to commit
them to paper, informed the proud wife at Windsor
of his happiness in the company of *'un Prince aussi
accompli, un homme doué de qualités si séduisantes et
de connaissances si profondes.'* The charm, of which
Lord Beaconsfield was one day to learn the secret,
began to work. The royal meeting, which provoked
leader-writers to moralise on the strangeness of
Napoleonic courtesies at the Camp of Boulogne, was
a profound success. *Punch*, with that ineptitude
which had not yet become a tradition, depicted a
convivial scene between the two princes *en garçon;*
and the strange friendship grew, as the Allied armies
landed in the Crimea to begin the war which had been
six months declared.

Winter shut down on the trenches before Sebas-

topol, and in Jersey M. Victor Hugo made a bitter
sneer at '*l'Empire qui recommence par* 1812.' Saint-
Arnaud had died almost in the saddle at the Alma,
and Canrobert was in command; Lord Raglan's army
had fought its way into popular recitation at Balak-
lava, and the Guards went in with the bayonet at
Inkerman. The Emperor (had he not studied siege-
warfare in his cell at Ham?) became critical; his
observations were much admired at the Tuileries, and
Imperial hints on gunnery followed one another by
every mail to the Crimea. General Niel went out as
his deputy; perhaps, if the Allies could agree, the
Emperor would follow to take the command himself.
Then, as the winter mist hung over the starving,
freezing camps, there was an odd revival of
diplomacy; statesmen got out their orders and took
their red boxes to Vienna; couriers came posting
in from St. Petersburg with clever arguments from
Prince Gortschakoff; and Piedmont, which had no
interest in the war except as a means of publicity for
a new power, joined the Allies, whilst Canrobert was
fumbling round the outworks of Sebastopol.

In the spring of 1855, as the guns were still playing
on the Russian lines, Napoleon resumed his international courtesies and steamed into British waters
at Dover through a fog believed by his subjects to be
perennial in those latitudes. The Empress was with
him; and as they drove across London to Paddington,
he showed her the corner of King Street where his
house had been. At Windsor the cheers died away,
and they passed into the domestic silence of the royal
circle, 'Vicky with very alarmed eyes making very
low curtsies.' Upstairs there was a panic before
dinner, because the Imperial trousseau had not ar-

rived. But someone had a blue silk dress; it might be made to fit, and wild-eyed women knelt stitching round the Empress. Half England was standing uneasily in its best, when Eugénie swept down to dinner in her plain blue dress with a single flower in her pale bronze hair: it was a French victory. The Emperor was charming to his hostess, smiling vaguely and speaking low. It was the first time in all her acquaintance with countless half-educated, clanking, military persons from the Courts of Europe that she had met a monarch who was also a gentleman, and the encounter left her strangely fascinated. He was odd, of course. There was that queer 'reliance on what he calls his *Star,* and a belief in omens and incidents as connected with his future destiny, which is almost romantic,' a strange faith 'in the realisation of hopes entertained from his very childhood, which borders on the supernatural.' But he was a most attractive person; and he spoke, one feels that he took care to speak, so charmingly of the dear country to which neither he nor his hostess owed official allegiance: 'the Emperor is as *unlike* a *Frenchman* as possible, being much more *German* than French in character . . . he is very well read in German literature, to which he seemed to be very partial.' The sharp little pen seemed to lose all its primness when it summed him up in an ecstasy of underlinings:

"That he *is* a very *extraordinary* man, with great qualities there can be *no* doubt—I might almost say a mysterious man. He is evidently possessed of *indomitable courage, unflinching firmness of purpose, self-reliance, perseverance,* and *great secrecy* . . . and at the same time he is endowed with wonderful *self-control,* great *calmness,* even *gentleness,* and with a *power* of *fascination,* the effect of which upon all those who become more intimately acquainted with him is *most sensibly* felt.

How far he is actuated by a strong *moral* sense of *right* and *wrong* is difficult to say. . . .'

The Queen sat wondering at her writing-table. And yet——

'My impression is, that in all these apparently inexcusable acts, he has invariably been guided by the belief that he is *fulfilling a destiny* which God has *imposed* upon him, and that, though cruel or harsh in themselves, they were *necessary* to obtain the result which he considered *himself as chosen* to carry out, and *not* acts of *wanton* cruelty or injustice; for it is impossible to know him, and not to see that there is much that is truly amiable, kind, and honest in his character. . . .

How could it be expected that the Emperor *should* have any *experience* in *public affairs,* considering that till six years ago he lived as a poor exile, for some years even in prison, and never having taken the slightest part in the *public* affairs of any country? It is therefore the more astounding, indeed almost incomprehensible, that he should show all those powers of Government and all that wonderful tact in his conduct and manners which he evinces, and which many a King's son, nurtured in palaces, and educated in the midst of affairs never succeeds in attaining.'

It was a strange, dazzled verdict with its doubts and its excuses and its little gasps of admiration. But then Napoleon was a gentleman, and amongst her equals the Queen had met little except royalty.

For a week Napoleon and Victoria, Albert and Eugénie walked a ceremonial minuet at Windsor. There was a review in the Great Park and a ball in the Waterloo Room. The Emperor of the French danced a quadrille with the little Queen, and Mr. Disraeli enjoyed the rare delight of making seven

reverences in his Court suit, each time to a different
royal personage.   Then they held a council of war
in the Emperor's room to dissuade him from going
to the Crimea and imposing that unity of command
which is so distasteful to Allies; and afterwards the
Queen came knocking at the door, and there was an
investiture of the Garter, with Napoleon wearing the
blue ribbon on his wrong shoulder and saying '*Enfin
je suis gentilhomme.*'   One evening they all went to
the opera and heard *Fidelio,* and in the morning
someone said it was the Emperor's birthday: his
hostess crowned her hospitality with the gift of a
pencil-case and took him to see the Crystal Palace
in its new home at Sydenham.   His lady had been
charming, and the children loved her.   Sometimes
(her origin might have led one to expect it) she was
found sitting on the edge of a table.   But the Queen
thought her 'very pretty and very uncommon-looking,'
although Mr. Disraeli confided to one of his old ladies
his disappointment with her 'Chinese eyes and a perpetual smile or simper which I detest.'   But the week
came slowly to an end: the Emperor recorded in the
Queen's album '*le sentiments qu'on éprouve pour une
reine et pour une sœur*'; and as the escort jingled off,
she was left 'quite *wehmüthig.*'

Eastwards across Europe the guns were booming
before Sebastopol.   Canrobert resigned to Pélissier;
but the Russians still held Malakoff and the Redan,
and in August the Italians paid their footing in the
war on the Tchernaya.   Two days later the Emperor
stepped out into the sunlight on the balcony of a
hotel at Boulogne.   Queen Victoria and her Consort
were at sea, and their host stood looking for the
British colours above the skyline.   Then he rode up

to the high ground behind the town and down again; the yacht came steaming into harbour, and a royal train went up the line to Paris. It was evening before they drove into the roaring streets; and the bells and the crowds and the Allied flags and the bands playing *God save the Queen* all seemed '*quite feënhaft*' to the little lady in the open carriage. Then there was a blaze of lights, and the new Imperial Guard was presenting arms at St. Cloud; the Empress was at the door, 'the dear and *very* charming Empress (whom Albert likes particularly),' and the Second Empire seemed canonised into dynastic respectability by the approval of its solemn guests. There were drives to Neuilly— 'poor Neuilly'—where the Queen sat beside a Bonaparte and saw the ruins of an Orleans palace, and an excursion through the streets of Paris, with the Emperor there to point out the Conciergerie and say so romantically '*Voilà où j'étais en prison.*' Or one could sit sketching the Zouaves at Versailles, whilst a military band played its very best; and one day there was a fascinating visit to Paris *incognito* to see the sights, with Vicky in a bonnet and mantilla, and her mother recognisable by every Parisian in her white English dress and her green parasol and sandals tied with black ribbons across the ankle. In the evenings they heard Alboni at the Opera, or went to great parties, where the Queen wore the *Koh-i-noor* in her hair, or sat next to General Canrobert in her geranium dress and could ask him about the war and tell him all about Albert in his green uniform; and once in the Galerie des Glaces she was introduced to a tall gentleman from Prussia named von Bismarck, who said behind his great moustache that Paris was '*sogar schöner als Petersburg.*' But sometimes they went

quite alone in the evening to a 'nice *vertrauliches* little
dinner' with the Emperor, and afterwards he 'repeated
with Albert all kinds of old German songs, and Albert
repeated some to him.' Then there was the Exhibition to be visited, and a great review in the Champ de
Mars with 'Bertie in his full Highland dress,' and a
queer evening visit to the Invalides where tall old men
held up torches and the thunder rolled outside, as
the organ muttered its way through *God save the
Queen,* and the Emperor of the French stood with the
Queen of England by Napoleon's grave. One day
it was Albert's birthday, and his sovereign presented
him with a pictorial set of 'Alliance and Crimean
studs, the third button having a blank, I hope, for
Sebastopol,' whilst his host avenged the pencil-case
of Windsor with the gift of a Meissonier called '*La
Rixe.*' It was all wonderful; the Emperor was 'very
fascinating, with that great quiet and gentleness'; and
when it was over and they were back again at Osborne,
Baron Stockmar was informed of his 'power of
attaching those to him who come near him and know
him, which is *quite incredible.*' Was he not 'quite
The Emperor, and yet in *no* way playing it?' Had
he not gone over old German airs with Albert? Were
not the children devoted to their kind new friend?
It was the first and the most unexpected conquest of
the Empire. In a few days it had its second, as the
Russians marched out in the falling dusk over the long
bridge to the north, and in the seventh month the
firing died away round Sebastopol.

THE Second Empire was essentially Parisian; and as the war with Russia trailed away into incoherence, Paris once more became the centre of the world. The crowds went by in the Champs Élysées to see the Exhibition, and the billowy proliferation of the crinoline was beginning to undulate in the imagination of M. Constantin Guys, whilst the harassed *bourgeois* of the comic papers stepped warily round its outer edges. The sightseers stood staring at the marvels of science in the Palais de l'Industrie; but it was all a shade more modish, a thought less improving, than the gleaming monument of good intentions with which Prince Albert had obliterated Hyde Park four years before. It was a rustling age of millinery and dance-music. At Fontainebleau some one turned the handle of a mechanical organ as the couples swung round the ball-room, because, as the Emperor said, an orchestra is so awkward: '*Ils racontent ce qu'ils ont vu ou ce qu'ils n'ont pas vu.*' They danced at Court or posed in fancy dress for M. Gavarni to draw them. They danced at the Ball *Mabille* and *Valentino*, and the town was beginning to sway to the measure which swung and quickened and rose until the Second Empire danced to an air of Offenbach out of the gaslight into the cruel sunshine of 1870.

At the Tuileries a lovely lady with sad, sloping eyebrows and a strange smile sat at innumerable angles to M. Winterhalter, whose kindly imagination had peopled the thrones of Europe with a race of beauties. But Eugénie had not inherited the accumulated ugliness of a dynasty; and as she sat amongst her ladies, he hardly needed, he almost forgot to flatter. She was still beautiful, and as her husband saw her on a great staircase, all in white with leaves of grass on her ball dress and a glitter of diamonds on the *tour de corsage,* he could say loud enough for the Queen of England to hear: *'Comme tu es belle!'*

Even the Emperor was a man of fashion, as he drove his curricle through the streets and smiled hehind his great moustache. He had held his own at Lady Blessington's; and now the world began to study the cut of his beard, until Mr. Trollope was exasperated by 'that mould into which so large a proportion of Parisians of the present day force their heads, in order that they may come out with some look of the Emperor about them. Were there not some such machine as this in operation, it would be impossible that so many Frenchmen should appear with elongated, angular, hard faces, all as like each other as though they were brothers. The cut of the beard, the long, prickly-ended, clotted moustache, which looks as though it were being continually rolled up in saliva, the sallow, half-bronzed, apparently unwashed colour—these may all perhaps be assumed by any man after a certain amount of labour and culture. But how has it come to pass that every Parisian has been able to obtain for himself a pair of the Emperor's long, hard, bony, cruel-looking cheeks, no Englishman has yet been able to guess.' The mystery was deepened for all readers of *Punch* by the diverting fun which Mr. Leech and Mr. Tenniel, who idealised no sovereign but their own, poked week by week at the

queer, foreign figure of their new ally. But the
Emperor continued to dominate his capital; and as
he took his drives abroad, respectful tourists, fresh
from the Dover packet, stood up to raise their hats.
One afternoon he passed an open cab and bowed
vaguely to an Admiral Swinburne and his lady; the
Admiral's hat came smartly off as the Emperor drove
by, but there was a white-faced under-graduate on the
box whose hat remained sternly perched on a great
pyramid of red, republican hair.

But the town where Napoleon took the air was
changing under his touch. Fine gentlemen with tilted
hats still sat outside *Tortoni,* and the carriages went
up and down between the Place de la Concorde and
the Bois. M. de Viel Castel, in whose irritable little
books the age found its Mr. Pepys, might sit at table
between Sainte-Beuve and de Musset or dine with M.
Houssaye to meet M. Théophile Gautier, whose style
was so preposterous, and M. Diaz, whose pictures were
so bad. But round them Paris was fading into something new and bright and regular. An ungainly man
named Haussmann had come to town and was remak-
ing it in his own image. Great avenues were hewn
through the old quarters, and nervous citizens walked
every Sunday to note the progress of the week. Sometimes he cleared a rookery round a great building;
sometimes he linked the outer barracks with the centre
of the town; always he left an excellent field of fire.
Militant democracy had loved to build barricades in
old, crooked corners. But M. Haussmann favoured
straight vistas, and he remodelled Paris with a queer
blend of town-planning and measures of police. The
broad, new streets which drove through the town were
beautifully accessible to light, air, and infantry. No

17

insurrection could live for an hour in those long, open avenues; and on the barricades of the future it would be difficult to do anything but die. The work went quickly on; and there was a pleasant stir among the building contractors, whilst claims for compensation provided a new and fascinating field for speculation.

Yet in the iridescence of its new *décor* the Empire did not forget its origins. Piety was perpetually devising fresh embellishments for the shrine of Bonapartism at the Invalides. A reverent Commission established by Imperial decree and protecting by its discreet omissions Imperial reputations, was searching Europe for the twenty thousand letters of Napoleon I. to include them in a monument twenty-eight volumes high to the First Empire. There was even a strange echo of old wars when the troops marched in behind Canrobert from the Crimea and the Emperor took the salute in the Place Vendôme. In the shadow of the Column twenty-five old men stood in the winter light: it was forty years since Waterloo, and they were in their own person the *Grande Armée,* two of them in red with the great two-foot plume above the battered *schapska* of the Red Lancers, and on the right of the line an old man in a tall, rusty bearskin with black gaiters buttoned up the thigh as they wore them, when the bugles sounded for Wagram, in the Grenadiers of the Guard.

On this bright Parisian scene, with its vivid new beginnings and its faint suggestions of an earlier past, there entered in the first months of 1856 an essembly of gentlemen all talking in different languages and intended to constitute a European Congress. They proposed to terminate the Crimean War and to settle beyond dispute the Eastern Question. Since the

The Empress Eugenie and her Ladies

After Winterhalter

Crimean War had ended itself by the exhaustion of the Russians and the tedium of the French (only Great Britain was still interested, because the British public in their queer way had discovered the war in its third year), it was not difficult to record its close in a treaty. But their settlement of the Eastern Question, which did not survive its next time of asking, was of less value. They assembled with gravity under the presidency of M. Walewski. He had a charming wife and was reputed to be Napoleon's son by a Polish countess; he denied the distinction, but the rounded profile which he kept clean-shaven seemed to confess his parentage. Lord Clarendon came from London, and the Russians sent a tall old man in green and gold who wore three miniatures of his Czar set in diamonds among his decorations. A small man in a fez and a black frock-coat represented the gorgeous East, and someone in spectacles named Cavour came from Turin. M. Benedetti, with his smooth head and his big, black bow, acted as Secretary; and the Congress went solemnly about its labours, whilst Count Cavour, with the vigorous irrelevance invariably displayed at Peace Conferences by the delegates of new nationalities, 'deposited the Italian Question upon the green cloth of the Congress table.' They dined with Lord Cowley; they dined at Court; they conferred upon the closing of the Black Sea and the navigation of the Danube; they drafted and re-drafted with exquisite skill; and they inquired discreetly after the health of the Empress. Then one Sunday morning (it was March 16, 1856) Paris heard twenty-one guns from the Invalides, and a pause, and eighty more. There was a prince born in the Tuileries, and the Emperor was half running, half crying through the rooms of the palace. Eugénie had suffered all one day and night, and when she turned to him to ask faintly: *'C'est une fille?'* he had said *'Non'*; then she asked again: *'C'est un garçon?'* and he said again, because he feared the shock for her, *'Non'*; and she asked, *'Mais alors, qu'est-ce que c'est?'* The Empire had an heir; the crowds were cheering outside the railings, and M. Gautier was scanning his lines to the Prince Imperial. Two weeks later the clever gentlemen at the Quai d'Orsay gave peace to Europe, and they signed the Treaty of Paris with the quill of an eagle (was not France once more an Empire?) from the Jardin des Plantes.

The reign went slowly on in the shining days of 1856. The Emperor danced at the British Embassy 'dressed quite *à l'Anglaise*: blue evening coat, with gilt buttons, and velvet collar; a white waistcoat; black breeches; black silk stockings; and buckled shoes: his only decoration that of the Garter; the blue ribbon crossing his waistcoat; the Star on the left breast; and the Garter below the left knee.' All the world danced or dined or strolled at Compiègne or saw, with Mr. Henry James and his brother William, 'the incomparable passage, as we judged it, of the baby Prince Imperial borne forth for his airing or his progress to Saint-Cloud in the splendid coach that gave a glimpse of appointed and costumed nursing breasts and laps, and besides which the *centgardes,* all light blue and silver and intensely erect quick jolt, rattled with pistols raised and cocked.' That was the Empire in the good days.

VI

IT was a queer, silent France that drifted contentedly
into the year 1857. Public life had been paralysed by
the *coup d'état,* and the nation's affairs were trans-
acted by an autocracy in which the absolutism of the
Emperor was barely tempered by the authority of his
ministers. In the silence of the country there was
hardly a sound beyond the steady running of the
Imperial machine. A faint reverberation of republican eloquence floated in from somewhere across the
frontier, and there was an audible titter of genteel
amusement from the *salons* whose Orleanist ex-
ministers displayed their superior wisdom to sympathetic callers. But an odd silence hung over the public
places from which the great voices of 1848 had once
governed France; and whilst M. de Morny presided
gracefully over a parliament of nonentities, the dismal
and unreported debates of an undistinguished Chamber were little more than a hollow echo in an empty
room.

Yet for the majority of Frenchmen prosperity was
an agreeable substitute for politics, and in the first
phase of the Empire France passed out of a romantic
period of insurrection into the more substantial blessings of the Nineteenth Century. The sporadic railways of the Forties were linked up into a national
system; commerce was startled by the marvels of the
electric telegraph; the seaward horizons were smudged

by the unlovely evolutions of steamboats; there was even a proliferation of banking facilities which developed large enterprises and produced a type of industrialist that was already familiar in Lancashire. It was an age of material activity in which men were disinclined to dwell unduly on the starvation of their political aspirations, a comfortable period in which a young man named Flaubert was charged before a criminal court with aiding and abetting the editor of a weekly magazine to subvert religion and morality, and sent a lean-faced professional gentleman with bushy whiskers into agonies of forensic propriety with the adventures of *Emma Bovary*.

The atmosphere was unfriendly to politics. There was a public funeral or so, with a few speeches at Père Lachaise; and the police enjoyed the occasional diversion of detecting a plot against the Emperor. But although the Empire was without serious competitors, it was disinclined to take risks; and at the elections of 1857 opinion was carefully manipulated in the manner which had become traditional. Prefects were instructed by their ministers to employ the machinery of government in support of the official candidates, and their opponents were reduced to the predestined futility of an unauthorised campaign. The regimentation of opinion was almost uniformly successful. There was a flicker of independence in Paris, which had never quite lost a taste for politics. But the provinces voted stolidly for the Emperor's nominees, and republicanism sat in the new Chamber only five members strong to confront the serried mass of Bonapartists. The little group seemed insignificant enough in the autumn of 1857; there was a dark young man in spectacles

named Ollivier and a strange shaggy creature called
Jules Favre, who seemed to have been left over from
1848 into a pleasanter, less rhetorical period. But
their advent into Imperial politics was a shade
ominous. Hitherto the republicans had confined
themselves to a statuesque refusal to take the oath
of allegiance, an obliging, if dignified, attitude which
had completely relieved the Empire from the unpleasantness of an Opposition. But *les Cinq*, after
a vast deal of heart-searching, correspondence, consultation of republican oracles, and debate, took a
more enterprising view and presented themselves in
the Chamber as an active party. It was a strange
intrusion of reality into the parliamentary charade
of the Empire, and nervous Deputies shuddered as
the shadows of three lawyers, one journalist, and a
gentleman from Lyons fell across the bright Imperial
scene.

The year faded out without any movement in
politics. Mr. Disraeli came to Paris, dined out eleven
nights running, and failed to impress the Emperor;
an exchange of hospitality brought to Napoleon and
his Empress the felicity of a few days at Osborne
with 'a little dance in a tent on Saturday (which was
very successful) and additional carriages and ponies';
the Prince Consort was gravely receptive as usual
whilst the Emperor talked at large about Europe and
the partition of North Africa; but when Albert
'expatiated a little on the Holstein question,' the topic
'appeared to bore the Emperor as *très compliqué*,'
and the Queen found it all 'very quiet and *gemüthlich*';
there was an informal return visit to the naval works
at Cherbourg, which startled Prince Albert and his
patriotic wife; then came autumn manœuvres at

Châlons and a meeting with the Czar at Stuttgart which set the world talking but left Europe precisely where it had been since the Peace of Vienna. But a bearded man from the Romagna named Orsini was flitting about the Continent with an admirable specification for the manufacture of bombs and a fixed obsession that the liberation of Italy was only to be achieved by the death of the Emperor and the inauguration of a revolution in France. His reasoning was confused, but it followed closely the teaching of Mazzini and the normal course of political conversation in back rooms in Soho. An order for six bombs was executed at a reasonable price in Birmingham; they passed the Belgian customs in the luggage of a Swiss waiter who declared them as gas-fittings; Orsini received them in Brussels and left for France with a British passport in a false name; the bombs followed him to Paris in charge of a simple-minded ostler, and in the second week of 1858 the parties to the attempt converged on the scene. All four were Italians; and their conversations, in a code which was rendered faintly convincing by Orsini's *alias* of 'Allsop,' ran principally upon the manufacture and sale of beer. In the failing light of a winter afternoon (it was January 14, 1858) they met in a little room, and each of them pocketed something wrapped in black silk. Then they walked out into Paris and waited in the cold for the Emperor to drive up to the Opera. One, by a queer chance, was arrested; but three remained in the crowd. There was a sound of distant cheering and the clatter of oncoming horses. The cheers came nearer, and the Lancers of the Guard jingled into the gaslight by the Opera. Then, as a closed carriage drove up, the bombs crashed into the

Napoleon III. (1863)

From the picture by Flandrin in the Musée de Versailles

roadway. The lights went out, and the street was filled with cries and broken glass and men and horses, as the Italians faded back into the crowd. There was a vague gleam of drawn swords, and the Empress, muttering, *'Les poignards maintenant,'* put herself between her husband and the street. Inside the Opera they were playing *William Tell,* and a few moments later the whole house stood up to cheer, as Napoleon and Eugénie walked into their box: her dress, after the dreadful street, was no longer white. There was a confused evening of arrests and congratulations. Orsini was taken in his bed that night, and the Emperor drove back to the Tuileries through the roaring streets; while the police were raking Paris for the murderers, he knelt with Eugénie in the half light of a nursery beside the child who was so nearly, never more nearly, Emperor of the French.

As the echoes died away, the attempt on the Emperor left its mark on French policy. The new Chamber was lectured on the need for firmness; the Empire turned sharply away from the path of parliamentary Liberalism, and emergency powers were conferred upon the executive by a *Loi de sûreté générale,* which enabled the Imperial authorities to detain or deport their enemies without trial. Since the soldierly illegality of this procedure was felt to be unsuitable for exercise by a civilian, there was a change at the Ministry of the Interior and General Espinasse was appointed to administer the new powers. *Son Excellence le général-ministre* was a simple-minded absolutist who had served his apprenticeship in the *coup d'état,* and he performed his duties by the unsubtle expedient of exacting a stated quota of arrests from every Department in France.

Society was to be saved once more; but it acquiesced less readily in its salvation than in 1851. There was a faint protest from *les Cinq,* and in the Senate General MacMahon stood up alone to speak against the system. But it passed into law; and when four hundred arrests were made under it, the Empire seemed to have parted company for ever with liberty.

Stranger still was the effect which the attempt had on foreign policy. There was a natural protest to Piedmont against against the export of Italian bomb-throwers. But the real resentment was against England, where one of the conspirators, who had remained in the peace of Bayswater, was acquitted by a Middlesex jury; and it was expressed in a demand on London that Great Britain should restrict the right of asylum which had enabled Orsini to meet his men behind Leicester Square. Lord Palmerston was sympathetic and proposed to deal in the Conspiracy to Murder Bill with persons conspiring to commit crimes outside the British jurisdiction. But he had taught his countrymen for too long to deride the ridiculous demands of foreign potentates, and British opinion was rendered more British still by the tone of falsetto militancy in which patriotic French officers had protested their resentment of foreign assassins and their haunts in London among the victors of Waterloo and the associates of Sir Hudson Lowe. The question passed from the sphere of intelligence to that of patriotism. Excited men made speeches in Hyde Park; *Punch* depicted its late allies as a crowing cock in a *képi*; and this discerning mood communicated itself to the House of Commons, where Mr. Kinglake (who had once admired the white shoulders of Miss Howard) struck patriotic attitudes

whilst the author of *Ten Thousand a Year* filled
thirteen and a half columns of Hansard with a full
statement of the law, several Latin quotations, and a
peroration on the subject of King Edward III. On
the second reading an amendment was carried against
the Government by a queer combination of Tory
speeches and Liberal votes. Mr. Gladstone and Mr.
Disraeli walked into the same lobby, and Lord
Palmerston was defeated. It was a blow to the
Anglo-French alliance which had ruled Europe since
1855; and even a royal visit to Cherbourg in the
summer did little to restore the old tone, although
Eugénie wore her best lilac and white silk dress
and white and black lace bonnet and 'Albert, who
is seldom much pleased with ladies or princesses,
is very fond of her.' The Queen spent an evening in
finishing 'that most interesting book *Jane Eyre,*' dined
on board a French battleship, and suffered those
peculiar agonies which are reserved for the wives of
after-dinner speakers—'the dreadful moment for my
dear husband, which was terrible to me, and which I
should never wish to go through again. He did it
very well, though he hesitated once. I sat shaking'
(the poor lady took no coffee, and even the Emperor
was quite pale) 'with my eyes *cloués sur la table.'*
But Englishmen came increasingly to regard the
Emperor as a military menace, a persistent construc-
tor of ironclads, the master of great armies whose
bayonets troubled old ladies' sleep at Dover and impelled young gentlemen to defend their country by
quoting Mr. Tennyson's patriotic lyric and joining
the Rifle Volunteers.

But the strangest echo of Orsini's bombs was in
Paris, where the conspirators were tried in that air of

eloquent inconsequence which is the atmosphere of
French jurisprudence. The defence was conducted
by Jules Favre; and since his client was indefensible,
he defended the far better cause of Italian nationalism. The Court listened to a letter from the prisoner in which he begged the Emperor to liberate Italy
(*'Qu' Elle délivre ma patrie, et les bénédictions de
25 millions de citoyens la suivront dans la postérité*),
and Maître Favre followed it with a pleading reference to the nationalist tradition of Bonapartism. In
the grey light of a French law-court that queer
haunting voice rose and fell and died away in the
cry which *Vittoria* sang to the dark, listening tiers
from the great stage of La Scala at Milan, '*Italia,
Italia shall be free!*' It was a strange appeal, which
the Emperor had himself made possible by sending
the letter to the lawyer. It was made in the hearing
of all France; and after conviction and sentence, when
the heads had fallen and the crime was half forgotten,
the Emperor seemed to sit wondering.

VII

On a summer morning in the year 1858 the Emperor
sat waiting in a room in Plombières; outside in the
little town his subjects took the waters, and to the
east the hills climbed up steadily through the trees
into the high Vosges which look down across Alsace
into Germany. He was expecting a caller who had
come in overnight from Switzerland, and about eleven
in the morning the stumpy, unimpressive figure of
Cavour, with its ill-fitting spectacles and its fierce,
myopic stare, was shown in. The invitation had
come, a little mysteriously, from the Emperor, and
his guest interrupted a *villeggiatura* of elaborate art-
lessness in the Alps to enjoy the Imperial conversation in the milder surroundings of the Vosges. The
two men talked for five hours; and when they rose,
the future of Italy had taken shape under their hands.
There was to be a war, of course; but France must
have a reputable *casus belli*. The Austrians might
be goaded into war with Piedmont, and then it would
be simple for France to come in with a fine gesture of
protection. When the war was over, Italy could be
remade. Piedmont might take the northern plain
from the Alps to Venice; there would be a kingdom
of Central Italy for somebody; one must leave the
Pope at Rome, since the faithful had scruples, but he
would hardly need his territory, and perhaps (he had
not had a change of title for centuries) he would care

to be President of a new Italian Confederation; then there was Naples—the Russians were always so peculiar about Naples, and one might safely leave it to become Italian by a revolution of its own. The quiet talk went on behind the Emperor's door at Plombières, and outside in the sunshine ladies in crinolines walked up and down beneath the balconies in the little street. There was still France to be considered (the Emperor's level voice was speaking again); France must have something; why not Savoy and Nice? His guest, who had been in the corn trade, contested the price; Savoy was too valuable, and then since Nice was Italian, it could hardly turn French if the new doctrine of nationality were sound. The Emperor sat twisting his long moustache and never found (no one has ever found) an answer. Questions of detail must wait; it was enough that in five hours of easy talk Cavour and his host had changed the face of southern Europe.

They met again, as the July afternoon wore on and the trees began to cast long shadows. The Emperor's phaeton was at the door, and he drove his guest through the little town and out along a white road into the hills. As the horses pounded along in the sunshine and Count Cavour hazarded the opinion that the vicinity of Plombières was among the most picturesque portions of France, the Emperor turned the conversation from politics to romance. He had a fine young cousin of thirty-seven; the King of Piedmont had a daughter of fifteen. If France was to unite with Italy, a union between the Courts might serve a useful purpose. He pressed his cousin's suit through the long afternoon; the young man had been wild perhaps, and the bride was a trifle young; but she might repose confidence in one so constant (had he not left town to see Rachel on her death-bed at Nice?) to his mistresses. The two men talked of the match without irony, as the hills grew dark along the road; and lights were beginning to shine in Plombières, as the phaeton clattered home through the streets with the strange allies.

The little man in spectacles slipped back across the frontier, and the Emperor was left alone on the European stage. He had pronounced, as he had written nearly twenty years before, '*le nom si beau d'Italie*,' and he had taken almost the first constructive step in Continental statesmanship which had been known since the Peace of Vienna. His action was in line with the doctrine of nationality which he had stated in the *Considérations sur la Suisse* and the *Idées Napoléoniennes*, which had haunted him when he took his men against Cività Castellana in 1831 and reminded an impatient friend of Italy in 1848 that his name was Bonaparte. The doctrine was a foreign policy in itself; it was to earn him the tittering commendation of a British diplomat upon 'his professional pursuits as *surgeon accoucheur* to the ideas of the nineteenth century'; but Sir Robert Morier, who regarded Baron Stockmar's as 'the noblest and most beautiful political life which this century has seen,' was rarely appreciative of ideas which were not Teutonic. The Emperor had found his doctrine: it remained to apply it to the reconstruction of Europe.

The name of Italy had been spoken in a whisper by two men at a health-resort. Before it could sound across the world, the quiet sentences of *diplomatie thermale* must be translated into the terms of war and

a peace-treaty, and the stage must be set for the final
tableau. As yet no one in France knew his part for
the new piece. The Emperor's ministers were told
nothing of the drastic nature of their sovereign's cure
at Plombières, and M. Walewski continued to rotate
gravely in the solemn movements of the European
minuet. The customary exchange of courtesies continued through the year 1858, and the Austrians
mounted guard at Milan. But the Emperor was
taking the autumn sunshine by the sea at Biarritz,
and on a September morning he walked down from
the Villa Eugénie along the sands in sight of the great
rocks and the surf and the long line of mountains
which is Spain. He walked with his cousin, Prince
Napoleon, for whom he had found a bride in a royal
nursery; and as they went, he trailed his stick in the
sand and told him of the future of himself and Italy.
The Empress knew nothing; but that night the
Prince left for Russia. In a week he was at Warsaw,
and the Czar was asked to take a hand against
Austria. He need not go to war unless the Prussians
came in against France. All that was required was
a Russian concentration on the Austrian frontier,
which would draw off troops from Italy, and Russia
would be well paid by a revision of the Black Sea
clauses of the Treaty of Paris. If the Germans gave
trouble and there was a general war, she might even
(the Emperor was a practising nationalist in Italy,
but one could hardly be sentimental about Poland)
get Galicia. It was a queer transaction; but the
isolation of Russia during the Crimean War had left
her with no love of Austria, and Prince Gortschakoff
stood amiably on one side to watch the blow fall on
Vienna. There was even an attempt to buy the

neutrality of Prussia; but the Hohenzollern were
nervous of the Bonapartes—*et dona ferentes,* and on
that side nothing was arranged. Yet before the year
was out, Cavour was contracting for a rising in Italy
and something brisk beyond the Hungarian border,
the stray talk of Plombières was written down and
signed in a treaty, and a girl was sobbing in a room
at Turin. On the day of the treaty, which pointed
straight to war, Lord Malmesbury assured his Queen
that no war 'is at present contemplated by the Emperor Napoleon (who has just contradicted the report
officially), and Count Beust is of the same opinion.'

Their illusions were respected for three weeks.
But at the New Year's reception of 1859 the
Emperor, wth a rare mastery of that meaningless
diction of which royalty possesses the secret, startled
the world by addressing to the amiable widower who
represented Austria in Paris an expression of hollow
solemnity: *'Je regrette que nos relations avec votre
gouvernement ne soient pas aussi bonnes que par le
passé; mas je vous prie de dire à l'Empereur que
mes sentiments personnels pour lui ne sont pas
changés.'* The sudden turn (it had happened to the
British ambassador in 1803) was in the Napoleonic
manner, and the poor gentleman was scared into
despatches of enormous length. Stocks fell, as the
electric telegraph took the grave and empty words
into every town in Europe, and beyond the Alps
Count Cavour muttered, *'Il paraît que l'Empereur
veut aller en avant.'* There was a nervous scurry
among the diplomats; and the Prince Consort was
left with grave misgivings, shaking his head and writing to a minister to warn him that the Emperor 'has
been born and bred a conspirator, and at his present

18

age will never get out of this turn of mind, scheming himself and suspicious of others.' The air was thick with *démentis* and explanations. But the King of Piedmont opened his Parliament with an impulsive announcement that he could not hear unmoved the bitter cry, the *'grido di dolore'* of Italy; the French Prince came to Turin to fetch his Italian bride; and General Niel was working with the soldiers on the military details of the new alliance. While the masters of British policy were wringing their hands and running up and down Europe in a frenzy of good intentions and Prince Albert in interminable memoranda was urging Prussia to 'be *German,* be *Volksthümlich,'* the French were buying draught-horses for their gun-teams and moving field-guns into Algeria, which, oddly enough, never got past Marseilles; troop-ships were put into commission, and French opinion was enlightened upon the issues by a pamphlet of which the Emperor saw the proofs. At Turin the buccaneering monarch, who had impressed Queen Victoria by his *'ganz besondere, abenteuerliche Erscheinung'* as being 'more like a Knight or King of the Middle Ages than anything one knows nowadays,' was talking to Garibaldi, strangely spruce and soon to appear in the sober dignity of a Sardinian general's uniform. As the winter faded into spring, Austria mobilised five army corps and Piedmont stood to arms. There was a last whirl of diplomacy; England offered mediation, Russia proposed a Congress, Piedmont was asked to disarm and argued, Cavour came posting to Paris to hold the Emperor to his treaty. French policy seemed to sway in the grasp of a minister who worked for peace and Prince Napoleon whose desire was war.

The Emperor played for time; time had been always on his side, and he checked the Italians, pressed for demobilisation and a Congress. At Turin Cavour was burning papers in a locked room; it was all to end in talk and treaties, and he was half minded to end with it. But the Austrians and their proud young Emperor were bewildered and angry; it seemed intolerable that Piedmont should emerge from its impertinence without humiliation, and they pressed their advantage as they were to press it more than fifty years away in a disastrous future, pressed it with a conviction that Germany was behind them, and pressed it too far. Someone in Vienna drafted a curt ultimatum, and in the last days of April, 1859, two officers in white coats awaited on Count Cavour to give Piedmont seventy-two hours to demobilise: it was a challenge, and he had his war. The news came upon Paris at Easter; and as the crowds poured out of the churches, the marching bugles went sounding through the Sunday streets, as the troops went off to the station. Southwards in the Italian sunshine Austria tramped stiffly through the streets of Lombardy, and little towns saw the great sight which *Vittoria's* friends had seen ten years before, 'when the crash of an Austrian regimental band was heard coming up the Corso. . . . The regiment, in review uniform, followed by two pieces of artillery, passed by. Then came a squadron of Hussars and one of Uhlans, and another foot regiment, more artillery, fresh cavalry. . . . Further distracting Austrian band-music was going by . . . came a regiment of Hungarian grenadiers, tall, swart-faced, and particularly light-limbed men, looking brilliant in the clean tight military array of Austria. Then a squadron of blue Hussars, and a Croat regiment; after which, in the midst of Czech Dragoons and German Uhlans and blue Magyar light horsemen, with German officers and aides about him, the victorious Austrian Field-Marshal rode. . . . Artillery, and some bravely clad horse of the Eastern frontier, possibly Serb, wound up the procession. It gleamed down the length of the Corso in a blinding sunlight; brass helmets and hussar feathers, white and violet surcoats, green plumes, maroon capes, bright steel scabbards, bayonet points—as gallant a show as some portentously magnified summer field, flowing with the wind, might be; and over all the banners of Austria—the black double-headed eagle ramping on a yellow ground.' The men marched away in the spring sunshine, and in nine days after Easter the two Empires were at war.

VIII

I⊤ has been for two centuries the misfortune of
Austrian generalship to provide with victories the
armies of other nations, and in 1859 its traditions
were well maintained. Five corps fumbled slowly
along the Piedmontese frontier, as King Victor
Emmanuel drew back behind his fortresses and
waited for the French. Napoleon and his Empress
were driving through cheering streets in an open
carriage, and his men were moving slowly down into
Italy. The cavalry went between the mountains and
the sea by the coast-road beyond Nice, and long lines
of infantry wound slowly through the passes of the
Alps. Transports from Toulon came steaming into
Genoa, and in mid-May the army of Italy was marching along dusty Italian roads, ill-found, short of
supplies, but with a cheerful confidence founded
mainly upon the French comic papers that it was to
meet a grotesque and panic-stricken enemy who wore
preposterous headgear and surrendered at the sight
of a single Zouave. The Emperor, with a supreme
gesture of Bonapartism, took the command; had not
his uncle in his gaunt, lank-haired youth made a campaign of Italy against the Austrians, and might not
one do the same with a *képi* and a cigarette and a
long moustache and a Staff of names out of the
calendar of Napoleonic saints—Ney de la Moskowa,
Reille, Joachim Murat, Montebello, Cadore, Clary,

Tascher de la Pagerie? Even the surgeon was called
Larrey, and it seemed almost, as the French swung
along between the rice-fields, as though the ghost of
the *Grande Armée* was walking Lombardy.   Yet
there were other, simpler names in the lists of 1859
that drifted up out of a dark future and seemed to
hang waiting round the Emperor — Forey for
Mexico, Bazaine for Metz, Lebœuf for the last button
of an army's gaiters, Uhrich for the red sky over
Strasburg, Wimpffen for the green hills round
Sedan.

But in the sunshine of 1859 the Emperor tilted his
képi and rode out of his headquarters at Alessandria;
somewhere across the river lay Marengo and the
Holy Places of Napoleonic strategy.   He had telegraphed, kept telegraphing to Paris for transport
and supplies; Randon at the Ministry of War was
reading returns and saying, '*Tout manquait sauf le
courage.*'   But General Bonaparte had once fought
a campaign in Italy without boots, and one could
always rely on the Austrians.   They moved elaborately against Turin, felt an enemy somewhere to the
south of them, and fell back to the frontier.   There
was a scuffle with the bayonet at Montebello, and
the Emperor began to move his pieces on the board.
When a Napoleon took the field, it would be as well
for him to be Napoleonic; and the Emperor, who had
consulted the oracles of military orthodoxy in Paris,
brought with him an authentic plan by an old master.
Almost past eighty, living in the suburban peace of
Passy was a Swiss soldier of the First Empire named
Jomini, who had ridden with Ney's staff at Ulm and
Jena and left his master as the clouds gathered after
Moscow.   The old man had made a plan for his

master's nephew, and he made it in the full tradition
of Soult and Berthier. The plan was palpable to
connoisseurs as a perfect Empire piece; one could
almost see the gleam of the brass gryphons on its
dark rectangular joinery. It ignored completely the
unauthorised innovation of railways, and it depended
for its success upon the obliging courtesy of an enemy
who would keep reasonably still. But since it was
for use against the Austrians, it was entirely successful; and the French enjoyed in 1859 the pleasing
experience of defeating with the methods of 1809 an
adversary whose military thought was that of 1759.
Jomini's plan, in the mode of the First Empire, was
victorious over generalship which had advanced no
further than the Seven Years' War; but if the
Austrians had been Prussians or if General von
Möltke had ridden to Pavia with the Feldzeugmeister
Giulay, the French would have been swept against
the Alps.

In the last week of May the Emperor lay to the
south of his enemy. In a march of four days along
their front, he circled round them, passed danger-
ously up the Austrian line, and on June 4 came down
upon them from the north at Magenta. Contact had
been established almost by accident; and strategy
seemed to have been replaced, as in the Middle Ages,
by mere collision. Then, in a long summer day of
fighting, the issue was left without control or generalship to the bayonet. The Emperor sat his horse in
the sunshine, as the Guard and the Zouaves and the
Turcos went in with the bayonet and his generals
fought with swords up village streets. The Austrians
were shaken but held on. That night Napoleon sat
by candlelight in a village inn: he had telegraphed a

victory to Paris, and when the world of *modistes* was startled by the new chemical dyes, ladies were to name the colour of their *garibaldis* and *polonaises* after Magenta.

In the morning the Austrians tramped heavily eastwards across Lombardy, heading for the fortresses of the Venetian border; and whilst in Paris Eugénie and the Italian princess were driving to bow right and left down the Rue de Rivoli, the Allies, with a greater aptitude for pageantry than pursuit, set their faces towards Milan. The white coats had marched away, and on a summer morning the bearskins of the Guard were massed in the Piazza d'Armi as the tall helmets of the *Cent-gardes* went by and the balconies rained flowers on a King and an Emperor going up on horseback through the roaring streets to the frozen magnificence of the Duomo. The Emperor rode slowly, and as lyric ladies ejaculated:

> 'Shout for France and Savoy!
> Shout for the council and charge!
> Shout for the head of Cavour;
> And shout for the heart of a King——'

one seems to see bounding by his side, with a clash of the cymbals and a shake of her dark ringlets, the impulsive spirit of Elizabeth Browning ingeminating her ardent, her unfortunate refrain

> 'Emperor
> Evermore.'

The army spent a pleasant evening in the lighted streets; young ladies waved handkerchiefs from windows, Lieutenant Galliffet of the *Spahis* dined with his friends, and there was a lively iteration of

the friendly syllables *'Liberatori! Liberatori!'* Far
away to the north Garibaldi in his dark Piedmontese
uniform was moving warily among the foothills of the
Alps, and from Osborne Queen Victoria was watching the Emperor nervously and waiting until 'should
he thus have rendered himself the master of the entire
Continent, the time may come for us either to obey
or fight him with terrible odds against us.' There
was an unpleasant rise in the tone of Germany; but
he stated the unselfish nature of his mission in a proclamation to the Italian people and plunged heavily
after the Austrians across Lombardy. The advance
took him under the guns of the four strong places
of the Venetian Quadrilateral, where the Austrians,
reinforced and commanded by their Emperor, were
waiting dully. Once more collision took the place
of strategy, and the two armies drifted into contact
on the hills south of Lake Garda, where for three days
of August, 1796, the gaunt infantry of the Republic
and its young generals had faced the white coats.
They fought in the blazing sun of June 24 at Solferino; and once more the bayonets thrust and lunged
in the sunshine, as the Emperor sat watching on his
horse and smoked, gave an order, smoked again, and
watched, muttering *'Les pauvres gens! les pauvres
gens! quelle horrible chose que la querre!'* It cost
him more than fifty cigarettes to sit the day out; and
when the shadows began to fall longer from the west,
a storm of rain and wind swept down between the
armies. As it drove away, the Austrians were filing
slowly eastwards behind the Mincio, and the Emperor
telegraphed to Paris *'Grande bataille, grande victoire'* for a weary woman to read in bed at St. Cloud.
There was a flutter of flags in the Paris streets, and

she drove with a boy of three between mounted officers, through a hail of flowers to the great cathedral.

The army moved slowly forward through the Italian summer, and the Emperor rode on with his doubts. Some infection was filling his hospitals; there was fever along the dusty roads, and at the end of them Austria stood waiting behind the great guns of the Venetian fortresses. The Empress wrote from Paris that the Prussians were massing troops behind the Rhine; the French army was in Italy and the road was open. It was not easy, if France was to be protected on the eastern frontier, to thrust after the Austrians into Venetia. If one succeeded, the Germans would 'regard any serious defeat of Austria in Italy, or anything that should seriously endanger her position in the Quadrilateral, as a danger to the left flank of the German position,' and they might be in Paris in a month. If one failed, Lombardy was lost and France would not be merciful to a defeated Bonaparte—'*ce serait fini*,' as the French ambassador had told the Queen, '*ave la Dynastie*.' The risks were too great, and on a summer evening Fleury drove through the Austrian lines into Verona. In the mcrning the dust of his carriage came back up the white road: there was an armistice, and Napoleon was telling his generals in a garden that France could not both besiege Verona and defend herself. Four days later, on July 11, a house lay in the morning sunshine on the road beyond Villafranca. Some officers stood waiting in the road, and inside the house two men sat talking in a hot room. One of them was Emperor of the French, the other was a tall young man of twenty-eight in a blue uniform:

he reigned in Austria as Franz-Joseph I., and he had
a young wife in Vienna and a boy of one named
Rudolph. Since he had hardly known defeat, he
carried himself well with his fair, bushy whiskers.
But half a century away he was to fade dismally out
of life in the thunder of a twilight of half the gods in
Europe, the bowed Emperor of a dwindling Empire,
husband of a murdered woman, and father of a son
mysteriously dead. Yet it was very far away in the
sunshine at Villafranca. The two men talked easily
in the little room; and without maps or papers, as
the French Emperor frayed some flowers, they made
peace between France and Austria. Lombardy was
to be surrendered; Venice would be reformed; and
the Pope might preside over an Italian Confederation. After an hour they rode away, and before dusk
Franz-Joseph was signing the treaty in a room at
Verona. Prince Napoleon stood by; and as he
signed, the Emperor said, *'Je souhaite, Prince, que
vous ne soyez jamais dans la nécessité de céder votre
plus belle province'*: the wish was not answered. But
the Peace of Villafranca became the law of Europe,
and the Emperor, who had promised to the Italians
their country from the Alps to the Adriatic, left his
work half done. Cavour was raving at his master;
Queen Victoria was busily objecting to Foreign
Office drafts; and Italian opinion was exclaiming
with Mrs. Browning:

> 'Peace, peace, peace, do you say?
>   What!—with the enemy's guns in our ears?
>   With the country's wrong not rendered back?
> What!—while Austria stands at bay
>   In Mantua, and our Venice bears
>   The cursed flag of the yellow and black?'

Yet a good deed half done was better than no deed. There was always time to resume; *il ne faut rien brusquer,* and the Emperor had only drawn back within a week of war with Germany. Before the month was out he was back in France, riding through the flowers and the cheers on a triumphal charger from Anderson's in Piccadilly, or taking the salute as the army of Italy marched across Paris with rolling drums and clanging bands and great wreaths of laurel on the colours, whilst battle-painters in tall studios laid on their reds and blues (with a flicker of white for the retreating Austrians) or posed him in attitudes of command for large, commissioned canvases. A Napoleon had led out the armies of France and ridden home again from victory: his effigy was wreathed on the coins and stamps of his victorious country, and the Empire was at high noon.

IX

EUROPE in 1860 had a strange master. When the
scene was set, the Queen of England with her stoutish
husband, the Holy Father murmuring 'Caro mio
Russell' to the British agent, a slim young man at
Schönbrunn, the mild, elderly moustache of Prussia,
a Czar, a comfortable Queen of Spain, and the comic
ferocity of the Rè galant'uomo at Turin seemed to
fall apart and sidle into the wings, as Napoleon III.
took the centre of the stage. He moved slowly, with
his cigarettes and his great moustache (it was at its
longest after the war of 1859) and the hair bunched,
after an earlier fashion, above his ears; and before
he spoke, he seemed always to wait for a hint from
the prompter. It was a quiet figure. Yet his pre-
eminence was no less than his uncle's and as great as
Frederick's a hundred years before, when the world
had centred on that tight-lipped man with hunted
eyes. But they seemed, those earlier effigies, to cast
a sharper shadow in the hard light of an older time.
His was a vaguer outline, a milder, perhaps a more
intelligent figure with its good manners and its taste
for modern ideas. 'Our friend,' as Lord Clarendon
wrote with a touch of the pitying characterisation of
Mr. Henry James, 'is an odd little fellow.' He is
visible in the years after the Italian war moving
quietly about his Court among the trees at Fontaine-

bleau, or by the sea at Biarritz, or in the two square
palaces at St. Cloud and the Tuileries, which were
caught up somehow in his fate and came crashing
down with him to a dull roar of flames. One seems to
see him, in those central years of the Second Empire,
with his long face bearded to look still longer and a
great waxed moustache, smoking among his papers
at the Tuileries (the heat in the little room was always
stifling, and it was filled with the dull gleam of
Empire furniture) or running upstairs with a cigarette when 'Ugénie' sounded her gong at the top of
the little staircase; strolling on the terrace by the
river in the *bourgeois* solemnity of a vast top-hat, or
driving a phaeton in the Bois; crossing the polished
floor of the great gallery at Compiègne, as the doors
swung back and the party saw the Emperor come
slowly into the circle, murmuring the meaningless
courtesies of royal conversation in his black coat and
knee-breeches with the shirt-front barred with the
vivid red of the Legion. One gets a sight of him
walking a little heavily on the sands at Biarritz, or
driving up hot Basque roads to the blue line of the
Pyrenees in brakes full of smiling ladies; sometimes
Eugénie wore her black *mantilla,* and they sat together through a *corrida* in the little bull-ring at
Bayonne, or they all went out in boats into the Bay
of Biscay or on the milder waters of the lake at
Fontainebleau. There were dances, hunts, drives,
shoots, reviews, receptions. He had acquired, in all
their fatal versatility, the multiple accomplishments
of royalty, sometimes a soldier in camp at Châlons,
sometimes (in tactful company) a *savant,* sometimes
a mere gesture of monarchy on a round-backed
Empire throne, sometimes a sportsman with the fine,

promiscuous bag of foreign shooting or following the
staghounds at Compiègne in a queer, Eighteenth
Century masquerade of three-cornered hats. But
mostly he was a kindly, aging man who inflicted
parlour games upon his circle or sat smiling a vague,
sleepy smile through the innumerable scenes of
Imperial magnificence. It was a strange figure.

Beside him sat the sad, perpetual smile of Eugénie,
as she bowed her way through the life of an Empress,
and the little head which Lulu bent above his toys.
Behind them there was the rustling, gleaming, shifting scene of the Imperial Court with the faces thrusting forward a little eagerly into the light. For the
most part it was the circle of 1850 which had gathered
round the President at the Élysée. But under the
Empire the circle seemed drawn into a bolder sweep.
One saw the old faces—M. de Persigny with his
solemn stare, the wry smile of M. Mérimée, Mocquard the secretary in his buttoned coat, General
Fleury, and the suave M. de Morny with his bald
head and his imperial. But they appeared in the
ampler dignity of more impressive characters; they
were all ministers, ambassadors, Senators of the
Empire; there was a profusion of decorations and
gold braid, and the intimates of the Élysée rotated
gravely as an Imperial aristocracy. Morny, who
had been born without a name and was to die a
Duke, was the most elegant (was he not the pious
founder of Deauville and the Grand Prix?) and
passed gracefully along 'dans son attitude,' as young
M. Daudet saw him from a desk in his office, 'de
Richelieu-Brümmel,' with the plaque of the Legion of
Honour on his coat and a faint flavour of finance and
the Ballet, President of the Chamber and ex-ambas-

sador at the Court of St. Petersburg. Fleury had
risen from a captain of *Spahis* to be colonel of the
Guides and a grave person who conversed with
foreign Emperors; Mocquard, who had once written
the Prince's letters in a hotel room in the Place Vendôme, drafted Speeches from the Throne; and Persigny was seen in Downing Street on his way to a
conference with Lord Palmerston.

Beyond the intimates there came the circle of the
ministers, solemn gentlemen in black suits who tilted
the great stove-pipe hats of 1860 and looked wise as
they came out of Council to their carriages at St.
Cloud or seemed a trifle out of place on the broad
steps at Compiègne. M. Fould, who was so clever
about money matters, was of the group, and M.
Billault who made such splendid speeches, and M.
Rouher spreading his broad shoulders and looking
burly, and M. Walewski confronting Europe with
the courage of his master's convictions.

But the stir, the rustling movement of the Court,
came from the ladies, from the tittering groups that
stood in corners, wives and daughters of the grave
gentlemen in knee-breeches. The Empress had her
ladies with the diamond monogram on the shoulder-
knot—two Murats, an Essling, a Bassano, a Montebello, a Latour-Maubourg (the list sounded like
army orders of the First Empire), an Aguado for
Spain and a Bouvet for her heavy beauty. Most of
the intimates were married; Morny had brought back
a Troubetzkoi from St. Petersburg who had small
features and lived on talk and cigarettes, Madame de
Persigny was a Ney who carried so much of London
with her from her embassy that they called her in
Paris 'Lady Persington,' and the Countess Walewska

was a dark Italian. There was an exotic world of Russians and bright-eyed, excited ladies from Italy; one repeated M. de Massa's elegant *facetiae* in three languages, and the ministers' ladies seeced to stand apart a little nervously in their great stiff skirts. It was a shifting sea of smiling faces with hair tortured into the strange shapes of old fashions, swaying gently to the new Viennese valses, posing a little stiffly in the *tableaux vivants,* or taking the floor in the fantastic dress which theatrical costumiers send out for fancy balls or M. Worth (it was the dawn of the *grands couturiers*) believed to represent the last authentic voice of fashion. A little world of pretty women believed (as they have believed so often since) that it had discovered the true life of friendship with their husbands and their husbands' friends; and the *cocodès* and their *cocodettes* (the Second Empire had not learnt to talk of Souls) swung slowly round to an air of Strauss. Solferino was avenged, and Pauline Metternich—'*ce remuant petit monstre*'—with the insolence of her ugliness and her great dark eyes and her preposterously whiskered diplomat of a husband set a tune for the Tuileries to dance to.

Somewhere beyond, in the lighted city, a whole town took its tone from its easy master and his smiling servants; and stranger, brighter figures drifted into the flaring gaslight of the Second Empire. He had been for so long, he was still one of Nature's bachelors, and a closed carriage sometimes clattered through the dark streets to a silent house. The world whispered, and women were left with strange memories, to fade miserably out of life with a codicil so piteously asking for burial in old fragrance and old frailty, for '*la chemise de nuit de Compiègne, batiste*

19

et dentelle, 1857,' when the lights were turned low, and Madame de Castiglione was a tarnished recollection, and the Empire was thirty years in its grave.

X

THE tinkling melody of the Second Empire was
played out to a deeper accompaniment from beyond
the frontier. Hostile opinion in France was still an
affair of nods and whispers; the drawing-room futili-
ties of elegant irony went on behind the closed doors
of Orleanist *salons,* and a malicious ingenuity of
historical parallel enabled intrepid persons to elicit
sly laughter with the curious felicity of their denunciations of Tiberius and Caligula. But in the freer
atmosphere of Brussels and Soho they took a higher
tone, and a long litany of disgust went up from the
'*proscrits barbus, crochus, moussus, poilus, bossus, et
obtus,*' who haunted the Channel Islands. For
eighteen years, until they crept one by one into
amnesty or the grave, they roared republican
choruses; and through the steady beat of their song
one could hear, like the throb of lighter music through
the song of *Tannhäuser's* Pilgrims, the mounting
notes of the Empire.

The centre of the little stage was held by a familiar
figure which had flitted about Paris in the grey
light of the *coup d'état,* hurried across Belgium, and
stepped off the steamer at St. Helier with the dignity
of an operatic baritone confronting a stage thunder-
storm. He brought with him to British territory a
burning indignation, a pale, impending forehead, an
astonishing vocabulary, and a middle-aged seraglio

of two; and he installed all of them with an unseasonable air of holiday in the mild discomfort of seaside lodgings. It was the astounding achievement of Victor Hugo to contemplate the eternal verities and to commune with the infinite from an address in Marine Terrace; and on this exiguous pedestal he posed that figure which was his masterpiece, his unsurpassable, his own, muffled in the dark draperies of exile and lit by the wild light of stormy seas.

His first winter was haunted by the memories of the *coup d'état,* the streets, the running feet, the gunshots in the Rue Tiquetonne; and behind it all he saw, like a row of grinning masks, the new masters of France. All history seemed to begin and end on the winter night when Paris lay silent under the mist:

> 'Trois amis l'entouraient.   C'était à l'Élysée.
> On voyait du dehors luire cette croisée.
> Regardant venir l'heure et l'aiguille marcher,
> Il était là, pensif . . .
> Comme ils sortaient tous trois de la maison Bancal.
> Morny, Maupas le grec, Saint-Arnaud le chacal,
> Voyant passer ce groupe oblique et taciturne,
> Les cloches de Paris, sonnant l'heure nocturne,
> S'efforçaient vainement d'imiter le tocsin.'

The events of the three days of December were embalmed in an elaborate and eloquent mythology, and a bitter litany went up from the republican dead:

> 'O morts, l'herbe sans bruit croît sur vos catacombes,
> Dormez dans vos cercueils!   Taisez-vous dans vos tombes!
> L'Empire, c'est la paix.'

The Emperor—'*pirate empereur Napoléon dernier*'—appears through the flames of a new Inferno in every attitude of infamy,

The Court at Compiègne (1857)

From a photograph

'cassé de débauches, l'œil terne,
Furtif, les traits pâlis,
Et ce voleur de nuit alluma sa lanterne
Au soleil d'Austerlitz!'

Sometimes he is almost a figure of comedy—*'ce Cockney d'Eglinton et d'Epsom'* or *'Tom-Pouce Attila'* or

'une espèce
De perroquet ayant un grand nom pour perchoir.'

But more often he wears a sinister air—*'ce vil masque à moustaches,' 'l'homme louche de l'Élysée'*—as his frantic showman waves an ironical pointing-pole towards the cage of

'l'homme aux yeux étroits
Que l'histoire appelle—ce drôle—
Et Troplong-Napoléon trois—'

or vociferates in a crescendo of invective:

'ce gredin taciturne
Ce chacal à sang-froid, ce Corse hollandais,
Étale, front d'airain, son crime sous le dais,
Gorge d'or et de vin sa bande scélérate,
S'accoude sur la nappe, et cuvant, noir pirate,
Son guet-apens français, son guet-apens romain,
Mâche son cure-dents taché de sang humain!'

The onslaught is sustained, with the assistance of Juvenal and the Apocalypse in equal parts, against the friends of the Élysée—*'Canrobert Macaire'* and the dying Saint-Arnaud—and the immoral spectacle (so distasteful to a practising bigamist) of the nascent gaiety of the Second Empire. The poet strains his eyes from Jersey through the mist and sees the whirling dance of an Imperial Brocken:

'Bal à l'hôtel de ville, au Luxembourg gala.
Allons, juges, dansez la danse de l'épée!

.   .   .   .

Valsez, Billault, Paricu, Drouyn, Lebœuf, Delangle!
Danse, Dupin! Dansez l'horrible et le bouffon!
Hyènes, loups, chacals, non prévus par Buffon,
Leroy, Forey, tueurs au fer rongé de rouilles,
Dansez! Dansez, Berger, d'Hautpoul, Murat, citrouilles!'

The invective rises to a shriek beside which the
Second Philippic must appear a piece of tasteless
flattery, and the poet strains his voice to breaking-
point in his search for more discordant notes.   In
Napoléon-le-Petit, which went to the printer before
he left Belgium, he had harnessed history to the base
purposes of the pamphlet.   Variations on the same
theme travelled with him to England in his luggage,
to appear twenty-six years later as *Histoire d'un
Crime.*   But his Muse was still distracted by the
obsession of the grey December days of 1851, and
in *Les Châtiments* he made her drunk with words and
sent her to reel across Europe and crouch, mouthing
her detestation, on the doorstep of the Empire.

The dreary business of denunciation went on for
eighteen years.   The scene shifted from the sea-front
at St. Helier to a corner house in Guernsey; bulky
parcels came and went with the proofs of *Les
Misérables;* the poet was caught by the watchful
camera in attitudes of profound reflection in which
the gloom of Lord Byron was artfully combined with
the expatriation of Ovid; he thought; he thought
more deeply still; he grew a beard.   But whenever an
anniversary came round in the republican calendar,
or a distant insurrection was detected in need of the
encouragement of a manifesto, or an exile died with-

out the consolations of a funeral oration, there was
an inexhaustible well of reverberating prose at
Hauteville House, in which little groups of hearers
could see reflected the broad and beating wings of
human effort as it strove upward towards the fixed
stars of an eternal Republic. The great voice came
across the sea into England, where its angry iteration
exasperated the old and its deep melody obsessed the
young. The English have always imported their
intellectual fashions from the Continent; and young
gentlemen, who had turned Greek with Lord Byron
and Italian with Mr. Browning, found it picturesque
to make themselves French with M. Victor Hugo.
The attitude had an attractive air of defiance, and
the temptation to strike it was deepened by the
frisson of feeling oneself one with Danton and Marat
and the more freely gesticulating figures of M. Victor
Hugo and M. Ledru-Rollin. The cold intelligence
of Mr. Bagehot had scandalised the readers of *The
Inquirer* by his approval of the coup *d'état*. But it
was not surprising that on a May evening in 1857 the
Oxford Union met in the Society's room (the fine
new figures which Mr. Morris and Mr. Rossetti
painted for their young friends were soon to gleam
vaguely from the high ceiling) to warn the listening
nations 'that the Despotism of Louis Napoleon, as
at present exercised over France, is both prejudicial
to the progress of that country and to the true interests of Europe.' Young Mr. Bowen of Balliol
sat on the President's left, and Mr. Dicey, unconscious of his own longer but less vivacious walk down
the dreary avenue of jurisprudence, denounced the
tyrant. Someone from Brasenose moved, with that
feeling for very old institutions which is normally

experienced by very young men, a Legitimist amendment; and when the debate was resumed a week later,
the House enjoyed the engaging spectacle of Mr.
Swinburne of Balliol, whose room was decorated with
a portrait of Mazzini, urging upon it with all the
inconsequence of true conviction (and in breach of
the Society's admirable rule that members may not
read their speeches) 'that although some benefits have
accrued from the rule of Louis Napoleon, the restoration of the Bourbons to the Throne of France is much
to be desired.' The amendment received no support
outside the four members who spoke in its favour;
and it may be supposed that the Bourbons, who
learnt nothing, were never aware that they had
engaged the momentary support of Mr. Swinburne.

The young gentleman, who ensured a successful
career of letters by competing unsuccessfully for the
Newdigate Prize, added an engraving of Orsini to his
republican gallery; but his attentions were readily
diverted to the more attractive figures of Astarte and
Aholibah. Yet even in the intervals of his devotions
to Dolores he found time for a muttered prayer
to see

> 'Buonaparte the bastard
> Kick heels with his throat in a rope.'

A respectful review of *Les Misérables* was followed
by a gracious letter from Hauteville House; and the
poet's craft, which was always a trifle rudderless,
was swept into the great stream of European insurrection which set from Guernsey against the coast of
France. Mazzini, Victor Hugo, Barbès, Garibaldi,
and a stray rebellion in Crete were all startled with
the tribute of mellifluous lyrics, and the singer sent

up his denunciations of the Empire and 'the worm
Napoleon' in a steadily mounting crescendo of invective which seemed sometimes to rise into a cracked
falsetto. In imagery which stated the republican
sentiments of Mr. Odger with a Dantesque imagination and a Biblical vocabulary his readers were
invited to wait hungrily for the Emperor's end:

> 'O Death, a little more, and then the worm;
> A little longer, O Death, a little yet,
> Before the grave gape and the grave-worm fret;
> Before the sanguine-spotted hand infirm
> Be rottenness, and that foul brain, the germ
> Of all ill things and thoughts, be stopped and set.'

The exercise was pleasantly titillating to a young
man with friends whose appetite for recitation was
fortunately insatiable; and he contributed (like his
friend Meredith) 'to the Song of French History' a
metrical Philippic in which the Emperor appeared as
'an evil snake-shaped beast' and 'Judas' and 'son of
man, but of what man who knows?' until a winter
day in 1873 when the little poet pranced about with
his 'funeral flowers' for the grave at Chislehurst and
screamed over the man

> 'Whose soul to-night stands bodiless and bare,
> For whom our hearts give thanks who put up prayer,
> That we have lived to say, The dog is dead.'

Equally apocalyptic in his inspiration but of more
uneven literary accompaniment was the Prophet
Baxter, who saw in the Emperor's career the fulfil-
ment of all prophecies and a plain indication (so
gratifying to true believers) of the approaching end
of the age between the years 1864 and 1873. A

vigorous pictorial treatment of the Beasts of the Apocalypse demonstrated that, as the eighth head, Napoleon might be expected to manifest himself as Antichrist; Apollyon faded imperceptibly into Apoleon; and the prophet argued with a wealth of quotation and slightly feverish exegesis that the Empire led inevitably to Armageddon, 'an unprecedented Revival of Religion and of Missionary effort among the Foolish Virgins,' a successful invasion of Great Britain, the Resurrection, and quite a number of other agreeable fixtures which might be expected to take place at regular intervals after the date of Mr. Baxter's researches. The Emperor, described forcibly as 'this great Antetypical, Papistico-Infidel, Democratico-Despotic, Personal Antichrist,' was to fall with the Pope into a new volcano conveniently opened for the occasion outside Rome after a crowded career including campaigns in Egypt and Palestine and the subjugation of America, to which references in the Apocalypse are unaccountably vague but may be inferred from an indication somewhere in the text of 'a wilderness.' Mr. Baxter's programme was packed with pleasing incident, and it was timed to end at latest in 1873. In that year dutifully ended Napoleon III.; but the universe, which had been kept in ignorance of Mr. Baxter's revelation, omitted to end with him.

XI

THE Second Empire in 1860 drifted into its last decade at a characteristic tilt. Whilst the Emperor, upon a somewhat Anglo-Saxon view that the composition of history forms an appropriate relaxation for men of action, was beginning to collect material for a life of Caesar and calling upon slightly embarrassed *savants* to produce 'documents *inédités*' of the period, Europe was fingering a little doubtfully the Italian question.

This problem, which provided well-informed persons with the agreeable form of intellectual distraction subsequently derived from the Balkan Peninsula, was set for solution beyond all hope of avoidance. Grave gentlemen considered the future of Central Italy and its minor monarchies and wrestled with the paradox of the French garrison in Rome, whilst the prospects of the Papacy, the continuance of Bourbon incompetence in the Kingdom of Naples, the obvious aggressions of Piedmont, and a vague menace of Mazzinian republicanism supplied a shifting background before which the Emperor held, in attitudes of Eleusinian mystery, the centre of the stage. He had permitted the war to end before it had solved its problems with the satisfying completeness of a *fait accompli,* and it was not simple to reconcile his divergent impulses in a single policy. His word to Austria, his faith in Italy, and an anxious eye upon French Catholic opinion drew him in three directions, and he seemed to seek refuge from an awkward choice in the imposing attitudes of oracular immobility. His tendency in the autumn of 1859, when the Peace of Villafranca was embodied in the definitive treaties of Zurich, was to impose a provisional adjustment of the Italian question and to defer for solution by a European congress the final reconstruction of Italy. His faith in the collective wisdom of Europe, which never left him, was pathetic and (in an observer familiar with the congresses which followed the Peace of Vienna, although necessarily debarred from acquaintance with the more rococo series subsequent to the Peace of Versailles) surprising. But upon the question of Italy it was never tested, since the congress never met. The sages displayed a marked disinclination for one another's company, and the project faded.

It was an unfortunate by-product of this design that Church opinion in France, to which all logic had been sacrificed in the protective occupation of Rome by a French army, was profoundly shocked by an intrusion of common-sense. A pamphlet had been written to prepare the public mind for the issues to come before the congress; it was known to have been approved by the Emperor, and since it contained a plain indication that the maintenance of the Pope's territories in a reuniting Italy was a political absurdity, the suspicion of enlightenment at the Tuileries sufficed to scandalise clerical opinion. The Catholic supporters of the Empire exchanged their loyalty for a succession of hostile convulsions, and a section of French journalism was devoted to solemn invective whilst the pulpits rang with the grave eloquence of admonitions to the Emperor.

A more fortunate by-product of the Italian question (although it resulted equally in the alienation of
a large body of French opinion) was the movement
of French policy closer to Great Britain. It was
obvious that if the Italian case was to be maintained
in Europe, it must rest on the support of France and
England. The subjects of Queen Victoria had been
startled by French armaments into the defensive
attitudes of the Rifle Volunteers, and the Emperor
was anxious to recover their esteem. By a fortunate
chance his Minister of Commerce was dining one
evening to meet the remarkable Mr. Cobden, whose
views upon fiscal matters were so original and (to
French opinion) so diverting. He had an odd notion,
which he had opened to a French economist in the
congenial air of the Great Exhibition, on the subject
of Free Trade between France and England, and he
was anxious to put his fantastic proposal before the
Emperor. On an autumn morning in 1859 he drove
out to St. Cloud for an audience, leaving Mrs. Cobden at the hotel. Reflecting a trifle obviously on the
sumptuary differences between the President of the
United States and the Emperor of the French, he
was shown into a room, where he saw a short man
with a large moustache whose 'eye is not pleasant at
first, but it warms and moistens with conversation,
and gives you the impression that he is capable of
generous emotions.' They discussed the new architecture of Paris and the ineptitude of British
journalists; Mr. Cobden said that Mr. Gladstone
would have a surplus in his next Budget and was
anxious to reduce duties on French imports; the
Emperor was prepared to make similar concessions
but regretted the embarrassment of a Protectionist

majority in his own Chamber. Then, with a pleasing
irony, the elderly parliamentarian and his host
arranged to elude the Chamber of Deputies by a pre-
rogative use of the treaty-making power of the
French Crown. Something was said about Sir
Robert Peel, and the Emperor observed that he was
'charmed and flattered at the idea of performing a
similar work in my country; but it is very difficult
in France to make reforms; we make revolutions in
France, not reforms.'

Mr. Cobden drove back to Paris and engaged in
conversations of detail with M. Fould. An invitation
to Compiègne was declined, and the electors of Roch-
dale were denied the pleasing spectacle of their
member and Mrs. Cobden displaying the urbanity
of Lancashire among the Imperial parterres. The
missionary of Free Trade returned to England and
found the imagination of the Prime Minister obsessed
by news of French orders for armour-plate and rifled
artillery, and a sinister story, which prevailed in
British politics for half a century before and half a
century after it haunted Lord Palmerston in 1859,
that someone in a foreign port had seen by a failing
light a flotilla of (*monstrum informe ingens horren-
dum*) flat-bottomed boats. But the negotiation went
on; Mr. Cobden returned to Paris and saw something of Napoleon in his home with his cigarettes and
his tall Empress; angry French gentlemen on depu-
tations ran the traditional gamut of Protectionist
argument; but in three months from that first morning at St. Cloud a Commercial Treaty was signed,
and whilst his sovereign offered to Mr. Cobden the
distinctions of baronetcy or membership of the Privy
Council, the Chancellor of the Exchequer was

enabled to refresh his countrymen with Gladstone clarets.

The Emperor was smoking quietly over his life of Caesar; M. Mérimée wrote notes for him on Roman religion, and the lady whom he had sent round the libraries when he was at Ham went on archaeological errands into Germany. But the Italian question continued to throw a long shadow. A new minister was installed at the Quai d'Orsay who had demonstrated his faith in the doctrine of nationality in the unpromising instance of Roumania; but M. Thouvenel was instructed in the danger of public adhesion to general principles by the immediate necessity of annexing some Italian territory. Nice and Savoy had stood in the bond of Plombières as the price of French assistance; and as Piedmont rapidly expanded, the Emperor was disinclined to forego his trifling honorarium. Europe was startled by an announcement that by the exigencies of geography (it was the old revolutionary doctrine of natural frontiers) and by a treaty with Cavour the French were entitled to advance their south-eastern frontier to the watersheds of the Alps. Queen Victoria wrote voluble despatches about 'spoliation'; Lord John Russell made firm speeches; the Prince Consort wrote wise letters; Mr. Kinglake denounced the French annexations with all the fire with which, twenty years earlier, he had resented the appropriation of the blonde Miss Howard; and there was even an odd little wrangle between the Emperor and the British ambassador at a Tuileries concert. But the world was reluctant to go to war for an Italian province. Mr. Bright, whose appetite for a patriotic *casus belli* was always of the faintest, said 'Perish

Savoy!' and M. Benedetti came back from Turin
with the Piedmontese consent. A *plébiscite* in the
new provinces welcomed the change of ownership.
Garibaldi was left staring at the tricolour over

> 'The little house my father knew,
> The olives and the palms of Nice,'

and before the year was out, M. Thiers was rejoicing
sotto voce that 'the worst humiliation of 1815 has
been wiped out,' whilst cheering crowds sent the
Emperor bowing through Savoy, and Napoleon and
Eugénie put out in a stage barge from the Pont des
Amours under a night of stars into the Lake of
Annecy.

But Italy was never still. There was a queer thrill
in the south where *Bomba's* son, with what Queen
Victoria called 'an unfortunate *Pietät* for the memory
of his father,' was shooting his prisoners; and from
an inn at Genoa Garibaldi was beginning to look
southwards. A few cases of condemned muskets
came in by rail; a little piracy secured two ships in
the harbour; and on a May night he stood under the
great moon on the rocks at Quarto, as the boats put
out to sea and the Thousand faced towards Sicily.
The Neapolitans fumbled with the invasion; and
whilst Queen Victoria discussed the ethics of revolution with Lord John Russell, the world looked on at
the hard fighting in the hills with the cold stare of
impartiality generally reserved by official Christendom for successful insurrections against the Sultan
of Turkey, until

> 'You've seen the telegram?
> *Palermo's taken, we believe.*'

The mad march went on; and Garibaldi drove up Italy in a brougham, whilst Napoleon talked amiably about non-intervention and permitted Italy to make itself. His troops stood in Rome with grounded arms, as the Thousand reeled through the roaring streets of Naples and the slow tide of the Piedmontese advance washed over the Pope's territory in the north. The judicious Leopold wrote feverish letters from Laeken about *'le Filibustive* movement at Naples' and scandalised Queen Victoria with the bitter contrast between the canonisation of Garibaldi at Naples and the execution of General Walker in Honduras. Anxious gentlemen from Turin posted over the mountains to Chambéry to consult the impassive face behind the large moustache. The oracle, as is the way of oracles, was silent; but silence, at a moment when the Garibaldians were destroying the Kingdom of Naples and the Piedmontese army had violated the Pope's frontier, was consent enough for Cavour; and soon all Italy believed that the Emperor (though he was not above a hint to Austria that the Italians might be checked) had muttered his blessing—*'Faites, mais faites vite'* or *'Fatte, ma fatte presto'*—and the queer Italian war went on. The Pope's army, commanded by Lamoricière, whose name was a reproach to Napoleon, trailed despondently into the Marches and broke at Castelfidardo. The Piedmontese marched into Naples and Umbria, and before the year was out Victor Emmanuel was proclaimed King of Italy.

The French attitude had exasperated the Catholics and alarmed the English. Germany was nervous; and when the Emperor saw the Regent of Prussia at Baden, *'le Prince Régent s'est conduit vis-à-vis de moi comme une jeune fille pudique, qui craint les propos d'un vert galant et qui évite de se trouver longtemps seule avec lui.'* It remained to emphasise the importance of France by those operations against unarmed aboriginal populations in distant quarters of the world which were to be accepted in the last half of the Nineteenth Century as an unfailing indication of the status of a Great Power. Disorder in Syria provoked a French expedition and an impressive demonstration of the traditional interest of France in the Levant (as well as the literal truth of the Imperial anthem *Partant pour la Syrie*), and the regrettable persistence of Chinese ideas in China resulted in a Franco-British invasion. The Taku Forts were stormed, and the allies marched on Pekin. The mission of western civilisation was amply demonstrated by the looting of the Summer Palace, and honour was elaborately satisfied. On the road to the capital the little army brushed aside forty thousand Chinamen armed with bows and matchlocks. The engagement was grotesque, but the French general took a title from its name. He was to be (how far away it seemed in 1860) the last minister of the Empire; and when the name of a Chinese village turned General Cousin-Montauban into Count Palikao, a faint sound of the thudding guns of 1870 seemed to come up the wind.

XII

In the grey dawn of the Second Empire, by the cold
daybreak of 1852 the issues had been very plain.
The broad alternatives of Empire and revolution
had been sharply outlined in that clear light; and it
seemed so easy to save society, so simple to strike
enlightened international attitudes on the European
stage. Slowly the day broadened, and under a
mounting sun the Empire moved towards high noon.
In the blaze of it there were French victories, an heir,
a smiling Empress, and the world seemed waiting for
Napoleon to remake it. But the day drew on, and
in the milder light of afternoon the outlines blurred.
The old certainties seemed to lose something of their
sharpness and to fade, as doubts began to grow on the
slow minds of France and Europe, and the paths of
the Empire became less clear. The sun was still
high, and the Emperor paced slowly in the sunlight.
Yet it was past noon, and the shadows began to fall
longer on the ground. There were deaths round the
Emperor: Jerome, the old King of Westphalia,
faded unimpressively out of life into the legend of
the First Empire, and the Empress wore black for
her sister, the Spanish duchess. There was a faint
air of evening upon the Empire. Soon the light
would fade, and it would be night.

It had been simple enough in the first movement
of the Empire for a man not far past forty to govern

France. Centralisation was the administrative tradition of Bonapartism, and a single will made all decisions. They were transmitted to the nation by the Imperial machine, and the functions of ministers rarely exceeded the limited duty of supervising its smooth running. Ability is not encouraged by absolutism of this order; his surroundings, as an observer wrote of them, were *'des outils et . . . pas de compagnons,'* and since the Emperor needed no collaborators, he had found none. *'Le maître,'* as M. Mérimée saw him, *'n'admet pas trop, je le crains, qu'il y ait des hommes nécessaires.'* But under the pressure of a later phase he began to be conscious of the need. His ministers had been little more than a procession of self-seeking mediocrities, each willing to subordinate his policy to the Emperor's, but all consolable for their subjection by the gratifying proximity of the public purse—M. Fould the banker, who drifted into statesmanship after a financial career that had been far, so very far, from exemplary; the grave Baroche pocketing sinecures for his unpleasant son; M. Walewski, whose policy was so apt to vary with his investments; the hungry Haussmann, whose municipal finance inspired irreverent comments on the *Comptes fantastiques d'Haussmann;* and the simpler appetites of the smaller men. Their master had been indifferent in the choice of his servants since he disbelieved in the efficacy of human action to change the course of events and was content to rely, for such action as he took, upon himself. But as the scene darkened and the Emperor began to grope in the gathering gloom, he needed (and never found) a minister of the great tradition. There was no Louvet and no Colbert; and for ten years he was left muttering, as he had said almost fretfully to the Prince Consort at Osborne: '*Où trouver l'homme?*'

His choice was cruelly limited by his circle. Persigny, who alternated between the embassy in London and the Ministry of the Interior, was loyal to the point of tactlessness; but he had been indelibly impressed by his early reading with the ruthless absolutism of the First Empire. M. Rouher had a lawyer's aptitude for detail and considerable eloquence; but his political ideals were those of a policeman; and when the Emperor's design drifted towards an infusion of parliamentarism into the Imperial system, the dilution of strong government was repellent to his minister, and M. Rouher permitted the fragile parliamentary experiment of the later Empire to fail under his heavy hands. One man perhaps might have made a minister of the first order. M. de Morny possessed the airy accomplishments of a diplomat of romance; but he was rarely employed abroad, since the Empire required all its diplomacy at home. He was a strange figure, with an aptitude for light comedy and the happy application of official information to his private speculations —'*un bandit,*' *as* someone saw him, '*tombé dans la peau d'un vaudevilliste.*' His elegance (they called his house in Paris '*le petit coin d'amour*') seemed to date from an earlier age of frivolity in high places; and when Flahaut was French ambassador in London and the memory of Hortense was embalmed in the aromatic sanctity of the Imperial legend, their son sauntered gracefully through French politics, facing the world with the well-dressed irony of Mr. Brummell. One of his clerks at the Palais Bourbon was a young man named Daudet—*'fantastique employé à crinière Mérovingienne'*—and when the Duke offered him the post, the solemn youth warned him, with all the pomposity of an extremist, that he was a royalist. There was a bland, slow smile, and Morny replied: *'L'Impératrice l'est aussi.'* He lounged in his easy way into French fiction; and M. Zola's documents compiled *M. de Marsy,* whilst M. Daudet's observation sketched the *Duc de Mora.* It was an engaging person; but he had few beliefs. Democracy did not alarm him, because one could always captivate the democrats; and in this mood he joined in the Emperor's drift towards parliamentary government. Yet he was never a minister, sitting always as President of the Chamber, standing between the Emperor and the politicians, holding himself perpetually in reserve, until he died.

French opinion in 1860 was beginning to stir. Its rest had been seriously interrupted, and the Imperial lullaby was ceasing to soothe it. *Moustachu* was still popular in the streets although they were sometimes disrespectful about his lady, *la Reine Crinoline.* But Mr. Cobden's Commercial Treaty had roused the manufacturing interests; the desertion of the Pope scandalised those numerous persons who confused their religious beliefs with an adherence to the Temporal Power; and the unheroic gentlemen who sat at the Palais Bourbon under the suave tutelage of M. de Morny and his bell were beginning to lose (it may have been due to the Emperor's policies or to the dreadful proximity, the republican contamination of the Five) their native docility. Morny observed the need and responded with a modest plan for increasing the liberties of the Chamber; he said

as much to M. Darimon, one of the reckless Five.
Someone consulted M. Thiers as a retired expert on
parliamentary institutions, and one afternoon at
Council the Emperor informed his ministers that he
proposed to make a change. Two days later, on
November 24, 1860, the decree was signed; and true
Bonapartist opinion was scandalised by the intrusion
of liberties which approximated to those enjoyed by
the Parliaments of Queen Elizabeth.

Under the new system the two Chambers were
permitted to vote (and even to discuss) an Address
in reply to the Speech from the Throne; the procedure on amendment was simplified; debates might
in future be reported in full; and the Government
proposed to justify its proceedings to the Chamber
by the arguments of a new class of ministers without
portfolio, whose sole official duty was eloquence. M.
Billault, a harassed-looking gentleman with considerable powers of speech, was appointed to wrestle
with the strange forces of democracy, and the Empire
passed into its new phase. M. de Morny asked M.
Ollivier whether he was satisfied, and the mild eyes
gleamed at him almost sternly behind the narrow
spectacles: 'Si c'est une fin, vous êtes perdus; si c'est
un commencement, vous êtes fondés.' It was a
strange admission for a republican. But the young
man (he was under forty) had travelled a long way
since he was a bewildered official of the Second
Republic. The treadmill of opposition (he was
perpetually delivering admirable speeches to a
mausoleum of indifference or an inferno of interrup-
tion) was beginning to impress its barrenness upon
his sensitive intelligence. The world is so much
simpler for bigots than for philosophers; and a less

active mind would have found it easy to solve every problem with a republican *cliché*. All round him the orthodox republicans were murmuring their incantations with religious monotony, and he met a bull-necked young barrister at the Manets one evening (the name was Gambetta) who was pounding the table-tops of the Café Procope with a heavier fist, as a new voice from the Midi sent the infamies of the Empire vibrating among the chandeliers. Yet Ollivier saw too much of the republicans to believe completely in the Republic; perhaps Lamennais had been right when he said in his bitterness, '*Les républicains sont faits pour rendre république impossible.*' One could not always strike Roman attitudes, and republican perorations were hardly in themselves a substitute for good government. If only one could believe that the Emperor's drift into constitutionalism was sincere, was deliberate, was a step in a system, then France might be governed in ordered liberty, and M. Ollivier might return from the husks of republicanism to take a prodigal hand in its government. The solution had a tepid air of compromise; it lacked the devastating logic of revolutions. But M. Ollivier could write, '*Mieux vaut vivre dans une constitution illogique que de mourir pour la logique.*' The sentiment was hardly French; but it was forming in the mind of at least one Frenchman, and one can see beyond it the faint dawn of the Liberal Empire.

The experiment, which began in 1860, was and odd one. It was an attempt to govern France by the collaboration of men who did not believe in liberty with men who did not believe in the Empire; and the Emperor's circle stared a little when M. Ollivier

opened the politics of 1861 with a speech in which
he seemed to offer republican support to a parliamentary Empire:

*'Quant à moi qui suis républicain, j'admirerais, j'ap-
puierais, et mon appui serait d'autant plus efficace qu'il
serait complètement désintéressé.'*

There were debates in the Chamber upon real
issues, and M. Mérimée, whose Liberalism was a
trifle rusty, wrote letters of grave concern to his
friend Mr. Panizzi of the British Museum. Controversy centred on the perpetual problem of Rome;
they sold a puzzle named after it in the streets; and
as the Pope became the leading figure in French
politics, the clericals began to give tongue against the
Empire. But stranger things than the new voices of
the Chamber were heard in Paris. Everybody was
at the Opera one evening in March to see the preposterous new piece, all pilgrims and discords, which
the Emperor had imported from Germany. They
called it *Tannhäuser,* and anyone could see that M.
Berlioz was right when he denounced the new barbarism of Herr Wagner. One could hardly doubt, if
one had heard enough Rossini and Meyerbeer, that
opera was a succession of tinkling melodies punctuated by a ballet, and persons of taste were outraged
by the sonorous anarchy of the new revelation. The
Emperor, who had no ear, might applaud as an act of
foreign policy; Madame de Metternich clapped holes
in her gloves and broke a fan; and M. Ollivier (he
was Liszt's son-in-law—it was just what one would
expect of a republican) must have felt quite at home
defying a hostile majority. But the house hooted,
and French culture was noisily upheld.

The drift of politics continued through the year,

Italy toiled wearily through the maze of the Roman question; Cavour died as impulsively as he had lived; French clericals were dragged by their loyalty to the Church into dislike of the Emperor; and the strange transformation of the Empire went on. Late in the year (the decree was dated November 14, 1861) Napoleon by a sudden gesture restored to the Chamber the control of the public purse. Supply was to be voted almost in the English fashion, and M. de Morny met someone at a first night (the play was by a young man named Sardou) and expressed himself well pleased. The Empire was becoming almost perceptibly parliamentary, and before the recess of 1862 M. Ollivier for the first time risked his republican chastity in the compromising privacy of Morny's room. They talked vaguely of the future, of a constitutional Empire, of a ministry in which M. de Morny might lead and M. Ollivier might serve, until (it was a little ominous) M. Benedetti came in from Turin.

Outside France the world lived in a succession of problems, to each of which the Emperor seemed anxious to apply a uniform solution consisting (it seemed ridiculous in 1860, but it was the wisdom of 1918) of a congress and the principle of nationality. The method had already been attempted in the case of Italy, where its success seemed only to be delayed by the illogical survival of the Papacy. The Emperor appeared to desire a repetition of the experiment when the Poles went out against their masters in 1863. There was a spate of Notes and despatches. But in a world which knew its lessons (and one could teach them as one sat smoking at the Tuileries) the Polish question and the hovering

problems of Rome, Greece, the Elbe Duchies, and
the Danubian Principalities would all be quite simple,
because all Italy would be Italian, Poland would be
Polish, Germany would be German, and even in
the Baltic the little kingdoms of the north would
combine in a logical unit. It was so easy to recon-
struct Europe with a blank map and a coloured
pencil, and nothing but the obstinate pretence that
the settlement of 1815 was immutable prevented the
reconstruction. The imagination of Napoleon III.
was haunted by the malicious shadow of the Peace of
Vienna. It had degraded his country, insulted his
family, and cramped his project. He was a Bonaparte, and to revise it would be almost to reverse
Waterloo. Twice at least, to the blushing Prince
Albert in 1857 and to the less easily scandalised Lord
Palmerston in 1863, he proposed a revision of the
political structure of Europe. The proposal was even
embodied in a general circular to the Powers. But the
Prince was stiffly discouraging and 'begged him,'
with a rare approach to gesticulation, 'to open the
book of history, which lay before him'; whilst Lord
Palmerston, who although he was a Liberal rarely
forgot that he was a landowner, felt that 'those who
hold their estates under a good title, now nearly half
a century old, might not be particularly desirous of
having it brought under discussion with all the alterations which good-natured neighbours might wish to
suggest in their boundaries.' The project was
rendered still more ridiculous by a romantic design
that the agenda of the conference should include the
limitation of European armaments—'*des armements
exagérés entretenus par de mutuelles défiances*'—
and when it dropped, the Emperor was left alone

with his large intentions. His policy was losing
something of its old directness, and he seemed to
stray among the diplomats with the lost air of a man
of principle in a Peace Conference. His fiendish
cunning (even Mr. Disraeli alarmed his old ladies
with mysterious allusions to 'the great Imperial
Sphinx') was one of the tenderest illusions of a
romantic age. But a Prussian ambassador, who
spent a few months in Paris, was more sceptical. His
name was von Bismarck, and he had already epito-
mised Russia as *Nitchevo*. He found that France
contained '*deux femmes amusantes, l'Impératrice, la
plus belle femme que je connaisse, et la Walewska,
mais pas un homme,*' and of the Imperial *façade* he
said: '*De loin c'est quelque chose et de près ce n'est
rien.*'

With a faint air of confusion the country drifted
into the elections of 1863. The Emperor was deep
in the career of Julius Caesar; archaeologists were
entertained by preposterous models of triremes, and
ballistae threw Roman projectiles about in the park
of St. Cloud, whilst his ministers concerted plans
with M. de Persigny for the regimentation of French
opinion. There was a vague stir of political ideas in
the country, and manipulation was obviously necessary if the admirable unanimity of 1857 was to be
retained in the new Chamber. The work was congenial to Persigny, who circularised his *Préfets* in
language that was almost apocalyptic: '*Fort de son
origine providentielle, l'élu du peuple a réalisé toutes
les espérances de la France.*' But in case opinion
was insufficiently informed of this axiom, the public
memory was to receive official assistance at the
Préfecture:

'Le suffrage est libre. Mais, afin que la bonne foi des populations ne puisse être trompée par des habiletés de langage ou des professions de foi équivoques, désignez hautement, comme dans les élections précédentes, les candidats qui inspirent le plus de confiance au Gouvernement. Que les populations sachent.' . . .

As the Minister of the Interior sat writing in his room, a sound of voices seemed to drift across the long silence of the Empire, like the first movements of a dawning day. The republicans were renewing their old incitements, and the royalists of every shade were crying their old wares. The clericals formed a strange opposition of the Right, and even M. Thiers took a hand. There was a queer coalition of republicans and bishops; old gentlemen who desired the Republic of 1848 combined with still older gentlemen who desired the monarchy of King Charles X., and gentlemen in middle life whose simpler aspirations were satisfied by the monarchy of King Louis Philippe. The language of the Government became more violent; the *Préfets* redoubled their persuasions in favour of the official candidates; and Persigny, who seemed to a contemporary *'enivré au cabaret de la puissance,'* dictated loudly to his countrymen. In the provinces his orders were obeyed; but the republicans swept Paris, and the elections of 1863 sent an Opposition of thirty-two Deputies to the Chamber, of whom seventeen were republicans. M. Ollivier sat with MM. Jules Favre, Jules Simon, and Thiers; and whilst their young friends Ferry and Gambetta sat cheering behind them in the gallery, one seems to see gliding into place the men of the Third Republic.

XIII

On a winter day towards the end of 1861 the port of Vera Cruz observed without enthusiasm the arrival of a Spanish fleet in Mexican waters. The troops were landed, and six thousand men in the uniform of Queen Isabella marched off in the sunshine to the empty forts. Early in the new year more ships appeared on the skyline. A British admiral came ashore, and a naval brigade swung up the narrow street. On the next day there was more movement in the harbour. A French squadron had put in, and they were landing some marines. A battalion of Zouaves went up into the town, and the adventure of Mexico had begun.

The Mexican expedition was, in its first phase, a bond-holders' war. The weakness of the Latin intelligence for homicide as a form of political argument has frequently endangered the security of foreign investors, and it is rarely consistent with the regular payment of interest. Mexico, which had enjoyed the amenities of civil war for a generation, was a cause of frequent anxiety. Each of its competing Presidents (there were two) had misappropriated foreign funds and responded to complaints with exquisite courtesy and a receipt for the stolen money; and the misgivings of its European creditors had been recently confirmed when President Juarez, who was at the moment in control of the capital and

318

the greater part of the country, suspended for two years the payment of foreign debts. The simple directness of his financial methods caused some alarm in London and Paris, where Mexican securities were largely held. Spanish interests were also concerned in the insolvency of Mexico, and the wheels of diplomacy began slowly to revolve. But from the first the motives of the three Powers lacked uniformity. Great Britain alone was actuated by the simple appetites of the debt-collector. In Madrid there were a vague desire to regild the glories of the Spanish flag, to castigate these rebellious colonists, perhaps (who knows?) to re-establish across America the old belt of Spanish domination; whilst a still stranger project haunted the brooding intelligence at the Tuileries. The Emperor had once stayed at the Washington Hotel, Broadway, and he suffered for thirty years from the hallucination that he understood America. Its problems had haunted him in his little room at Ham, when gentlemen from Nicaragua waited on him and he made sketch-maps of the *Canale Napoleone;* and the fascination remained with him. His facile imagination was obsessed by the importance of Central America; it seemed to him to lie central to the whole world, and with the control of it one might even redress the balance of races and check with a strong barrier of Latin culture the rising tide of expansion, which seemed to set southwards from the United States and to threaten the absorption of the American continent by the mercenary and phlegmatic Anglo-Saxon. The slow drift of his project (it had other phases more intimately connected with the affairs of Europe) was quickened by the political exiles whom

Mexican revolutions, like another Gulf Stream, brought steadily to the coasts of Europe. Paris was full of little men from Mexico with magnificent names and unimpressive appearances, who could talk Spanish to the Empress and assure her husband that their unhappy country (had he not written eloquently on the subject in the days of his own exile?) was thirsting for good government, a monarchy, and the kindly tutelage of the Church. The conversation of refugees is rarely a sound foundation for policy. But the Emperor listened impassively and went back to his old plan. As early as 1857 he had discussed the romance of a European, even a Bourbon monarchy in Mexico in the congenial company of Mr. Disraeli. Sometimes he was less interested in the Mexican monarchy than in its monarch. It was becoming difficult to recruit for thrones. A deputation of embarrassed Greeks even pursued Lord Derby with a crown. But Archdukes were always to be had; and an offer of the new Mexican throne in Vienna might please Franz-Joseph. With Austrian goodwill the Emperor could perhaps complete his work in Italy, carry the new Kingdom 'from the Alps to the Adriatic' and restore Venetia. *Le spectre de Venise erre dans les salles des Tuileries.* As it beckoned, the Emperor went forward into Mexico and took with him Maximilian.

The moment, late in 1861, was not ill chosen. The Americans were certain to object; but they were deep in their own Civil War, and one might make a new Mexico whilst their armies were busy fumbling for one another on the Potomac. The Empress was gratified by the atmosphere of royalism and orthodoxy in which one could chastise the erring republic, and M. de Morny was friendly to the idea; by a happy coincidence he was entitled to one third of the profits which would accrue to M. Jecker, a person of the indeterminate nationality peculiar to bankers, upon the expulsion of President Juarez. Shares rose in Paris when men said *'Morny est dans l'affaire.'* So the Emperor was sympathetic to the cause of the French bondholders; and when a Spanish general followed him to Vichy with proposals for a joint expedition, his Catalan vehemence was well received. The three Powers made an agreement in London, to which the United States were invited to become a party. But the State Department was disinclined to involve Mr. Lincoln in a second war in the American continent; and Secretary Seward, whose urbanity had been severely tried by the Odyssey of Messrs. Slidell and Mason, replied with a pious reference to the father of his country and the distasteful nature of entangling alliances. The expedition proceeded without American approval, and two admirals and General Prim sailed for Vera Cruz to embody the mixed feelings of their Governments.

Their arrival, with one exception, was unimpressive. But the spectacular disembarkation of General Prim (he brought a considerable staff and a military reputation obtained chiefly in Morocco) impressed a local journalist with his marked resemblance to the angel of death, a number of historical characters, and almost all the more prominent figures of classical mythology. He was an active little man with a Mexican wife; and if there was to be a monarchy in Mexico, he was not averse to being cheered in the streets of Vera Cruz. But promiscuous equitation and gratuitous reminiscences of heroic deeds on the

21

Tetuan road got the allies little further. The Mexican government seemed politely indifferent to the presence of an invasion at Vera Cruz. Immigrants in that region were offered the uninviting alternatives of yellow fever and *vomito negro;* and as the expeditionary force began to evacuate its casualties to Havana, the allies formulated their demands. By agreement with the Mexicans they moved forward from the fever zone into the more tolerable *hinterland,* and a conference was arranged in convenient proximity to a volcano. But it never met. Allied relations had been chilled by the inclusion in the French claim of an immediate payment for M. Jecker; and as the political design underlying the French *démarche* became gradually obvious, the alliance was resolved into its atoms. The knowledge that Mexican *émigrés* were approaching an Austrian Archduke at Trieste extinguished General Prim's interest in the expedition, and the British minister was frankly hostile to the idea of disturbing President Juarez for the furtherance of reactionary ambitions. Trouble had already been caused by the appearance at Vera Cruz of a rival President *in partibus infidelium;* and when the French insisted upon protecting a Mexican of doubtful antecedents for no better reason than his hostility to the government of his country, their allies abandoned the expedition and the sails of their transports faded away into the Gulf.

The French admiral was recalled, reinforcements sailed from Cherbourg, and General Lorencez was left looking for a royalist party in the hot distances of the *tierras calientes.* As the spring of 1862 deepened into summer, Mexico lay unmoved in the

sunshine. The *émigrés* at French headquarters grew
eloquent upon the approaching rising of their people.
A few Mexicans trailed in with their sandals and
their brown women, and some generals came over in
search of further promotion. Lorencez clamoured
for an Archduke to proclaim and inform his government that he was the master of Mexico: it was
a strange delusion. Late in April he moved up from
the coast to take possession of the country. Mexico
City was a hundred miles away, and he had six thousand men. In the first week of May they reached La
Puebla. The local royalists were curiously silent;
there was no loyal demonstration, and the bells were
not ringing. The Mexicans misunderstood their kind
invaders; it became necessary to force an entrance,
and in a scuffle for an outwork of the town the French
were beaten off. Lorencez fell back towards the sea,
and his name was tossed into the new grave of military reputations.

By a broad window on the Adriatic a tall young
man was watching the queer struggle in Mexico.
His name was Maximilian, and his brother was
Emperor of Austria. He had a dark young wife
(she was a Coburg from Brussels) and that diversity
of accomplishments which passes, in the case of
royalty, for culture. After a creditable career in the
Austrian navy (he looked well in uniform) and a
brief, embarrassed interlude in the Governor's palace
at Milan, he had withdrawn to a castle by the sea
where his good manners, his botanical collections and
the finest pair of whiskers in Europe impressed his
contemporaries with his aptitude for kingship. But
when vague murmurs of an empire in Mexico floated
down to Miramar, he replied that the Mexican people

must first express their will. Such familiarity with modern principles was highly creditable in a Hapsburg, and he watched without enthusiasm the manifestation of Mexican opinion which swept the French half-way back to the coast.

Lorencez had stumbled into defeat before La Puebla, and he dragged the Empire after him into war in Mexico. The first, instinctive movement of official opinion in France was an invincible feeling that military honour must be retrieved by a victory over the egregious subjects of President Juarez: after that, it would be time enough to consider the future of Mexico. As the French held their ground at Orizaba between the Mexicans and the mosquitoes of the fever zone, the Emperor from the cool shade of Vichy abounded in telegraphic advice upon the discomforts of the climate. He proposed a new tropical uniform; he suggested the construction of a line of railway from Vera Cruz; and the monopolised the only good map of Mexico which his country possessed. An army corps was concentrated at the ports, and the command of the new expeditionary force was transferred to General Forey; his divisional generals (the names were a trifle ominous) were Félix Douay and Bazaine. Late in the year they stumbled up to Orizaba, and in the first months of 1863 Forey prepared with Mexican deliberation to advance up-country. There was heavy fighting outside La Puebla; the town was fortified, and the French settled down to a siege of nine weeks. A relieving army hovered vaguely round; but it was beaten off by Bazaine, and La Puebla surrendered. The road to Mexico was open; and as the French marched westwards, President Juarez trailed out of the city

to the north, taking the republic in his waggons.
Early in June Bazaine and the advance guard rode
in; and when General Forey made his formal entry,
the Mexicans, with that courtesy which the Latin
races rarely refuse to the victor, received him with
clanging belfries and a hail of flowers. The invaders
were overwhelmed in a cataract of official compli-
ments, and the traditional superlatives of Spanish
courtesy so far affected the literal intelligence of
Forey that he reported to his Government that the
population was 'avide d'ordre, de justice, de liberté
vraie.' These laudable cravings were promptly
satisfied (since the climate was hardly favourable to
the full application of the principles of 1852) with
a nominated assembly of notables, who indicated the
dawn of a new, monarchical day by voting the Empire and appointing a Regency. Two hundred
gentlemen invited Maximilian to Mexico, and General Forey enjoyed the pleasurable emotions of a
king-maker. Paris was mildly startled by the news.
Ministers who had regarded the monarchist intrigue
as an excuse for a brilliant razzia were chilled by the
slow march on Mexico. A treaty and a triumphant
return of the army was all that they hoped for; and
when Forey performed in 1863 the promises of 1862,
he was all but disavowed. Napoleon acquiesced
politely in the new Empire; his general was thanked
and promoted Marshal; but he was recalled to France,
and in his place Bazaine entered the melancholy
dynasty of the Mexican command.

While French society was deriving a pleasant
thrill from the spectacle of Captain de Galliffet on
his crutches (his reminiscences of La Puebla became classical) and Napoleon was presenting

Mexican trophies to the Guard on the steps of his new *châlet* at Vichy, a picturesque deputation drove out from Trieste to Miramar and offered the Archduke a step in the *Almanach de Gotha*. Bazaine was sweeping the republicans into the corners of their country, and the offer had quite an air of reality. Maximilian and his wife made a gleeful tour of the Continent and collected the half-hearted felicitations of their relatives. At Brussels the judicious Leopold omitted a unique opportunity for lugubrious foresight, and in Paris Eugénie gave Maximilian a medal—'*Monseigneur, elle vous portera bonheur*'—but the Emperor seemed more concerned with limiting the liability of France than with the prospects of his young *protégé*. Yet there was a definite agreement for the maintenance of French troops in the country until 1867; and if the claims of France precluded all possibility that the Mexican budget would ever balance, the new Emperor seemed almost assured of a sufficiency of foreign bayonets. The mysterious transactions which preceded the displacements of royalty were prolonged into the spring of 1864. Precise old gentlemen exercised a wealth of conveyancing ingenuity on the renunciation of Maximilian's rights as a Hapsburg; and as the drafts went backwards and forwards between Miramar and the Hofburg, he seemed to lose interest in the adventure. But a French general brought him a curt reminder of his pledges; and his wife, whose mother had only been a Queen, was wild to be an Empress. The Mexicans became insistent, and Franz-Joseph came to Miramar to sign the final document. The two men parted in the station at Trieste, and on an April afternoon the new Emperor sailed in an Austrian

cruiser; in four years it brought him silently home
again.

His ship went down the Adriatic in the sunlight,
and in the long summer days they crossed the
Atlantic. A great mountain stood up out of the sea
behind the dismal port of Vera Cruz, and they went
ashore into the new Empire. The wind swept down
the wretched arches which were there to welcome
them, and that night the Empress wept. But they
drove into the capital in a clatter of Mexican lancers,
and far to the north Juarez and his republic were
hunted along the United States frontier. The censers
swung in the great Cathedral, and the new Empire
was consecrated and installed with every recommen-
dation to Mexican confidence (including an obstinate
refusal on the part of the United States to recognise
it).

The Imperial experiment in Mexico, which diverted
French investors during the years 1864 and 1865,
was a queer medley. Down on the coast, where the
great *zopilotes* flapped dismally over Vera Cruz, a
French base lay in the heat. The town was held by
a few Egyptians in white uniforms, and French
drafts hurried nervously through the fever zone into
the interior. A rudimentary armoured train steamed
warily up the little line to railhead, and the winding
roads led through the glare to Mexico. In the capital
a mild-eyed gentleman, whose profuse blonde beard
captivated native opinion and concealed a deficiency
of chin, discussed a perpetual insolvency with his
ministers or inspected strange units of Hungarian
hussars and Belgian legionaries. Sometimes he
rambled vaguely through his sun-baked territory.
There was a dull blaze of civil war at every point of

the horizon; but Maximilian's attention wandered
easily from politics to botany; and what should have
been an Emperor in the saddle was too often an intelligent tourist. He even ordered nightingales from
Styria to moderate to his Austrian ear the song of
Mexican birds. Yet his part in the queer piece was
faintly supernumerary. Cast to play Emperor of
Mexico, he could hardly put his name to a decree
without French money to finance the policy and
French bayonets to enforce the signature. The
extent of his authority coincided exactly with the area
covered by the French flying columns; and the real
master of the new Empire, who could win or lose it
a province by the movements of his troops, was a
heavy-eyed, burly man with a good Spanish accent
who lumbered into the palace in a French Marshal's
uniform and took from Mexico to Metz the name of
Bazaine. In the streets of the capital staff officers
rode up and down, and hands went smartly up to
French *képis* as the carriages went by behind the
jingling mules and Mexican *brunettes* bowed to their
visitors on their evening drive. There was an odd
little world of Parisians in exile who mitigated their
transportation with an intermittent opera season,
whilst the faint sounds of civil war floated down
to the capital from the north.

Juarez and his phantom republic flitted along the
frontier, and an interminable war of *guerrillas* and
flying columns trailed on. French opinion was insufficiently nourished upon an enervating diet of victories without finality and casualties without results,
and gradually the glamour of the Mexican adventure
began to fade. Its finance, which had opened with
high promises and low interest, declined upon the

vulgar stimulant of lottery bonds; and in the Chamber a Mexican debate became a dismal exercise in which M. Rouher displayed an unconvincing eloquence and sardonic republicans made Mexico a symbol of Imperial failure. The enterprise had the distasteful air of an expedition to stifle a republic; if Juarez lacked the principles of the Gracchi, he was at least capable of the mobility of de Wet; and even official members began to listen sceptically when ministers asked for further votes of credit. There was a new temper of economy in France, and even at the Tuileries the call of distant adventures was growing fainter. Fresh problems were forming in the mists of Central Europe, and the Rhine was nearer to Paris than the Rio Grande. This tendency, which became marked towards the end of 1865, was accelerated by the new tone of the United States. The Civil War had flickered out, and the French had concealed their preference for the South behind the decencies of international law. But the incidents of a long neutrality had put a manifest strain upon American affections. The Emperor had permitted his shadow to fall across the American continent, and the violation of that republican sanctuary by a foreign monarch scandalised Mr. Lincoln and his successor. The presence of a Hapsburg across the Mexican border was distasteful to the vicar of George Washington upon earth, and the tone of American diplomacy became audibly sharper. The war sputtered along the Rio Bravo del Norte; and as the gunfire rolled round Matamoros, the knowledge which American citizens had so recently gained of the subtleties of neutrality was exploited in favor of Mexican rebels, and Brownsville, Texas, took an obliging hand in the republican game. There was a curt refusal to recognise Maximilian, and a representative was even appointed by the State Department to follow the peripatetic government of Juarez. Napoleon lost interest in the argument: he valued American goodwill, and he valued more highly still the army which was scattered across Mexico. Early in 1866 France and the world were informed that French troops would be withdrawn, and the Mexican adventure dropped sharply to the haunting minor of its last movement.

The news came to Mexico in the summer heat, and Maximilian knew that his Empire had begun to fade. There was no money and no loyalty, and soon there would be no troops. His Empress flung bravely out of the country in a last effort to persuade the world that Maximilian was betrayed. The crowds were silent at Vera Cruz as she drove down, a little wild-eyed, to the quay; and she spoke little on the long voyage home. At Paris (their trouble had come from Paris, and she brought it back) they had sent no one to receive her at the station. The carriages were waiting somewhere else, and she drove off miserably in a cab to a vast new hotel. Eugénie called, and the visit left her shaken and wretched. For a day she waited for the summons to the Emperor, and then she drove to St. Cloud on an August afternoon. The Emperor was ill, but he saw her; and for two cruel hours she begged him to support her husband. It was, as Bazaine had called it, *une agonie dans l'impossible,* and the pale man with the large moustache would not, could not help her. When they brought her some *naranjada,* she looked oddly at the glass; and when she fainted and

Eugénie gave her water, she shrieked out in mad woman's fear of poison. There was a dreadful drive back to Paris, and she trailed off unhappily across the Continent to see the Pope. At every hour, in every face murderers from Mexico flitted before her, and in the Vatican she raved out her wretched fear. The old Pope watched her with sad eyes. A Cardinal fetched a doctor, and that night two women slept in the Vatican. It was a dreadful end to her little reign; but it was kinder than the news from Mexico.

The Empire was crumbling as the French marched down to the sea, and Bazaine presided gloomily over its disintegration. The new American cable brought to Maximilian the ghastly news from Europe; and he wandered vaguely from town to town, wavering between abdication and the hopeless gesture of resistance. His luggage was sent to the coast; but a crowd had cheered his name in Vienna, Franz-Joseph would hardly welcome his return, and his mother wrote that his position at home would be questionable. The French bugles died away down the long road to Vera Cruz, and early in 1867 he was left alone with Mexico. The republican tide crept slowly back over the country, and he went out of the city by the north road to Queretaro with fifteen hundred men. There was a hopeless siege and a surrender, and the republicans rode in. Maximilian was a prisoner, and nervous diplomats fluttered round the new government. A good deal was said about mercy and the importance of the ex-Emperor's relations in Europe, and considerable eloquence was displayed by two members of the Mexican Bar. But there was no change on the impassive, Indian face of Juarez: the republic had come back out of the north, and mercy was a new notion in Mexican politics. There was a court-martial before the glaring drop-scene of a provincial theatre, and a firing party; and as the smoke of an irregular volley drifted across Queretaro, the Mexican adventure ended. It was a morning of bright sunshine, and the cracked bells were tolling.

Maximilian was dead; Charlotte was mad; Morny was dead; Jecker dragged on until the Commune shot him; the French dead lay in their graves; and to Napoleon the sudden fall of an Empire in Mexico must have come with the vague menace of lightning below the horizon

XIV

THE note of the later Empire (and in 1863 it began to swing slowly into the last phase) was uncertainty. New questions seemed to crowd upon it to which the simple catchwords of the *coup d'état* provided no answer. The Emperor was an aging man; the long moustache began to droop, and the hair hung raggedly above his ears. The mild manner was becoming touched with hesitancy, and when public business forced him to decisions, he fumbled a little with the problems of French policy. The slow drift of the Empire seemed to be floating him into a new world, among strange faces. But M. Mérimée, who had an eye for character, could see the truth: '*Le maître n'aime pas les visages nouveaux.*' The old *personnel* was hastily adapted to the new problems; an old minister (it was the secret of Napoleon's failure to reconcile the Empire with democracy) was instructed to strike a new attitude; and his sovereign returned with obvious relief to the less exacting companionship of Julius Caesar.

The elections of 1863 confronted the Empire with the problem of a Parliament. Napoleon was disinclined as yet to become a parliamentary monarch of the English type. But although his ministers continued to govern France without condescending to explain themselves in the Chamber, its existence was recognised by the appointment of a *Ministre d'État* whose functions, since he predominated in Council and spoke for the Government in the House, approximated to the duties of a Prime Minister. The first nominee was M. Billault, whose talent for exposition had even found reasons for the earlier phases of French policy in Mexico—'*Pas un homme d'État,*' in M. Mérimée's judgment, '*mais . . . un instrument merveilleux entre les mains d'un homme d'État.*' But he died before the Chamber met, and with the nomination of his successor the broad shadow of M. Rouher fell across the Second Empire. To the end of that long career (and before it was over, the Empire itself had ended) he remained, as he had begun, a successful lawyer with a professional aptitude for detail and a forensic profusion of second-rate reasoning. Never at a loss for an argument and untroubled by the doubts which oppress finer, if less professional, intelligences, his burly figure dominated the Chamber, and in the steady boom of his uninspired, his inexhaustible eloquence the later Empire had found its accompaniment.

The session opened in a mood of mild Liberalism. Imperial policy seemed to be passing into a tone of English sobriety and M. Fould was effecting Gladstonian economies at the Ministry of Finance; indirect communications were even opened with Hawarden through M. Mérimée, who got his clothes at Poole's, and Mr. Panizzi, who got his ideas from Paris. M. Thiers, a pontifical little figure with gleaming spectacles and a wintry smile, enlightened his countrymen in speeches of enormous length upon the march of progress; there were understood to be five '*libertés nécessaires*'—of the individual, the press, the vote, the Deputy, and the Chamber. But the real movement of the Empire towards constitutionalism was determined less obtrusively. M. de Morny continued his discreet conversations with M. Ollivier. Claiming credit for the dismissal of Persigny, who had become a retired Duke and a grotesque incarnation of reaction, he bluntly requested his young friend to collaborate *'pour organiser la liberté,'* and as an evidence of his good faith he put M. Ollivier in charge of a Government measure which legalised trade unions and conferred upon an ungrateful proletariat the right to strike. The result upon M. Ollivier's relations with his republican colleagues was immediate: suspicions were aroused, he parted from M. Jules Favre after one of those public quarrels which enliven French parliamentary life, and through the year 1864 he drifted steadily into the orbit of Morny. Republican pedantry was distasteful to a practical intelligence, and if the Empire could be reconstructed upon Liberal lines, M. Ollivier was prepared to take a hand in the work. But it did not begin. Quite suddenly, early in 1865, M. de Morny passed out of politics; and when the experiment was tried, it came too late.

The Duke (they were all dukes now) was not well. A few nights earlier he had been in his box for the *première* of M. Offenbach's *Belle Hélène;* M. Rochefort was in the house that evening, and his face (he wrote impertinences in the *Figaro*) haunted Morny a little. Doctor Oliffe was beginning to look anxious, and there was a consultation. His lady was seen at a ball; but he had forced her to go, and in his neat, curt way he prepared for his *'départ.'* They burned his papers in the room, as he lay back and watched them; Flahaut, his father, came to take his hand;

and on a winter evening the footmen were lined up
in the great hall, as a carriage drove up from the
Tuileries and two figures went up the broad staircase.
'*La femme montait droite et fière, enveloppée de ses
noires mantilles d'espagnole; l'homme se tenait à la
rampe, plus lent et fatigué, le collet de son pardessus
clair remontant sur un dos un peu voûté qu'agitait un
sanglot convulsif.*' The brothers parted; and in the
parting Napoleon lost his shrewdest man. On a cold
March day (there was a little sunshine as they left
the Madeleine) the long line of bayonets went up
the road to Père Lachaise, as the Empire wore
mourning for Morny; but almost it might have worn
it for itself.

A little wearily the Emperor went back to his
papers, and the movement towards a Liberal Empire
was sharply checked. Morny was no longer there to
introduce M. Ollivier, and Prince Napoleon was an
inadequate advocate of progress. His manners had
never been good; his political activity was normally
confined to resignations; he had the air of an *Égalité*
presumptive, and when he startled an audience at
Ajaccio with a radical speech, the Emperor disavowed
him and M. Rouher was left in charge of his grateful
countrymen. One could leave so much to M. Rouher;
he found reasons for everything, and if he hardly
directed the Empire towards progress, it was for the
sufficient reason that there were so few precedents
for progress. If he were ever guilty (and few lawyers are) of political generalisation, he was probably
of the opinion expressed by King Louis Philippe to
a young inquirer: '*Soyez sans inquiétude, jeune
homme; la France est un pays qu'on mène avec des
fonctionnaires publics.*' At any rate he left his mas-

The Emperor and the Prince Imperial

From a photograph

ter to himself; and in the days when the polite world was thrilled by Gounod's Mass and M. Théophile Gautier was seen at the Salon, 'a "shocking bad hat" attached to the back of his huge head by some process of adhesion known to himself alone, masses of dishevelled hair hanging anywhere but in the right place, and catalogue in hand, making and destroying reputations by the glance of his eye or the stroke of his pen,' Napoleon escaped from the tedium of administration into the more distinguished leisure of a historian. Early in 1865 his subjects were rejoiced by the appearance of the first volume of his *Vie de César*. Its loyal readers were presented with a doctrine of Caesarism which took a slightly Messianic tinge and hinted at the resemblance (which had escaped earlier writers) between the murder in the Senate House and the darker crimes of St. Helena and Calvary. Taking a longish run before delivering his actual theme, he began his story with the foundation of Rome and, noting the significant succession of a monarchy, a republic and an Empire, travelled sedately towards Caesar through regions hallowed by the measured tread of Niebuhr and Dr. Arnold. The margins displayed a creditable profusion of erudite notes, and the text contained a reputable range of historical analogy, although the learned author was precluded by the exigencies of his foreign policy from developing the comparison (so dear to Continental scholars) of Carthage to Great Britain. Caesar, when he appeared, had a faintly Napoleonic manner; something of a *littérateur* and more of a fatalist, he was familiar with the principles of the *coup d'état* and had almost assimilated the doctrine of nationality. The author's views were visible

22

beneath the scholarship of his collaborators. The
portrait of the artist was excellent; but it was less
easy to reconcile it with the hard features of Julius
Caesar. The Parisians of 1865 were less critical;
there was something mildly entertaining in their
master's erudite diversions, and one could make little
jokes about *Madame César*. MM. Émile Augier,
Octave Feuillet, and Jules Sandeau were honoured
with presentation copies, and the straining limits of
the French language barely sufficed to contain their
transports. Madame George Sand scandalised her
republican friends with the revelation that, as literature, it was faultless, and only consoled them with
the prediction that it would not sell; whilst from
beyond the Rhine came the solemn reverberations of
academic courtesy, as Professor Ritschl and his
friends expressed their gratitude above signatures
that are more familiar among the staccato objurga-
tions of controversial footnotes. Archaeology even
filtered as far as the great house-party at Compiègne,
where the autumn charade (M. Viollet-le-Duc was
generally so clever about the *tableaux vivants,* but
this year M. de Massa had written a whole *revue*) was
called *Les Commentaires de César* and Madame de
Metternich sang a song about the cab strike and the
Prince Imperial, as *l'Avenir,* appeared as a Grenadier
of the Guard. A second volume followed early in
1866, in which the awkward question of assassination
was tactfully eluded by interrupting the narrative at
the crossing of the Rubicon. The word had strange
memories for Napoleon, and his Caesar was provoked
to civil war in circumstances which bore a startling
resemblance to the December days of 1851, when a
Prince-President wrote *Rubicon* upon a file of

papers and handed them to his friends at the Élysée.
Caesar's campaigns in Gaul were patiently narrated,
and the footnotes contained copious evidence of the
official taste for archaeology which had set exasperated Engineer officers digging in *tumuli* and sent
Baron Stoffel of the Artillery, who was so soon to
have another, a more immediate mission beyond the
Rhine, on little errands of research round France in
quest of Caesar's camps. The book compelled the
blushing admiration of Professor Zumpt, and even
Mommsen complimented the Emperor on his scholarship. All Germany, the international, scholarly
Germany of 1866 whose arid ingenuity lies embalmed
in the *apparatus criticus* of every classic, poured its
gratitude into the Tuileries letter-bag, and from the
Emperor's correspondence it almost seemed as
though Europe from the Rhine to the Russian
frontier was populated by an inpecunious race of
scholars animated by a single ambition to possess
(without paying for it) a copy of his book: a com-
poser even asked leave to dedicate a Julius Caesar
march.

By the mild light of the later Empire Napoleon
sat writing in his study. M. Émile Ollivier was
struggling with his conscience, and M. Rouher was
drowning democracy with the measured enunciation
of the obvious. But as they looked up, a long shadow
fell across the European scene and Prussia came
slowly from the corner of the stage. *Un formidable
réaliste avait frappé les trois coups.* His name was
Otto Eduard Leopold von Bismark-Schönhausen.

XV

The appearances of Prussia in history have something of the suddenness, if not all the agility, of the bad fairy. The polite pantomime of the Eighteenth Century had been sharply interrupted in 1740 as King Frederick the Great emerged from the trapdoor and crouched for his spring on Silesia. The Prussian effort after Jena, which confronted Napoleon in seven years with an unbroken front of German resistance, was a performance of astounding rapidity. And there was something of the same quality in the sudden emergence of Prussia which filled the years between 1864 and the end of the Second Empire.

Prussia in 1850, with a king whose exuberant eloquence has been variously interpreted as a symptom of Romanticism, dementia, alcoholism, and the Hohenzollern manner, was a secondary state. It had an unaccountable legacy of military achievement; but Blücher and Ziethen had faded into history, and Rossbach and Ligny seemed almost as distant from contemporary Prussia as the broad sweep of the operations of Gustavus Adolphus from the mild activities of Swedish policy. Its interests were dissipated by a frontier of eccentric conformation, and the motives of Prussian policy seemed mostly to be found in the will of Austria. It was a dismal fate for the heirs of a great tradition. Old gentlemen in

lecture-rooms flavoured their scholarship with politics, and a strong tide of patriotism began to set from
the universities. But the world of 1850 seemed
determined to exist without assistance from Prussia.
Even in Germany it stood for nothing. There had
been a flicker of nationalism in 1848, which set Prince
Hohenlohe complaining that a man 'could not say
abroad "I am a German," could not pride himself
that the German flag was flying from his vessel,
could have no German consul in time of need, but
had to explain "I am a Hessian, a Darmstädter, a
Buckebürger: my Fatherland was once a great and
powerful country, now it is shattered into eight and
thirty splinters." ' But Prussia had not yet mastered
the German idea. Nationalism got involved somehow with democracy, a Parisian import which (outside South Germany) was regarded with grave
suspicion, and Prussia settled down once more to
rotate demurely in the orbit of Vienna.

Gradually, as Europe drifted under the control of
Napoleon III., a change came. Discreet encourage-
ments of Prussia were wafted from Paris to Berlin,
as the Emperor, who based French policy upon his
maritime alliance with Great Britain, felt gently for
an ally on the Continent. There was a show of
independence in some fiscal negotiations with Vienna;
and when Austria began to waver towards the Allies
in the Crimean War, a drinking squire in the
Prussian diplomatic service (the name was von Bismarck and the drink was champagne and beer)
manipulated the minor German states, controlled the
Diet, and checked the drift of Austria by the insistence of Prussia upon strict neutrality. His
design, since his imagination was obsessed by the

crushing war on two fronts which had broken Frederick in the Seven Years' War, was to rest Prussian policy upon a firm alliance with Russia; and for the first time in 1855 he earned for his government the gratitude of St. Petersburg. Berlin was slowly mounting in the scale, and Germany passed under the joint control of Austria and Prussia. When the march of the French across North Italy alarmed German patriots in 1859, Prussia caught and led the national drift; Prussian troop-movements on the Rhine checked Napoleon after Solferino, and Prussian policy forced him into peace. For the first time Prussia had stood for Germany. Von Moltke and von Roon were taking their places among the soldiers. But von Bismarck was playing with his bear-cubs in the embassy at St. Petersburg; his master governed Prussia with the precarious authority of a Regent; and for a few years longer Prussian policy lingered on in incoherence. Then, when a new King brought in a new minister, Bismarck became Prussia; and in eight years Prussia had become Germany.

In the first movement he put his own house in marching order. Berlin in 1862 contained a Parliament which (such was the perilous infection of the age) was in violent conflict with its King. His wishes had been scandalously disregarded by the electors; and since they related to a vital, almost a sacred (since it was a military) matter, he persisted in them. The mobilisation of 1859, which had checked the French on the Adige and made the Peace of Villafranca, was an imperfect operation; it had revealed the weakness of the Prussian army, and the King and his military advisers resolved upon a drastic reorganisation of the forces. Military reform is the most costly of all government activities, and the *bourgeois* parliamentarians of Berlin had no enthusiasm for the high taxes which denote military efficiency or for the discomforts which accompany military service. The resulting conflict aligned against King William almost the whole civilian population of Prussia, and it became the congenial business of Bismarck to restore to Prussian politics the enviable simplicity of the drill-ground. A *Junker* training had impressed him with the sanctity of royal wishes, and he was coldly determined that Prussia should have its army. The battalions which his master regarded with simple piety as the instruments (if adequately armed) of the Most High were in Bismarck's view the last and most useful branch of the Foreign Office. War was a form of policy, and without an army (since Prussia had not the preposterous prestige which enabled Lord Palmerston to dictate to Europe with a peace establishment of 100,000 men) Bismarck would find himself reduced to the futility of Alberoni or the expedients of Cavour. It was a good cause; and as he defied his Parliament in attitudes which owed something to Strafford, he exercised to the full his native gifts of insolence.

But the affairs of Europe found more useful employment for him. Beyond the frontier Russia was at grips with a Polish insurrection, and French policy precipitated St. Petersburg into the waiting embraces of Berlin. In the years which followed the Crimean War Napoleon had sedulously cultivated Prince Gortschakoff and his Czar. But at the faint, far call of Polish nationalism he seemed to sacrifice French interests to modern principles. The Russian alliance,

upon which his uncle had built a new Europe, was
almost in his grasp. Sebastopol was half forgotten,
and the two Emperors seemed to control Europe
from either end. But somewhere in the mists of
the Vistula a nation was struggling to be free, and
Napoleon forgot all his statecraft in his theories.
He was the man of his age; he could never forget
(had he not made Italy?) that it was the age of
nationalities: 'I think on Poland as I thought in
1831.' He pestered the Russians with Notes, protests, circulars, and special missions, as they entered
with gusto upon the congenial business of repression.
But humanity was an injudicious guide in 1863 (and
possibly at even later dates) for foreign policy, and
the Emperor's initiative chilled Russian friendship
and gave to Bismarck his first opportunity. Whilst
France pullulated with generous emotions and British statesmen dispensed those heartening phrases
which they so rarely supported with British troops,
the Prussian frontier was closed to Polish rebels.
Bismarck abstained, since the master of Posen could
sympathise with the master of Warsaw, from the
despatch of humanitarian essays to St. Petersburg,
and there was a helpful *cordon* of Prussian frontier-
guards on the Polish border. His calculated kindness had its reward: when Bismarck performed a
service, he made a friend. Napoleon, with a less
certain touch, had failed to grasp his allies. He
had shared a war with England; but his friends in
London were startled by the doctrinaire flavour of
his policy and the aimless construction of armoured
warships, the futile gesture of the fortification of
Cherbourg. He had befriended Russia after the
Crimea; but Gortschakoff was chilled by the Polish

aberration. He had cheated Italy; but the annexation of Savoy cost him half the credit of Magenta;
and gradually, as the French sentries stood before
the Vatican, he let the bright waters of Italian gratitude stray and vanish in the sands of the Roman
question. Bismarck was less impulsive in his benefactions, less interested, perhaps, in the goodness of
the deed than in the richness of the reward. But in
1863 he had served Russia well; and until he left
office a generation later in a changed world (and
he, more than any other man, had changed it) Prussia
knew no fear for the long line of her eastern frontier,
and leaving Russia in grateful inactivity behind her,
turned westwards upon Europe a bright, acquisitive
gaze. Late in the year it encountered a vague,
familiar outline, as a king died in Denmark and be-
queathed to Europe the tangled inheritance of the
Elbe Duchies.

The problem of Schleswig-Holstein, which provoked a volume of state-papers almost equal to the
area of the Duchies, had whitened the hair of diplomats for fifteen years. Its complexities, which could
have been handled by any competent solicitor, were
publicly referred to in tones of amused awe. Prince
Albert was believed to have taken a thorough knowledge of it to his grave at Frogmore; and Lord
Palmerston, although still capable of a stirring
speech on it, had forgotten the point. But its elements were strangely simple. Two Duchies lay
between North Germany and the Danish frontier.
The King of Denmark held them as Duke by a
cession of 1460, and in moments of Danish patriotism
there was always an effort to absorb the Duchies in
the Danish kingdom. German opinion was equally

interested, since ethnology came into fashion, in their
fate; and German nationalism was usually expressed
in an effort to resume for Germany the lost Duchies.
In 1848, when tempers mounted in both countries,
there was a clash of these conflicting tendencies. A
pretender seized the Duchies in the German interest;
the Danes contested the decision; and in a queer,
half-hearted war, which swayed obscurely up and
down the peninsula for three years, Prussians
and Saxons and Holsteiners with Prussian officers
struggled in forgotten battles with the Danes for the
disputed lands. But Europe intervened; there was
a conference in London, and in 1852 the Treaty of
London restored the Duchies to the Danish crown.
The pretender sold his claims for a generous remit-
tance of *rixdalers,* and under the clearing sky Denmark re-entered upon its possession. But German
patriots, 'painfully conscious,' as Mr. Disraeli con-
descendingly observed, 'that they do not exercise that
influence in Europe which they believe is due to the
merits, moral, intellectual, and physical, of forty millions of population, homogeneous and speaking the
same language,' were still muttering about Holstein;
and when the Danish king with obvious good sense
(since Schleswig was predominantly Danish in population and Holstein predominantly German) incorporated Schleswig in his kingdom of Denmark
and granted local self-government to his duchy of
Holstein, German opinion grew shrill in its resentment of this scandalous partition of the Duchies. It
was indelicate, it was quite unpardonably crude, in
the government of Copenhagen to solve a cherished
European problem by a sudden application of common-sense; worse still, it ignored a treaty of 1460,

and the reckless Danes were recalled from reality to politics by a curt demand of the German Diet that their new constitution should be withdrawn. There was a mild flutter in Europe, and even England caught the infection of excitement. It was barely four months since the Prince of Wales had taken a Danish wife and Mr. Tennyson, the Laureate, had informed the world that the subjects of Queen Victoria were, in spite of their mixed ethnological origins, all of them Danes in their welcome of Princess Alexandra. Lord Palmerston spoke movingly in the House of Commons of 'the independence, the integrity, and the rights of Denmark,' and added with a menace which its extreme familiarity deprived of none of its effect, 'that if any violent attempt were made to overthrow those rights, and interfere with that independence, those who made the attempt would find in the result that it would not be Denmark alone with which they would have to contend.' The rosy gentlemen of 1863 cheered loudly; but their favourite's prediction was dismally unfulfilled. The Danish resistance was stiffened by the brave language of Lord Palmerston; the Germans insisted and directed Hanover and Saxony to enforce the decision of the Diet by an occupation of Holstein; and at that supreme moment the King of Denmark died. His death brought into the field a pretender to the Duchies, the son of the former claimant, who gravely contended that his father's sale of the claim could not be taken to include the rights of a son. This solemn nonsense was countenanced in Germany, and the young man entered Holstein in the wake of the Saxon army. But whilst the pretender was striking ducal attitudes in Kiel, a colder intelligence surveyed

the problem from Berlin, and Bismarck resolved that
Prussia should take a hand. Troubled waters were
eminently congenial to his fishing, and he came
sharply to the conclusion that if the Duchies were
to change hands, Prussia could find a place for them.
His ruling motive was rather a desire to exclude the
pretender, who would have created in Schleswig-
Holstein yet another minor German state that took
its tune from Austria, than any long prevision of
a Prussian navy with a base at Kiel. The diplomats
began to flit about between the capitals; Fleury
brought good advice from Paris, and Lord Wode-
house urged Denmark to be gentle with the Germans.
British opinion, always so sympathetic to the resistance of small nations to other empires, had been
prepared by Palmerston for heroic intervention; but
the Government could hardly move without the other
parties to the treaty of 1852. Russia was silent, and
even Napoleon seemed strangely inactive. He had
a vague notion that the population of the Duchies
was predominantly German; if that were so, intervention on the Danish side would be a sin against
the doctrine of nationality. But the true cause of
his inaction was more human. England had disappointed him earlier in the year when he sought support against Russia in the cause of Poland, and he
was disinclined to oblige Lord Palmerston by joining England in support of Denmark. 'He felt himself' (Mr. Disraeli could see the point) 'in a false
position with respect to his own subjects, because he
had experienced a great diplomatic discomfiture,' and
he was in no mood for fresh adventures. British
heroics dwindled into protests; Lord Palmerston was
sobered into a cautious neutrality; and the tone of

Germany, when Denmark was deserted, rose sharply. Prussia asked leave to enforce the decision of the Diet; the Austrians, unwilling that King William should figure as the sole champion of German rights, joined in the application; and the combined forces of the two monarchies were authorised to invade and occupy the Duchies in the name of Germany. The result, since the Danish army had a strength of only 40,000 men, was hardly doubtful.

Early in 1864 the troop-trains were rolling northwards across Germany. Three army corps, with von Wrangel in command, were charged with the dismal duty of crushing Denmark; and the Prussian Guard moved on Kiel, as the Austrians on their left crossed the Elbe at Hamburg and went north. They marched proudly forward past the Saxon cantonments in Holstein; but there was little scope in a narrow peninsula for brilliance against a retreating enemy, and the Prussian *verve* of 1870 hardly appears (although the Red Prince was a corps commander) in the cautious operations of 1864. In the first days of February they fumbled at the fortified line of the Danevirke; but the Danes slipped away to the north, fell back before the invasion, and turned at Düppel in the Sundevit to bar the road to Copenhagen and the Islands. The redoubts of Düppel, which lined the little hills above Sonderburg, were a faint reflection of the lines of Torres Vedras; and as the Prussians lumbered after them, the Danes stood to their guns. Outside the lines of Düppel, Schleswig was almost cleared. The invaders even exceeded their authority by passing the frontier of the Danish kingdom, pressing forward into Jutland, and reaching Kolding. Europe vociferated its protests; but no

Power moved. Bismarck was bland and the war went on. As Earl Russell drafted those clever Notes of his and wrestled silently with the German sympathies of his sovereign (Albert, she felt sure, would have sided with Bismarck even though Albert Edward's pretty wife was a Dane), the guns were booming in the green fields before Düppel. The Danish lines held for two months; but in the last week of April they fell, and Prussia came to a conference in London with all the comfort of a *fait accompli*. For two months more the collective wisdom of Europe struggled with the Duchies. The French (how amusing it seemed in 1864 and how like the fantastic Emperor) proposed a *plébiscite*. At one moment, after the Danes had beaten the Austrians at sea off Heligoland, Lord Palmerston looked fierce and threatened Austria with the Channel Fleet. 'I determined,' as he informed his Foreign Secretary with sporting jocularity, 'to make a notch off my own bat.' But he could hardly bombard Vienna and Berlin from the sea; the guns of the *Warrior* did not range far into Central Europe. A field-force of 20,000 men was useless without an ally on the Continent; and the Emperor, who might have moved, was sitting gloomily in Paris, tracing new frontiers on the map of Schleswig-Holstein. Diplomacy wrung its hands and withdrew once more, and the war was resumed. There was a last flicker of Danish bravery at Alsen; but the pace was faster, since von Wrangel had gone home and the Red Prince was in command with Count von Moltke at his elbow. The war died down; there was an armistice, and by the Peace of Vienna the King of Denmark ceded his Duchies to the conquerors.

Düppel was the first part of the Prussian trilogy.
Bismarck had fought his war, and in the last months
of 1864 Schleswig-Holstein was the joint property
of Austria and Prussia: it was a queer result. But
the stake in the game was not a few fields north of
Hamburg or a port on the Baltic coast. He was
playing steadily for control of the German machine,
of the complex of kingdoms and duchies which regu-
lated their common affairs in the Diet of Frankfort
under a system which neatly combined the verbiage
of a parliament with the deliberation of diplomacy.
At present Prussia shared it with Austria; but
Austria could be beaten in the field if one had an
army, an ally and a *casus belli*. Prussia had (General
von Roon had seen to it) an army; and General
Count Helmuth von Moltke, who was always writing
in his room, had a sheaf of plans. The ally, since
Russia was always too late and (when she arrived)
too powerful, must be Italy; and the awkward *condominium* in the Duchies could provide a quarrel
whenever one was wanted. The parts for the new
piece were obvious. Victor Emmanuel was to play
Pylades to King William's Orestes, while Napoleon
was cast for a thinking part in attitudes of dignified
neutrality; and during 1865 Bismarck attended dili-
gently to the rehearsals. The manipulation of Italy
was easy, since the direction of Italian policy was
determined by an irresistible craving for Venice, and
Prussia felt no difficulty in promising this amputa-
tion from the territory of her late ally. The Prussian
ambassador appeared in Florence with a discreet
offer for the hand of Italy, who replied with becoming modesty that the kind gentleman must ask the
Emperor Napoleon. So French neutrality became

the chief essential in the new combination, and in the next phase Bismarck devoted his ingenuity to obtaining it. The Emperor on general principles had always been favourable to Prussia; as a statesman of the old type he welcomed this solid counterpoise to Austria, and his private convictions were gratified by the spectacle of a busy German state which might one day do for Germany what Piedmont had done for Italy. The revelation of St. Helena had included *'l'agglomération, la concentration des mêmes peuples géographiques';* Napoleon I. had prophesied a new European order based upon *'l'agglomération et la confédération des grands peuples.'* German unity was a respectable cause over which an intellectual Emperor might preside if he wished to keep abreast of the time; and he was always inclined to graciousness when his callers came from Berlin. King William had displayed his excellent manners at Compiègne; M. Bismarck was a most entertaining person; and when General von Roon came to the French manœuvres of 1864, there was a charming scene at Châlons on a September day with the little Prince Imperial stretching up to hand the Legion of Honour to his father's guest—they made quite an anniversary of it in Germany, since it was the second of the month and six years later the Emperor spent it at Sedan. With this amiable mood prevailing at the Tuileries French diplomats were politely receptive when Bismarck, in his expansive way, began to speak casually of French advances on the Rhine or in French-speaking countries. His policy commenced to defer elaborately to the Empire, and his ambassador in Paris professed an admiration of Eugénie that was faintly grotesque. Late in 1865, when the

Court was at Biarritz, he came himself to consult the
dull eyes of the oracle. The big, bald man drove up
to the Villa Eugénie; and as the great Biscayan
rollers broke along the coast, he talked interminably
to the Emperor. There were no promises; but as
their talk trailed slowly across the map, Bismarck
could see that Venice still haunted *il muto Imperator,*
that he would abet a war in which Venice might be
won for Italy. *Le spectre de Venise erre dans
les salles des Tuileries.* It had beckoned once;
and Napoleon sent Maximilian to Mexico. It
beckoned again; he stared and sent the Prussians to
Sadowa.

That autumn there were storms along the Basque
coast. The waves thundered outside the Emperor's
windows, and Bismarck went back to Berlin. He
returned with persistent gallantry to the courtship
of Italy. But the Italians were unnaturally coy, full
of suspicion, nervous that their martial wooer had no
real intention of fighting Austria. Eager to prove
his sincerity (the situation had all the charm of
novelty) the Prussian minister hastened to pick his
quarrel with Vienna, and the invaluable Duchies came
in play once more. The *condominium* in Schleswig-
Holstein had ended in partition; after a mild course
of medicinal diplomacy, with a royal conference at
Carlsbad and an inter-allied convention at Gastein,
Austria had taken Holstein and left Schleswig to
Prussia. But such cures are rarely final, and early
in 1866 the effects of the treatment began to wear
off. The Austrian command in Altona permitted a
public statement of the claims, the forgotten claims,
of the pretender to the Duchies for which Germany
had gone crusading against Denmark in 1864. Bis-

23

marck was scandalised. After the war, it seemed, his tender conscience had been tortured by legal doubts as to the true ownership of Schleswig-Holstein, and his torments had been allayed by the opinion of some obliging jurists in Berlin, who advised that the King of Denmark had been the rightful owner after all. That might have seemed, in view of the fact that he had been expelled by force of arms, unfortunate. But Bismarck, haunted by few idle regrets, derived infinite consolation from the fact that the Danish title, which was above suspicion, had been transferred by treaty to Austria and Prussia. It followed that in tolerating the antics of the pretender in the Austrian zone, von Gablenz was trifling with sedition, and a solemn complaint was transmitted to Vienna. The debate rapidly became acrimonious, and Italy was invited to observe the drift of Prussia towards war. The effect upon Italy was immediate. Napoleon was hastily consulted as to the propriety of a combination with Prussia against Austria; and when he blessed the union, Italy yielded gracefully to the embraces of Bismarck. An Italian soldier appeared in Berlin; his mission related to the technical improvements in the Prussian needle-gun, but his time was spent almost entirely in the more enlivening company of Count Bismarck. Their conversation strayed from the needle-gun into *haute politique*. By a fortunate coincidence General Govone was empowered to negotiate, and in April, 1866, they signed a secret treaty of alliance for a war against Austria, provided (Italy was a trifle impatient) that it opened within three months.

The problem before Bismarck had passed from the

uncertainties of diplomacy into the more congenial precision of arithmetic. If he could force Austria into war within twelve weeks, he would have Italy for an ally. He steadied his hand, made a war in nine weeks, and won it in seven weeks more. In the spring days of 1866, when the Prussian artillery was buying horses and the Austrians were moving cavalry up into the northern provinces, both sides turned nervous eyes to Paris. The Emperor might throw an army into either scale, and he was the master of Italian policy. Prince Metternich, whose lady stood so well at Court, fluttered round with offers from Vienna; and the Prussian ambassador asked Napoleon to name his price. He fumbled a little with the maps (the Emperor was not well that year) and muttered something about Belgium—or Luxemburg, perhaps—or was there a town or so in the Saar basin? It had been so simple to make one's terms with Cavour in 1858. But somehow the world seemed more crowded now; the provinces which one might have asked for were full of Germans, and it would be awkward for the high-priest of nationalism to transgress the sacred dogma of nationality. *'Ah! si vous aviez une Savoie!'* said the Emperor a little helplessly, and fell back into silence. He made no terms with Prussia, because (it was a strange confession for an Emperor, and his country never forgave it) he was disinterested. He was asked to approve the reconquest of Venice and the promotion of Prussia in Germany; and since he approved already, there was no need to purchase his approval. Besides, the Prussians might not win; one must wait for the result; as always, *il ne faut rien brusquer.* Napoleon was ill that summer, and he had a sick

man's fear of sharp decisions. Anxious ambassadors
flitted in and out of his study; but they saw little in
his dull eyes beyond the reflection of their own uncertainty. Sometimes he dropped a hint about the
Rhine or seemed to promise Venice to Italy without
a war. Only once, as the troop-train rumbled slowly
across Prussia and the *Süd Armee* stood to its arms
in the Italian sunshine, the veil seemed lifted at the
Tuileries, and the Emperor emerged from his inaction. There had been a little trouble in the Chamber, where M. Thiers, whose taste was always for an
active foreign policy, pointed a menacing finger
towards the lengthening shadow of Prussia and re-
proved the Empire for its half-hearted expedients.
Napoleon replied with a firm speech at a provincial
meeting, and a bucolic audience at an agricultural
show was startled and edified by an emphatic statement of its sovereign's detestation of the treaty-
system of 1815. With a sudden recollection of his
responsibilities as the arbiter of Europe he invited
the world once more to bring its troubles to a congress. Prussia and Italy had mobilised; yet both
accepted the Emperor's invitation. The neutral
Powers consented to attend; but Austria, with an
angry fling of the madness which had thrown her
into war in 1859, refused the congress unless it were
pledged beforehand to maintain the *status quo*. The
Emperor could do no more, and in two weeks Central Europe was at war.

The war of 1866 was designed to secure for Prussia
the mastery of Germany, and Bismarck's objectives
were neatly combined in the *casus belli*. A promise
of Venice and the quarrel with Austria over Holstein
brought Italy into play. The German states were

still neutral. But when Prussian troops moved into
Holstein and challenged the Austrian garrison,
Austria went in quest of allies to the German Diet.
There was a vote in June upon Prussia's action, and
South Germany went into the war behind Austria
whilst Saxony and the blind King of Hanover waited
for the first impact of the Prussian forces. Before
the month was out, the Hanoverians had fought at
Langensalza and were prisoners; the Saxons were
falling back into Austria, and the Prussian armies
were feeling their slow way down through the hills
into Bohemia. Away to the south in Italy the Archduke Albert had broken the Italians at Custozza;
the Austrian cavalry went sabring down the road to
Villafranca, and the old taste of victory came back
to the white coats. But a victory less in Italy and
two corps more in the north might have saved Austria.
The Prussians trailed slowly down into Bohemia, and
von Benedek stood uneasily on the defensive. Gradually, as the needle-guns cracked in the green valleys
of the Riesengebirge, he was driven in upon the position of Königgrätz. The Prussians began to feel
their advantage at Gitschin and Nachod; and
although the Austrians held their ground at Trau-
tenau, Benedek could see the slow converging of
defeat. He had lost heavily in the opening movements, and he telegraphed desperately to Vienna for
an immediate peace. Franz-Joseph answered him on
July 1 with curt orders for a battle; and twenty-
four hours later, when a royal train steamed into
Vienna in the dark hours of a summer night, the
King of Saxony found the station all decorated with
flowers to receive him, and on the platform he could
see by the flaring lights an Emperor whose face was

as white as his uniform.   Franz-Joseph had the news
of his battle, and its name was Sadowa.

As the Austrians stumbled back towards Vienna
and the astonished eyes of Europe followed them
down the dusty roads, the French Emperor made a
hesitating reappearance on the stage.   It had been
his design to let the war take its course and, when the
combatants were panting, to make a dazzling re-
entry as the *deus ex machina* whose neat adjustment
of the crisis would close the play; and he seemed
to have his cue when the Austrians, in an adroit
attempt to disengage themselves from the war on the
southern front and throw all their weight northwards
against the Prussians, invited Napoleon to mediate
and surrendered Venice to the French to abide the
mediator's award.   Prussia and Italy were promptly
notified of the Emperor's good offices, and he waited
with dignity to award the prizes.   In his old impetuous mood he might have struck a firmer attitude.
The Prussian armies were in Bohemia and the
western frontier lay open to the French; mobilisation
and a peremptory summons to Berlin would have
satisfied French vanity, which smarted a little under
the sudden revelation that other armies could win
victories in Europe.   But there was an uneasy feeling
in Paris that supplies were low and munitions which
might have served on the Rhine had been diverted to
Mexico; the Emperor dragged wearily to Council in
cruel pain; and when he saw a diplomat from Vienna,
he could only mutter, '*Je ne suis pas prêt à la
guerre.*'   The French mediation, since there was to
be no armed intervention, trailed off into diplomacy;
and since Bismarck was disinclined to be given prizes
which he had already taken, the Emperor was left

making dignified gestures to an empty class-room.
Even the Italians marched into Venetia without waiting for his permission, and the French ambassador
pursued the Prussian Government with offers which
were not required. The adventurous Bismarck, who
always derived an unnatural enjoyment from wearing uniform, had the habit, peculiar in a statesman,
of accompanying the Prussian army in the field. He
had ridden wildly about on the night after Sadowa,
and it was his practice to direct Prussian policy in a
pickelhaube and spurs from a wandering chancellery
at the royal headquarters. Napoleon communicated
with him through the tactful medium of (how the
omens were beginning to accumulate) M. Benedetti;
and the French ambassador, a little scared and dis-
consolate after trailing exhaustingly through the
back areas of an advancing army, came upon the
Prussian minister late at night in an empty house.
The big man was writing by candle-light, and a large
revolver lay on the table beside him. He played a
little brutally with the French offer of mediation,
whilst the Prussian armies came slowly within sight
of the tall spire of Vienna. The last embers of
Austrian resistance were stamped out or scattered
eastwards into Hungary, where the little Rudolph
was clinging to his mother's skirts and staring with
round eyes at the cheering Magyars; the Italians
were beaten at sea off Lissa; but there was cholera
in the Prussian camp, and it was time to break off
the war and count the spoil. Whilst France stood
waiting to crown the victors, Bismarck borrowed a
gesture from the first Napoleon and crowned himself.
Checking the soldiers, who were anxious to march
behind their beating drums into Vienna, he signed

peace with Austria at Nikolsburg in the last week of
July. Franz-Joseph ceded Holstein and Venetia
and paid a trifling indemnity; the German Diet
ceased to exist; and in its place there was to be a new
union of Germany, from which Austria was now
excluded. The new unit would be dominated by
Prussia, and its members were warned by the annexation of Hanover that submission to Berlin was the
sole condition of existence. It was a rich result.

The war was over, and France was left in a commanding attitude without the pride of having ended
it. The oracle had spoken, but there were no sup-
pliants in the temple. *Chantecler* had crowed, and
the sun had risen; but there was an uneasy suspicion
that the sunrise owed little to his efforts. Paris was
sullen. French opinion had been stung by the Prussian victory and the Emperor's failure to preside over
the readjustment of Central Europe; and in the next
phase his policy was driven to a dismal competition
for a consolation-prize. It was the policy, as Bismarck called it, of *Trinkgeld*. The positions were
altered now; where once a Prussian minister had
walked delicately on the sands at Biarritz, deferential
French diplomatists held out a hat to Prussia for a
trifle of the Rhineland, a cast-off fortress, an old
pair of German towns. The Emperor had made no
stipulation before the event; but after the war he
came to ask for his reward, to present, as they said
in 1866, *la note de l'aubergiste*. It was a poor-
spirited expedient. But French opinion was discon-
tented in the pervading air of Prussian victory, and
M. Rouher (it was just one of his *rouhereries,* as the
Emperor called them) was so anxious to have something to show in the Chamber. Parliamentary

management is an injudicious guide for foreign
policy; but France seemed restive and the Emperor
was far from well, 'like a gambler,' as Mr. Disraeli
wrote, 'who has lost half his fortune and restless to
recover; likely to make a *coup,* which may be fatally
final for himself.' He made the *coup;* but in those
hot days of 1866 his hand shook a little.

King William was riding through the cheers in the
Berlin streets, and Napoleon was huddled in pain,
sipping his water at Vichy, when the first demand
came to Bismarck. Mainz and the left bank of the
Rhine seemed a good deal to ask for; but M. Benedetti was suave and did his best. Quite blandly,
with a vague hint that some other article might
perhaps take his customer's fancy, Bismarck refused.
Whilst Benedetti posted off to France for further
instructions, his offer became a useful card in Bismarck's hand. It was gravely reported to St. Petersburg as a disturbing indication of restless French
ambitions, and a calculated indiscretion to a journalist informed the world of the rebuff to France and
alarmed good Germans with the news that Napoleon
was waiting hungrily beyond the Rhine. Napoleon
was sick with dumb pain at Vichy, and he seemed to
turn blindly like a weary bull as Bismarck planted
the *banderillas.* For a few days Imperial policy was
distracted by the sunlit tragedy of Mexico, as the
Empress Charlotte came to Paris for her audience
and the Emperor dragged back to meet her, sat
wearily through a bitter afternoon of heat and rail-
ing, and watched the slow drift of an Empire to
disaster. Then Benedetti was back at his post again
with a new proposal. One might take Luxemburg
and Belgium, if Bismarck would agree, with a free

hand to Prussia in Germany and an alliance between
Paris and Berlin if England took a pedantic view of
Belgian neutrality.   It was a simple treaty, and
Bismarck took a draft of it in M. Benedetti's writing.
Then he refused.   The draft was useful, since he
showed it to Bavaria to prove that France had sold
South Germany for Belgium; and one day he might
show it to England.   Austria had signed peace in a
hotel at Prague; Bavaria entered the Prussian alliance; and the new North German Confederation was
under construction.   Bismarck had planted his
banderillas, and soon it would be time for the *espada.*
He had fought Düppel and Sadowa; but the Prussian piece was a trilogy, and he was waiting for
Sedan.

XVI

IT was the year 1867, and the brilliance of the Empire (for it had still brilliance) was a glow of evening, a vivid light upon quiet hills that face a sinking sun. The sky was still bright; but there was a strange chill upon the Empire. The clear dawn of 1852 seemed half a century away, and quite suddenly the Emperor had become an old man. Something in Eugénie's sad-eyed beauty was beginning to fade, and the Court had aged. Where once Bacciochi had played the barrel organ for the dancers, there was a grave succession of distinguished visitors; and the only sounds about the palace were the young voices of the Prince Imperial and his small friends. Slowly the Emperor seemed to fade into the background, to smoke his cigarettes and speak low behind the great moustache in that far-away voice of his, to turn the *regard vague et doux* of his *visage muet et triste* with the *air de rêve* with which he drifts through that story into which M. Bergeret has put so much of the art of M. Anatole France. He was becoming the shadowy figure of a second Napoleonic legend, and Imperial policy turned increasingly to the preparation of a future in which an Empress-Regent should govern France in the name of a pale young Emperor. The boy was not strong; but Eugénie was slowly schooled to stand behind his throne, and gradually the smiling figure of *la Reine*

Crinoline faded into the stiff outline of a Regent. She had governed with a Council of Regency during the Italian war and later when the Emperor was in Algeria, and M. Mérimée, who could see the change in her, had a faint, ironical regret: '*Il n'y a plus d'Eugénie, il n'y a plus qu'une impératrice. Je plains et j'admire.*' In earlier years romantic critics of the Emperor's policy, who loved to detect a hidden hand, to catch a low whisper in his ear, had exaggerated her influence, her Spanish prejudices, her distaste (which M. Mérimée hardly shared) for anti-clericals. But under the later Empire, since the future belonged to her and to Lulu, she played a larger part.

It was an uncertain future, since the old certainties of 1852 seemed to have lost their hold upon the generation of 1867. The Empire had been made because France was haunted by the confused, ignoble vision of 1848. But the men who had seen the great crowds go roaring round the Hôtel de Ville and heard the dreadful silence as Cavaignac's infantry stormed the barricades were in middle life now, and their sons could remember little of the Empire except the police, the censorship, and the heavy-handed *Préfets* who seemed to have remade France in their own image, as M. Haussmann had remade Paris in his. The Revolution had been the *raison d'être* of the Empire; and in 1867 the Revolution was half forgotten. It was even regretted a trifle sentimentally by the Parisian undergraduates, who displayed their aptitude for public life by shouting jokes about *Badinguet* round corners at policemen and dreamed wistfully of the past glories of the *jeunesse des écoles* behind the barricades. The Empire was failing in its appeal to youth. It had made few recruits; *le maître n'aime pas les visages nouveaux,* and his ministries were dismal alternations of elder statesmen. Young gentlemen preferred to write ingenious pamphlets in which Machiavelli expounded the principles of Bonapartism to a scandalised Montesquieu (and the learned Nilus found forty years later the raw material for his *Protocols of the Elders*—so far removed from the Tuileries—*of Zion*). The glamour of the Empire had begun to fade; it had not made a lucky throw since 1859: Rome was a riddle, Sadowa was a shame, and Mexico was a regret. The new generation seemed to turn away, found small encouragement to enter a service where all the rewards were earmarked for M. Rouher, and preferred to snigger over the ingenious side-hits of the *Propos de Labiénus* at Augustus and his simple enjoyment of the company of Drusilla and Tertulla and Terentilla and Rufilla and Silvia Titiscenia and even more. The Empire persevered in its performance; but it was beginning in 1867 to find the public a trifle sceptical.

It was the paradox of the Emperor's system that, like Lord Palmerston, he preached liberty to foreign countries and maintained reaction in his own. But although his Liberalism began abroad, there was no reason (since he was not the leader of a Whig Party) why it should end there, and he returned with some vigour to the project, which Morny had let drop in 1865, for a Liberal Empire. It was the only hope, if youth was to be reconciled to the Empire, if Lulu was to inherit the future; and M. Walewski, who had followed Morny as President of the Chamber, seemed to catch an echo of his views. There was still the haunting question with which the Emperor was

always faced: *'Où trouver l'homme?'* Perhaps the
legacy of Morny's odd friendship with M. Ollivier
would answer it. The dark young man in spectacles
had been once or twice at the Tuileries; once he had
gone to an evening party when the Emperor was
away, and Eugénie discussed a cab strike and told
him that she was a socialist at sixteen, and once she
sent for him, and as they sat talking, a quiet door
half opened; Eugénie made a sign, and the Emperor
walked in; there were some courtesies and M. Ollivier
lectured his sovereign upon liberty. The movement
of parties in the Chamber was drifting him to the
leadership of a group which lay midway between the
stiff Imperialists and the republicans of the Left.
Now he was taken at his word; the Empire was
inclined to take the plunge into constitutionalism,
although Eugénie felt that it was premature and
would have preferred to postpone it, with other fire-
works, for her son's accession; and in the first days
of 1867 Walewski offered M. Ollivier the Ministry
of Public Instruction with duties as official advocate
in the Chamber. In the failing light of a winter
afternoon M. Ollivier slipped into the Tuileries and
saw his sovereign. The Deputy pointed the way to
a more constitutional Empire with parliamentary
ministers and freedom of public meetings and the
press, and Napoleon was anxious to do *'quelque chose
de résolu et de libéral.'* Only one must avoid *'l'air
de vouloir me faire pardonner mes échecs au Mexique
et en Allemagne. Par des raisons qu'il serait trop
long d'expliquer je n'ai pas pu profiter des affaires
allemandes et je suis obligé de revenir du Mexique.
Dans cette situation de concessions ne m'affaibli-
raientelles pas?'* M. Ollivier thought not, and he

went out into the dark streets with a promise to come
back and talk to the Empress. He found her a shade
unfriendly to the movement, but the Emperor wrote
him a letter full of decision: ,

> 'Pour frapper les esprits par des mesures décisives je
> voudrais d'un coup établir ce qu'on a appelé le couronne-
> ment de l'édifice; je voudrais le faire, afin de ne plus y
> revenir . . .'

Unfortunately M. Ollivier in 1867 clung to the
virtuous detachment of a private member; his tender
conscience shrank from the indignity of office; and his
sovereign, who might have gained a Liberal minister,
received only enlightened advice. Napoleon's good
impulses remained in the official charge of M.
Rouher, and the coyness of M. Ollivier sentenced the
whole project to futility. The new programme was
embodied in a public letter from the Emperor to the
Minister of State, in which 'le couronnement de
l'édifice élevé par la volonté nationale' was to be
achieved by a revision of the press-law and the attendance of ministers in the Chamber to debate and
answer questions. It was not easy to feel enthusiasm
for the Imperial manifesto of January 19, 1867,
since the promises which it contained were of the
mildest, and even they were to be performed by a
ministry which profoundly disbelieved in them. Once
more the Empire had made a vague gesture of
Liberalism and relapsed into the easier exercises of
reaction. There was a faint revival of parliamentary
life; M. Walewski brought the tribune out of store,
and after certain drastic alterations required by the
stature of M. Thiers it was installed once again in the
Chamber. The sweeping toga of an earlier day

seemed to have been cut down to fit the frosty little gentleman in spectacles, and from his new rostrum he delivered interminable disquisitions upon the teaching of history and the errors and imperfections of Imperial policy. But in spite of the Liberal aspirations of the Emperor's letter, France was not yet the mistress of its own destinies. M. Rouher still governed in his master's name, and M. Ollivier pointed the bitter moral:

> *'Les attributions du ministère d'état ont dû s'accroître démesurément; l'avocat des ministres est d'abord devenu leur conseil, puis leur directeur, et aujourd'hui il est, non pas comme on l'a dit, premier ministre, maire du palais ou grand vizir, mais un Vice-Empereur sans responsabilité.'*

There was a roar in the Chamber; and the Emperor replied to his impulsive adviser with a gracious letter to Rouher and the Grand Cross in diamonds. It was a strange preparation for the future.

But Paris in 1867 was not conspicuously interested in the future. Students of foreign policy were vaguely disquieted by the sudden emergence of Prussia, and they followed anxiously a queer negotiation about Luxemburg in which M. de Moustier, the new Foreign Minister, made a fresh attempt to secure some small advantage for France in the readjustment of European relations which followed Sadowa. Prussia had absorbed Hanover and one of the Hesses; the North German Confederation—'a congress of roaches presided over by a very big pike' —was a new commonwealth of Germany north of the Main with Berlin for its capital; and the last hope of detaching South Germany from Bismarck's combination was removed by his publication of treaties of alliance with Bavaria, Baden, and Württemberg. French jealousy burned bright, and the directors of French policy snatched eagerly at any chance of a set-off. Luxemburg, by an eccentric complication of past treaties, belonged to the King of Holland, and in view of Bismarck's notorious appetite for outlying Duchies, this isolated *enclave* on the Franco-German frontier was regarded by cautious persons at the Hague as an embarrassing *casus belli* with Prussia. The French obligingly offered to relieve Holland of the Grand-Duchy, and the Prince of Orange, who was a familiar figure on the more frivolous side of Parisian life under the less impressive appellation of *Prince Citron,* notified the Emperor of his father's consent. Mr. Disraeli heard of the offer from the Rothschilds, and there was a nervous flutter of 'all the cousins' round Windsor. But at this stage Prussia intervened; German opinion was mobilised to demonstrate the Teutonic origin of Luxemburg, and the Franco-Dutch transaction was sharply interrupted. With some adroitness Moustier changed his ground and, abandoning his claim to the Grand-Duchy, pressed for the withdrawal of the Prussian garrison. There was an uneasy pause, in which French agents bought remounts in Hungary and Prussian engineers worked by torchlight on the forts at Luxemburg. But Austria assumed the exhausting functions of an angel of peace; the soothing ministrations of diplomacy were invoked, and after a four days' conference in London the destinies of Luxemburg were settled by a treaty which dismantled the fortress, withdrew the Prussian garrison, and conferred upon the Grand-Duchy the questionable blessings of neutrality.

24

Whilst French policy struggled a shade inadequately with its perennial problem to *porter haut le drapeau de la France,* expert opinion was gravely exercised as to the simpler exigencies of national defence. Sadowa had set the soldiers thinking. Manpower and the needle-gun had swept the Prussians to victory; and although the French infantry was to be rearmed with the excellent *Chassepot,* there was an uneasy feeling that the big battalions would be on the German side. Prussia had adopted a system of conscription which followed the formula of the *Volk in Waffen* and brought the whole population to the colours. The French, with a more limited system which permitted the purchase of substitutes, had a smaller establishment of higher quality; there was even a tendency towards professionalism, and the Empire aligned against the Prussian masses an army which had seen service in Italy, Mexico, the Crimea and approximated more nearly to the long-service soldiers of Mr. Cardwell and Queen Victoria. There was a hasty movement of reform; the house-parties at Compiègne became predominantly military, and the soldiers sat in committee with the Emperor. Randon, who had been at the Ministry of War since Magenta, was sceptical. But Trochu was voluble, and Ducrot sent nervous reports from Strasburg upon the movements of Prussian agents in the frontier provinces. The country was informed that the first-line army would be increased, exemptions curtailed, and the existing forces supplemented by a *Garde mobile* modelled upon the Prussian *Landwehr.* A new minister came to the War Office; and as Marshal Niel was settling down to his papers, Napoleon stated in the Chamber that a nation's influence must depend upon the size of its army. It was a strange termination of the age of Congresses; and when General Trochu published a disturbing pamphlet on *L'Armée française en* 1867, with its gloomy motto from Tacitus and its dismal prevision that France might one day have a Benedek, men bought it into its hundredth edition and began to look nervously towards the eastern frontier.

But Paris in 1867 had more immediate interests. Once again the Empire fell back upon the simple expedient of government by Exhibition, and the crowds stood in the Champ de Mars to see the miracles of science—the steam locomotives, the marvellous featherweight metal *aluminium,* and the new American rocking-chair. Paris once more became the capital of Europe; and anxious couriers propelled their charges through the staring crowds, whilst stupid foreigners talked broken French and the provincials fumbled with their purses. In the Exhibition there was a baroque profusion of kiosks, of gleaming show-cases, of strange, insistent salesmen, and young ladies who waited upon their customers in the outlandish costumes of their own countries. Missionary societies amused an enlightened public with trophies of heathen weapons, and Herr Friedrich Krupp of Essen exhibited a great gun which showed its black muzzle to the French and won a prize. The whole city was a lodging-house, and its lodgers swung gaily into the Parisian dance. In the day one tramped the Exhibition open-mouthed, and at night one sat in the stalls to hear Carvalho sing *Juliet* in M. Gounod's new opera or to see Ristori as *Queen Elizabeth,* or (best of all) one nodded a responsive head at the Alcazar to the lilt of Thérésa's *C'est dans l'nez qu'ça me chatouille* or raised an eyebrow at her deep-voiced, her classical insistence that *Rien n'est sacré pour un sapeur,* which had inspired Cham to retort with a picture of scandalised Engineers ejaculating *Rien n'est sacré pour Thérésa.* Paris had gone mad for the divine Patti when she sang *Lucia* and *Sonnambula;* but the authentic Muse of the Second Empire was Thérésa.

It seemed in 1867 that the whole Empire had been set to music; and the *maestro* was a tall, lean-faced man with drooping whiskers and perpetual pince-nez who had come out of a synagogue choir at Cologne and was named Offenbach. He drifted from serious composition to ballet-music (with Taglioni to arrange his dances), and then in the great days of the Empire *opéra bouffe* found its master. *Orphée aux Enfers* had set all Paris humming; and as Bazaine's officers rode down to the hot, blue sea at Vera Cruz, their vision of home was Paris and a box for *la Belle Hélène.* The armies of the Second Empire went into action to an air of Offenbach, and his leading lady was a national, almost a European figure. In the year of the Exhibition he gave her royal rank; and when Hortense Schneider played *la Grande-Duchesse de Gerolstein,* it was an international event. The librettists pointed fingers of French derision at a minor German state; and when the whole *Almanach de Gotha* came to Paris to see the Exhibition, she played, like Talma at Erfurt, to a *parterre de rois* her travesty of German royalty. It was the last joke of the Empire; and since the Empire was to fall so soon under German guns, it tasted a little bitter in the mouth.

In the last years of the Empire the little figures of
Parisian gaiety jigged on a broad and lighted stage.
The scene, lit by the flaring gas-jets of the Second
Empire, was set by the tall buildings of M. Haussmann's avenues; and as the *maestro* Offenbach drew
a tinkling melody from the orchestra, one seems to
see them simpering prettily in their great skirts and
their little hats, the lost anonymas of the Second
Empire.   They crossed the stage to a lively air, as
young M. Rochefort fought his duel with Prince
Achille Murat and the *cocodès* settled their great
cuffs into place—Cora Pearl, the Englishwoman,
with her fair curls (she once played Cupid in
Orphée), Mogador, *Nana* herself with her scarlet
liveries and her pair of Russian trotters, and
Marguerite Bellanger whom an extensive public
knew as *Margot la Rigoleuse* before discreet equerries transported her to Vichy and Biarritz, where a
Cher Seigneur was waiting and grave officials laid
before an Emperor the letters of his Marguerite.
'Pourtant,' as Fleury said, *'nous nous sommes
diablement bien amusés.'*   The Empire in 1867
seemed to centre in Paris, and Paris in the year of
the Exhibition was at its most Parisian.

But there was a flutter of *haute politique* in the
streets when the kings of Europe drove by to see the
show.   A Swede, a Jap, a Czar, a Prince of Wales, a
Sultan in his fez went past at the salute, and the
Emperor seemed always to be waiting in uniform at
the station to meet a royal train. King William came
from Berlin with his strapping Chancellor in *Landwehr* uniform, and Bismarck sat laughing at the
Grande-Duchesse.   One day in the summer (there
had been bad news from Mexico by the new Ameri-

can cable) the Emperor sat by the Sultan of Turkey to award the prizes; there was a silence as he made his speech, because it was known in Paris that Maximilian was lying shot at Queretaro. But the greatest day in the year was a June afternoon when the crowds stood in the sunshine at Longchamps and the Emperor sat his horse with the Czar and the King of Prussia to watch Marshal Canrobert take the troops by at the salute. It was the last pageant of the Empire, and it passed with a gleam of helmets and the flicker of sunlight on fixed bayonets. The shakoes of the infantry went by and the green *Chasseurs* and the great drum-majors and the little *vivandières* in their bright petticoats. There was a great stream of red and blue as the Zouaves swung past, and then the cavalry went jingling by—the *Guides* in green and gold, the Lancers in their *schapskas* with a flutter of pennons, and the tall helmets of the heavy cavalry who were to pound so soon across the hills at Mars-la-Tour and down into the hollow at Reichshoffen. The little brass guns went clanking past behind their gun-teams, and the Emperor sat in the sunshine with his great moustache between the tall Czar and the narrow eyes of Prussia. As the sun dropped towards the west, they drove back into Paris, and a Polish boy snapped a pistol at the Emperor of Russia. The troops marched off through the June dust, and Longchamps had seen in the blaze and jingle of the great review the Indian summer of the Empire.

XVII

As the shouting died away and the last flags hung limply on the autumn air in the Exhibition grounds, Napoleon was left alone again with his problems. Paris and the younger generation were palpably hostile to the Empire; and new pieces with astounding moves were beginning to appear on the European chess-board. The old gambits had lost something of their value. The game was ending, and the Emperor seemed to fumble a little with the pieces. His health had recovered partly from the breakdown of 1866; but he remained an aging man, and he was too often in pain to command a clear eye and a steady hand.

The most pressing of his problems was the balance of European power. Bismarck had tilted the scale sharply, and French policy had found no means to redress it. There was something a little sinister in the silent progress of Prussia. The light was failing; and through the gathering dusk the North German Confederation, to the imagination of Sir Robert Morier, 'looms out like some huge ironclad from which no sounds are heard but the tramp of men at drill, or the swinging upon their pivots of monster guns.' It was an uneasy spectacle for an Emperor without allies; and as it slowly took shape in the mist, he seemed to stare a little helplessly. Foreign politics had been like a bad dream since 1866; he had waved his wand and made his passes; but nothing had happened and his public was growing impatient. The centre of European gravity was shifting to Berlin. Napoleon still looked enigmatic and made significant speeches; but he no longer held the centre of the stage. Once a respectful Continent had watched the Tuileries to guess its future; now it looked further east, where something seemed crouching in the shadows.

It was an obvious resource for France to seek alliances, and Austria seemed the natural counterpoise to the new power of Germany. A queer irony sent Napoleon to make advances to Franz-Joseph; ten years of French policy had stripped him of his Italian dominions, and Magenta, Solferino, the French bayonets which had captured Milan, and the French hint which had sent the Italians into Venice seemed an odd prelude for the new friendship. But the two Empires drew together, like tall ships under a stormy sky; they had need of one another, and statesmen in difficulties have short memories. One could change partners in the European dance with astonishing rapidity, and Austria might care to take the floor with France. It would be a brave repartee to Prussia to set up once more the old Austro-French alliance which had taken the field against Frederick the Great in the Seven Years' War; and the agile Count von Beust, who had migrated from Dresden to Vienna and entered Austrian politics from the top as Chancellor, seemed just the man (had he not brought Saxony into the war against Prussia in 1866?) to take the new, the daring turning. No royalty from Vienna had visited the Exhibition, since a Mexican firing-party at Queretaro had put the

Court in mourning. But at the turn of the year Napoléon and Eugénie left France with elaborate informality for a private visit to Franz-Joseph. As the train wound through South Germany, the kings stood bowing in their stations; and at Augsburg in Bavaria the Emperor showed Eugénie his school, his mother's house, and the old streets where a German schoolboy had once learnt to be Emperor of the French. At the Austrian frontier the royal train steamed into Salzburg, and Napoléon met on the platform the tall young man whom he had last seen on the white road to Villafranca in 1859. There were five days of courtesy, of drives and visits; and one evening a thoughtful Court assisted nature to be picturesque by lighting bonfires on the hills. Whilst Eugénie dressed quietly and sat with her queer, vivacious hostess, the two Emperors talked politics. M. de Gramont, from the embassy at Vienna, was full of plans. But Beust was cautious and Napoléon was not, was never in a hurry. *Il ne faut rien brusquer;* and the visit closed upon a note of peaceful friendship. The Emperor took the train again to France; and as it stopped at Lille, he seemed a little anxious. His speech said something of the past glamour of the Empire—*'J'entrevoyais pour notre patrie une nouvelle ère de grandeur et de prospérité'*—then, with a sudden drop to the minor key, he peered uncertainly into the future: *'des points noirs sont venus assombrir notre horizon. De même que la bonne fortune ne m'a point ébloui, de même des revers passagers ne me décourageront pas.'* It was an odd confession; Napoléon was a silent man, but he seemed for once to be thinking aloud. His courtesy to Franz-Joseph was returned a few weeks later, when

the Austrian Emperor visited him at Paris. The
streets were crowded; and the young man, whom
defeat and bereavement had rendered interesting,
was well received. The diplomats took up the work
of friendship; and for a year or more, as M. Rouher
dabbled in *haute politique* and M. de Gramont
strolled over to the Ballplatz to talk *'académique-
ment'* to Count von Beust about a European war,
the correspondence trailed on. Drafts passed from
hand to hand; solemn gentlemen exchanged significant nods; the atmosphere was highly confidential,
and there were *'échanges d'idées et de projets'*
between Paris and Vienna. How much, how little
had been said came later into controversy. But,
although the bright perspective of alliance kindled
the warm imagination of M. de Gramont, nothing
was signed. There was a vague contact of the two
Empires; but Austria, to an experienced eye,
belonged 'to the mollusc category,' and Napoleon's
initiative was little more than a tired gesture. There
was no treaty, and even the letters provided for little
beyond co-operation in diplomacy. An Austrian
army corps in Bohemia might one day save the
French; but even M. Rouher might well doubt
whether the same results would attend an Austrian
Note. The Emperor had gone to Salzburg in search
of an ally; he had found only a neutral.

His natural allies were in Italy, which was the
creation of his policy. But gratitude is an unusual
sentiment in statesmen; and Italy, with Venice and
Milan, had little more to hope from the French alliance. An offer of the Trentino went to Florence
with a draft treaty of alliance. But the long fatality
of the Roman question had estranged the two

countries, and at the moment when France most
needed Italian friendship, it rose once more between
them. For a few months in 1867, when the Italians
undertook to guard the Pope's territory and the last
French sentries sailed for home, it had seemed to
pass away. But before the year was out, Garibaldi
was on the move again. That incorrigible liberator,
whom Italian guns had already turned back from
Rome at Aspromonte in 1862, took the road once
more by way of a Peace Congress at Geneva attended
principally by belligerent revolutionaries, who waved
their international olive-branches a shade ferociously.
There was a nervous flutter in Italy, and the Legion
began to filter into the Papal States under the eyes
of grinning Piedmontese police. There was a
crackle of musketry; and the *Papalini* fell back fighting on the city, whilst France sent Italy a sharp
reminder of her duty to protect the Pope. The
Italians wrung their hands, regretted, condoled,
apologised, explained. But the Garibaldians moved
slowly on, and France was insistent. An expeditionary force was concentrated at Toulon and sent
the Emperor's mind back to the distant days when
a President sat at the Élysée and General Oudinot
marched slowly up the road to Rome. Garibaldi
slipped out of Caprera to take the field against the
Pope, and the Zouaves were marching down to the
transports as Napoleon struggled with his doubts.
Orders to Toulon went and were recalled. But the
fleet sailed at last, as the arms of the semaphores
flapped out the last hesitations of the Government
from the coast-guard stations of Provence; and in the
last weeks of October the French were back in Rome.
They marched out by the Porta Pia before dawn, and

at Mentana on a Sunday they found Garibaldi and
his men. The Legion was broken in a running fight,
and General de Failly, proud of his new rifles, reported to Paris in words which were never forgiven
in Italy;

'Les fusils Chassepot out fait merveille.'

The Pope was saved; but France had saved him by
Italian casualties, and Italy was less than ever likely
to ally herself with the Emperor. M. Rouher struck
an attitude in the Chamber and announced in his
big voice, *'au nom du gouvernement français, l'Italie
ne s'emparera pas de Rome! Jamais, jamais la
France ne supportera cette violence à son honneur et à
la catholicité.'* His sovereign gently remarked, *'En
politique, il ne faut jamais dire "Jamais" '*; and the
advice, for an Empire without allies, was wise.
Finality could hardly be attained in French policy
at a time when the first impression of a new ambassador from London was that Napoleon had 'reigned
eighteen years, and they were getting tired of so much
of the same thing and want novelty.'

One other event in foreign politics had its influence
upon the Empire. Spanish affairs under Queen
Isabella had passed through rapid alternations
of stagnation and comic opera. Public life was
crowded with fierce military gentlemen who clanked
into office and out again with bewildering rapidity,
and the combined efforts of the entire corps of
generals had reduced the national finances to the condition which induced Lord Macaulay to observe to
his banker: 'Active Spanish Bonds profess to pay
interest now, and do not. Deferred Spanish Bonds
profess to pay interest at some future time, and will

not. Passive Spanish Bonds profess to pay interest neither now, nor at any future time. I think that you might buy a large amount of Passive Spanish Bonds for a very small sum.' A *pronunciamiento* of artillery sergeants was followed by a *pronunciamiento* of sailors at Cadiz; shiploads of generals went into exile and returned with enlightened views; and gradually, in the later years of the Second Empire, the country drifted towards unanimity. The Queen's ministers had succeeded in uniting Spanish opinion; but unfortunately they had united it against the Queen. In the late summer of 1868 her *villeggiatura* at San Sebastian was interrupted by four separate *pronunciamientos;* she looked wildly round the great curve of the bay and scuttled across the bridge at Irun into France, leaving a debt of fourteen millions and a cash balance in the Treasury of something under five shillings. One more ruler of Spain and the Indies had justified Lord Clarendon's gloomy diagnosis: 'Spanish dynasties go and come; Spanish kings and queens go and come; and Spanish ministers go and come; but there is one thing in Spain that is always the same—they never answer letters.' The Queen passed the frontier, and the little houses of St. Jean de Luz slid by her carriage window. The Emperor was at Biarritz for the autumn, and he had the courtesy to come to the station as her train went through. There was a vacancy for the throne of Spain; and before it was filled, it had made a gap at the Tuileries.

In his own country the Emperor watched the half-hearted execution of the programme of 1867. Whilst his concessions to democracy were imposed upon a suspicious public by sceptical ministers, army reform was gravely debated in the Chamber, and Count von Moltke was reported to be interesting himself in the geography of the eastern frontier. But French opinion was gratified by the devastating possibilities of the *mitrailleuse,* and Marshal Niel's proposals were steadily reduced in effectiveness by an Opposition which never hesitated to reproach the Emperor for supineness in face of Prussia but declined, with that levity which is the privilege of Oppositions, to provide him with the means of action. Colonel Stoffel reported voluminously from the embassy at Berlin upon the growing efficiency of the Prussian service; the French field-gun was outranged, the most careful attention was being given to musketry, and even the Court circular showed how assiduously the elderly King devoted himself to his army. The tactful *attaché* alluded cautiously to the manifest superiority of the Prussian higher command; apart from the genius of Count von Moltke, a Staff College presided over the education of his officers in that art of war which had lately become so complex. Railways and rifles and steel artillery were making European warfare into something beyond the comprehension of dashing French colonels in tight uniforms, and it was no longer enough for a successful soldier to combine a knowledge of the names of Napoleonic victories with the display of personal courage in the *hinterland* of Algeria.

The Liberal promises of 1867 were gingerly fulfilled by M. Rouher. Whilst the public crowded to hear Christine Nilsson as *Ophelia,* cautious legislators conferred upon it the privilege of meeting to discuss unpolitical questions and even (with official permission) to talk politics. The law of press-offences was

reformed, and there was a queer revival of public life
in France. The sudden resumption of activity was
almost convulsive. Once more, after the long
silence of the Empire, public speakers began to gesticulate to public meetings, and journalists wrote
almost what they thought. The strait-waistcoat of
1852 had been relaxed, and the Empress, whom half
Paris regarded as an agent of reaction, was devoting
herself to the harmless pursuit of charity and the
posthumous reinstatement of Lesurques after the
long martyrdom of his tragic confusion with Dubosc,
who robbed the Lyons mail in his own person and
fascinated a generation of British playgoers in someone else's. But there was little gratitude in France
for the new liberty. The Emperor drafted newspaper articles in which the country was to be informed, with a desperate homœopathy, of its continued
devotion to his person, to *'la bienveillance extrême du
chef de l'État, sa modestie et sa simplicité'* in spite of
the imperfections of his domineering subordinates;
there was a queer admission that *'l'Empereur est resté
aussi populaire qu'il y a quinze ans, tandis que son
gouvernement ne l'est pas.'* He even interrupted his
journalism to sketch the scenario of a novel in which
an intelligent traveller returned to France in 1868
and wandered open-mouthed through the rich perspective of the Empire—ironclads at Brest (*'l'invention de l'Empereur. Revêtus de fer, ils sont à l'abri
du boulet, et cette transformation a détruit jusqu'à un
certain point la suprématie sur mer de l'Angleterre'*),
railways, electric telegraphs, low prices and Free
Trade, a country at peace, and all the beneficent
apparatus of a modern state. But French opinion
was restive and unimpressed. Paris seemed to want

a new toy, and Lamartine might have said once more
'*la France s'ennuie.*'

The uneasy temper of 1868 reacted upon a cheerful
and crowded Opposition. Little remained of the
Five of 1857; M. Darimon was seen now at official
receptions, M. Émile Ollivier was under grave suspicion of having permitted his reasonableness to
outrun his logic, and only M. Jules Favre seemed to
survive, with the gift of peevish invective which had
delighted French audiences for twenty years and an
appearance which came increasingly to suggest an
unsuccessful impersonation of Mr. Lincoln. But
M. Thiers had returned to the stage and was forget-
ting his Orleanism in the enjoyment of eliciting
republican cheers by the measured enumeration of
someone else's mistakes; and gradually the sedate
republicans of the early Empire were reinforced, were
superseded by a younger, more violent generation.
M. Ollivier's young friends at the Bar forsook him as
his views assumed the fatal caution of middle age;
and since the claims of clients had not yet absorbed
their leisure, they were always available to speak at
meetings or to cheer in the Chamber, to write for the
papers or to publish pamphlets. One voice seemed
even then to carry above the rest, where the southern
verve of *Numa Roumestan* sent Léon Gambetta rock-
eting volubly across the Parisian scene. But there
were grave elements in the Opposition; successive
amnesties had released the exiles of 1852, and they
returned to France with all the memories of the
Second Republic and all the bitterness of the *coup
d'état*. There was even a recrudescence of the old
ideal of the social revolution, of the *République
sociale* which Cavaignac had blown off the Paris

streets in the June days of 1848. Working-class
opinion had been gratified by the condescension of the
Prince-President's early writings on *l'Extinction du
Paupérisme*. But gradually, as the development of
industrialism under the Second Empire huddled the
workers in the large towns, it was attracted by
Proudhon's more vigorous enunciation of the principle *La propriété c'est le vol*. The system of Karl
Marx was largely unreadable and mostly unread; but
a dangerous contact with the revolutionary movements
of Europe was established by the well-intentioned
institution of the *Internationale*. Designed by a
modest group of Parisian trade unionists to secure the
co-operation of organized labour in all countries, it
was assailed in France with the embarrassing attentions of more experienced agitators, who seemed
anxious to embellish its drab economic programme
with the more vivid attractions of republicanism,
irreligion, free love, and Nihilism. Their harmless excursions to pass resolutions at international conferences brought the delegates of the *Internationale* in
contact with the main stream of European revolution,
and those simple-minded exponents of working-class
solidarity were soon to be found murmuring the deep-
chested incantations of insurrection in unison with the
fuller voices of Mazzini, Garibaldi, and Bakunin.
French opinion in the industrial areas was rapidly
affected by the strange contagion, and one more
ingredient was added to the effervescence of Paris.

There was a surge of journalism as the restrictions
came off, and anxious gentlemen sat at the Ministry
of the Interior scanning the new publications for
signs of *lèse-majesté*. Their quest was amply satisfied
in the summer of 1868 when M. Rochefort, who had

made something of a reputation for seditious in-
nuendo in the newspapers, brought out a paper in a
bright red cover and called it *La Lanterne.* He was
a remarkable young man with black hair and a
piercing eye; his gifts combined a rare genius for
burlesque with that verbal felicity which can maintain a steady flow of witticisms; and he had not yet
discovered his total incapacity for living contentedly
under any form of government whatever. The bland
impertinence of his first number, of which he hoped
to sell four thousand copies, brought him a circula-
tion of one hundred thousand, and his malice set Paris
tittering every Saturday. Sheets of the same type
had circulated furtively in Madrid under the late
dynasty. The note was struck in his opening sentence—*'La France contient, dit l'*Almanach impérial,
*trente-six millions de sujets, sans compter les sujets
de mécontentement'*—and he ran easily through every
tone of derision from irony to abuse. The ways of
ministers, the Empress and her crinolines, the Emperor and his dog made a weekly appearance in his
sardonic *revue;* the accomplishments of Queen Hortense and the paternity of her son, the dialectic of
M. Rouher, the antics of the police, the stale flavour
of old scandals about Mexico, and the whole under-
side of the Imperial scene were M. Rochefort's stock-
in-trade. But he was at his best in passages of sustained irony:

> *'Comme bonapartiste, je préfère Napoléon II. . . . Per-
> sonne ne niera qu'il aît occupé le trône, puisque son succes-
> seur s'appelle Napoléon III. Quel règne! mes amis,
> quel règne! Pas une contribution; pas de guerres inutiles
> avec les décimes qui s'ensuivent; pas de ces expéditions
> lointaines dans lesquelles on dépense six cents millions pour*

aller réclamer quinze francs, pas de listes civiles dévorantes,
pas de ministres cumulant chacun cinq ou six fonctions
à cent mille francs pièce; voilà bien le monarque tel que
je le comprends. Oh! oui, Napoléon II. je t'aime et je
t'admire sans réserve. . . .'

The public reputation of French institutions, which
depended under the Empire upon a romantic venera-
tion, is peculiarly susceptible to ridicule. Humour
is an innocuous weapon in British politics; but in
the more sensitive Parisian *milieu,* in which the
Lanterne circulated, it produced a serious influence
upon the prestige of the Empire. M. Pinard, who
had conducted the prosecution oî M. Flaubert for
the improprieties of *Madame Bovary,* was at the
Ministry of the Interior, and his sense of humour was
unequal to M. Rochefort's scurrility. He displayed
a laudable activity in persecuting the exasperating
pamphlet; and the intemperate little paper, which
blushed scarlet in every suburban railway-carriage
on Saturdays in 1868 and lay in heaps along the
boulevards like the autumn leaves of the Empire, was
suppressed after eleven issues. Whilst his *facetiae*
were gravely investigated by a court of law, Rochefort escaped to Belgium and settled down in the
congenial company of Victor Hugo to lampoon the
Empire from beyond the frontier. The *Lanterne*
continued to be printed in Brussels, but its sole contributor dated occasional issues from towns in England, Holland and even Prussia (which he did not
visit) out of consideration for the responsibilities of
the Belgian Government to its neighbours. The
tone of his invective became progressively more violent, and every artifice of comic opera was adopted
through the year 1869 to introduce copies of the

Lanterne into France. The paper was printed on a reduced scale and posted to its subscribers in envelopes; a consignment of fifteen plaster busts of the Emperor was found to contain a whole edition—six copies in each epaulette and seven inside the *Grand Cordon* of the Legion of Honour; and an antique picture-frame was filled with sedition and despatched to an art-dealer in Paris. The success of the *Lanterne* came to depend less upon its contents, which were a trifle monotonous, than upon the pleasing mystery of its distribution. Even the dullest paper becomes interesting, if it is delivered at the house by smugglers. Its author, who had never cultivated anonymity, gradually became a popular figure, and at a by-election in 1869, M. Rochefort was returned to the Chamber by a working-class constituency of Paris: it was a strange symptom.

French opinion, in the *malaise* which had prevailed in public life since 1866, was becoming profoundly sceptical as to the Empire, and the doubts in the public mind were expressed in a critical examination of its tradition and its origins. The sanctity of the First Empire had been an axiom of the reign of Napoleon III.; but M. Lanfrey's handling of the subject showed a strange departure from the reverent attitude of earlier writers, and the indivisible collaboration of MM. Erckmann and Chatrian displayed a scandalous indifference to the fascinations of sentimental militarism. The Emperor's own antecedents were exposed to still more searching criticism, and the shrill abuse of M. Rochefort was supplemented by a revival of public interest in the dark circumstances of the *coup d'état*. The exiles had employed their leisure in constructing an elaborate mythology of the

crowded days of December, 1851; and since every
cause requires a martyr, the republicans were fortunate in a belated recollection of the part played by
M. Baudin. Shot gallantly (if a trifle superflu-
ously) on a barricade and subsequently forgotten
by his supporters for seventeen years, this obscure
victim became in 1868 a symbol of insurrection. Stray
references to him began to appear in print; crowds
learned to cheer his name; the national genius for
political funerals was thwarted by the unfortunate
circumstance that he was already buried, but it was
not, it was never too late for the posthumous distinction of a monument, and some newspapers opened
a subscription-list. There was even a notion that the
Emperor might head the list of subscribers. But his
ministers foresaw the unpleasantness of an eloquent
unveiling, and the papers were prosecuted. A brief
for the defence was delivered, by some fortunate
chance, to Maître Gambetta; and on a November day
in 1868 France heard for the first time the great voice
that was to reverberate through politics for fourteen
years. French procedure has rarely insisted upon the
distinction, so dear to the arid formalism of British
jurisprudence, between a theatre and a court of law;
and the dramatic possibilities of a trial were never
more generously exploited. There was no defence;
but with a lively change of scene the defence became
the prosecution. The Empire was challenged in its
origins, and Maître Gambetta launched with gusto
into a crashing denunciation of the *coup d'état*. Rele-
vance and forensic courtesy were swept aside; he
shook his mane; he roared; he quoted Sallust. All
the wild vigour of his southern verbiage came together in a declamatory tornado of invective; and

when he dropped, rumpled and panting, into his seat,
Paris had found a new sensation, and the vague
republican murmur of *'En voilà assez!'* which George
Sand seemed to catch in the earth and the trees and
the sky of 1868 was suddenly articulate. His clients
were convicted; but an advocate's reputation rises
superior to such trifles, and one talked as much of M.
Gambetta that autumn as one did of Rossini's death
and M. Doré's drawing of the dead *maestro* and a
clever young pianist named Saint-Saëns.

The evening of the Empire was unrestful, and
Napoleon moved uncertainly through the failing
light. He was more alone now than in the early days;
the Imperial circle had grown old with him, and so
many of his men had died. A new mood of impatience
was growing on the public mind; Lord Lyons had
noticed it when he came to Paris, and the Empress
was to say bitterly in later years, *'En France, au
commencement, on peut tout faire; au bout d'un
certain temps, on ne peut même plus se moucher.'*
The country was a little wearied by the apparent opportunism of Imperial policy, in which dexterity
seemed to have been substituted for principle; and the
Emperor had nothing new to offer. Early in 1869
he alarmed international opinion with an unfortunate
transaction in his later manner. A private negotiation by a French railway company for running rights
over a Belgian system alarmed the Belgians. Lord
Clarendon instantly suspected 'a sneaking attempt
to incorporate Belgium by means of a railway company and its employés.' There was a flutter at
Osborne, where the Queen had always felt a tender-
ness for her uncle Leopold and his subjects; and
Mr. Gladstone stayed his axe at the foot of the Irish

upas tree for the composition of emphatic memoranda
upon Belgian neutrality. Anxious gentlemen hurried
from Brussels to Paris; and when the Belgian attitude seemed to resist the peaceful French penetration,
Napoleon and his ministers irritably suspected the
hand of Bismarck. M. Rouher stamped out of a
room proclaiming *'Tôt ou tard, cette guerre est inévi-
table; le prince impérial ne régnera pas si Sadowa
n'est pas effacé; eh bien! s'ils la veulent, la guerre,
soit!'* Even the Emperor made inquiries of Marshal
Niel about a campaign in Belgium and was answered
'Je suis prêt.' Mr. Gladstone was sounded by
Bernstorff as to his readiness to take the field with
Prussia in the sacred cause of Belgian neutrality, and
Lord Clarendon muttered angrily about *'sales tri-
potages'* and 'all the jobbery and *pots de vin* that are
passing.' But the mood changed in Paris; peace was
maintained, and Mr. Gladstone went back to the
Irish Church Bill.

The Emperor turned an anxious eye upon France,
where an election was bringing all his enemies into
line. The new republicans were massed a shade
menacingly behind the elder statesmen of the
Opposition, and the Ministry of the Interior no longer
felt equal to the deliberate manipulation of the electorate which had produced the unanimous majorities
of 1857 and 1863. Even his official candidates spoke
in the strange new dialect of constitutionalism. Outside Paris the country remained loyal to the Empire
with Liberal reservations; but in the capital an impatient surge of advanced opinion swept aside the
sedate republicanism of the older type and substituted
the wilder gestures of MM. Gambetta and Rochefort
for the more measured utterance of MM. Jules Favre

and Garnier-Pagès. M. Ollivier was defeated in
Paris, and even M. Thiers found difficulty in retaining his seat. The election was followed by a strange
week of disorder. Crowds hung about the streets on
summer nights; there was some hooting and the
sound of broken glass, and they burnt a cabmen's
shelter in Belleville. At the Tuileries there were
lights in the great windows, and nervous guests looked
out at a sea of surly faces in the Carrousel. There was
a ball at the palace that evening; but the floor was half
empty as the band swung to the gentle lilt of Wald-
teufel's valses, and between the dances one could hear
sharp voices shouting orders and the angry surge outside as the police charged the crowd. The rioting died
down, and when the Emperor drove out with Eugénie
in an open carriage, they were tolerably well received.
There was a coal strike in the provinces, and a legacy
of bitterness was left by an unfortunate collision with
the troops at La Ricamarie. The Emperor affected
to be satisfied with the results of the election. But
the country was uneasy, and Lord Lyons interpreted
its temper as weariness 'of the uncertainty and dis-
quiet in which they are kept by the fact that peace
and war, and indeed everything, depend upon the
inscrutable will of one man whom they do believe
capable of giving them surprises, and whom they no
longer believe to be infallible.' The real verdict of
the country in 1869 was a condemnation of autocracy
and of its most prominent agent, M. Rouher. Even
Persigny admitted in public that the generation of
the *coup d'état* had played its part; and in his unhurried fashion, whilst the new Deputies took the
road for Paris, the Emperor prepared to face the
new demand.

The Chamber met after midsummer, and Napoleon's incurable taciturnity permitted it to meet in total uncertainty as to his intentions. There was a strange failure on the part of the Emperor to put himself at the head of the Liberal movement which was manifestly sweeping the country, and the British ambassador reported gloomily on his dwindling prestige:

> 'When one looks at the position in which things stood, I will not say before the election, but between the election and the meeting of the Chamber, one is astonished at the rapid descent of the personal power and the reputation. Whether concessions will come in time to enable him to stop before he is dragged to the bottom of the hill, is even beginning to be questioned.'

The concessions came; but they had an unfortunate air of following rather than leading the political tendencies of the day. There was a general promise of constitutional reform, and the new era was consecrated by the sacrifice of M. Rouher.

The *Vice-Empereur* had ceased to reign; but the Emperor had a return of his illness in August, and his resolution was unequal to the shock of a new departure into genuine constitutionalism. Rouher was out; but the Liberals were not yet in, and when an obviously transitional ministry was formed, opinion was impressed that finality had not yet been reached. The Constitution was amended by the complete emancipation of the Chamber; freedom of debate and legislation, questions to ministers, and financial control were restored to the Deputies, and even the Senate caught a breath of the new air. It was a strange celebration of the centenary of Napoleon I. But the Liberal Empire had not yet enlisted

the support of the Liberals, and Lord Clarendon was
left with an uneasy 'instinct that they will drift into
a republic before another year is over.' In the autumn
the Empress went off to attend the opening of the
Suez Canal, after alarming Lord Lyons with the suggestion of a visit to India. The Empire seemed to be
jolting uncomfortably through a period of transition,
with strikes in the industrial areas and some incompetent rioting in Paris, when Eugénie confided to her
'bien cher Louis' her impressions of a journey to Port
Said by way of Constantinople. Her spelling was
not invariably faultless, but her emotions were always genuine—in Venice, *'cette ville du silence, ou
tout semble glisser,'* at 'Majenta' where she laid a
wreath by torchlight, on board the *Aigle* with a *bora*
blowing down the Adriatic and all the Turkish guns
banging at the Dardanelles. The Sultan was charming, and the Khedive *'d'un galant à te faire dresser les
cheveux.'* The French yacht steamed through the
Canal at the head of the line, and everybody went to
see the wonderful new Egyptian opera *Aïda,* which
Ismail had ordered from the *maestro* Verdi for the
occasion. With startling rapidity the electric telegraph brought to the Comtesse de Pierrefonds (for
Eugénie had acquired the supreme royal affectation
of *incognito*) the news from home, and the Egyptian
campaign of the Second Empire was crowned by a
bulletin from Compiègne:

> *'Tu as vu les Pyramides et les quarante siècles t'ont
> contemplée: nous t'embrassons tendrement.*
>
> NAPOLÉON.'

But politics went on in France, whilst the Emperor
consoled his solitude by giving small dances at the

Tuileries for some American young ladies. Even
Eugénie seemed to advise an honest acceptance of
the new Liberalism:

> '*Je pense malgré tout qu'il ne faut pas se décourager et
> marcher dans la voie que tu as inaugurée, la bonne foi dans
> les concessions données . . . plus il est nécessaire de
> prouver au pays qu'on a des* idées *et non des* expédients.
> *. . . Je n'aime pas les coups, et je suis persuadée qu'on ne
> fait pas deux fois dans le même règne un coup d'état. . . .*'

The autumn deepened in disorder, and Napoleon
seemed to drift for support towards the Liberals.
M. Ollivier was discreetly approached in October and
responded in voluminous letters with a quotation
from Machiavelli and an offer of service, '*prêt à
prendre la responsabilité de la lutte et à prendre la
révolution corps à corps comme ministre.*' Judicious
intermediaries flitted up and down with messages,
and on a November evening he left by the Gare du
Nord for Compiègne; a large muffler and the absence
of his spectacles lent him an unusual air of mystery.
At the country station a secretary tapped him on the
arm; he was spirited to the Château in a closed
carriage, and the Emperor was waiting in his study.
They talked until midnight, and a night train took
M. Ollivier back to Paris. Napoleon seemed to hesi-
tate, to shrink from the full logic of a Liberal
ministry, and to prefer an innocuous blend of Liberal
elements with his present ministers. There was an
interval of correspondence in which the Emperor
confided to M. Ollivier '*la grandeur du rôle que vous
êtes appelé à jouer*' and M. Ollivier imparted to his
sovereign his emotion at '*l'élévation calme et douce
. . . la sérénité simple qui respirent dans la lettre de*

votre Majesté.' But in the intervals between his
graceful genuflexions he found time for sound advice.
*'Appelez à vous la jeunesse, Sire, elle seule peut sau-
ver votre fils, les vieillards égoïstes qui vous entourent
ne songent qu'à eux. . . .'* It was a wise diagnosis of
the failing powers of the Empire, of the creeping de-
bility which nothing but the new Liberalism could
arrest. Names were discussed and ministries were
allocated. Before the transaction was complete, the
Chamber met, and the Emperor publicly indicated
his new programme: *'La France veut la liberté, mais
avec l'ordre; l'ordre j'en réponds. Aidez-moi, Messieurs, à sauver la liberté.'* It was Napoleon's reply
to the election of the egregious M. Rochefort for a
division of Paris, and a month later he made his
meaning clear by inviting M. Ollivier to form a parliamentary ministry. The invitation was accepted;
solemn gentlemen consulted their consciences and
took office from the highest motives; there was a pleasant flutter at the opening of a new year, and only one
shadow fell across the bright hopes of M. Ollivier and
his friends. It was the year 1870.

XVIII

THE faint dawn of 1870 broke over France with a pale gleam of hope, and the last winter of the Empire had almost an air of spring. New men, new names, new notions seemed to come crowding on the scene, and the stiff outlines of autocracy were melting in the rebirth of the *Empire libéral* into the simpler, younger form of a modern monarchy. One could see, like shadows on the blind of a lighted room, the Emperor's tired, gracious gesture of surrender and M. Ollivier standing erect to take up, in the name of France, the burden of the Empire. And outside, in the sky above them, the dawn of 1870 was breaking.

The year opened in the pleasant stir of the new ministry. The decree which appointed it bore date January 2, and for a few months it lived a busy life of fresh endeavour. Someone had called it the *ministère des honnêtes gens;* and the old, faded figures of the Empire seemed to go back into their corners, as the band struck up an air of good intentions and M. Ollivier and his colleagues took their blameless way down the centre of the stage. M. Rouher was a retired grandee in the Senate; M. Haussmann faded inconspicuously out of public life; and even M. Thiers seemed satisfied. The Emperor played little games with the monkey which Eugénie had brought from Egypt or sat at Council with his

back to the great fire, between M. Ollivier and the
fierce moustache of General Lebœuf, drawing on his
papers and making tentative suggestions. That
winter there were great parties in Paris; Madame
Ollivier wore the little dresses which made them
call her *Sainte Mousseline* at the palace, and among
the uniforms one saw queer, half-forgotten figures
where M. Guizot came out once more to hear the
talk and M. Odilon Barrot abounded with twenty
years' accumulation of good advice. There was a
strange, refreshing air of new beginnings, and the
older men seemed to stand aside to watch the slow
dawn of the *Empire libéral*. But it was the dawn of
a day that never came.

There was a flicker of disorder before the month
was out which showed the quality of the new ministers. The Emperor had a faintly raffish cousin
named Pierre Bonaparte, who lived in the suburbs
after a somewhat violent career in the more congenial
air of the Balkans and South America. His private
life, in spite of an aptitude for minor poetry, was
mainly morganatic; and his energies, which were frequently offered to the Imperial service and invariably
refused, were principally devoted to the more dangerous forms of sport. By an unhappy inspiration he
had intervened with some violence in a controversy
with two republican newspapers; and having invited
MM. Rochefort and Paschal Grousset to challenge
him to fight, he was waiting at home at Auteuil on a
January afternoon in 1870 with a bad cold and (by
an unfortunate mannerism) a large revolver in his
pocket. Two strangers were announced, and a young
man named Victor Noir walked in with his friend to
convey to the Prince a challenge from M. Grousset.

The Prince was surly; M. Noir was an offensive
young man in a new pair of gloves; someone slapped
someone's face, and there was a shot. Victor Noir
reeled dying into the street, and his friend scrambled
behind the chairs and tried to get in a shot at the
Prince. The young man in the new gloves died outside, and by six o'clock nervous policemen were
arresting Prince Pierre Bonaparte. This Mexican
interlude, if the republicans exploited it, might shake
the Empire. The grave news met the Emperor at a
Paris railway station, and he was helped to his
carriage. M. Rochefort devoted the evening to the
composition of a staccato invective against the
Emperor's family *'où le meurtre et le guet-apens
sont de tradition et d'usage,'* and on the next day his
paper appeared with deep black borders. The
body of Victor Noir would afford an exquisite, an un-
paralleled excuse for a political funeral, and all
Paris was invited to follow the hearse from Neuilly.
But M. Ollivier and his mild-eyed colleagues were
disinclined to submit to the violence of the streets,
and his spectacles had an unusual gleam in the
Chambers as he informed the excited Deputies that
*'nous sommes la loi; nous sommes le droit; nous
sommes la modération; nous sommes la liberté; si
vous nous y contraignez, nous serons la force.'* The
Liberal Empire was beginning to have an uncomfortably metallic ring, and the benevolent legal gentleman
who presided over it had a business-like conversation
with General Lebœuf, Marshal Canrobert, and Marshal Bazaine as to the best disposition of the troops.
In the morning a huge crowd gathered at Neuilly for
the funeral; and whilst eager spectators hung in
bunches from the trees outside, M. Rochefort argued

with his friends in a little room as to whether the great procession should march heroically across Paris to Père Lachaise or withdraw for speech-making to the safety of a suburban cemetery. There was a scuffle at the horses' heads; but the driver of the hearse preferred the more cautious route, and the crowd trailed obediently after him towards Auteuil. M. Rochefort sat on the hearse; but he fainted before the burial-ground was reached, and the funeral orations were delivered without his assistance. Late in the afternoon the crowd marched back to Paris by the line of the Champs Élysées. They were singing the *Marseillaise,* and Rochefort drove with them in a cab. At the Arc de Triomphe they clambered up and shouted *'Vive la République!'* but the troops were out in the broad avenue between the trees and the Emperor was waiting in uniform at the Tuileries. The cavalry trotted towards the crowd with drawn swords, and its republican principles evaporated before this disturbing spectacle. The road emptied suddenly, and the Liberal Empire had survived its first *journée.*

The ministry of good intentions pursued its amiable way through the cold weather of 1870. There was a generous proliferation of committees to inquire into administrative and educational reform. But national discipline was maintained by the arrest and prosecution of M. Rochefort; he was dining with Madame George Sand that evening, and the police took him later on the way to a crowded meeting. There was a little shouting in the streets; the troops were under arms in barracks, and the police had a busy night. Someone made a stupid speech at a dinner, proposing the health of a regicide bullet—

'*à la petite balle libératrice, à la petite balle humanitaire, à la petite balle de bon secours que le monde
attendait*'—and there was some trouble in M.
Schneider's works at Le Creusot. But France found
it possible to conduct public affairs without the
voluble assistance of M. Rochefort, who passed
his time in prison; and the mutter of insurrection died
away like a distant storm.

A mild glow of enlightenment even fell on the dark,
twisted mass of Imperial foreign policy. M. Ollivier
held conversations, quite in the modern taste, about
disarmament; and Great Britain was invited through
Lord Lyons to approach the Prussians. The Liberal
ministers in both countries had no enthusiasm for
large armaments and high taxation; Lord Clarendon
was full of distaste for 'a state of things that is
neither peace nor war, but which is so destructive
of confidence that men almost desire war with all its
horrors in order to arrive at some certainty of peace,
a state of things that withdraws millions of hands
from productive industry and heavily taxes the people for their own injury and renders them dis-
contented with their rulers'; Mr. Gladstone was
impressed that the object of the proposed *démarche*
was 'noble,' and even Queen Victoria was prepared
to write to the King of Prussia with her own hand.
The subject of disarmament was opened in Berlin.
Bismarck was in an idyllic mood. He wrote to correspondents about unclouded skies and universal
peace. But when the British ambassador proposed
that Prussia should disarm *pari passu* with the
French, he seemed disinclined to include Germany
in the idyll. Mr. Gladstone in his happy island could
afford such dreams; but for Prussia there was still,

26

there was always the haunting fear of French invasion; and then Napoleon was so incalculable. The talk trailed on through the winter; but it got no further than 'a sort of opening as to a conference between Powers as to proportionate reductions and exchange of guarantees.' Bismarck would 'not decline to share in any deliberations,' would 'carefully sift the question,' might even estimate the value of the proffered guarantees. But when he thought of Prussia's defencelessness in Central Europe, he began to wring his hands; France had been so restless as recently as 1869 (one remembered the disturbing transaction of the Belgian railways), and though 'the inclinations of a Nation may be essentially peaceful . . . neither the most powerful Monarch, nor the most influential Minister is able to estimate or guarantee the duration of peaceful Inclinations.' It was all infinitely distressing to a peace-loving Chancellor, and in the outcome France was left to show its good faith by a reduction of 10,000 men in the conscription of 1870, which Count von Moltke noted in his papers. But the work of the General Staff went on, and Lord Clarendon's *démarche* had failed. It was a queer interlude; and after he had died in the crowded summer weeks of 1870 'in the very act,' as Lord Granville said, 'of trying to arrange a matter necessary to civilisation in Europe,' Bismarck told his daughter in the British embassy at Berlin that if her father had lived, there would have been no war. It may be doubted.

The bright prospect of disarmament faded, as the politicians of the Empire settled down to the congenial task of debating a new Constitution. The form and powers of the Senate were to be modified, and the Constitution of 1870 was submitted to the electorate for the final consecration of a *plébiscite.* There was a vigorous campaign, in which the army was sedulously canvassed by the republicans, and the orators of the Opposition explored the Apocrypha of political invective in search of appropriate descriptions of the Empire. But the tyranny which they denounced blandly tolerated their declamations, except when assassination was openly advocated. M. Ollivier abstained from the use of official pressure, and on May 8, 1870, the Liberal Empire was approved by a majority of almost six millions on a poll of nine millions. There was a little uneasiness about the vote of the army; but the Emperor and Eugénie were well received in the Paris barracks, and the Empire seemed refreshed by its new contact with democracy. M. Ollivier was radiant; M. Gambetta regarded the result as *'un écrasement';* M. Jules Favre advised a young friend to stay at the Bar, because *'il n'y a plus rien à faire en politique';* and even the Comte de Paris (though pretenders are rarely susceptible to changes of opinion) felt that little remained for an Orleans prince beyond a discreet withdrawal to America.

In the world beyond the French frontier the Emperor had resumed his slow manipulation of the alliance with Austria. The Archduke Albert, who had beaten the Italians at Custozza in 1866, came to Paris in March; the ministers saw little of him, but he talked strategy to Napoleon. Nothing was put on paper; but the feeling grew that the two Empires would stand together against Prussia, and when a change of Foreign Ministers in May brought M. de Gramont from the embassy at Vienna to the Quai

d'Orsay, he came with a simple faith in the unsigned
Austrian alliance which he had pressed on the two
Emperors at Salzburg and discussed so eagerly with
Count von Beust. There was a talk in Paris, where
four generals sat round a table with the Emperor:
within four months all of them heard the thudding
German guns in the sunshine outside Metz or in
the echoing hollow of Sedan. But in May 1870, they
bent over their maps and catalogued the victories of
the new triple alliance over Count von Moltke. It
was to be a most enjoyable campaign: whilst the
Prussians were held in Lorraine, the French would
pass the Rhine and grateful South Germans would
observe their meeting with the Austrians in Bavaria,
as eager Italians came pouring northwards through
the Tyrol and indignant Danes avenged, under the
guns of a French fleet, the defeats of 1864. It was a
noble plan, which required little for its success beyond
an alliance or so and the sympathy of South Germany. There was a faint uneasiness about the opening weeks: it would be awkward if the Prussians
moved before the Austrians were ready to strike at
them from the south. But the Archduke was so
obliging, and in June General Lebrun went off to
Austria to seal the bargain. He found the Archduke, in the less heady air of his own country, a shade
inclined to withdraw from exciting realities into the
shadowy sphere of military theory; and they discussed academic campaigns according to the best
principles of the art of war. He saw the Austrian
Emperor privately under some trees in a great park.
Franz-Joseph was full of friendliness and highly
confidential; but there was a disquieting tendency
to postpone the Austrian move until after the first

French victory.   Lebrun came back to Paris in the
hot June days.   The world seemed very still; Mr.
Hammond noticed the lull in foreign affairs, and M.
Ollivier informed his colleagues in the Chamber that
at no time had European peace seemed more assured.
Three days later (it was a Sunday, and M. Ollivier
had gone to the country for the day) a telegram
from Madrid informed M. de Gramont that Marshal
Prim proposed to make Prince Leopold of Hohenzollern-Sigmaringen King of Spain.

The news was unexpected, and on the Sunday
Gramont drove out to St. Cloud to see the Emperor.
But the idea was not an entire novelty at the Quai
d'Orsay.   The Spanish throne had been in the market for almost two years; judicious king-makers in
Madrid ignored their own pretenders and thumbed
the *Almanach de Gotha;* there were always Coburgs
to be had, and Austria would never miss an Archduke; the waiting list was full of Bourbons; a taste
for novelty suggested an Italian prince, or one might
even ask Queen Victoria to spare a son—the Duke
of Edinburgh, who played the violin so charmingly.
The notion of a Hohenzollern seemed to come from
the Prussian papers.   The Catholic branch was
obviously eligible; one son had already been placed
in Roumania; and after a Prussian agent had
appeared in Madrid to appease his passionate interest
in the battle-fields of the Peninsular War, the name
of Prince Leopold was launched with touching spontaneity by a Spanish Deputy.   The proposal had
alarmed Paris in 1869, and the acute M. Benedetti
was directed to make a complaint in Berlin.   But
Count Bismarck had been blandly reassuring, and
the disturbing notion of a Prussian colonel on the

throne of Spain seemed to fade away. The family was mildly disappointed: it was never easy to provide for younger sons; Charles seemed quite happy as a sort of king at Bucharest, and a young man with a fair moustache and a taste for adventure might do far worse than go to Madrid. Napoleon had supported the Roumanian appointment; he was always kind (was he not urging Charles to marry in Germany —*les princesses allemandes sont si bien élevées?*)— and perhaps he would put up with a younger brother at Madrid. Bismarck knew better: Napoleon would not, could not tolerate a second Prussia beyond the Pyrenees, and the project meant war with France. Since German unity required a German war, it was not unwelcome. Moltke was ready, and one had better fight the French before they found their allies; Beust's drift towards France looked dangerous, one could never trust the Italians, and Fleury, the new French ambassador at St. Petersburg, was driving about in the Czar's sleigh. It was a good moment, and early in 1870 there was a solemn committee of the Hohenzollern at Berlin. The Catholic branch was informed that it was a national duty to accept the Spanish crown; they seemed to comply, and if Leopold would not go to Madrid, an enterprising father was prepared to send Fritz. Spanish gentlemen began to appear in Germany, and Prussian agents flitted about Spain. Prince Leopold conquered his doubts in June, and Prim was informed that Bismarck had found a king for him. There was a pleasant lull in Europe. The Emperor, who was ill again, was resting at St. Cloud, and the King of Prussia was at Ems to take the waters. The statesmen were on holiday; Count Bismarck was at

Varzin, M. Benedetti was on leave, and even the indomitable Prim was in the hills behind Toledo. But the news got out: the French ambassador at Madrid asked questions; and when his report reached Paris on a quiet Sunday in July, the stage was set hurriedly for the first act of a tragedy.

The French case was obvious, and it was promptly stated in the language of diplomacy at Berlin and Madrid and repeated in the fuller tones of journalism by the whole French press. On the Tuesday the Emperor asked Baron Rothschild to telegraph to his London house for pressure to be put on Mr. Gladstone to secure the withdrawal of Prince Leopold. Someone gave notice of a question in the Chamber, and on a Wednesday morning the Council met at St. Cloud. Lebœuf, who had succeeded Niel at the Ministry of War, was asked whether he could face the prospect of hostilities, and assented; there was a vague talk about alliances, and the Emperor took two letters from a drawer and read them to his ministers. The letters were from Franz-Joseph and Victor Emmanuel; they were a year old and expressed a polite predilection for the French alliance. Gramont's draft of his reply for the Chamber was revised in Council, and before two o'clock the ministers drove back to Paris. The question was answered by the Foreign Minister in a firm statement:

> 'Nous ne croyons pas que le respect des droits d'un peuple voisin nous oblige à souffrir qu'une puissance étrangère, en plaçant un de ses princes sur le trône de Charles-Quint, puisse déranger à notre détriment l'équilibre actuel des forces en Europe, et mettre en péril les intérêts et l'honneur de la France.'

There was a roar in the Chamber, and M. Ollivier

explained his colleague's policy to the excited Deputies: '*Le Gouvernement désire la paix! Il la désire avec passion, mais avec l'honneur.*' There was a sudden flutter in Europe. It was only the day before that the permanent under-secretary had been telling Lord Granville of the lull in foreign affairs, and the new Foreign Secretary confessed a little helplessly to Lord Lyons that the news, which arrived whilst they were debating the Irish Land Bill, 'took Mr. Gladstone and me by surprise.' But the expedients of British policy were unheroic: the prescient Hammond drafted despatches for Lord Granville, and the Queen might write a letter. Russia was apathetic; and Beust fell back on good advice proposing, with a rare instinct for comic opera, that a French cruiser should intercept Prince Leopold on his way to Spain. Whilst the streets of Paris began to stir and mutter and excited men opened their newspapers in the sudden enjoyment of a bold foreign policy, the French sent messengers in all directions. Someone might see Marshal Serrano in Madrid and persuade him to withdraw Prim's candidate for the throne; a Roumanian came to St. Cloud before dawn on a summer morning and left the Emperor with a mission to Sigmaringen. And Benedetti (his moment had arrived) went to Ems.

Prussia had been elaborately unapproachable since the crisis opened. Bismarck had gone to ground at Varzin; his subordinates in Berlin were studiously obtuse; and their innocuous sovereign was sipping his water in the Kurhaus at Ems. French policy appealed to the valetudinarian Caesar, and M. Benedetti unpacked his luggage at the Hôtel de Bruxelles. He saw the King of Prussia twice; William declined to put pressure on Prince Leopold. But suddenly relief came from an unexpected quarter: the Prince and his father succumbed to the increasing volume of grave advice, and after nine days of crisis the Hohenzollern candidature was withdrawn. It was a triumph for France; Bismarck had come to town to start his war, but he sat staring at the news in Berlin, whilst M. Ollivier, who had been handed a telegram in the Tuileries Gardens and ran home to tell his wife, was spreading the good news in the Chamber. There was to be no war; troop-movements in Algeria stopped, and the King of Italy went off to shoot. That afternoon (it was Tuesday, July 12) the Emperor drove back from the Tuileries to St. Cloud; he was cheered on the road, but he found the Court a shade sceptical of the latest triumph of French policy. The Prussian government was not a party to the renunciation, and Sadowa was still unavenged. The Empress seemed gravely dissatisfied, and General Bourbaki of the Guard threw down his sword and struck an angry attitude. Gramont was there, and in the late afternoon a hasty talk produced a fresh policy. The King of Prussia was to be asked to join in the renunciation and to guarantee that the Hohenzollern candidature would never be resumed: then the angry ladies and gentlemen at St. Cloud would be satisfied, and the Empire might claim a victory over the *parvenu* power of Prussia. M. Ollivier had said to M. Thiers at the Chamber: '*Nous tenons la paix, nous ne la laisserons pas échapper.*' He was wrong.

The new instructions were telegraphed to Ems through the darkness of the summer night, while M. Ollivier tried to get some sleep and played with

the notion of resignation; and in the morning sunshine M. Benedetti was waiting under the trees at
Ems to see the King of Prussia. The old gentleman
had drunk his water and was strolling benevolently
along the Kurgarten on that Wednesday morning.
But Benedetti seemed to reopen the whole affair
with his fresh demand for guarantees. The King
refused a little shortly, and they parted near the
bandstand. He asked three times to see the King
again; but polite gentlemen came to the Hôtel de
Bruxelles and informed the ambassador that the case
did not require . . . that no useful purpose . . . that
Majesty had nothing to add. That morning there
was a wrangle at St. Cloud over the French mobilisation; M. Ollivier insisted on delay, and the Empress
was rude to him at lunch. That evening Bismarck
dined in Berlin with von Moltke and von Roon.
Their *casus belli* had faded, and the three men sat
gloomily round the table. But a telegram came in
from Ems with the story of King William's morning.
The Chancellor altered it for publication, and in the
new version the King's attitude was represented as
a final dismissal of the French ambassador. Dinner
was resumed in a more convivial mood; the frigid
Moltke became almost uproarious, and von Roon
vociferated his renewed faith in an old German God.
That night the news was known in Berlin, and a
great crowd was roaring 'Nach Paris!' outside the
Schloss. A bellicose Deputy was dining at St. Cloud,
and the Emperor was still fumbling with French
policy.

The news reached Paris on the next morning (it
was Thursday, July 14), and all that summer afternoon the ministers sat in Council with the Emperor

at the Tuileries. About four o'clock they decided to
call out the reserves, and Lebœuf went off to the
Ministry of War to give his orders. There was a
nervous silence at the Council; one minister muttered
to Napoleon that a defeat would bring a revolution,
and someone with a last gleam of hope proposed a
Congress. The Emperor welcomed the familiar
expedient, and his eyes filled with tears. M. Ollivier
drafted something eloquent for the Chamber; but it
was too late to make a statement that evening, and
the Council adjourned. When it met again after
dinner at St. Cloud, there was a change of tone;
Bismarck had sent the news from Ems to every capital in Europe, and the French ministers could not
face their country with a compromise. They talked
until nearly midnight, and drove back to Paris under
the summer stars. The streets were full of men shouting '*à Berlin!*' and at the Opera, by special leave,
for the first time in eighteen years someone was singing the *Marseillaise*.

On the Friday morning the Council met early at
St. Cloud. Gramont read over the draft of a statement for the Chamber, and the Emperor clapped his
hands. Lebœuf said that the army was ready and
that the chances in a war with Prussia would never
be better. Benedetti was waiting at the Quai d'Orsay,
a little mystified by the significance which the world
seemed to attach to his adventure with the King at
Ems; and M. Ollivier went down to the Chamber.
He made his statement in the proud tone of a minister
announcing war, and he was followed by M. Thiers.
By a singular irony this indomitable critic of Imperial
policy, who had reproached Napoleon since 1866 with
the rise and the menace of Prussia, became suddenly

reasonable. He was heard with impatience by an excited House, and M. Ollivier returned to the tribune to make his meaning clear. He re-stated the insulting publication of the report from Ems, and having argued the soundness of his cause, he made a sudden gesture:

> '*Oui, de ce jour commence pour les ministres mes collègues et pour moi, une grande reponsabilité. Nous l'acceptons, le cœur léger!*'

The phrase rang later with a tragic ineptitude, and the speaker passed forty years more of a long life in arguing it away. But the Chamber was cheering on that July afternoon in 1870. The debate trailed on, and the House went into committee to hear the ministers *in camera.* Lebœuf praised the *Chassepot* and the *mitrailleuses;* Gramont, when someone asked about alliances, looked mysterious and mentioned the Austrian ambassador and the Italian minister. The day was almost over. In London a red box was passed along the Treasury Bench to Mr. Gladstone, and he said in such a strange tone, 'War declared against Prussia.' There was an evening session of the Chamber which voted credits and called up the *Garde mobile,* whilst M. Rouher was felicitating his sovereign at St. Cloud and the Emperor was walking slowly round among his Senators and saying, '*Ce sera long et difficile, il faudra un violent effort.*' They were cheering in the streets of Berlin; and whilst Paris roared '*à Berlin!*' in the failing light, *Nana* was dying in her room on the *boulevard,* and in a garden at Blackheath Mr. Morley was telling the news to Mr. John Stuart Mill. The war had come.

XIX

THE sky was dull over Paris when the Emperor left
St. Cloud. There was a hint of thunder in the air,
and a few early leaves had fallen. He had a word
with his ministers about an offer of mediation from
the Pope and went gravely round the *salon* with a
cigar in his fingers to say good-bye. Then he took up
his *képi* and walked for the last time out of a French
palace. The carriages were waiting, and he stared
in front of him as they drove down to the little station
in the park. At the train he took Eugénie in his
arms: they never met again in France. The Prince
Imperial was with them, and in the silence she drew
the sign of the cross on the boy's forehead in the
Spanish fashion. As the train moved, she called out
'*Louis, fais bien ton devoir!*' and the Emperor waved
his hand from the great window of his saloon. Hats
came off on the platform, and there was a faint cheer
of '*Vive l'Empereur!*' from the little crowd. The
Empress drove back in an open carriage with her face
hidden. The train clanked over a level crossing, and
some people cheered. That night the Emperor was
at Metz.

The French armies were strung out awkwardly
along the line of the frontier; and there was an uneasy
pause before the great advance began, which was to
swing MacMahon across the Rhine and stretch a

hand to Austria over the neutral kingdoms of South
Germany. A fleet was fitting out at Cherbourg for
the Baltic, and Trochu was to command an army
which would land under its guns, force Düppel, and
raise Hanover against the Prussians. But French
diplomacy was still piping to the Danes, and they
would not dance; Italy and Austria had developed
a belated passion for peace; and the South Germans,
who had been imperfectly rehearsed for their parts
in the Emperor's plans, were mobilising under von
Moltke's orders. Even the neutrals became faintly
hostile when Bismarck startled Mr. Gladstone's sus-
ceptibilities (and set him asking Mr. Cardwell questions about 'the means of sending 20,000 men to
Antwerp') by publishing Benedetti's draft treaty of
1866 for the annexation of Belgium to France; and
there was a sudden, tragic echo when the French
minister at Washington gave way in the great heat
and shot himself. The *Cent-gardes* were clattering
through the streets of Metz on a summer evening, as
the Emperor drove from the station; and there was
a pleasing discussion among the foreign diplomats
in Paris as to whether, in view of the early prospect
of French victories, they should illuminate the
embassies. But on the frontier Lebœuf was telegraphing for ammunition, and Frossard was inquiring a little helplessly for a few maps of France in
place of the copious issues of German sheets which
he found *'inutiles pour le moment'*; recruits were
trailing about France in search of their units; a
brigadier arrived in Belfort and failed to find his
command; and Metz was calling hungrily for a million rations. There was a hasty conference when
the Emperor arrived, and on the next day he was

inspecting troops at St. Avold. Bazaine and Frossard met him, and there was a casual talk about a raid on Saarbrück. The town had no importance; but it was on Prussian territory, and an advance into Germany would look well in the French papers. Napoleon had written home rather dispiritedly to the Empress; he was driving miserably round the cantonments outside Metz, and in a letter to M. Ollivier he made a dismal confession: *'Nous avons tout intérêt à traîner la guerre en longueur, puisqu'il nous est impossible de la terminer par ce qu'on appelle un coup de foudre.'* But after an army corps, with bands playing the *Marseillaise,* had driven in a screen of Prussian infantry and shelled the railway-station at Saarbrück on August 2, his mercurial Parisians were invited to rejoice over the first French victory, and a courtly *communiqué* informed the nation that the Prince Imperial had received his 'baptism of fire.' The boy found it rather enjoyable; he was allowed to keep a shot that fell near them, and as they waited on the hillside under fire, it almost seemed as though the four-leaved clover which Eugénie had sent from St. Cloud had brought them luck. But his father suffered cruelly on horseback; he had been in pain all the morning and kept his horse at a walk. The firing died away about one o'clock, and the Emperor stumbled heavily to the ground muttering to Lebrun, *'Je souffre horriblement . . . je préfère marcher un peu; cela me soulage.'* It was a queer, pitiable ending to the long tale of Bonapartes in the field which had begun with a gaunt young general in the sunshine at Montenotte.

The sick Emperor fumbled with his armies round

Metz, and slowly in the first weeks of August von Moltke's troop-trains began to pour his men along the French frontier. Douay was caught at Wissembourg; and on August 6, whilst Frossard was driven in on the French masses in front of Metz, MacMahon eighty miles to the south-east was fighting for Alsace among the trees of Wörth. His field guns were outranged, but the Zouaves went stumbling forward through the hedges with the bayonet; fresh German troops came up to the sound of the guns; and as the Crown Prince sat watching on his horse across the valley, the French were checked, were held, were forced back up the slope. There was a sudden drumming of hoofs, a gleam of tall steel helmets, a flutter of waving horsehair as the *Cuirassiers* crashed into a charge and plunged forward through the sunshine to be shot to pieces in a village street. Somewhere to the left the *Turcos* were yelling and lunging with bayonets among the trees; and as the sun dropped behind the blue line of the Vosges, the French went trailing westwards in retreat.

When the news came to Metz, there was an evening of dull confusion. The Emperor sat staring in the *Préfecture,* and angry soldiers argued round him. In Paris, where the Empress was turning over the pages of her Bible in search of lucky passages, false news of a victory had sent a great crowd surging into the Place de la Concorde; two figures stood above the sea of faces and sang the *Marseillaise* from an open carriage, and M. Ollivier made a speech from a balcony. But the news faded; and as the telegrams came in from Metz, a sullen crowd began to trail about the streets. It was a warm evening, and they were shouting in time:

'Ollivier!
Ollivier!
Des nouvelles!
Des nouvelles!'

Scared ministers were staring at a telegram with the news of two defeats, and at St. Cloud a pale, handsome woman was fighting down her tears and saying, *'La dynastie est perdue, il ne faut plus songer qu'à la France.'* Someone broke down, and she turned sharply on her: *'Ne m'attendrissez pas, j'ai besoin de tout mon courage.'* In the dark hours of the summer night she drove into Paris for the last time, and a Council met among the sheeted furniture at the Tuileries. General Trochu was there, and he became voluble about his colleagues' errors. He was still speaking when the Council adjourned, and someone stayed behind to listen to him. They had decided to call the Chamber, and in the dawn M. Ollivier walked home through the silent streets.

That day (it was a Sunday) the Emperor drove by the first light to his train at Metz. He was to join the army at St. Avold for a general advance; but at the station they gave him a telegram, and his doubts returned. He showed it to Lebœuf and drove back to the *Préfecture.* All that day they were full of plans and good advice. Someone was bold enough to urge that the Emperor should leave the army and go back to Paris. A tactful general referred to 1812, but the Emperor sat quietly on a sofa and took the Prince Imperial on his knee. He asked his heir: *'Je veux que tu sois juge de la question.'* The boy was excited, and he replied: *'C'est impossible, rentrer avant de nous être battus, ce serait un déshonneur.'*

27

The point of honour seemed a trifle childish; but
French opinion would be childish also, and it had
been plainly stated by a child.

For four days more, whilst Eugénie took chloral in
an empty palace and Paris stared at the news of
Wörth, he fumbled with his armies. Metz seemed
full of plans and each one had its turns. Sometimes
they were to stand and give battle in Lorraine; sometimes they were to fall back on Châlons and cover
Paris in the great plain of Champagne. The weary
columns tramped up and down in the driving rain
(the season had broken), and the armies of the
Empire wheeled interminably with the shifting
strategy of their master. One day a thin old man
came to headquarters and gave, with a queer flavour
of old republican debates, the name of Changarnier;
they found him a uniform, and he peered about to
see men whom he had known in Africa. But the
Emperor still trailed his doubts about the *Préfecture;*
and when M. Ollivier begged Eugénie to bring him
back to Paris, she turned angrily: *'Avant une
victoire, c'est impossible! . . . c'est le déshonneur!'*
They pressed her to recall the Prince Imperial. She
said that he knew how to ride, and then, in a sudden
flare, *'Il peut se faire tuer! Oh! laissez-le se faire
tuer!'*

The chamber met and helped, as is the way of
Chambers, to win the war by making a crisis. The
Empress had struggled helplessly with her ministers;
but she found an excited crowd of Deputies to rid
her of them. The streets were full of angry men,
when M. Ollivier spoke for the last time in the
Chamber and then resigned; the hunt for scapegoats
had begun. His place was taken by an elderly

cavalry officer named Cousin-Montauban, whom the campaign of China in 1860 had decorated with the fantastic title of Palikao; and the last ministry of the Empire (it was formed on August 10 and lasted for twenty-four days) was the familiar war-time masquerade of reaction in the bright clothes of patriotism. Paris was pleasantly excited by the cheers in the Chamber and the shouts in the street. But at Metz the days passed slowly. The Prussians were feeling their way into France and Uhlans were beginning to trot into startled villages, as the sick man at the *Préfecture* fingered the cards uncertainly. In the first movement the Emperor of the French had commanded his armies, as he did in the days when Berthier wrote out the orders and Murat rode jingling with the cavalry. But Lebœuf had failed him; angry telegrams were pouring in from Paris; and Bazaine was given the command. The tired battalions turned once more to fall back from Metz on Verdun. There was a brisk rear-guard action beyond the river, as the Emperor's escort clattered through the empty Sunday streets and he drove out of Metz saluting with a tired hand. That night he lay at Longeville; from his house they could see the smoke drifting over Borny, and he was in bed when Bazaine rode up to report. The Emperor was almost cheerful—'*vous venez de rompre le charme*'—and he was waiting, still waiting for an answer from Franz-Joseph: one must be careful of the army and take no risks which might discourage dubious allies. MacMahon had lost an army in Alsace; but there was still Bazaine and the Army of (how far away it seemed) the Rhine. One must fall back into France and then begin again—*tout peut se rétablir.*

Napoleon had been eighteen days at Metz, and on the next morning (with the ghastly ineptitude of anniversaries it was the *fête* of the Empire) he rode slowly up the hill to Gravelotte. There was a village on the bare ridge, and he rested at a little inn. All day the troops went marching by; there was silence in the ranks, but sometimes they stared sullenly at the Emperor's carriages by the roadside. Late in the afternoon Bazaine rode up; the burly man had brought some flowers for his sovereign. That night, as they slept in little houses at Gravelotte, the Germans circled slowly round Metz to the south; and in the early light the Emperor took the road again in an open carriage. Bazaine saluted, as Napoleon said, *'Je vous confie la dernière armée de la France; songez au Prince impérial'*; and when the artillery drivers touched their team, the carriage went down the long white road. A line of vans went slowly with it; the servants wore the Emperor's livery of green and gold, and one could see the *chefs* in their white coats on top of a heavy *fourgon*. The Lancers of the Guard and some Dragoons rode with them. But on the road he changed his escort. The heavy cavalry seemed too slow. The Emperor (he was wrapped in a long cloak and looking ill) said something faintly to a general, and he clattered out of Conflans with the *Chasseurs d'Afrique*. They took the road for Verdun, and behind them a plodding company of infantry could hear the guns of Rezonville. Scared faces watched the Emperor go by, and they stopped at a little town to telegraph to Paris. Napoleon's message was vague; but the Prince Imperial confided to Eugénie his delighted experiences of war:

'Ma chère Maman,—Je ais très bien, ainsi que papa; tout va de mieux en mieux. . . .'

The dismal drive went on, back down the white roads into France. At one o'clock they were at Verdun. The streets were silent, and they waited whilst a train was made up. Some third-class carriages were coupled to an engine; a few carriage-cushions were laid on the wooden seat, and the Emperor left for Châlons. Somewhere behind them, on the slope of Mars-la-Tour, the long cavalry trumpets were sounding the charge and mounted men in red and blue and white went crashing forward over the hills. The green trees of the Argonne slid past the window, and at a little station in Champagne General Trochu came to the door. He had travelled from Paris to take command of an army corps, and the dazed man with the great moustache asked him twice, a little stupidly, for news of the King of Prussia. It was evening when they reached the camp at Châlons, and the Emperor drove to his quarters in a cart.

For four days they waited at Châlons. The trains came steaming in from the east with MacMahon's broken regiments from Wörth, and disorderly young *mobiles* from Paris bawled insults at Napoleon. On the first morning, whilst Bazaine was falling back on Gravelotte, there was a hasty talk in the Emperor's room at Châlons. When they told him that his place was either on the frontier or in Paris, he replied: *'C'est vrai, j'ai l'air d'avoir abdiqué.'* Someone pressed him to send Trochu back to the capital as Governor, to follow him, and concentrate the troops round Paris. He agreed, and Trochu drove to the station; he found the line blocked near Épernay with

trains full of material for the siege of Mainz. But
Napoleon was no longer master of his movements;
the government was in Paris, and the new plan was
equally distasteful to the Empress and M. de Palikao.
The return of the Emperor seemed a fatal admission
of defeat; the retreat of the army would isolate
Bazaine. She made a scene with Trochu and sent
indignant telegrams to Châlons. There was a desperate insistence that MacMahon should advance on
Metz and, above all, that the Emperor should keep
away from Paris. But von Moltke was tracing his
circle round Bazaine; the French were locked in
Metz by the long day's fighting at Gravelotte on
August 18, when Canrobert stood in St. Privat and
the Prussian Guard came storming up the bare slopes
which look down towards France; and when Mac-
Mahon made a move from Châlons three days later,
the game was lost. He marched on Rheims, and the
Emperor trailed after him. That night M. Rouher
came to headquarters to urge the army forward
towards Metz. The Marshal refused; but when a
message came through from Bazaine that he was
breaking out of Metz to the north by way of Mont-
médy, they marched uncertainly towards him, and
the *fourgons* of the Emperor rumbled in the dust of
the army. For eight days more, whilst MacMahon
felt blindly for Bazaine, the Emperor dragged after
him into the north-east. The Prince was sent away;
but the *Cent-gardes* still clattered into villages with
gleaming helmets, and scared countrymen were half
afraid to call out *'Vive l'Empereur!'* as a carriage
went by with a dull-eyed, weary man: his ragged hair
was long and almost white. They made little meals
for him, but he would not eat; and at night someone

outside his door heard him crying out in pain. Once he mounted a horse to watch the fighting by the Meuse at Beaumont. He telegraphed the news to the Empress and went to his quarters. But that night at dinner they ordered him to take a train to the north; the army was falling back along the river, and he trailed patiently after it. About eleven o'clock the train stopped at a dark station. The platform was almost empty as the Emperor got down, and he walked out into the silent streets of a little town. It was called Sedan.

On the next morning (it was the last day of August, and his faithful Parisians were hunting Prussian spies) he stood on a tower and watched the Germans shelling the last train which got through the slow converging movement of von Moltke's columns. The last army of the Empire was trapped between the Germans and the Belgian frontier; and when a general said something about his safety, the tired Emperor was almost curt: *'Je suis décidé à ne pas séparer mon sort de celui de l'armée.'* There was a dark night; and as the sun came up on September 1, 1870, the guns were thudding in the river mist at Bazeilles. A captain clattered up to the *Sous-préfecture* after dawn with word that the Marshal was wounded. There were tears in Napoleon's eyes as he took the news. But he rode out with his staff; his great moustache was waxed again, and he had put colour on his white face. On the road he passed MacMahon, and for four hours he sat his horse under the German gun-fire. All that morning he strayed along the French line on horseback; twice he dismounted in pain; and once, as he sat behind a battery in action, the men turned to cheer him. Near Givonne he sent his staff to cover and waited for death in the open. Yet it never came. One of his men was killed and three were wounded. But the painted Emperor galloped across the heights amongst the falling men, as his last army reeled into its last defeat. Before noon he was back in the town, and German shells were dropping in the streets. There was no pause in the thunder of the guns, and M. de Galliffet took the *Chasseurs d'Afrique* in a last wild charge at Floing. The little town was quivering with the gun-fire; there was a crash of falling roofs, and the pale flames were licking broken houses in the sunshine. They were urging him to break out of Sedan in a mad *sortie*. But the Emperor took his last decision. Someone was sent to the Citadel to hoist a white flag. Still the guns went on, and the tortured man turned helplessly to his officers: he would see the King of Prussia, but firing must cease—'*Il faut absolument que le feu cesse . . . Il faut faire cesser le feu, il faut faire cesser le feu. Il n'y a que trop de sang versé.*' But shells were still bursting in Sedan and angry soldiers on the hills outside drove at the Germans in the last rush. Two Prussian officers came through the lines and summoned the fortress to surrender. The Emperor had his chance and sent, in that fine writing of his, a letter to the King:

'*Monsieur mon frère,—N'ayant pu mourir à la tête de mes troupes, il ne me reste plus qu'à remettre mon épée entre les mains de Votre Majesté.*

'*Je suis de Votre Majesté le bon Frère,*

NAPOLÉON.'

A French general (the name, with a flavour of old victories, was Reille) rode out to La Marfée with the letter, and the firing died away round Sedan.

There was a night of conferences; the French commander saw von Moltke by lamplight in a little room, and Bismarck talked of peace with an indemnity and the surrender of Alsace-Lorraine. The day came slowly, and at six in the morning of September 2 the Emperor drove over the bridge and out of Sedan in a pair-horse carriage. Some Zouaves were lounging at the gate, and for the last time he heard them call *'Vive l'Empereur!'* But down the road some soldiers threatened him, as he drove through the early mist between the trees to Donchery. Bismarck rode up in uniform, and Napoleon took off his *képi.* The tall man did the same, and the Emperor's tired eyes seemed to follow the movement of his cap. As they came to a big revolver in his belt, the sick man changed colour. There was a little talk between the two men in a cottage by the road. Something was said about terms; and as they sat on a bench outside, the Emperor struggled against the surrender of his army. But Bismarck rode off, and the carriage went down the road to a little house with feudal spires and a conservatory. It was called the Château de Bellevue; and the Emperor went in. They made him take some wine and a piece of bread; and he was reading Montaigne when the King of Prussia came. The tall old man dismounted, and the Emperor stood on the steps with a white face; his cheeks were wet with tears. There was a murmur of courtesy as they went in together. That day he wrote to Eugénie in his agony:

'*Ma chère Eugénie,—Il m'est impossible de te dire ce que j'ai souffert et ce que je souffre. Nous avons fait une marche contraire à tous les principes et au sens commun; cela devait amener une catastrophe. Elle est complète.*

J'aurais préféré la mort à être témoin d'une capitulation si désastreuse, et cependant, dans les circonstances, c'était le seul moyen d'éviter une boucherie de 60,000 personnes.

'Et encore si mes tourments étaient concentrés ici! Je pense à toi, à notre fils, à notre malheureux pays. Que Dieu le protège! Que va-t-il se passer à Paris?

'Je viens de voir le Roi. Il a eu les larmes aux yeux en me parlant de la douleur que je devais éprouver. Il met à ma disposition un de ses châteaux près de Hesse-Cassel. Mais que m'importe où je vais! . . . je suis au désespoir. Adieu, je t'embrasse tendrement.

NAPOLÉON.'

Outside he gave a hand to the Crown Prince, and with the other he wiped away his tears. When the King had gone, he said, '*Messieurs, nous allons à Wilhelmshöhe.*' The reign was over.

XX

THREE days later (it was September 5, 1870) the Emperor came by train through the driving rain into Cassel. There was a crowd at the station, and he walked slowly at the salute past a Prussian guard of honour. Then they drove off among the dripping trees to Wilhelmshöhe, and the cruel journey ended. After a night at the Château de Bellevue (there was a novel of Lytton by his bed) he had left Donchery on an autumn morning in his carriage. The road wound round Sedan among the halted German infantry. People stared at him from the fields, and sometimes a column of French prisoners shook fists and hooted. In the last French village he gave his money to some soldiers, and they drove quickly among the trees into Belgium. That night he lay at Bouillon and sent word to Eugénie of his agony —'*La marche d'aujourd'hui au milieu des troupes prussiennes a été un vrai supplice.*' But France lay behind him, and he stared out at little Belgian towns. Their next halt was at Verviers. In Neufchâteau he took the train for Germany, and at Verviers a boy went calling newspapers along the railway platform. '*Chute de l'Empire!*' (he heard the news) '*Fuite de l'Impératrice!*' That night Napoleon did not sleep.

The news had reached Paris on September 3. The Empress faced it with a cold stare of horror. She stood on the little staircase in the Tuileries where

427

Napoleon used to come up from his study with his cigarette when he heard her gong, and she asked men angrily whether it could be true. Her nights of chloral and her days of coffee were ending in disaster, and for one dreadful minute she was swept into wild rage with her husband. Then she went off to Council. They sat till dinner; and when the Chamber met at midnight, M. Jules Favre gave notice of motion to depose the Emperor and his family. The House rose before dawn; but Paris did not sleep. A great crowd was roaring round the dark palace half the night, and they had found a chant of three syllables, without which no Parisian riot can hope to be successful:

> 'Déchéance!
> Déchéance!'

The shouts drifted across the dark garden into the empty rooms where Eugénie was waiting. But the new day came up brightly over Paris. Early the next morning (it was a Sunday) she heard mass; and they were calling papers in the streets with cries of 'Napoléon III. prisonnier.' The last Council met at eight, and they fumbled with plans for a new Regency. But a crowd was gathering in the Place de la Concorde, and the Empress telegraphed despairingly to her mother at Madrid:

> '. . . Du courage, chère mère; si la France veut se défendre, elle le peut. Je ferai mon devoir. Ta malheureuse fille, Eugénie.'

Outside the sun was shining in the great square, and the crowds were staring across the river at the Palais

Bourbon. There was a line of mounted police on the bridge; and Sir Charles Dilke strolled round to see the sights, whilst his friend Mr. Labouchere made comic speeches to the crowd in the most amusing characters. About mid-day the square was almost empty (it was lunch-time, and the sun beat down on the broad pavement between the fountains), and some solemn gentlemen walked over from the Chamber to persuade the Empress to abdicate. She had few ambitions left; but to desert her post in face of a German invasion was distasteful. She was quite calm and consented, with an unusual respect for the Constitution, to act as her ministers might decide. But the decision was taken elsewhere. The streets were filling again, and the troops were disinclined to fight. A disorderly crowd broke into the Palais Bourbon, and about three o'clock in the afternoon of September 4, 1870, M. Gambetta was informing the Chamber in his great voice that the dynasty had ceased to reign, whilst M. Jules Favre said something encouraging about a Provisional Government. They met General Trochu on his horse outside and, with a quaint flavour of 1848, five gentlemen went off once more to make a new world at the Hôtel de Ville. The streets were shouting '*Vive la République!*' and M. Mérimée was writing his last letter at the Senate. Somewhere across Paris, in the sunshine and the shouting, a Spanish woman was waiting, like his *Carmen* outside the bull-ring, for the blow. They came round her at the Tuileries with terrified advice. Someone went out of the room to fetch a revolver, and she slipped away with Prince Metternich and the Italian minister. They got into the Louvre, and their steps went echoing down the great empty galleries; there were bare spaces on the walls where the best of the pictures had been sent to Brest for safety. At the foot of a staircase she came out into the sunshine. The street was full of men; they were all shouting; but when a youth saw her face and turned to give the news, his voice was swept away in the uproar of the crowd. They found a closed cab, and she drove slowly through the press in the Rue de Rivoli with her veil down and a hand to her face. She could see them taking down the eagles as she went; it tasted bitter, and she said, a little ruefully, '*Déjà!*' At the first house of refuge no one was at home; the cab had been sent away, but they found another and drove to an American dentist's in a quiet street. He was quite startled when he came in and found her waiting. At the Tuileries her adventurous cousin, M. de Lesseps, in whose honour she had gone to Suez, was wrangling with a tall young man in uniform named Sardou; and outside the Palais Bourbon they were chalking up the names of the Provisional Government on the great pillars—Trochu, Jules Favre, Gambetta, and a republican constellation which even included the stormy star of Rochefort. On the next day the enterprising dentist drove her to the coast. That night the Emperor came to Wilhelmshöhe.

The days passed slowly among the trees at Cassel. There was a vague flavour of the First Empire about the place; Jerome had lived there when he was King of Westphalia, and on the first morning Napoleon found a portrait of his mother. It seemed to be always raining; and they sat about and talked, or read the letters which came in a slow trickle from France. The Government of National Defence was

striking attitudes; and Paris, the bright, bedizened
Paris of the Second Empire, was stripping for a
siege. But whilst the naval guns were mounted outside the city and Eugénie and the Prince were staring out of the bow-windows of the Marine Hotel at
Hastings, Napoleon was smoking in his little room
at Cassel. He wrote a pamphlet, *Des causes qui
ont amené la capitulation de Sedan,* and a second on
*Les relations de la France avec l'Allemagne sous
Napoléon III.;* they were published in Brussels without his signature. The Prussian army seemed to
fascinate him; all that autumn, whilst he went for
little walks in the park and eyed the uniforms of the
German sentries, he was collecting technical material
for a book on German military organisation; and
once in the barracks at Cassel he was allowed to see
a battery of the new breech-loading field-guns. It
was always hot in the little room where the Emperor
wrote, and the group of silent Frenchmen had a
faint, despairing air of St. Helena. General Castel-
nau played Bertrand to the Hudson Lowe of an
obliging German count. But Hesse-Cassel was less
impressive than the South Atlantic, and Bonapartist
piety never compiled a *Mémorial de Wilhelmshöhe.*

Politics seemed very far away; the Russians were
quietly tearing up treaties in the confusion, and at
Rome the French had gone and the Italians were
marching in; but the Emperor sat in the silence of
his provincial park, whilst the great guns began to
boom round Paris. At Hastings the Empress had
made a vague attempt to enlist Franz-Joseph and
the Czar in support of France, and an equivocal
gentleman named Régnier flitted about with a
strange project for a peace-treaty between the Ger-

mans and the Empire. His credentials consisted of
an air of mystery and a photograph of the sea-front
at Hastings signed (under false pretences) by the
Prince Imperial. But he was received with the
utmost gravity at German headquarters. Bismarck
had hoped to make peace with the Emperor at Sedan,
and he was half inclined to put his peace terms up
to auction between the Empire and the Third Republic. Crushing victories are frequently embarrassing to the victor when he comes to strike his
bargain; and an Emperor with an army seemed at
once a more stable and a more congenial contracting
party than the incalculable rhetoricians who were
gesticulating in the Government of National Defence. M. Régnier went off, under German auspices,
to Metz to ascertain whether Bazaine's army was
disposed to re-establish the Empire. General Bourbaki was permitted to run the blockade and came to
England; he saw the Empress, but there was no
result. A few weeks later there was a queer attempt
to secure Eugénie's consent to an Imperialist *pronunciamiento* on the best Spanish model by the garrison of Metz; Bazaine was still holding out, and the
Germans seemed to countenance his incursion into
politics. But the Empress was unresponsive, and
Bazaine never played Monck in the new Restoration.
The fortress fell; and as they burned their flags, the
last eagles of the Empire faded into history.

Napoleon was still watching the German sentries
at Wilhelmshöhe. It seemed like the distant misty
days at Ham; Conneau was there, and when an
American came to see him, he discussed the old faded
project of a Panama canal. But one quiet Sunday
a cab drove up from the station; a young man mut-

tered something to Napoleon, who stared and said, *'Est-ce possible? Qu'elle vienne vite!'* He stood quite quietly on the steps, and Eugénie walked up. They had not met since that dull morning at St. Cloud; and when a door closed behind them, he was sobbing in her arms. She stayed for two days and slipped back across Belgium into England. The war trailed on into the hard winter of 1870, when strange, impromptu armies took erratic courses across France; dramatic ministers alighted from balloons, and admirals rode on horseback commanding queer mixed units of *gendarmes* and *Spahis,* whilst Garibaldi led *francs-tireurs* in Burgundy and Chanzy's *moblots* died in the snow outside Le Mans to show that France was still unbeaten. They skated a little at Wilhelmshöhe, and a galaxy of Marshals arrived, fresh from the surrender of Metz. Bazaine was there, looking a little dull, and Canrobert, and Lebœuf, whom no one seemed to speak to. There was a mild revival of politics; Fleury and Piétri were perpetually departing on mysterious errands into Switzerland; and there was even a fantastic request to the King of Prussia that his captive Guard should be interned round the captive Emperor. But Paris was beginning to starve, and the war was ending. The guns spoke slower now from Mont-Valérien, and Bourbaki's army trailed across the snow into Switzerland. Bismarck had made his King an Emperor among the mirrors at Versailles, and once more he seemed to play with the notion of a Bonaparte restoration. Bewildered Frenchmen brought their hopes to him; but he signed peace with the Republic, and Napoleon was left at Cassel, muttering, *'Je suis désolé!'* In February, 1871, he broke his silence—

28

'ce profond silence qui est le deuil du malheur'—
with a manifesto to the French; the illegality of the
republican dictatorship was denounced, and there
was a grave appeal to the electorate. But the new
Assembly at Bordeaux confirmed the deposition of
the Emperor and proclaimed a queer Republic—*'la
République sans les républicains'*—under M. Thiers.
There was a faint protest from Wilhelmshöhe; but
the Empire went obediently into exile. On a March
day in 1871 Napoleon's carriages drove down to the
station. The place was crowded (it was a Sunday);
but as the train started, there was no sound from the
people. On the way to the frontier news reached
them of the Commune: Paris had gone mad; but
Napoleon was smoking in a German railway-carriage,
and M. Thiers was left to deal with the pleasing
problems of repression. At Cologne the station was
decorated for the returning troops, and they could
read the great names of German victories on the
decorations. They reached Herbesthal in the dark,
and passed the frontier into Belgium. On the next
day Eugénie and the Prince were waiting at the Lord
Warden Hotel to see the Ostend boat steam into
Dover harbour. Napoleon met them; his train ran
up the line through the little fields of Kent to Chislehurst, and they were all together once more at Camden Place. It was the house where Miss Rowles had
lived, whom he nearly married in 1847; and by way
of the Tuileries and Sedan he had reached it at last.

There was a mild glow of evening over the little
house in Kent. It seemed to stand under a quiet
sky among the trees. They had shelled St. Cloud
into ruins, and there were flames in the Tuileries as
the *pétroleuses* ran crouching through the drifting

Napoleon III. (1871)

From a photograph

smoke and the troops marched in from Versailles.
But at Chislehurst the birds wheeled slowly over a
silent garden, and Napoleon sat writing in his little
study or smoked in the big chair after dinner. He
was mostly writing; there was a little pamphlet on
French policy—*Les Principes*—which its author
signed in a pitiably modest name—*'par un ancien
diplomate.'* Later he wrote a fuller work on the war
and the military preparation of the Empire, *Les
Forces Militaires de la France et la Campagne de
1870*; it was a mild strategic *apologia* for Sedan.
Sometimes they had visitors; the Queen came, with
Princess Beatrice and Prince Leopold; the county
called; Mr. Borthwick of the *Morning Post* was
often there, and once Mr. Sullivan played the piano
for hours together. On Sunday mornings they
walked across the Common to church, and Napoleon
raised his great top hat, as little groups of loyal
French from London bowed and curtseyed by the
road. There were always callers at the house; Lord
Malmesbury and old Earl Russel came, Archbishop
Tait impressed his new neighbours, and Christine
Nilsson sang for them all one afternoon. Sometimes
busy gentlemen called from France, and Napoleon
almost became an Emperor again; M. Rouher was
still, was always faithful, and one might yet (who
knows?) disturb M. Thiers and his singular Republic. But life went on quietly at Chislehurst.
The little hall was full of flowers for the *fête* of the
Empire, and on fine afternoons the ladies took tea on
the lawn. It was a quiet *envoi*.

Sometimes they went away. In the first autumn
Napoleon was at Torquay—*'charmant endroit
quoique triste'*—whilst Eugénie was in Spain with

her mother, and some of her jewellery was being sold in London: it fetched good prices, because they were buying diamonds for the Prince of Wales to give as presents to the Indian princes on his travels. In 1872 they spent the summer in a little house at Cowes, quite close to Ryde, where the Empress had landed after her dreadful crossing from Trouville with Sir John Burgoyne; and once or twice Napoleon went up to town to the photographer's. They even saw the Prince of Wales drive to St. Paul's for the Thanksgiving after his recovery from typhoid fever. That year Napoleon was busy with vague beneficent plans for improving the condition of the people; he drafted schemes for old age pensions and made little ingenious drawings of economical stoves for working-class dwellings. His mind strayed actively across innumerable problems, as he paced the long corridor at Chislehurst. One might abolish the *octroi;* one might even (he was talking to a gentleman from London) abolish war. Europe had been politely amused by the Emperor and his Congresses; but its entertainment would have bordered on discourtesy if it had fathomed his strange design —a Council in regular session to settle the world's affairs and an Assembly of the nations meeting to legislate in terms of international law. The fantastic project provoked incredulous smiles, which have scarcely faded before its realisation at Geneva.

But his eye was fixed on a nearer future. The Prince was at Woolwich now, and in France a throne was waiting. Late in 1872 Napoleon made his last plan. One might slip over to Ostend, by Germany into Switzerland, and then to Annecy, past the great lake where Eugénie had stood with him under a night of stars, and by the dim hills above Aix where Hortense had once sat sketching. Bourbaki commanded at Lyons; he was always loyal, and one might march his troops on Paris. But armies do not follow ill men in carriages: one must ride again. He tested himself bravely in the quiet drive at Chislehurst; and riding was not easy. Even the train was exhausting now; and he faced the doctors quietly. There must be an operation; and the surgeons came to Camden Place in the first week of 1873. They seemed to be successful; but he failed suddenly. It was January 9, and Eugénie was with him. As he drowsed into the last unconsciousness, he muttered something to Conneau about Sedan: those thudding guns under that leaden sky haunted him to the end, and the story was over.

XXI

SIX years later, on a South African June morning (it was Whitsunday of the year 1879) Lieutenant Carey rode eastwards out of Itelezi camp with six troopers and the Prince Imperial.

For reasons which were a trifle mysterious to most of her subjects the armed forces of Queen Victoria were engaged in hostilities against the Zulus, and Cetewayo's *impis* disturbed that Peace which (with Honour) had been so recently promised by Lord Beaconsfield to the British electorate. The war was an unwelcome legacy from an active Colonial Secretary, who had figured impressively in the Cabinet as Lord Carnarvon but was rendered faintly ridiculous to his contemporaries by the nickname of 'Twitters.' It had resulted immediately from the uncontrolled policy of a bellicose High Commissioner, who earned the obloquy of his countrymen but must be taken to have derived consolation from his sovereign's prompt gift of 'the fourth Volume': the work to which she referred was Sir Theodore Martin's *Life of His Royal Highness the Prince Consort,* and there is something almost endearing in the Queen's assumption that his first three instalments were universally in the possession of public servants.

The military conduct of the Zulu War was in the cautious but incompetent hands of Lord Chelmsford,

whom the Prime Minister retained in the command
from motives of delicacy, because he was the son of
a distinguished lawyer whom the family incompetence had compelled him to exclude from the Wool-
sack eleven years previously. The cogency of the
reason will be readily apparent to any student of the
British system. His columns, shaken but reinforced
after the disaster at Isandhlwana, moved slowly
towards the Zulu concentration at Ulundi, and the
Prince Imperial rode with them, studying savage
warfare, designing field fortifications, and writing to
his mother. His inclusion had raised questions of
some difficulty at home, since Lord Beaconsfield regarded without enthusiasm the addition to the British
forces in the field of a young man from Woolwich
who was a claimant to the throne of a friendly Power.
But his mother enlisted the support of the Queen.
Victoria and Eugénie in conjunction formed a
powerful constellation, which baffled even Disraeli's
remarkable capacity for influencing elderly ladies.
'I did all I could to stop his going,' he grumbled
afterwards. 'But what can you do when you have
to deal with two obstinate women?'

The Prince vanished into Zululand on Lord
Chelmsford's staff, and rode out on a Sunday morning with Lieutenant Carey. Late in the afternoon
they off-saddled in an empty kraal by the Imbazani.
No guards were posted, and the Prince talked
quietly to Carey of the first campaign of the first
Napoleon. Then, at a vague alarm, the party was
ordered to remount. But before they were all in the
saddle, there was a volley from the long grass, and
the Zulus came at them with the assegai. One man
went down; the horses bolted; and Carey, who had

only served in a West Indian foot-regiment with unmounted officers, became too much absorbed in the pressing problems of horsemanship presented by a runaway horse to look behind him. Outside the kraal the Prince was in tragic difficulties. His horse was bolting after the retreating troop, and with the enemy coming on he ran alongside in a desperate effort to mount. The saddle swung round with him, and he went down.

Then, as the galloping horses pounded away into the distance, he walked slowly towards the Zulus with a revolver in his left hand. Three shots were fired, before the long spears flashed; and they left him stripped in the trampled grass. The sun which had set over Longwood and Schönbrunn and Chislehurst went down behind Itelezi. Only the Empress lived on. . . .

AUTHORITIES

BONAPARTISM

I

BOURGEOIS, ÉMILE. *Manuel Historique de Politique Étrangère.* 3 vols. 1909.

Cambridge Modern History. Vol. ix. 1907.

FISHER, H. A. L. *Bonapartism: Six Lectures.* 1908.
Studies in Napoleonic Statesmanship: Germany. 1903.

FOURNIER, AUGUST. *Napoleon I.: a Biography.* 2 vols. (Translated) 1911.

GUEDALLA, PHILIP. *The Partition of Europe, a Textbook of European History, 1715-1815.* 1914.

LAVISSE AND RAMBAUD. *Histoire Générale.* Vol. iv. 1905.

ROSE, J. HOLLAND. *Life of Napoleon I.* 2 vols. 1903.

SOREL, ALBERT. *L'Europe et la Révolution Française.* 8 vols. 1885-1903.

VANDAL, ALBERT. *L'Avènement de Bonaparte.* 2 vols. 1902-1911.

II

GONNARD, PHILIPPE. *The Exile of St. Helena* (translated). 1909.

GOURGAUD, G. *Sainte-Hélène: Journal inédit de 1815 à 1818.* 2 vols. 1899.

LAS CASES, E. P. D. *Mémorial de Sainte-Hélène.* 4 vols. 1823.

MEREDITH, GEORGE. *Odes in Contribution to the Song of French History.* 1898.

MONTHOLON, C. J. *Récits de la Captivité de l'Empereur Napoléon à Sainte-Hélène.* 2 vols. 1847.

ROSEBERY, EARL OF. *Napoleon: the Last Phase.* 1900.

III

BARTHÉLEMY AND MÉRY. *Napoléon en Egypte, Waterloo, et Le Fils de l'Homme.* Illustrated by Horace Vernet and Hippolyte Bellangé. 1842.

BÉRANGER, P. J. de. *Œuvres.* 2 vols. 1847.

Cambridge Modern History. Vol. x. 1907.

DAYOT, ARMAND. *Napoléon: Illustrations d'après des Peintures, Sculptures, Gravures, Objets du Temps.* 1910.

LAURENT, P. M. *Histoire de Napoléon Ier.* Illustrated by Horace Vernet and Hippolyte Bellangé.

MUSSET, ALFRED DE. *Confession d'un Enfant du Siècle.* 1836.

NORVINS, M. DE. *Histoire de Napoléon.* Illustrated by Raffet. 1839.

THE PRINCE

GENERAL

BONAPARTE, LOUIS-NAPOLÉON. *Œuvres.* 2 vols. 1848.

BONAPARTE, PRINCE NAPOLÉON-LOUIS. *Des Idées Napoléoniennes.* 1839.

CHEETHAM, F. H. *Louis Napoleon and the Genesis of the Second Empire.* 1909.

GIRAUDEAU, F. *Napoléon III.* 1895.

JERROLD, BLANCHARD. *The Life of Napoleon III.* 4 vols. 1874-1882.

SIMPSON, F. A. *The Rise of Louis Napoleon.* 1901.

THIRRIA, H. *Napoléon III. avant l'Empire.* 2 vols. 1895.

I

NAPOLÉON IER. *Correspondance.* Vol. xvii. 1865.

II

BULLOCH, WILLIAM, M.D., F.R.S. *Unpublished notes on illness and death of Prince Napoleon-Louis-Charles.*

NAPOLÉON IER. *Correspondance.* Vol. xv. 1864.

III

SERGEANT, PHILIP W. *The Empress Joséphine.* 2 vols. 1908.

IV

BOURGUIGNON, J. *Les Adieux de Malmaison*. *L'Illustration*. May 1921.
HOUSSAYE, HENRY. *1815*. 3 vols. 1903.

VII

PERSIGNY, DUC DE. *Mémoires*. 1896.

VIII

JAMES, HENRY. *Washington Square*. 2 vols. 1881.

IX

BEACONSFIELD, EARL OF. *Endymion*. 3 vols. 1880.
GREVILLE, CHARLES C. F. *A Journal of the Reign of Queen Victoria, 1837-1852*. 3 vols. 1885.
MONYPENNY, W. F. AND BUCKLE, G. E. *Life of Benjamin Disraeli, Earl of Beaconsfield*. 6 vols. 1910-1920.
WIKOFF, H. AND GRANT, G. *Biographical Sketches of Louis Napoleon Bonaparte and Poetical and Prose Writings of Louis Napoleon*. 1850.

X

CROKER, J. W. *Correspondence and Diaries*. 3 vols. 1884.

XI

BRIFFAULT, F. T. *The Prisoner of Ham*. 1846.

THE PRESIDENT

GENERAL

GORCE, PIERRE DE LA. *Histoire de la Seconde République Française*. 2 vols. 1887.
LEBEY, ANDRÉ. *Louis-Napoléon Bonaparte et la Révolution de 1848*. 2 vols. 1907-1908.
THIRRIA, H. *Op. cit.*

I

Hugo, Victor. *Choses Vues.* 1900.
Senior, Nassau W. *Conversations with M. Thiers, M. Guizot, and other Distinguished Persons during the Second Empire.* 2 vols. 1878.

II *and* III

Cham and Lireux, A. *Assemblée Nationale Comique.* 1850.
Dayot, Armand. *Les Journées Révolutionnaires: 1830-1848.*
Simpson, F. A. *Op. cit.*
Victoria, Queen. *Letters.* 3 vols. 1907.

IV

Clough, Arthur Hugh. *Poems and Prose Remains.* 2 vols. 1869.
Garibaldi, Giuseppe. *Autobiography* (translated). 2 vols. 1889.
Trevelyan, G. M. *Garibaldi's Defence of the Roman Republic.* 1907.

V

Ollivier, Emile. *L'Empire Libéral.* Vol. ii. 1897.
Persigny, Duc de *Op. cit.*

VI

Casse, Baron A. du. *Les Dessous du Coup d'Etat.* 1891.
Histoire Anecdotique du Second Empire. 1887.
Hugo, Victor. *Napoléon-le-Petit.* 1852.
Histoire d'un Crime. 1877.
Maupas, M. de. *Mémoire sur le Second Empire.* 1884.
Ollivier, Émile. *Op. cit.*

VII

Ashley, Hon. Evelyn. *Life of Viscount Palmerston: 1846-1865.* 2 vols. 1876.
Gorce, Pierre de la. *Histoire du Second Empire.* Vol. i. 1908.
Lachaud, E. *Circulaires, Rapports, Notes et Instructions Confidentielles: 1851-1870.* 1872.

MAUPAS, M. DE. *Op. cit.*
PERSIGNY, DUC DE. *Op. cit.*
VICTORIA, QUEEN. *Op. cit.*

THE EMPEROR

GENERAL

BOURGEOIS, ÉMILE. *Op. cit.*
Cambridge Modern History. Vol. xi. 1909.
DAYOT, ARMOND. *Le Second Empire: d'après des Peintures, Gravures, Sculptures, Dessins, Médailles, Autographes, Objets du Temps.*
GORCE, PIERRE DE LA. *Histoire du Second Empire.* 7 vols. 1908.
JERROLD, BLANCHARD. *Op. cit.*
OLLIVIER, ÉMILE. *L'Empire Libéral.* 17 vols. 1895-1915.
Papiers Secrets et Correspondance du Second Empire. 1877.
Papiers Secrets brûlés dans l'Incendie des Tuileries. 1871.
SEIGNOBOS, C. *Le Second Empire.* 1921.
            Le Déclin de l'Empire. 1921.
VICTORIA, QUEEN. *Op. cit.*
VIEL CASTEL, COMTE H. DE. *Mémoires sur le Règne de Napoléon III.* 6 vols. 1884.

I

FLEURY, COMTE, AND SONOLET, LOUIS. *La Société du Second Empire: 1851-1858.* 1918.

II

CARAN D'ACHE. *Nos Soldats du Siècle.*
DETAILLE, EDOUARD. *L'Armée Française.* 2 vols. 1885-1889.

III

FILON, A. *Souvenirs sur l'Impératrice Eugénie.* 1920.
FLEURY, COMTE, AND SONOLET, LOUIS. *Op. cit.*
            Memoirs of the Empress Eugénie (translated). 2 vols. 1920.

IV

MARTIN, SIR THEODORE. *Life of H.R.H. the Prince Consort.*
5 vols. 1871-1880.
SENIOR, NASSAU W. *Op. cit.*
　　　　*Conversations with Distinguished Persons
　　　　during the Second Empire.* 2 vols. 1880.

V

FRASER, SIR WILLIAM. *Napoleon III: My Recollections.* 1896.
GOSSE, EDMUND. *Life of Algernon Charles Swinburne.* 1917.
HÜBNER, COMTE DE. *Neuf Ans de Souvenirs d'un Ambassadeur
　　d'Autriche à Paris: 1851-1859.* 2 vols. 1904.
JAMES, HENRY. *A Small Boy and Others.* 1913.
MAXWELL, SIR H. *Life and Letters of the Fourth Earl of
　　Clarendon.* 2 vols. 1913.
TROLLOPE, A. *The Three Clerks.* 3 vols. 1858.

VI

DARIMON, A. *Histoire de Douze Ans: 1857-1869.* 1883.
FLAUBERT, GUSTAVE. *Madame Bovary: Réquisitoire, Plaidoirie
　　et Jugement.* 1857.
LACHAUD, E. *Op. cit.*
MARTIN, SIR THEODORE. *Op. cit.*

VII

MORIER, SIR ROBERT. *Memoirs and Letters.* 2 vols. 1911.
ORSI, PIETRO. *Cavour and the Making of Modern Italy.* 1914.
TREVELYAN, G. M. *Garibaldi and the Thousand.* 1909.

VIII

BROWNING, ELIZABETH BARRETT. *Poems before Congress.* 1860.
CHAM. *Les Zouaves.* 1859.
MASSA, MARQUIS PHILIPPE DE. *Souvenirs et Impressions: 1840-
　　1871.* 1897.
VIAL, J. AND C. *Histoire Abrégée des Campagnes Modernes.*
　　2 vols. 1910.

IX

FLEISCHMANN, H. *Napoléon III. et les Femmes.* 1913.

LOLIÉE, F. *Le Duc de Morny et la Société du Second Empire.* 1909.

Les Femmes du Second Empire. 1906.

La Fête Impériale.

ZOLA, ÉMILE. *Son Excellence Eugène Rougon.* 1875.

X

BAGEHOT, WALTER. *Literary Studies.* 3 vols. 1878.

BAXTER, REV. M. *Louis Napoleon the Destined Monarch of the World, Foreshown in Prophecy to confirm a seven years' Covenant with the Jews about seven years before the Millennium, and (after the Resurrection of Saints and Ascension of Watchful Christians has taken place two years and from three to five weeks after the Covenant) subsequently to become completely supreme over England and most of America, and all Christendom, and to cause a great persecution of Christians during the later half of the seven years, until he finally perishes at the descent of Christ, at the end of the War of Armageddon, about or soon after 1873.* 1865.

DUCLAUX, M. *Victor Hugo.* 1921.

GOSSE, EDMUND. *Op. cit.*

HUGO, VICTOR. *Les Châtiments.* 1853.

Actes et Paroles: Pendant l'Exil, 1852-1870. 1875.

SWINBURNE, A. C. *Songs before Sunrise.* 1871.

Songs of Two Nations. 1871.

Posthumous Poems. 1917.

XI

MÉRIMÉE, PROSPER. *Lettres à M. Panizzi, 1850-1870.* 2 vols. 1881.

MORIER, SIR ROBERT. *Op. cit.*

MORLEY, J. *Life of Cobden.* 2 vols. 1881.

Life of Gladstone. 3 vols. 1903.

SENIOR, NASSAU W. *Op. cit.*

TREVELYAN, G. M. *Garibaldi and the Making of Italy.* 1911.

XII

DARIMON, A. *Op. cit.*

DAUDET, ALPHONSE. *Le Nabab.* 1877.

FLEURY, COMTE, AND SONOLET, LOUIS. *La Société du Second Empire: 1858-1863.* 1918.

FRASER, SIR WILLIAM. *Op. cit.*

HANOTAUX, GABRIEL. *Histoire de la France Contemporaine.* Vol. i. 1903.

LACHAUD, E. *Op. cit.*

MÉRIMÉE, PROSPER. *Op. cit.*

ZOLA, ÉMILE. *Op. cit.*

XIII

FLEURY, COMTE, AND SONOLET, LOUIS. *La Société du Second Empire: 1863-1867.* 1918.

MASSA, MARQUIS PHILIPPE DE. *Op. cit.*

VIAL, J. AND C. *Op. cit.*

XIV

BORDIER, H. *L'Allemagne aux Tuileries de 1850 à 1870.* 1872.

DAUDET, ALPHONSE. *Op. cit.*

LOLIÉE, F. *Le Duc de Morny, op. cit.*

MÉRIMÉE, PROSPER. *Op. cit.*

NAPOLEON III. *Histoire de Jules César.* 2 vols. 1865-1866.

PEAT, A. B. NORTH. *Correspondence (1864-1869).* 1903.

XV

ASHLEY, HON. EVELYN. *Op. cit.*

BENEDETTI, COUNT. *Studies in Diplomacy* (translated). 1895.

BEUST, COUNT VON. *Memoirs* (translated). 2 vols. 1887.

BURDIN D'ENTREMONT, F. M. *L'Armée Danoise et la Défense du Sundevit en 1864.* 1885.

HEADLAM, J. W. *Bismarck and the Foundation of the German Empire.* 1904.

HOHENLOHE, PRINCE CHLODWIG. *Memoirs* (translated). 2 vols. 1906.

HOZIER, SIR H. M. *The Seven Weeks' War.* 2 vols. 1867.

KLACZKO, J. *Deux Chanceliers: le Prince Gortchakof et le Prince de Bismarck.* 1877.

MOLTKE, COUNT VON. *Projects for the Campaign of 1866 against Austria* (translated). 1907.

XVI

ANONYMOUS. *The Truth about 'The Protocols.'* 1921.
CARTIER, V. *Le Général Trochu.* 1914.
FLEISCHMANN, H. *Op. cit.*
KAHN, GUSTAVE. *Europas Fürsten im Sittenspiegel der Karikatur.*
LOLIEE, F. *La Fête Impériale, op. cit.*
ROCHEFORT, H. *Les Aventures de ma Vie.* 5 vols.

XVII

BEUST, COUNT VON. *Op. cit.*
CLARKE, H. BUTLER. *Modern Spain: 1815-1898.* 1906.
DAUDET, ALPHONSE. *Numa Roumestan.* 1881.
DESCHANEL, PAUL. *Gambetta.* 1920.
FILON, A. *Op. cit.*
LAMY, ÉTIENNE. *Etudes sur le Second Empire.* 1895.
MORIER, SIR ROBERT. *Op. cit.*
NEWTON, LORD. *Lord Lyons.* 2 vols. 1913.
NEWTON, LORD. *Op. cit.*
ROCHEFORT, H. *Op. cit.*
　　　　　Les Lanternes (reprinted). 3 vols. 1880.
STOFFEL, BARON. *Reports on the Military Forces of Prussia: 1868-1870* (translated). 1872.

XVIII

MAXWELL, SIR H. *Op. cit.*
MORLEY, J. *Op. cit.*
NEWTON, LORD. *Op cit.*
ROCHEFORT, H. *Op. cit.*

XIX

BAZAINE, MARSHAL. *L'Armée du Rhin.* 1872.
EVANS, T. W. *Mémoires.* 1910.
FILON, A. *Op. cit.*
FRASER, SIR WILLIAM. *Op. cit.*

NEWTON, LORD. *Op. cit.*

PICARD, E. *1870: Sedan.* 2 vols. 1912.

ROUSSET, LIEUT.-COL. *Histoire Général de la Guerre Franco-Allemande.* 2 vols. (Illustrated.) 1912.

TROCHU, GÉNÉRAL. *Œuvres Posthumes.* 2 vols. 1896.

VIAL, J. AND C. *Op. cit.*

ZOLA, ÉMILE. *Le Débâcle.* 1892.

XX

BEUST, COUNT VON. *Op. cit.*

EVANS, T. W. *Op. cit.*

FILON, A. *Op. cit.*

FRASER, SIR WILLIAM. *Op. cit.*

GIRAUDEAU, F. *Op. cit.*

GWYNN, S. AND TUCKWELL, G. M. *Life of Sir Charles Dilke.* 2 vols. 1917.

HANOTAUX, GABRIEL. *Op. cit.*

MONTS, COMTE. *La Captivité de Napoléon III.* (translated). 1908.

NAPOLÉON III. *Œuvres Posthumes.* 1873.

XXI

BLUNT, W. S. *My Diaries.* 2 vols. 1919-1920.

FILON, A. *The Prince Imperial* (translated). 1917.

MONYPENNY, W. F. AND BUCKLE, G. E. *Op. cit.*

INDEX

EMINENT VICTORIANS

By LYTTON STRACHEY

8vo. With Portraits

A selection from a host of reviews of this brilliant and extraordinarily witty book:

The New York Times—"There is every temptation to quote from this volume, for it abounds in striking stories and brilliant interpretations. . . . Mr. Strachey has not written history in the usual fashion, but he has made a notable contribution to that prodigious undertaking, the history of the Victorian Age."

The Outlook—"Brilliant."

The Metropolitan—"It is one of the few current books that I would specially recommend as worth reading. He is a refreshing, brave, witty, and large-minded biographer."—*Clarence Day, Jr.*

The Chicago Daily News—"Lytton Strachey can write circles around any living biographer; can give handicaps to any living essayist and match the most touted workers in the language with one hand tied behind his back. . . . When you have read the last line of these soul-portraits you are aware of the stark truthfulness of the work. It is not only art—it is reality."

The New York Tribune—"We receive Mr. Strachey's volume with gratitude and joy. . . . Profound sincerity of both constructive and destructive criticism, sanity of judgment and splendor of spirit make this volume a memorable tribute to one of the most memorable eras in the history of the human intellect."

The Chicago Tribune—"One of the outstanding biographical works in English literature. . . . In a generation that produces one Strachey there bob up several thousand professional mourners, who model their style and general appreciation of the truth upon epitaphs. . . . Strachey wields one of the most engaging pens now employed in literature. His humor is unfailing, but always smooth, unforced, ironic. He knows the satiric value of hyperbole and antithesis. His book is altogether a remarkable performance. . . . In his gallery are portraits of familiar personages wearing new expressions, and the manner of presentation is that of a cultivated and penetrating artist. The volume is recommended eagerly to all lovers of vivid and daring biography."

The Springfield Republican—"Mr. Strachey's wit gives stimulating piquancy to a style at once brilliant and pure. His power of illuminating the figures which he presents is matched by his ability to interest the reader in his craftmanship."

The Hartford Times—"Under his pointed, facile, and illuminating pen dry-as-dust facts become of absorbing interest. It is astonishing what he can do to make a 'life' worth reading."

The Indianapolis News—"Mr. Strachey has succeeded notably in making biography more dramatic and fascinating than fiction."

New York   **G. P. PUTNAM'S SONS**   London